"This book is informative, well written and just like Todd Lammle's other books. I recommend them all. I read the whole book twice, went through the written labs and review questions, as well as the extra questions on the CD and the flashcards. Whew! It was a lot of work, but it paid off because this book prepared me fully for the Remote Access exam. Study hard and you will pass the exam using this book."

"If you want to know what is on the new Remote Access exam, then look no farther then Sybex. This book covered absolutely everything I found on the exam. I passed and am now a CCNP!"

"I just keep moving towards my CCNP with Sybex! This is a great written book and it really helped me understand the ISDN troubleshooting technique that is so difficult on this exam. To pass the Cisco CCNP Support exam, you MUST know your troubleshooting techniques for ISDN and Frame Relay really, really well. Everything on the exam was in this book. I recommend this book for the exam and for a desk reference as well."

"I'm not going to lie, the Support 2.0 exam is very hard! If you have hopes in passing the exam the first time, I recommend you to study this book cover to cover. On top of that, this is the only resource I used to prepare. If you do not have access to a router, you can follow the excellent examples in the book by writing down the commands and their results a few times to jog your memory. Bottom line, this may be the easiest way to prepare for such a hard exam."

"(The *CCNP: Switching Study Guide*) was very well written. I couldn't put it down. It was technical, but funny, and prepared me for the exam. The written labs, review questions, and flashcards were exactly what I needed to help me pass the exam. I scored a 910, which isn't bad since I hadn't worked on a switch before reading this book. The amount of in-depth information on the Catalyst switch series, mostly the 5000, was amazing. The exam had questions based on the Catalyst 1900 and 5000 series, and this book had everything needed on the Catalyst switch series to pass the exam. I am ... pleased with all the Sybex books for Cisco certification."

"Sybex has a winner with this Switching book. This book is right up there with the Todd Lammle CCNA study guide. It has a great format and is easy to read. I not only learned a lot about switching with Cisco Catalyst switches, but also pass the CCNP Switching exam, which is a cool bonus."

CCNP
Routing
Study Guide

CCNP™
Routing
Study Guide

Todd Lammle

Sean Odom

with Kevin Wallace

San Francisco • Paris • Düsseldorf • Soest • London

Associate Publisher: Neil Edde
Contracts and Licensing Manager: Kristine O'Callaghan
Acquisitions and Developmental Editor: Jeff Kellum
Editor: Linda Recktenwald
Production Editor: Molly Glover
Technical Editor: Eric Quinn
Book Designer: Bill Gibson
Graphic Illustrators: Tony Jonick, Jerry Williams!
Electronic Publishing Specialist: Nila Nichols
Proofreaders: Nancy Riddiough, Nanette Duffy, Yariv Rabinovitch, Jennifer Campbell
Indexer: Ted Laux
CD Coordinator: Kara Eve Schwartz
CD Technicians: Keith McNeil, Siobhan Dowling
Cover Designer: Archer Design
Cover Photographer: Tony Stone Images

Software License Agreement: Terms and Conditions

I would like to dedicate this book to all the hard-working staff at GlobalNet Training, Inc.

Todd Lammle

I would like to dedicate this book to my family—Erin, Mikayla, Sean Jr., and Hillary.

Sean Odom

To my daughters Stacie and Sabrina, who constantly remind me of the joy found in learning new things, and to my wife, Vivian, an endless source of encouragement, support, and love.

Kevin Wallace

Acknowledgments

This book would not be on the shelf if it were not for the hard work and dedication of the Sybex editing crew, especially Molly Glover and Jeff Kellum, who kept us all on track. Many thanks! My thanks also to Linda Recktenwald (editor), Eric Quinn (technical editor), Nila Nichols (EPS), Tony Jonick and Jerry Williams! (illustrators), Nancy Riddiough, Nanette Duffy, Yariv Rabinovitch, and Jennifer Campbell (proofreaders), and Ted Laux (indexer).

T.L.

I need to thank Todd Lammle for trusting me to grace the pages of another one of his books. It's always exciting when you get to the acknowledgments because that means the book is almost finished. I must thank Erin for putting up with me during the writing of this book. She is a wonderful person who is as smart as she is good looking and puts up with a lot of extra responsibility while I am working on books. I need to also thank some of those who helped me in the writing process, such as Hanson Nottingham, Doug Hammond, and John Turner, who have made me consider myself an expert at BGP and EIGRP. And finally, I'd like to thank everyone at Sybex who worked so hard at completing this project.

S.O.

I would like to thank John Swartz for introducing me to Todd Lammle and thanks to Todd for all his encouragement and advice. My family also deserves acknowledgment for their patience while I was secluded in my office. Now that the book is finished, Daddy can get back to the really important things like coloring pictures and working puzzles.

K.W.

Contents at a Glance

Contents

Introduction

This book is intended to help you continue on your exciting new path toward obtaining your CCNP and CCIE certification. Before reading this book, it is important to have at least read the Sybex *CCNA: Cisco Certified Network Associate Study Guide, Second Edition*. You can take the CCNP tests in any order, but you should have passed the CCNA exam before pursuing your CCNP. Many questions in the Routing exam are built upon the CCNA material. However, we have done everything possible to make sure that you can pass the Routing exam by reading this book and practicing with Cisco routers.

The new Cisco certifications reach beyond the popular certifications, such as the MCSE and CNE, to provide you with an indispensable factor in understanding today's network—insight into the Cisco world of internetworking.

Cisco—A Brief History

A lot of readers may already be familiar with Cisco and what it does. However, those of you who are new to the field just coming in fresh from your MCSE, or maybe even with 10 or more years in the field but wishing to brush up on the new technology, may appreciate a little background on Cisco.

In the early 1980s, a married couple who worked in different computer departments at Stanford University started up cisco Systems (notice the small *c*). Their names are Len and Sandy Bosack. They were having trouble getting their individual systems to communicate (like many married people), so in their living room they created a gateway server to make it easier for their disparate computers in two different departments to communicate using the IP protocol.

In 1984, Cisco Systems was founded with a small commercial gateway server product that changed networking forever. Some people think the name was intended to be San Francisco Systems, but the paper got ripped on the way to the incorporation lawyers—who knows? But in 1992, the company name was changed to Cisco Systems, Inc.

The first product it marketed was called the Advanced Gateway Server (AGS). Then came the Mid-Range Gateway Server (MGS), the Compact Gateway Server (CGS), the Integrated Gateway Server (IGS), and the AGS+. Cisco calls these "the old alphabet soup products."

In 1993, Cisco came out with the amazing 4000 router and then created the even more amazing 7000, 2000, and 3000 series routers. These are still around and evolving (almost daily, it seems).

Cisco Systems has since become an unrivaled worldwide leader in networking for the Internet. Its networking solutions can easily connect users who work from diverse devices on disparate networks. Cisco products make it simple for people to access and transfer information without regard to differences in time, place, or platform.

Cisco Systems' big picture is that it provides end-to-end networking solutions that customers can use to build an efficient, unified information infrastructure of their own or to connect to someone else's. This is an important piece in the Internet/networking-industry puzzle because a common architecture that delivers consistent network services to all users is now a functional imperative. Because Cisco Systems offers such a broad range of networking and Internet services and capabilities, users needing regular access to their local network or the Internet can do so unhindered, making Cisco's wares indispensable.

Cisco answers this need with a wide range of hardware products that are used to form information networks using the Cisco Internetworking Operating System (IOS) software. This software provides network services, paving the way for networked technical support and professional services to maintain and optimize all network operations.

Along with the Cisco IOS, one of the services Cisco created to help support the vast amount of hardware it has engineered is the Cisco Certified Internetworking Expert (CCIE) program, which was designed specifically to equip people to effectively manage the vast quantity of installed Cisco networks. The business plan is simple: If you want to sell more Cisco equipment and have more Cisco networks installed, ensure that the networks you installed run properly.

However, having a fabulous product line isn't all it takes to guarantee the huge success that Cisco enjoys—lots of companies with great products are now defunct. If you have complicated products designed to solve complicated problems, you need knowledgeable people who are fully capable of installing, managing, and troubleshooting them. That part isn't easy, so Cisco began the CCIE program to equip people to support these complicated networks. This program, known colloquially as the Doctorate of Networking, has also been very successful, primarily due to its extreme difficulty. Cisco continuously monitors the program, changing it as it sees fit, to make sure that it remains pertinent and accurately reflects the demands of today's internetworking business environments.

Building upon the highly successful CCIE program, Cisco Career Certifications permit you to become certified at various levels of technical proficiency, spanning the disciplines of network design and support. So, whether you're beginning a career, changing careers, securing your present position, or seeking to refine and promote your position, this is the book for you!

Cisco's Installation and Support Certifications

Cisco has created new certifications that will help you get the coveted CCIE, as well as aid prospective employers in measuring skill levels. Before these new certifications, you took only one test and were then faced with the lab, which made it difficult to succeed. With these new certifications that add a better approach to preparing for that almighty lab, Cisco has opened doors that few were allowed through before. So, what are these new certifications, and how do they help you get your CCIE?

Cisco Certified Network Associate (CCNA) 2.0

The CCNA certification is the first certification in the new line of Cisco certifications and it is a precursor to all current Cisco certifications. With the new certification programs, Cisco has created a type of stepping-stone approach to CCIE certification. Now, you can become a Cisco Certified Network Associate for the meager cost of the Sybex *CCNA: Cisco Certified Network Associate Study Guide, Second Edition,* plus $100 for the test. And you don't have to stop there—you can choose to continue with your studies and achieve a higher certification called the Cisco Certified Network Professional (CCNP). Someone with a CCNP has all the skills and knowledge they need to attempt the CCIE lab. However, because no textbook can take the place of practical experience, we'll discuss what else you need to be ready for the CCIE lab shortly.

Cisco Certified Network Professional (CCNP) 2.0

This new Cisco certification has opened up many opportunities for the individual wishing to become Cisco-certified but who is lacking the training, the expertise, or the bucks to pass the notorious and often failed two-day Cisco torture lab. The new Cisco certifications will truly provide exciting new opportunities for the CNE and MCSE who just don't know how to advance to a higher level.

So, you're thinking, "Great, what do I do after I pass the CCNA exam?" Well, if you want to become a CCIE in Routing and Switching (the most popular certification), understand that there's more than one path to that much-coveted CCIE certification. The first way is to continue studying and become a Cisco Certified Network Professional (CCNP). That means four more tests, and the CCNA certification, to you.

The CCNP program will prepare you to understand and comprehensively tackle the internetworking issues of today and beyond—not limited to the Cisco world. You will undergo an immense metamorphosis, vastly increasing your knowledge and skills through the process of obtaining these certifications.

Remember that you don't need to be a CCNP or even a CCNA to take the CCIE lab, but to accomplish that, it's extremely helpful if you already have these certifications.

What Are the CCNP Certification Skills?

Cisco demands a certain level of proficiency for its CCNP certification. In addition to those required for the CCNA, these skills include the following:

- Installing, configuring, operating, and troubleshooting complex routed LAN, routed WAN, and switched LAN networks, and Dial Access Services.

- Understanding complex networks, such as IP, IGRP, IPX, Async Routing, AppleTalk, extended access lists, IP RIP, route redistribution, IPX RIP, route summarization, OSPF, VLSM, BGP, Serial, IGRP, Frame Relay, ISDN, ISL, X.25, DDR, PSTN, PPP, VLANs, Ethernet, ATM LAN-emulation, access lists, 802.10, FDDI, and transparent and translational bridging.

To meet the Cisco Certified Network Professional requirements, you must be able to perform the following:

- Install and/or configure a network to increase bandwidth, quicken network response times, and improve reliability and quality of service.

- Maximize performance through campus LANs, routed WANs, and remote access.

- Improve network security.

- Create a global intranet.

- Provide access security to campus switches and routers.

- Provide increased switching and routing bandwidth—end-to-end resiliency services.

- Provide custom queuing and routed priority services.

How Do You Become a CCNP?

After becoming a CCNA, the four exams you must take to get your CCNP are as follows:

Exam 640-503: Routing   This exam continues to build on the fundamentals learned in the CCNA course. It focuses on large multiprotocol internetworks and how to manage them with access lists, queuing, tunneling, route distribution, router maps, BGP, OSPF, and route summarization. This book covers everything you need to pass the new CCNP Routing exam.

Exam 640-504: Switching   This exam tests your knowledge of the 1900 and 5000 series of Catalyst switches. The Sybex *CCNP: Switching Study Guide* covers all the objectives you need to understand for passing the Switching exam.

Exam 640-506: Support   This exam tests you on troubleshooting information. You must be able to troubleshoot Ethernet and Token Ring LANS, IP, IPX, and AppleTalk networks, as well as ISDN, PPP, and Frame Relay networks. The Sybex *CCNP: Support Study Guide* covers all the exam objectives.

Exam 640-505: Remote Access   This exam tests your knowledge of installing, configuring, monitoring, and troubleshooting Cisco ISDN and dial-up access products. You must understand PPP, ISDN, Frame Relay, and authentication. The Sybex *CCNP: Remote Access Study Guide* covers all the exam objectives.

If you hate tests, you can take fewer of them by signing up for the CCNA exam and the Support exam, and then take just one more long exam called the Foundation R/S exam (640-509). Doing this also gives you your CCNP—but beware, it's a really long test that fuses all the material listed previously into one exam. Good luck! However, by taking this exam, you get three tests for the price of two, which saves you $100 (if you pass). Some people think it's easier to take the Foundation R/S exam because you can leverage the areas that you would score higher in against the areas in which you wouldn't.

Remember that test objectives and tests can change at any time without notice. Always check the Cisco Web site for the most up-to-date information (www.cisco.com).

Cisco Certified Internetworking Expert (CCIE)

You've become a CCNP, and now you fix your sights on getting your CCIE in Routing and Switching—what do you do next? Cisco recommends that before you take the lab, you take test 640-025: Cisco Internetwork Design (CID) and the Cisco authorized course called Installing and Maintaining Cisco Routers (IMCR). By the way, no Prometric test for IMCR exists at the time of this writing, and Cisco recommends a *minimum* of two years of on-the-job experience before taking the CCIE lab. After jumping those hurdles, you then have to pass the CCIE-R/S Qualification exam (exam 350-001) before taking the actual lab.

To become a CCIE, Cisco recommends the following:

1. Attend all the recommended courses at an authorized Cisco training center and pony up around $15,000–$20,000, depending on your corporate discount.

2. Pass the Qualification exam ($200 per exam—so hopefully you'll pass it the first time).

3. Pass the two-day, hands-on lab at Cisco. This costs $1,000 per lab, which many people fail two or more times. (Some never make it through!) Also, because you can take the exam only in San Jose,

California; Research Triangle Park, North Carolina; Sydney, Australia; Brussels, Belgium; Sao Paulo, Brazil; Beijing, China; Bangalore, India; Tokyo, Japan; Seoul, Korea; Halifax, Nova Scotia; Singapore; or Johannesburg, South Africa, you might just need to add travel costs to that $1,000. Cisco has added new sites lately for the CCIE lab; it's best to check the Cisco Web site at `http://www.cisco.com/warp/ public/625/ccie/exam_preparation/lab.html` for the most current information.

The CCIE Skills

The CCIE Routing and Switching exam includes the advanced technical skills that are required to maintain optimum network performance and reliability, as well as advanced skills in supporting diverse networks that use disparate technologies. CCIEs just don't have problems getting a job. These experts are basically inundated with offers to work for six-figure salaries! But that's because it isn't easy to attain the level of capability that is mandatory for Cisco's CCIE. For example, a CCIE will have the following skills down pat:

- Installing, configuring, operating, and troubleshooting complex routed LAN, routed WAN, switched LAN, and ATM LANE networks, and Dial Access Services.

- Diagnosing and resolving network faults.

- Using packet/frame analysis and Cisco debugging tools.

- Documenting and reporting the problem-solving processes used.

- Having general LAN/WAN knowledge, including data encapsulation and layering; windowing and flow control, and their relation to delay; error detection and recovery; link-state, distance-vector, and switching algorithms; management, monitoring, and fault isolation.

- Having knowledge of a variety of corporate technologies—including major services provided by Desktop, WAN, and Internet groups—as well as the functions, addressing structures, and routing, switching, and bridging implications of each of their protocols.

- Having knowledge of Cisco-specific technologies, including router/ switch platforms, architectures, and applications; communication servers; protocol translation and applications; configuration commands and system/network impact; and LAN/WAN interfaces, capabilities, and applications.

- Designing, configuring, installing, and verifying voice over IP and voice over ATM networks.

Cisco's Network Design and Installation Certifications

In addition to the Network Installation and Support certifications, Cisco has created another certification track for network designers. The two certifications within this track are the Cisco Certified Design Associate and Cisco Certified Design Professional certifications. If you're reaching for the CCIE stars, we highly recommend the CCNP and CCDP certifications before attempting the lab (or attempting to advance your career).

These certifications will give you the knowledge to design routed LAN, routed WAN, and switched LAN and ATM LANE networks.

Cisco Certified Design Associate (CCDA)

To become a CCDA, you must pass the DCN (Designing Cisco Networks) test (640-441). To pass this test, you must understand how to do the following:

- Design simple routed LAN, routed WAN, and switched LAN and ATM LANE networks.
- Use Network-layer addressing.
- Filter with access lists.
- Use and propagate VLAN.
- Size networks.

The Sybex *CCDA: Cisco Certified Design Associate Study Guide* is the most cost-effective way to study for and pass your CCDA exam.

Cisco Certified Design Professional (CCDP) 2.0

If you're already a CCNP and want to get your CCDP, you can simply take the CID 640-025 test. If you're not yet a CCNP, however, you must take the CCDA, CCNA, Routing, Switching, Remote Access, and CID exams.

CCDP certification skills include the following:

- Designing complex routed LAN, routed WAN, and switched LAN and ATM LANE networks

- Building upon the base level of the CCDA technical knowledge

CCDPs must also demonstrate proficiency in the following:

- Network-layer addressing in a hierarchical environment

- Traffic management with access lists

- Hierarchical network design

- VLAN use and propagation

- Performance considerations: required hardware and software; switching engines; memory, cost, and minimization

What Does This Book Cover?

This book covers everything you need to pass the CCNP Routing exam. It teaches you how to configure and maintain Cisco routers in large internetwork. Each chapter begins with a list of the topics covered, related to the CCNP Routing test, so make sure to read them over before working through the chapter.

Chapter 1 covers the introduction to large internetworks and how to clear up network congestion. This chapter also covers the Cisco three-layer model and how to use that when designing and maintaining your large routed internetwork. The requirements needed to scale large internetworks are discussed at the end of the chapter.

Chapter 2 covers the campus network and the basic fundamentals of routing. Both classful and classless routing are discussed, as well as the routing protocols available with Cisco routers and the differences between them.

Chapter 3 covers advanced IP routing, including VLSM and route summarization. This is important information to understand before reading the OSPF, EIGRP, and BGP chapters.

Chapter 4 covers Open Shortest Path First (OSPF) and how to configure OSPF with Cisco routers.

Chapter 5 continues with OSPF, but with more advanced configurations, such as multiple-area configurations.

Chapter 6 introduces you to the Cisco Enhanced IGRP routing protocol. This is a proprietary protocol designed by Cisco for large internetworks.

Chapter 7 introduces the Border Gateway Protocol and the terminology used with it, as well as when to use and not use BGP in an internetwork.

Chapter 8 continues with our BGP discussion and shows how to configure BGP with Cisco routers.

Chapter 9 is also a continuation of BGP and demonstrates how to scale BGP to a large Cisco internetwork, including how to connect to two ISPs.

Chapter 10 ends the book with a detailed discussion on route optimization, including redistribution, controlling routing update traffic, and policy-based routing.

Each chapter ends with review questions that are specifically designed to help you retain the knowledge presented. To really nail down your skills, read each question carefully, and, if possible, work through the hands-on labs in some of the chapters.

Where Do You Take the Exam?

You may take the exams at any of the Sylvan Prometric or Virtual University Enterprises (VUE) testing centers around the world. For the location of a testing center near you, call Sylvan at (800) 755-3926 or VUE at (877) 404-3926. Outside of the United States and Canada, contact your local Sylvan Prometric Registration Center.

To register for a Cisco Certified Network Professional exam:

1. Determine the number of the exam you want to take. (The Routing exam number is 640-503.)

2. Register with the nearest Sylvan Prometric or VUE testing center. At this point, you will be asked to pay in advance for the exam. At the time of this writing, the exams are $100 each and must be taken within one year of payment. You can schedule exams up to six weeks in advance or as soon as one working day prior to the day you wish to take it. If something comes up and you need to cancel or reschedule your exam appointment, contact the testing center at least 24 hours in advance. Same-day registration isn't available for the Cisco tests.

3. When you schedule the exam, you'll get instructions regarding all appointment and cancellation procedures, the ID requirements, and information about the testing-center location.

Tips for Taking Your CCNP Exam

The CCNP Routing test contains about 60 questions to be completed in about 75 minutes. However, understand that your test may vary.

Many questions on the exam have answer choices that at first glance look identical—especially the syntax questions! Remember to read through the choices carefully because "close doesn't cut it." If you put commands in the wrong order or forget one measly character, you'll get the question wrong. So, to practice, do the hands-on exercises at the end of the chapters over and over again until they feel natural to you.

Unlike Microsoft or Novell tests, the exam has answer choices that are really similar in syntax—although some syntax is dead wrong, it is usually just *subtly* wrong. Some other syntax choices may be right, but they're shown in the wrong order. Cisco does split hairs, and it is not at all averse to giving you classic trick questions. Here's an example:

> `access-list 101 deny ip any eq 23` denies Telnet access to all systems.

This item looks correct because most people refer to the port number (23) and think, "Yes, that's the port used for Telnet." The catch is that you can't filter IP on port numbers (only TCP and UDP). Another indicator is the use of an extended access list number but no destination address or "any" for the destination.

Also, never forget that the right answer is the Cisco answer. In many cases, more than one appropriate answer is presented, but the *correct* answer is the one that Cisco recommends.

Here are some general tips for exam success:

- Arrive early at the exam center, so you can relax and review your study materials.

- Read the questions *carefully*. Don't just jump to conclusions. Make sure that you're clear about *exactly* what each question asks.

- Don't leave any questions unanswered. They count against you.

- When answering multiple-choice questions that you're not sure about, use a process of elimination to get rid of the obviously incorrect answers first. Doing this greatly improves your odds if you need to make an educated guess.

- As of this writing, the written exams still allow you to move forward and backward. However, it is best to always check the Cisco Web site before taking any exam to get the most up-to-date information.

After you complete an exam, you'll get immediate, online notification of your pass or fail status, a printed Examination Score Report that indicates your pass or fail status, and your exam results by section. (The test administrator will give you the printed score report.) Test scores are automatically forwarded to Cisco within five working days after you take the test, so you don't need to send your score to them. If you pass the exam, you'll receive confirmation from Cisco, typically within two to four weeks.

How to Use This Book

This book can provide a solid foundation for the serious effort of preparing for the Cisco Certified Network Professional Routing exam. To best benefit from this book, use the following study method:

1. Take the Assessment Test immediately following this Introduction. (The answers are at the end of the test.) Carefully read over the explanations for any question you get wrong, and note which chapters the material comes from. This information should help you plan your study strategy.

2. Study each chapter carefully, making sure that you fully understand the information and the test topics listed at the beginning of each chapter. Pay extra-close attention to any chapter where you missed questions in the Assessment Test.

3. Complete all hands-on exercises in the chapter, referring to the chapter so that you understand the reason for each step you take. If you do not have Cisco equipment available, make sure to study the examples carefully. Also, check www.routersim.com for a router simulator. Answer the review questions related to that chapter. (The answers appear at the end of the chapter, after the review questions.)

4. Note the questions that confuse you, and study those sections of the book again.

5. Take the Practice Exam in this book. You'll find it in Appendix A. The answers appear at the end of the exam.

6. Before taking the exam, try your hand at the bonus practice exam that is included on the CD that comes with this book. The questions in this exam appear only on the CD. This will give you a complete overview of what you can expect to see on the real thing.

7. Remember to use the products on the CD that is included with this book. The electronic flashcards, the Boson Software utilities, and the EdgeTest exam-preparation software have all been specifically picked to help you study for and pass your exam. Study on the road with the CCNP: *Routing Study Guide* eBook in PDF, and be sure to test yourself with the electronic flashcards.

 The electronic flashcards can be used on your Windows computer or on your Palm device.

8. Make sure you read the Key Terms list at the end of each chapter, and Appendix B includes all the commands used in the book, along with explanations for each command.

To learn all the material covered in this book, you'll have to apply yourself regularly and with discipline. Try to set aside the same time period every day to study, and select a comfortable and quiet place to do so. If you work hard, you will be surprised at how quickly you learn this material. All the best!

What's on the CD?

We worked hard to provide some really great tools to help you with your certification process. All of the following tools should be loaded on your workstation when studying for the test.

The EdgeTest for Cisco Routing Test-Preparation Software

Provided by EdgeTek Learning Systems, this test-preparation software prepares you to successfully pass the Routing exam. In this test engine you will find all of the questions from the book, plus an additional Bonus Exam that appears exclusively on the CD. You can take the Assessment Test, test yourself by chapter, take the Practice Exam that appears in the book or on the CD.

To find more test-simulation software for all Cisco and NT exams, look for the exam link on www.lammle.com and www.boson.com.

Electronic Flashcards for PC and Palm Devices

After you read the *CCNP: Routing Study Guide*, read the review questions at the end of each chapter and study the practice exams included in the book and on the CD. But wait, there's more! Test yourself with the flashcards included on the CD. If you can get through these difficult questions, and understand the answers, you'll know you'll be ready for the CCNP Routing exam.

The flashcards include more than 100 questions specifically written to hit you hard and make sure you are ready for the exam. Between the review questions, practice exam, and flashcards, you'll be more than prepared for the exam.

CCNP: Routing Study Guide in PDF

Sybex is now offering the Cisco Certification books on CD so you can read the book on your PC or laptop. The *Dictionary of Networking* and the *CCNP: Routing Study Guide* are in Adobe Acrobat format. Acrobat Reader 4 with Search is also included on the CD.

This will be extremely helpful to readers who travel and don't want to carry a book, as well as to readers who find it more comfortable reading from their computer.

Boson Software Utilities

Boson Software is an impressive company. It provides many services for free to help you, the student. Boson has the best Cisco exam-preparation questions on the market, and at a very nice price. On the CD of this book, Boson has provided for you the following:

- IP Subnetter
- Superping
- System-Logging
- Wildcard Mask Checker and Decimal-to-IP Calculator
- Router GetPass

CCNA Virtual Lab AVI Demo Files

The *CCNA Virtual Lab e-trainer* provides a router and switch simulator to help you gain hands-on experience without having to buy expensive Cisco gear. The demos are .avi files that you can play in RealPlayer, which is included. The .avi demo files on the CD will help you gain an understanding of the product features and the labs that the routers and switches can perform. Read more about the CCNA Virtual Lab e-trainer at `http://www.sybex.com/cgi-bin/rd_bookpg.pl?2728back.html`. You can upgrade this product at `www.routersim.com`.

How to Contact the Authors

You can reach Todd Lammle through Globalnet System Solutions, Inc. (`www.globalnettraining.com`)—his training and systems integration company in Colorado.

To contact Sean Odom, you can e-mail him at `sodom@rcis.com`.

You can send e-mail to Kevin Wallace at `kevinwallace@mail.com`.

Assessment Test

1. What determines the Router ID used in OSPF virtual-link configuration?

   A. A router interface's MAC address

   B. The IP address of the first interface on a router

   C. The lowest IP address configured on a router

   D. The highest loopback IP address configured on a router

2. Which of the following protocols support VLSM routing? (Choose all that apply.)

   A. RIPv1

   B. RIPv2

   C. IGRP

   D. EIGRP

3. What is the `default-metric` command used for?

   A. It ensures proper metric conversion when redistributing routes from the same routing protocols.

   B. It ensures proper metric conversion when redistributing routes from different protocols.

   C. It changes the administrative weight of a route.

   D. It changes the administrative distance of a route.

4. Which of the following are used specifically to break up collision domains?

   A. Repeaters

   B. Routers

   C. DLC

   D. Switches

   E. Bridges

5. What does the MTU metric component indicate?

   A. Mean Time Unit

   B. Maximum Threshold Unspecified

   C. Minimum TCP UNI

   D. Maximum Transmission Unit

6. RIPv2 provides which of the following benefits over RIPv1?

   A. RIPv2 is link-state.

   B. RIPv2 uses a topology table.

   C. RIPv2 supports VLSM.

   D. RIPv2 uses Hello messages.

7. When an OSPF is not physically adjacent to the backbone area (Area 0), which of the following offers a solution?

   A. A virtual link

   B. An NSSA

   C. A Summary Link Advertisement

   D. A Type 7 LSA

8. Choose the three layers that Cisco uses for building its hierarchical internetwork model. (Choose all that apply.)

   A. Fundamental

   B. Distribution

   C. IGRP

   D. Core

   E. Backbone

   F. Access

9. Which of the following pertain to link-state routing protocols? (Choose all that apply.)

    A. They use the Hello protocol to establish adjacencies.

    B. They use several components to calculate the metric of a route.

    C. Updates are sent only when changes occur in the network.

    D. They are better protocols than distance-vector protocols.

10. Which command provides an EIGRP process to run on a Cisco router?

    A. `ip router eigrp autonomous-system-number`

    B. `router ip eigrp autonomous-system-number`

    C. `router eigrp process-id`

    D. `router eigrp autonomous-system-number`

11. Which of the following is the IOS command to set a router's priority?

    A. `ip ospf no-default priority_number`

    B. `ip ospf no-summary priority_number`

    C. `ip ospf priority priority_number`

    D. `ip ospf-priority priority_number`

12. What IP address represents a local loopback?

    A. 127.0.0.2

    B. 255.255.255.255

    C. 127.1.0.0

    D. 127.0.0.1

13. Which of the following algorithms is used by EIGRP to determine the best path?

   A. Open Shortest Path First Algorithm

   B. Diffusing Update Algorithm

   C. Distance-Vector Algorithm

   D. Link-State Algorithm

   E. Advanced Distance-Vector Algorithm

14. If a route advertised by EIGRP has a load metric of 100, approximately what percentage of the link is being utilized?

   A. 2.5 percent

   B. 25 percent

   C. 39 percent

   D. 100 percent

15. BGP uses which of the following TCP ports to open a session with another BGP peer?

   A. Port 20

   B. Port 21

   C. Port 179

   D. Port 23

16. Which of the following describes the main purpose of the Core layer?

   A. To distribute client-server router information

   B. To provide an optimized and reliable transport structure

   C. To provide access to various parts of the internetwork, as well as to services

   D. To provide access to corporate resources for a workgroup or users on a local segment

17. Which protocols use a topology table? (Choose all that apply.)

   A. EIGRP

   B. IGRP

   C. RIP1

   D. OSPF

18. If you wanted to see the status of all BGP connections by using only one IOS command, which one would that be?

   A. `show ip bgp`

   B. `show ip bgp status`

   C. `show ip bgp all`

   D. `show ip bgp summary`

19. What is the administrative distance of directly connected routes?

   A. 0

   B. 1

   C. 90

   D. 100

   E. 110

20. What are the first two bits in the first byte that defines a Class B network?

   A. 00

   B. 01

   C. 10

   D. 11

21. Which of the following identify the characteristics of a scalable internetwork?

    A. Reliability

    B. Responsiveness

    C. Efficiency

    D. Adaptability

    E. Accessibility

    F. All of the above

22. Which of the following are ways of managing routes advertised by BGP routers? (Choose four.)

    A. Using route maps

    B. Using prefix lists

    C. Using distribute lists

    D. Using path filters

    E. Using re-distribution lists

23. When configuring an OSPF area as a totally stubby area, which of the following routers need to be configured as totally stubby?

    A. All routers in the area

    B. Only the ABRs

    C. Only the ASBRs

    D. Only the internal routers

24. Which subnet mask will support 50 IP addresses?

    A. 255.255.255.240

    B. 255.255.255.248

    C. 255.255.255.192

    D. 255.255.255.224

25. Which IOS command is used to clear all the entries in the BGP table?

    A. `clear ip route *`

    B. `clear ip bgp *`

    C. `clear route`

    D. `reset bgp table`

26. If the `seq` syntax is not used, in what sequence are numbers assigned and in what increment?

    A. 3 (3,6,9...)

    B. 5 (5,10,15...)

    C. 15 (15,30,45...)

    D. 25 (25,50,75...)

27. Route summarization is best described in which of the following?

    A. A router's ability to take a group of subnetworks and summarize them as one network advertisement

    B. The Cisco IOS feature that permits serial interfaces to borrow an IP address from another specified interface

    C. The ability to tunnel IP address information inside an AURP encapsulated frame

    D. EIGRP's ability to isolate discontiguous route advertisements from one AS to another

28. When should BGP be used? (Choose all that apply.)

    A. When multi-homing

    B. When connecting multiple ISPs

    C. When connecting routers within the same AS

    D. When configuring backup links

29. Which routing algorithm does OSPF use for route calculation?

    A. Dijkstra

    B. SPF

    C. Link-state

    D. Distance-vector

30. The IOS command `show ip ospf process-id` shows which of the following?

    A. The information contained in each OSPF packet, such as Router ID and Area ID

    B. Information about a router's OSPF database, such as router link states and network link states

    C. Area information, such as the identification of the ABR

    D. The status of a router's virtual links

31. Which of the following are used in confederations?

    A. iBGP

    B. eBGP

    C. Sub-ASes

    D. Sequence numbers

    E. Confederation identifier

32. When do DR/BDR elections occur? (Choose all that apply.)

    A. When two routers are connected via point-to-point.

    B. When multiple routers are connected via NBMA point-to-multipoint.

    C. When multiple routers are connected via broadcast multi-access.

    D. When multiple routers are connected via NBMA broadcast.

33. What is the MED command used for in BGP?

    A. Provide emergency medical updates on a BGP routing table

    B. Provide Medium Extra Documentation on BGP attributes

    C. Inform neighboring external AS routers as to which link to use to receive traffic

    D. Inform neighboring internal AS routers as to which link to use to receive traffic

34. What parameter of IGRP and EIGRP must be the same if automatic route redistribution is to take place?

    A. process-id

    B. area

    C. metric

    D. weight

35. Which IP address is used as the OSPF Router ID?

    A. Highest IP address

    B. Highest loopback IP address

    C. Lowest IP address

    D. Lowest loopback IP address

36. When a BGP peer tries to open a session with another endpoint, the peer is in which of the following states?

    A. Active state

    B. Connection state

    C. Open state

    D. Established state

37. The multicast address 224.0.0.5 is assigned to which of the following?

    A. AllOSPFRouters

    B. AllDR

    C. AllRouters

    D. AllSPFRouters

38. Which of the following use Type 7 LSAs?

    A. Stub areas

    B. Not-so-stubby areas

    C. Totally stubby areas

    D. Internal routers

39. What is the purpose of a passive interface?

    A. To stop unwanted route information from entering the specified interface

    B. To allow route information to be filtered by an access list

    C. To allow routes to be sent out the specified interface, but deny route information to enter the interface

    D. To allow routes to enter the interface, but deny any route information to exit the specified interface

40. How is a BGP session established between two routers?

    A. Telnet

    B. Hello packets

    C. UDP (SYN, ACK, SYN)

    D. TCP (SYN, ACK, SYN)

41. The neighbor table is used to collect information on which of the following?

    A. Directly connected workstations

    B. All routes through the network

    C. Neighboring routers in other autonomous systems

    D. All directly connected neighboring routers

42. How is the IANA involved in BGP?

    A. They are not involved.

    B. They assign your Internet security.

    C. They provide the IP addresses you use.

    D. They are responsible for assigning ASNs.

43. What is the purpose of the `set` clause in a route map?

    A. To test traffic patterns against a specified access list

    B. To change such routing parameters as default route

    C. To create a specific traffic pattern for the `match` clause to act upon

    D. To translate an entry to the internal port translation table

44. What BGP command syntax identifies the AS of the remote router that the local router will initiate a session with?

    A. `remote-as`

    B. `aggregate-paths`

    C. `connect bgp-all`

    D. `network as-10`

45. BGP is a non-proprietary protocol. However, Cisco provides some proprietary attributes. Which of the following is Cisco proprietary?

    A. Weight attribute

    B. Next-hop attribute

    C. MED attribute

    D. Atomic Aggregate attribute

46. Which of the following are multi-homing classifications for BGP?

    A. Centralized

    B. Basic

    C. Medium

    D. Full

    E. Low

47. Which of the following describes the main purpose of the Distribution layer?

    A. To distribute client-server router information

    B. To provide an optimized and reliable transport structure

    C. To provide access to various parts of the internetwork, as well as to services

    D. To provide access to corporate resources for a workgroup or users on a local segment

48. Why would a BGP router be called a non-client router?

    A. A route reflector not participating in a route reflector cluster in an iBGP network is a non-client router.

    B. A route reflector participating in a route reflector cluster in an iBGP network is a non-client router.

    C. A route reflector not participating in a route reflector cluster is a non-client router. It usually wouldn't be the reflector itself.

    D. A route reflector participating in a route reflector cluster is a non-client router.

49. What routing protocol is based on the work of Edsger Dijkstra?

   A. RIP

   B. IGRP

   C. OSPF

   D. EIGRP

50. Which of the following are considered link-state protocols? (Choose all that apply.)

   A. RIP

   B. RIPv2

   C. IGRP

   D. EIGRP

   E. OSPF

   F. IS-IS

Answers to Assessment Test

1. **D.** In the IOS command `area area-id virtual-link router-id`, the `router-id` is the highest loopback IP number configured on a router. If a loopback interface has not been configured on the router, then the `router-id` is the highest IP address configured on the router. For more information, see Chapter 5.

2. **B, D.** VLSM is compatible only with classless routing protocols. Classless routing protocols have the ability to carry subnet information in their route advertisements. RIPv1 and IGRP are classful, whereas RIPv2 and EIGRP are classless. For more information, see Chapter 3.

3. **B.** The `default-metric` command ensures proper metric conversion when redistributing routes from different protocols. See Chapter 6 for more information.

4. **D, E.** Even though routers do break up collision domains, only bridges and switches are used specifically to break up collision domains. See Chapter 1 for more information on segmentation of a network.

5. **D.** The MTU size metric component is the Maximum Transmission Unit (in bytes) over a specified interface. For example, the default MTU size for an Ethernet interface is 1,500 bytes. For more information, see Chapter 10.

6. **C.** RIPv2 is still distance-vector and acts accordingly. However, it sends prefix routing information in the route updates so it can support VLSM. See Chapter 2 for more information on RIPv2.

7. **A.** When designing OSPF networks, each area within an OSPF routing process should have a link to the backbone area (Area 0). However, when an area is not physically adjacent to Area 0, a virtual link can be used to connect across the transit area, which separates the area from Area 0. For more information, see Chapter 5.

8. B, D, F.   The Cisco three-layer model includes the Core, Distribution, and Access layers. See Chapter 1 for more information on the Cisco three-layer model.

9. A, C.   Link-state protocols do not send entire routing table updates like distance-vector protocols do. Link-state uses Hello messages to make sure that neighbor routers are still alive, and then when a change in the network does occur, it sends only the necessary information about the change. See Chapter 2 for more information on the link-state routing protocols.

10. D.   The command `router eigrp` is used followed by the AS number to implement EIGRP. You must then identify the attached networks using the `network` command. See Chapter 6 for more information.

11. C.   The IOS command to set a router's priority is `ip ospf priority priority_number`, where `priority_number` is a number from 0 to 255. See Chapter 4 for more information.

12. D.   Network 127 is reserved for loopback purposes (e.g., for trouble-shooting diagnostics). With a local loopback address, a host can send a test packet to itself without generating network traffic. For more information, see Chapter 3.

13. B.   The Diffusing Update Algorithm (DUAL) is used to calculate routes in EIGRP. See Chapter 6 for more information.

14. C.   Values for the load metric range from 1 through 255. Therefore, a load metric of 100 indicates an approximate load of 39 percent (100/255 = 39.2). For more information, see Chapter 10.

15. C.   Port 179 is used by BGP to establish a session with another BGP peer. Ports 20 and 21 are used by FTP, and port 23 is used by Telnet. For more information, see Chapter 7.

16. B.   The Core layer should provide a fast transport between Distribution layer devices. See Chapter 1 for more information on the Cisco three-layer model.

17. A, D. EIGRP and OSPF both use a topology table to help maintain a loop-free network. See Chapter 2 for more information on the use of topology tables.

18. B. The `show ip bgp status` command displays the status of all BGP connections. The `show ip bgp summary` command displays the BGP configuration. The other two commands are not valid. For more information, see Chapter 8.

19. A. Directly connected routes have an administrative distance of zero. See Chapter 2 for more information on administrative distances.

20. C. A leading bit pattern of 0 indicates a Class A network. A leading bit pattern of 10 indicates a Class B network. A leading bit pattern of 110 indicates a Class C network. For more information, see Chapter 3.

21. F. An internetwork should be reliable, responsive, efficient, adaptable, and accessible. See Chapter 1 for more information on scalable internetworks.

22. A, B, C, D. There is no such item as a re-distribution list using BGP. The others listed are all valid ways of manipulating routes advertised by BGP. For more information, see Chapter 9.

23. B. When configuring an area as totally stubby, we are stopping summary Link State Advertisements from being injected into the area. Therefore, the IOS router configuration command `area area-id stub no-summary` only needs to be issued on the area border routers (ABRs). However, all of the other routers within the area need to be configured as stubby. Typically, an area will have only one ABR. For more information, see Chapter 5.

24. C. The formula $2^n - 2$ = number of hosts (where n is the number of host bits in the subnet mask) tells us how many hosts can be supported for a particular subnet. For more information, see Chapter 3.

25. B. The `clear ip bgp *` command is used to clear all the entries in the BGP table. For more information, see Chapter 8.

26. B.   Sequence numbers are assigned in increments of five when no sequence number was assigned when the prefix list statements were configured. See Chapter 9 for more information.

27. A.   Route summarization, which works best with contiguous address space, reduces the memory and processor burden on routers by representing multiple subnets in a single route advertisement. For more information, see Chapter 3.

28. A, B.   BGP should be used when multi-homing and when connecting multiple ISPs. For more information, see Chapter 7.

29. A.   SPF is the type of path created by the Dijkstra algorithm. See Chapter 4 for more information.

30. C.   The IOS command show ip ospf process-id shows area information, such as the identity of the area border router (ABR) or autonomous system boundary router (ASBR). For more information, see Chapter 5.

31. A, B, C, E.   Confederations use iBGP on routers in sub-ASes and then use eBGP to connect the sub-ASes. The sequence number is used in prefix lists. The confederation identifier is the number assigned to all the routers to identify that all the routers in the confederation using sub-ASes reside in the same autonomous system. See Chapter 9 for more information.

32. C, D.   There must always a DR and a BDR for each multi-access segment. See Chapter 4 for more information.

33. C.   The MED attribute is used to inform other external AS routers as to which route to use in order to receive traffic. For more information, see Chapter 8.

34. A.   If the IGRP and EIGRP processes are both running on the same router, their routes will be automatically redistributed if their process-ids are equal. This is possible because IGRP and EIGRP use very similar metrics. Note that in some of the literature, the process-id may be referred to as an Autonomous System. For more information, see Chapter 10.

35. B. The highest IP address is used if no loopback interfaces are configured. See Chapter 4 for more information.

36. B. This connection is in the Connection state until a message is sent to identify each peer. When the connection is established, it transitions to the Open state. Once the connection is accepted by the other peer, the connection transitions to Established state. If the connection is lost, possibly due to a version mismatch, the peer goes to the Active state and actively tries to reestablish the connection using the proper version properties. For more information, see Chapter 7.

37. D. AllOSPFRouters does not exist. See Chapter 4 for more information.

38. B. Not-so-stubby areas (NSSAs) import external routes (Type 7 Link State Advertisements) via route redistribution and then translate these Type 7 LSAs into Type 5 LSAs. For more information, see Chapter 5.

39. D. Passive interfaces are used for such interfaces as BRI, where you do not want to have routing updates sent out the interface. See Chapter 6 for more information.

40. D. A BGP session is established between two routers by using a TCP SYN, TCP ACK, and then another TCP SYN. For more information, see Chapter 7.

41. D. The neighbor table tracks all the directly connected routers running EIGRP. The table also tracks the smooth round-trip timer (SRTT), the retransmission timer (RTO), and the hold timer, which are all used by the neighbor table to track its neighboring routers. See Chapter 6 for more information.

42. D. The Internet Assigned Numbers Authority (IANA) is responsible for delegating autonomous system numbers. Other organizations may assign numbers, but only if they are authorized by the IANA. See Chapter 7 for more information.

43. B. After a traffic pattern has been identified by a route map's match clause, the `set` clause sets route parameters such as next-hop address or default route. For more information, see Chapter 10.

44. A. The `remote-as` syntax identifies the peer router that the local router will enable a session with. The IP address identifies the interface attached to the peer router. If the ASN is the same number as the internal ASN, it identifies an internal AS; if it is different, it identifies an external AS. See Chapter 8 for more information.

45. A. The Weight attribute is a Cisco proprietary BGP attribute used as a metric to find the best routes through the networks. See Chapter 8 for more information.

46. B, C, D. When you use multi-homing with only static routes, it is considered a Basic classification. When you use static routes and BGP learned routes, it is considered a Medium classification. When you use only BGP learned routes, it is considered a Full classification. See Chapter 9 for more information.

47. C. The Distribution layer connects Access layer devices together and provides users with network service connections. See Chapter 1 for more information on the Cisco three-layer model.

48. C. Routers not participating as a route reflector client are called non-client routers. Non-client refers to any iBGP peer that is not participating in the route reflector cluster as a client. See Chapter 9 for more information.

49. C. Sometimes referred to as the Dijkstra Algorithm, OSPF uses the Shortest Path First Algorithm to generate its composite metric. For more information, see Chapter 10.

50. E, F. Although EIGRP is really a hybrid routing protocol, it is considered an advanced distance-vector protocol, not link-state. See Chapter 2 for more information on link-state protocols.

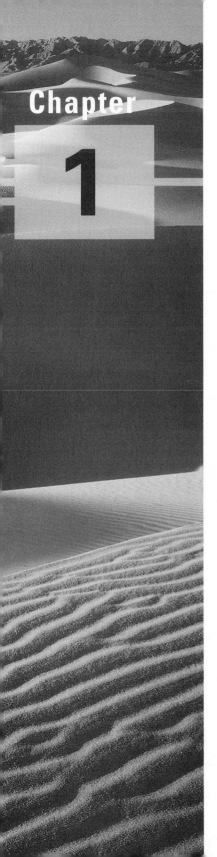

Chapter

1

Scaling Large Internetworks

THE CCNP ROUTING EXAM TOPICS COVERED IN THIS CHAPTER ARE AS FOLLOWS:

✓ Describe causes of network congestion

✓ List solutions for controlling network congestion

✓ Describe the key requirements of a scalable internetwork

✓ Select a Cisco IOS feature as a solution for a given internetwork requirement

We'll begin this book with a review of internetworks and a discussion of the typical business requirements for their implementation in today's marketplace. This discussion will lead naturally into exploring the ubiquitous but avoidable problem of network congestion. Examining both its causes and the solutions for controlling it, we'll describe the key requirements for a scalable internetwork. We'll also look to the Cisco three-layer model for the inherent solutions it provides and unveil helpful Cisco IOS features that will aid us in scaling large internetworks.

Internetworks

An *internetwork* is the communication structure that works to tie LANs and WANs together. Its primary goal is to efficiently move information anywhere within a corporation quickly, upon demand, and with complete integrity. Today's users have become increasingly dependent on their networks—just make a group of users' server or hub go offline and watch the chaos that results around the office.

Where this has led—and what this means for corporations that want to remain capable of competing in today's global market—is that the networks they depend on today have to efficiently manage, on a daily basis, some or all of the following:

- Graphics and imaging
- Files in the gigabyte range
- Client/server computing
- High network traffic loads

To be able to amply meet these needs, the IS department must provide the following to users:

- More bandwidth

- Bandwidth on demand

- Low delays

- Data, voice, and video capabilities on the same media

Also, the network of today must be adaptable in that it must be ready to suit the applications of tomorrow. In the not-too-distant future, networks will need to be equipped to handle

- High-definition imaging

- Full-motion video

- Digitized audio

In short, for an internetwork to realize its purpose, it must be able to efficiently connect many different networks together to serve the organizations that depend on it. This connectivity must happen regardless of the type of physical media involved. Companies expanding their networks must overcome the limitations of physical and geographic boundaries. The Internet has served as a model to facilitate this growth.

Clearing Up Network Congestion

With a combination of powerful workstations, audio and video to the desktop, and network-intensive applications, 10Mbps Ethernet networks no longer offer enough bandwidth to fulfill the business requirements of the typical large business.

As more and more users are connected to the network, an Ethernet network's performance begins to wane as users fight for more bandwidth. As when too many cars try to get onto a freeway at rush hour, this increased utilization causes an increase in network congestion as more users try to access the existing network resources. Congestion causes users to scream for more bandwidth. However, simply increasing bandwidth can't always solve the problem. A slow server CPU or insufficient memory on the workstations and servers can also be the culprit, and these need to be considered as well.

One way to solve congestion problems and increase the networking performance of your LAN is to divide a single Ethernet segment into multiple network segments, which maximizes the available bandwidth. Some of the ways to do that are as follows:

Physical segmentation   You can segment the network with bridges and routers, thereby breaking up the collision and broadcast domains. This minimizes packet collisions by decreasing the number of workstations on the same physical network.

Network switching technology (microsegmentation)   Like a bridge or router, switches can also provide LAN segmentation capabilities. LAN switches (for example, the Cisco Catalyst 5000) provide dedicated, point-to-point, packet-switched connections between their ports. Since this allows simultaneous switching of packets between the ports in the switch, it increases the amount of bandwidth open to each workstation.

Using full-duplex Ethernet devices   Full-duplex Ethernet can provide almost twice the bandwidth of traditional Ethernet networks. However, for this to work, both the switch port and the network interface cards (NICs) must be able to run in Full Duplex mode.

Using Fast or Gigabit Ethernet   Using Fast Ethernet and gigabit switches can provide up to 100 times the amount of bandwidth available from 10BaseT.

It's no surprise—reducing the number of users per collision domain increases the bandwidth on your network segment. By keeping the traffic local to the network segment, users have more bandwidth available to them and enjoy a noticeably better response time than if there was simply one large backbone in place.

Okay, now let's explore some different ways to clear up nasty network congestion problems:

- Segmentation with bridges

- Segmentation with routers

- Segmentation with switches

Segmentation with a Bridge

A bridge can segment, or break up, your network into smaller, more manageable pieces. However, if it's placed incorrectly in your network, it can cause more harm than good.

Bridges perform at the MAC sublayer of the Data Link layer. They create both physical and logical separate network segments to reduce the traffic load. There are solid advantages to bridging—by segmenting a logical network into multiple physical pieces, it secures network reliability, availability, scalability, and manageability.

As Figure 1.1 shows, bridges work by examining the MAC or hardware addresses in each frame and, only if necessary, forwarding the frame to the other physical segments. These devices dynamically build a forwarding table of information composed of each MAC address and the segment that address is located on.

FIGURE 1.1 Segmentation with a bridge

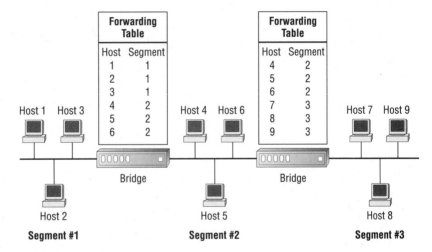

Now for the bad news.... A drawback to using bridges is that if the destination MAC address is unknown to the bridge, it will forward the frame to all segments except the port from which it received the frame. Also, a 20–30 percent latency period can occur for the processing of frames. This delay can increase significantly if the frame cannot be immediately forwarded due to current activity on the destination segment.

Bridges will forward broadcast and multicast packets to all other segments to which they're attached. Since, by default, the addresses from these broadcasts are never seen by the bridge, and hence are not filtered, broadcast storms can result. The same problem can happen with switches because, theoretically, switch ports are bridge ports. A Cisco switch is really a multiport bridge that runs the Cisco IOS and performs the same functions as a bridge.

Segmentation with a Router

As you know, routers work at the Network layer and are used to route packets to destination networks. Routers use routing tables to make routing decisions. However, in the routing tables, routers keep information on how to get to networks in their tables, not to hosts, using that information to route packets through an internetwork. Routers use logical network addresses instead of hardware addresses when making their routing decisions. They maintain a routing table for each protocol on the network—a Cisco router will keep a routing table for AppleTalk, a different one for IPX, and still another for IP, as shown in Figure 1.2.

FIGURE 1.2 Routing tables are kept for each Network layer routing protocol.

IP ROUTING TABLE			IP ROUTING TABLE	
Subnet	Interface		Subnet	Interface
172.16.10.0	E0		172.16.30.0	E0
172.16.20.0	S0		172.16.20.0	S0
172.16.30.0	S0		172.16.10.0	S0

IPX ROUTING TABLE			IPX ROUTING TABLE	
Network Number	Interface		Network Number	Interface
117	S0		10	S0
108	E0		108	E0
10	S0		117	S0

AppleTalk ROUTING TABLE			AppleTalk ROUTING TABLE	
Cable Range	Interface		Cable Range	Interface
2–2	E0		1–1	E0
10–10	S0		10–10	S0
1–1	S0		2–2	S0

Here are the pros regarding routers:

Manageability Multiple routing protocols give the network manager who's creating an internetwork a lot of flexibility.

Increased functionality Cisco routers provide features that address the issues of flow, error and congestion control, fragmentation, reassembly, and control over a packet's lifetime.

Multiple active paths   Using path metrics, routers can make informed routing decisions. This allows routers to have more than one active path between networks. Multiple paths can provide load balancing, which provides more bandwidth to remote networks as well as redundancy.

To provide these advantages, routers must be more complex and more software intensive than bridges. Routers provide a lower level of performance in terms of the number of frames or packets that can be processed per unit.

Segmentation with LAN Switches

LAN switching is a great strategy for LAN segmentation. LAN switches improve performance by employing Layer 2 frame switching, which permits high-speed data exchange.

Just like bridges, switches use the destination MAC address to ensure that the packet is forwarded to the right outgoing port. Cut-through switches begin forwarding the packet before reception is complete, keeping latency to a minimum. Store-and-forward switching receives the entire frame onto its onboard buffers, runs a CRC, and then forwards the frame out the destination port.

There are three different switching-method terms:

Port configuration-switching   Allows a port to be assigned to a physical network segment under software control. It's the simplest form of switching.

Frame-switching   Increases available bandwidth on the network. Frame-switching allows multiple transmissions to occur in parallel. This is the type of switching performed by all Catalyst switches.

Cell-switching (ATM)   Uses small, fixed-length cells that are switched on the network, similar to frame-switching. It's the switching method used by all Cisco Lightstream switches.

A LAN switch supplies you with considerably higher port density at a lower cost than standard bridges. Since the largest benefit of LAN switches is fewer users per segment, the average available bandwidth per user increases. This fewer-users-per-segment trend is known as *microsegmentation*, which lets you create dedicated segments. When you have one user per segment, each one enjoys instant access to the full lot of available bandwidth instead of competing for it with other users. Because of this, the collisions that are common with shared, medium-sized networks that use hubs (half-duplex) just don't happen.

A LAN switch bases the forwarding of frames on the frame's Layer 2 address (Layer 2 LAN switch) or on the Layer 3 address of the packet (multi-layer LAN switch). LAN switches are sometimes referred to as *LAN frame switches* because they generally forward Layer 2 frames in contrast to an ATM switch, which forwards cells. Do not confuse this with Frame Relay, which is a WAN technology.

LAN switches uniquely support some very cool new features, including the following:

- Numerous, simultaneous conversations

- High-speed data exchanges

- Low latency and high frame-forwarding rates

- Dedicated communication between devices

- Full-duplex communication

- Media rate adaptation (10,100, and 1000Mbps hosts can work on the same network)

- The ability to work with existing 802.3-compliant network interface cards and cabling

Thanks to dedicated, collision-free communication between network devices, file-transfer throughput is increased. Many conversations can occur simultaneously by forwarding or switching several packets at the same time, which expands the network capacity by the amount of supported conversations.

The Cisco Three-Layer Model

Cisco has created its own three-layer hierarchical model. The Cisco hierarchical model is used to help you design, implement, and maintain a scalable, reliable, cost-effective hierarchical internetwork. Cisco defines three layers of hierarchy, as shown in Figure 1.3, each with specific functionality.

FIGURE 1.3 The Cisco hierarchical model

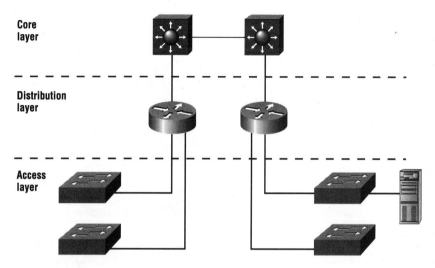

The three layers are:

- The Core layer

- The Distribution layer

- The Access layer

Each layer has specific responsibilities. Remember, however, that the three layers are logical and not necessarily physical. Three layers do not necessarily mean three separate devices. Consider the OSI model, another logical hierarchy. Its seven layers describe functions but not necessarily protocols, right? Sometimes a protocol maps to more than one layer of the OSI model, and sometimes multiple protocols communicate within a single layer. In the same way, when we build physical implementations of hierarchical networks, we may have many devices in a single layer, or we might have a single device performing functions at two layers. The definition of the layers is logical, not physical.

Before you learn about these layers and their functions, consider a common hierarchical design, as shown in Figure 1.4. The phrase "keep local traffic local" has almost become a cliché in the networking world. However, the underlying concept has merit. Hierarchical design lends itself perfectly to fulfilling this concept.

FIGURE 1.4 Hierarchical network design

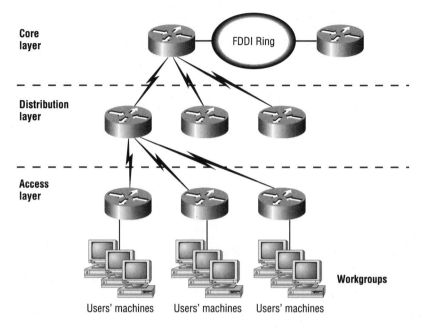

Now, let's take a closer look at each of the layers.

The Core Layer

The *Core layer* is literally the core of the network. At the top of the hierarchy, the Core layer is responsible for transporting large amounts of traffic both reliably and quickly. The only purpose of the Core layer of the network is to switch traffic as fast as possible. The traffic transported across the core is common to a majority of users. However, remember that user data is processed at the Distribution layer, and the Distribution layer forwards the requests to the core if needed.

If there is a failure in the core, every single user can be affected. Therefore, fault tolerance at this layer is an issue. The core is likely to see large volumes of traffic, so speed and latency are driving concerns here. Given the function of the core, we can now consider some design specifics. Let's start with some things that we know we don't want to do:

- Don't do anything to slow down traffic. This includes using access lists, routing between virtual local area networks (VLANs), and packet filtering.

- Don't support workgroup access here.

- Avoid expanding the core when the internetwork grows (i.e., adding routers). If performance becomes an issue in the core, give preference to upgrades over expansion.

Now, there are a few things that we want to make sure to do as we design the core. They include:

- Design the core for high reliability. Consider data-link technologies that facilitate both speed and redundancy, such as FDDI, Fast Ethernet (with redundant links), or even ATM.

- Design with speed in mind. The core should have very little latency.

- Select routing protocols with lower convergence times. Fast and redundant data-link connectivity is no help if your routing tables are shot!

The Distribution Layer

The *Distribution layer* is sometimes referred to as the *workgroup layer* and is the communication point between the Access layer and the Core layer. The primary function of the Distribution layer is to provide routing, filtering, and WAN access and to determine how packets can access the core, if needed. The Distribution layer must determine the fastest way that user requests are serviced, for example, how a file request is forwarded to a server. After the Distribution layer determines the best path, it forwards the request to the Core layer. The Core layer is then responsible for quickly transporting the request to the correct service.

The Distribution layer is the place to implement policies for the network. Here, you can exercise considerable flexibility in defining network operation. There are several items that generally should be done at the Distribution layer. They include

- Implementing tools such as access lists, packet filtering, and queuing

- Implementing security and network policies, including address translation and firewalls

- Redistribution between routing protocols, including static routing

- Routing between VLANs and other workgroup support functions

- Broadcast and multicast domain definition

Things to avoid at the Distribution layer are limited to those functions that exclusively belong to one of the other layers.

The Access Layer

The *Access layer* controls user and workgroup access to internetwork resources. The Access layer is sometimes referred to as the *desktop layer*. The network resources that most users need will be available locally. The Distribution layer handles any traffic for remote services. The functions to be included at this layer include

- Continued (from the Distribution layer) access control and policies

- Creation of separate collision domains (segmentation)

- Workgroup connectivity into the Distribution layer

Technologies such as DDR and Ethernet switching are frequently seen in the Access layer as well as the Distribution layer. If you are using DDR to connect to a remote office, then it has to be a Distribution layer device. Static routing (instead of dynamic routing protocols) is seen here as well.

As already noted, three separate levels does not have to imply three separate routers. It could be fewer, or it could be more. Remember, this is a *layered* approach.

Requirements of the Scalable Internetwork

Today's internetworks are experiencing extraordinary growth due to increasing demands for connectivity both in businesses and at home. Therefore, it's very important for them to be scalable. It's now vital for administrators to understand what a scalable network is, as well as what is required to effectively manage its incessant growth.

Since a scalable internetwork undergoes continual growth, it must be both flexible and easily appended. An ideal design is based on the hierarchical model to simplify management and permit well-planned growth that honors the network's requirements. Here are the requirements of a scalable internetwork:

It must be reliable and available.   The Cisco IOS provides features for implementing redundancy, load balancing, and reachability with protocols such as OSPF and EIGRP.

It must be responsive.   Because network growth often occurs on a daily basis, the administrator's duty to maintain the network's responsiveness can become overwhelming. The Cisco IOS provides solutions to provide Quality of Service (QoS) that will allow multiple protocols to be supported on the network, without compromising QoS requirements.

It must be efficient.   Efficiency, in a nutshell, means keeping the bandwidth from becoming saturated. A central goal of this book is to arm you with information on fine-tuning your router to optimize the existing bandwidth on your internetwork. You'll learn how to achieve that objective through innovative techniques such as using access lists, optimizing route update operations, and scaling IP addresses.

It must be adaptable.   The internetwork must be designed to respond masterfully to change and to accommodate disparate networks as well as older legacy technologies.

It must be easily accessible while being secure.   It is a network administrator's foremost obligation (obsession?) to meet business requirements by ensuring that network resources remain available to users at all times, while managing to keep out any and all hackers. The Cisco IOS provides dedicated and switched WAN support such as Frame Relay, SMDS, X.25, and ATM to equip networking professionals with options to meet cost, location, security, and traffic requirements. The Cisco IOS also provides exterior routing support with the Exterior Gateway Protocol (EGP) and Border Gateway Protocol (BGP) to permit routing on the Internet with maximum security.

We will talk about each of these requirements in the following sections.

Reliability and Availability

Because a network is depended upon so heavily—ideally, it's up and running 24 hours a day, 365 days a year—failures and downtime must be kept to a minimum. It's also vital that when a failure does occur, it's easy to isolate, reducing the time needed for troubleshooting. When it comes to reliability, the internetwork's Core layer is the most critical. Cisco's definition of *reliable* is an internetwork that can respond quickly to changes in the network topology and accommodate failures by rerouting traffic.

Some Cisco IOS features that serve to provide stability and availability are as follows:

Reachability   OSPF and EIGRP use expanded metrics that can go beyond the hop-count limitations of distance-vector routing algorithms. These routing protocols analyze a combination of factors to establish the real cost of a path to a network, making Cisco routers able to support very large internetworks.

Convergence   Scalable routing protocols can converge quickly because of each router's complete understanding of the internetwork and ability to detect problems.

Responsiveness

Since it's the network administrator's responsibility to make sure users don't experience delays in responsiveness as the internetwork grows, they must be keenly aware of the latency factor that each piece of equipment (routers, switches, and bridges) contributes to the internetwork. The Cisco IOS provides mitigation for the latency needs of each protocol running on your internetwork, with features such as

Alternate paths routing   Because OSPF and EIGRP build a complete map of the internetwork, a router can easily reroute traffic to an alternate path if a problem occurs.

Load balancing   Through the EIGRP and OSPF routing algorithms, the Cisco IOS is able to perform load balancing. This allows for redundant links and for more bandwidth to be available to locations needing more than just one link. For example, if two T1 WAN links were installed between buildings, the actual bandwidth between them would reach approximately 3Mbps.

Tunneling   Running a tunneling protocol affords the ability to communicate across WAN links that were previously unreachable. For example, if you have a WAN link that supports only TCP/IP and you want to manage a Novell NetWare server that supports only IPX, you could tunnel IPX packets inside of IP packets to achieve your goal.

Dial backup   You can configure dial-backup links for redundancy on your WAN links and to add extra bandwidth whenever it becomes saturated, enhancing the link's reliability and availability.

Efficiency

The task of creating smoothly running, efficient LANs and internetworks is obviously very important, but optimizing the bandwidth on a WAN can be very difficult. The best way to reduce the bandwidth usage is to reduce the amount of update traffic on the LAN that will be sent over your WAN. The Cisco IOS features available to help reduce bandwidth usage are as follows:

Access lists   Used to permit or deny certain types of traffic from entering or exiting a specific router interface. They can stop basic traffic, broadcasts, and protocol updates from saturating a particular link. TCP/IP, IPX, and AppleTalk can all be filtered extensively.

Snapshot routing   Commonly used for ISDN connections when running distance-vector protocols, it allows routers to exchange full distance-vector routing information at an interval defined by the administrator.

Compression over WANs   The Cisco IOS supports TCP/IP header and data compression to reduce the amount of traffic crossing a WAN link. Link compression can be configured, which compresses header and data information into packets. This is accomplished by the Cisco IOS prior to sending the frame across the WAN.

DDR (Dial-on-Demand Routing)   DDR allows wide area links to be used selectively. With it, the administrator can define "interesting" traffic on the router and initiate point-to-point WAN links based upon that traffic. What denotes interesting traffic is defined by access lists, so a great deal of flexibility is afforded to the administrator. For instance, an expensive ISDN connection to the Internet could be initiated to retrieve e-mail, but not for a WWW request. DDR is an effective tool in situations where WAN access is charged according to a quantified time interval—it's best to use it in situations where WAN access is infrequent.

Reduction in routing table entries   By using route summarization and incremental updates, you can reduce the number of router processing cycles by reducing the entries in a routing table. Route summarization occurs at major network boundaries, which summarize all the routes advertised into one entry. Incremental updates save bandwidth by sending only topology changes instead of the entire routing table when transmitting updates.

Switched access   Packet-switched networks such as X.25 and Frame Relay provide global connectivity through a large number of service providers with established circuits to most major cities.

Adaptability

Another important goal for an administrator is to design an internetwork that responds well to change. To achieve this goal, internetworks need to be able to

Pass both routable and nonroutable network protocols   Examples would be TCP/IP, which is routable, and Microsoft's NetBEUI (NetBIOS Extended User Interface), which is not routable, only bridgeable.

Create islands of networks using different protocols   This allows you to add protocols used by the network islands to Core layer routers or use tunneling in the backbone to connect the islands, which keeps you from having to add unwanted protocols to the core backbone.

Balance between multiple protocols in a network   Each protocol has different requirements, and the internetwork must be able to accommodate the specific issues of each one.

The Cisco IOS also has many different features that contribute to network adaptability:

EIGRP   Cisco's proprietary EIGRP allows you to use multiple protocols within one routing algorithm. EIGRP supports IP, IPX, and AppleTalk.

Redistribution   Allows you to exchange routing information between networks that use different routing protocols. For example, you can update a routing table from a network running IGRP on a router participating in an RIP network.

Accessibility and Security

Access routers must be both accessed and used to access a variety of WAN services, while maintaining security to keep hackers out.

The Cisco IOS features that support these requirements are as follows:

Dedicated and switched WAN support   You can create a direct connection with Cisco routers using basic or digital services (a T1, for example). Cisco routers also support many different switched services, such as Frame Relay, SMDS, X.25, and ATM, to give you options to meet cost, location, and traffic requirements.

Exterior protocol support   Both Exterior Gateway Protocol (EGP) and Border Gateway Protocol (BGP) are supported by the Cisco IOS. BGP (discussed in detail in Chapters 7 through 9) is used primarily by Internet Service Providers (ISPs) and has mostly replaced EGP.

Access lists   Used to filter specific kinds of traffic from either entering or leaving a Cisco router.

Authentication protocols   Cisco supports both Password Authentication Protocol (PAP) and Challenge Handshake Authentication Protocol (CHAP) for providing authentication on WAN connections using PPP.

Summary

In this chapter, we covered the network congestion issues and showed how to solve them. For an internetwork to realize its purpose, it must be able to efficiently connect many different networks together to serve the organizations depending on it. However, the more users and networks that you tie together, the more network congestion results.

The way to solve congestion problems and increase the networking performance of your LAN is to divide a single Ethernet segment into multiple network segments using bridges, routers, and switches.

We also discussed in this chapter that the key requirements of a scalable internetwork are based on an ideal design using the Cisco hierarchical model to simplify management, which permits well-planned growth that honors the network's requirements.

The following issues were discussed as mandatory requirements of a scalable internetwork:

- Reliability and availability

- Responsiveness

- Efficiency

- Adaptability

- Easy accessibility while maintaining security

Key Terms

Before taking the exam, make sure you're familiar with the following terms:

Access layer

Core layer

Distribution layer

internetwork

microsegmentation

Written Lab

1. Match the following letters to the *numbered* list below:

   A. Reliable and available

   B. Responsive

   C. Efficient

   D. Adaptable

   E. Accessible but secure

   Numbered Term   Letter

   1. Authentication protocols

   2. Reachability

   3. Create islands of networks using different protocols

   4. DDR (Dial-on-Demand Routing)

   5. Convergence

   6. Alternate paths routing

   7. Compression over WANs

   8. Exterior protocol support

   9. Balance between multiple protocols in a network

   10. Switched access

Review Questions

1. Which of the following can you use to alleviate congestion in an internetwork (if used correctly)?

   A. Repeaters

   B. Routers

   C. DLC

   D. Switches

   E. Bridges

2. Choose the three layers Cisco uses for building its hierarchical internetwork model.

   A. Fundamental

   B. Distribution

   C. IGRP

   D. Core

   E. Backbone

   F. Access

3. Identify the characteristics of a scalable internetwork.

   A. Reliability

   B. Responsiveness

   C. Efficiency

   D. Adaptability

   E. Accessibility

   F. All of the above

4. What is the primary function of the Core layer?

    A. To distribute client/server router information

    B. To provide an optimized and reliable transport structure

    C. To provide access to various parts of the internetwork, as well as to services

    D. To provide access to corporate resources for a workgroup or users on a local segment

5. What is the primary function of the Distribution layer?

    A. To distribute client/server router information

    B. To provide an optimized and reliable transport structure

    C. To provide access to various parts of the internetwork, as well as to services

    D. To provide access to corporate resources for a workgroup or users on a local segment

6. What is the purpose of the Access layer?

    A. To distribute client/server router information

    B. To provide an optimized and reliable transport structure

    C. To provide access to various parts of the internetwork, as well as to services

    D. To provide access to corporate resources for a workgroup or users on a local segment

7. How do LAN switches improve performance on a LAN?

    A. By filtering via logical address

    B. By regenerating the digital signal

    C. By employing packet-switching that permits high-speed data exchanges

    D. By employing frame-switching that permits high-speed data exchanges

8. What is a benefit of bridge segmentation?

   A. Regeneration and propagation

   B. Segmenting, or breaking up, your network into smaller, more manageable pieces

   C. LAN queuing

   D. Forwarding the frame before reception is complete

9. How does cut-through switching provide better performance than other switching methods?

   A. By using LAN queuing

   B. By using microsegmentation

   C. By receiving the entire frame onto onboard buffers, running a CRC, and then forwarding the frames out the destination port

   D. By forwarding the frame before reception is complete

10. LAN segmentation with switches is also called what?

   A. Filtering

   B. Microsegmentation

   C. Bridging

   D. Routing

11. Which Cisco layer governs access to Core layer resources?

   A. Distribution

   B. Core

   C. Backbone

   D. Access

12. Which layer should have the most redundancy?

    A. Backbone

    B. Core

    C. Distribution

    D. Access

13. How do bridges filter a network?

    A. By logical address

    B. By IP address

    C. By hardware address

    D. By digital signaling

14. How do routers filter a network? (Choose all that apply.)

    A. By logical address

    B. By IP address

    C. By digital signaling

    D. By hardware address

    E. By IPX address

15. How do switches segment a network?

    A. By logical address

    B. By IP address

    C. By hardware address

    D. By IPX address

16. What is a drawback of filtering a network with bridges?

    A. It segments the network.

    B. It creates internetworks.

    C. It forwards all broadcasts.

    D. It filters frames.

17. How can you reduce routing table entries?

    A. Route summarization

    B. Incremental updates

    C. IP filtering

    D. VLANs

18. Which Cisco IOS features are available to help reduce bandwidth usage? (Choose all that apply.)

    A. Access lists

    B. Snapshot routing

    C. Compression of WANs

    D. TTL

    E. DDR

    F. Incremental updates

19. Which Cisco IOS features serve to provide stability and availability? (Choose all that apply.)

A. Reachability

B. Convergence

C. Alternative path routing

D. Snapshot routing

E. Tunneling

F. Dial backup

G. Load balancing

20. Which Cisco layer is responsible for breaking up collision domains?

A. Core

B. Backbone

C. Distribution

D. Access

Answers to Written Lab

1.

Numbered Term	Letter
1. Authentication protocols	E
2. Reachability	A
3. Create islands of networks using different protocols	D
4. DDR (Dial-on-Demand Routing)	C
5. Convergence	A
6. Alternate paths routing	B
7. Compression over WANs	C
8. Exterior protocol support	E
9. Balance between multiple protocols in a network	D
10. Switched access	C

Answers to Review Questions

1. B, D, E. Routers, switches, and bridges are used to segment a network and alleviate congestion on a network segment.

2. B, D, F. The Cisco three-layer model includes the Core, Distribution, and Access layers.

3. F. An internetwork should be reliable, responsive, efficient, adaptable, and accessible.

4. B. The Core layer should provide a fast transport between Distribution layer devices.

5. C. The Distribution layer connects Access layer devices together and provides users with network service connections.

6. D. The Access layer is the connection point for users into the internetwork.

7. D. LAN switches are Layer 2 devices that filter by hardware address in a frame.

8. B. Bridges filter the network by using the hardware address in a frame and create smaller collision domains.

9. D. Cut-through LAN switching begins forwarding the frame to the destination device as soon as the destination hardware address is read in the frame.

10. B. Microsegmentation is a term for breaking up collision domains into smaller segments.

11. A. The Distribution layer is responsible for connecting the Access layer devices together and managing data flow to the Core layer.

12. B. If there is a failure in the core, every single user can be affected. Therefore, fault tolerance at this layer is an issue.

13. C. Bridges use the hardware address in a frame to filter a network.

14. A, B, E. Routers use logical network addresses. IP and IPX are examples of logical network addresses.

15. C. Switches, like bridges, use hardware addresses in a frame to filter the network.

16. C. Both switches and bridges break up collision domains but are one large broadcast domain by default. All broadcasts are forwarded to all network segments with a bridge or switch.

17. A. Route summarization is used to send fewer route entries in an update. This can reduce the routing table entries.

18. A, B, C, E, F. Access lists, snapshot routing, compression techniques, Dial-on-Demand Routing (DDR), and incremental updates all can help reduce bandwidth usage.

19. C, D, E, F. Alternate path routing, which provides redundancy and load balancing, along with snapshot routing, tunneling, and dial backup, all provide stability and availability in an internetwork.

20. D. The Access layer is responsible for breaking up collision domains.

Chapter

2

Routing Principles

THE CCNP ROUTING EXAM TOPICS COVERED IN THIS CHAPTER ARE AS FOLLOWS:

- ✓ List the key information routers need to route data
- ✓ Describe the use of the fields in a routing table
- ✓ Describe classful and classless routing protocols
- ✓ Compare distance-vector and link-state routing protocol operation
- ✓ Given a pre-configured laboratory network, discover the topology, analyze the routing table, and test connectivity using accepted troubleshooting techniques

In this chapter, you will learn the difference between distance-vector and link-state routing protocols. The idea of this chapter is to provide you with an overview of the different types of routing protocols available, not how to configure routers. Distance-vector protocols will be covered in more detail in this chapter than link-state because link-state routing protocols are covered very thoroughly starting at Chapter 4, "OSPF Areas."

This is an important chapter to understand before moving on to the link-state routing protocol chapters. Having a fundamental understanding of the distance-vector and link-state concepts is important, as it will help you when you design internetworks and the routing protocol implementation.

Fundamentals of Routing

Routing is the process of forwarding packets from one network to another; this is sometimes referred to as a *relay system*. Logical addressing is used to identify each network as well as each device on the network. The actual movement of transient traffic through the router is a separate function; it is actually considered to be the switching function. Routing devices must perform both a routing and a switching function to be effective.

For a routing decision to take place on a relay system, three major decisions must be made:

- Is the logical destination address a known protocol? Is this protocol enabled on the router and active? This does not have to be IP; IPX, AppleTalk, and other protocol suites can be used as well.

- Is the destination logical address in the routing table? If not, discard the packet and send an ICMP (Internet Control Message Protocol) message to the sender.

- If the destination logical address is in the routing table, to which interface will the packet be forwarded? Once this exit, or forwarding interface, is chosen, the router must have an encapsulation in which to place the packet. This is called *framing* and is required to forward the packet to the next-hop logical device.

Once the packet is framed, it is forwarded from hop to hop until it reaches the final destination device. Routing tables in each device are used to pass the packet to the correct destination network.

Routing Tables

All the routing information needed for a router to forward packets to a next-hop relay device can be found in the router's *routing table*. Again, if a destination logical address is not found in the table, the router discards the packets. A gateway of last resort can be set on the router to forward packets not listed in the routing table. This is called *setting the default route*.

However, this is not a default gateway, nor does it act as a default gateway, so it is important to not think of setting the gateway of last resort as setting a default gateway. Default gateways are used on hosts to direct packets to a relay device if the destination logical device is not on the local segment. Gateway-of-last-resort entries are used to send packets to a next-hop relay device if the destination logical address is not found in the routing table. If the destination logical address is in the routing table, then the gateway of last resort will not be used.

A sample routing table is shown below:

```
2600B#sh ip route
Codes: C - connected, S - static, I - IGRP, R - RIP, M -
mobile, B - BGP, D - EIGRP, EX - EIGRP external, O - OSPF,
IA - OSPF inter area. N1 - OSPF NSSA external type 1, N2 -
OSPF NSSA external type 2, E1 - OSPF external type 1, E2 -
OSPF external type 2, E - EGP, i - IS-IS, L1 - IS-IS
level-1, L2 - IS-IS level-2, * - candidate default
        U - per-user static route, o - ODR
        T - traffic engineered route
```

```
Gateway of last resort is not set

     172.16.0.0/24 is subnetted, 6 subnets
C       172.16.60.0 is directly connected, BRIO/0
C       172.16.50.0 is directly connected, Ethernet0/0
S       172.16.10.0 [1/0] via 172.16.50.1, Ethernet0/0
S       172.16.11.0 [1/0] via 172.16.50.1, Ethernet0/0
R       172.16.50.0 [120/3] via 172.16.10.2,
        ↳FastEthernet0/0
R       172.16.40.0 [120/2] via 172.16.10.2,
        ↳FastEthernet0/0


2600B#
```

At the top of the routing table are the different codes that describe the entries found in a routing table. In the example above, the entries include both directly connected static routes and RIP entries.

Let's take a look at a static route entry:

```
S       172.16.10.0 [1/0] via 172.16.50.1, Ethernet0/0
```

The list below describe the different parts of the routing table entry:

S The means by which the entry was learned on this router. S is for static entry, which means that the administrator added the route manually.

172.16.10.0 The logical destination remote network or subnet.

[1 The administrative distance, or trustworthiness, of a route. (We discuss this in the next section.)

/0] The metric value. Since it is a static route, the value is 0 because the router is not learning the route; thus the router has nothing to compare the route with. This value will vary widely depending on the routing protocol used.

via 172.16.50.1 The address of the next relay device to forward packets to.

Ethernet0 The interface from which the path was learned and to which the packets will be forwarded.

Administrative Distances

When configuring routing protocols, you need to be aware of *administrative distances*. These are used to rate the trustworthiness of routing information received on a router from a neighbor router. An administrative distance is an integer from 0 to 255, where 0 is the most trusted and 255 means no traffic will be passed via this route.

Table 2.1 shows the default administrative distances that a Cisco router will use to decide which route to take to a remote network.

TABLE 2.1   Default Administrative Distances

Route Source	Default Distance
Connected interface	0
Static route	1
EIGRP summary	5
External BGP	20
EIGRP	90
IGRP	100
OSPF	110
IS-IS	115
RIP	120
EDP	140
External EIGRP	170
Internal BGP	200
Unknown	255 (This route will never be used.)

If a network is directly connected, it will always use the interface connected to the network. If an administrator configures a static route, the router will believe that route over any other learned routes. However, you can change the administrative distance of static routes, but, by default, they have an administrative distance of 1.

Packet Switching

After a router is started up, the routing protocol tries to establish neighbor relationships in order to understand the network topology and build the routing table. All routing protocols perform this differently; for example, some use broadcast addresses to find the neighbors and some use multicast addresses.

Once the neighbors are found, the routing protocol creates a peer relationship at Layers 4 through 7 of the OSI model. Routing protocols either send periodic routing updates or exchange Hello messages to maintain the relationship.

Only after the topology is completely understood and the best paths to all remote networks are decided and put in the routing table can the forwarding of packets begin. This forwarding of packets received on an interface to an exit interface is known as *packet-switching*.

There are four basic steps for a router to packet switch:

1. The router receives a frame on an interface, runs a CRC (cyclic redundancy check), and if it is okay, checks the hardware destination address. If it matches, the packet is pulled from the frame. The frame is discarded and the packet is buffered in main memory.

2. The packet's destination logical address is checked. This address is looked up in the routing table for a match. If there is no match, the packet is immediately discarded and an ICMP message is sent back to the originating device. If there is a match, the packet is switched to the forwarding interface buffer.

3. The hardware address of the next-hop device must be known. The ARP cache is checked first and if it is not found, an ARP broadcast is sent to the device. The remote device will respond with its hardware address.

4. A new frame is created on that interface and the packet is placed in this frame. The destination hardware address is the address of the next-hop device. Notice that the packet was not altered in any way.

Dynamic Routing

Dynamic routing is the process of using protocols to find and update routing tables on routers and to maintain a loop-free, single path to each network. This is easier than static or default routing, but you use it at the expense of router CPU processes and bandwidth usage on the network links. A routing protocol defines the set of rules used by a router when it communicates between neighbor routers.

Once the router process knows the metric values of each path, then routing decisions are made. When a route is learned from different sources, the router will first choose the route with the lowest administrative distance. If two routes have the same AD, then the router will use the routing metrics to determine the best path to the remote network. If the AD is the same in both routes, as well as the metrics, then the routing protocol will load balance.

There are two types of dynamic routing protocols used in internetworks: Interior Gateway Protocols (IGP) and Exterior Gateway Protocols (EGP). IGP routing protocols are used to exchange routing information with routers in the same *autonomous system (AS)*. An AS is a collection of networks under a common administrative domain. EGPs are used to communicate between ASes. An example of an EGP is the Border Gateway Protocol (BGP), which is discussed in Chapters 8 through 9.

Routing Protocols

There are two classes of dynamic routing protocols:

Distance-vector   The *distance-vector protocol* uses the distance to a remote network as a determination of the best path to a remote network. Each time a packet goes through a router, it's called a *hop*. The route with the least number of hops to the remote network is determined to be the best route. The vector is the determination of direction to the remote network.

 Examples of a distance-vector protocol are RIP and IGRP.

However, not all distance-vector protocols use hop count in their metric. IGRP uses bandwidth and delay of the line to determine the best path to a remote network. It is considered a distance-vector protocol because it sends out the complete routing table at periodic intervals. The periodic routing updates from a distance-vector router are sent only to directly connected routers and sent as a broadcast of 255.255.255.255. Since the updates include all routes that the sending router knows about, this is sometimes referred to as "routing by rumor" because a router will accept information from a neighbor as correct. The disadvantage to distance-vector protocols is that the periodic updates consume bandwidth even if there are no topology changes to report.

Link-state   Typically called shortest path first, *link-state routers* create three separate tables. One of these tables keeps track of directly attached neighbors, one determines the topology of the entire internetwork, and one is used for the routing table. Link-state routers know more about the internetwork than any distance-vector protocol. An example of an IP routing protocol that is completely link-state is OSPF.

To send routing updates, the link-state router uses a triggered-update type of announcement. These announcements are sent from a router only when a topology change has occurred within the network. The advantage of link-state routing over distance-vector is that when an update occurs, only the information about the link that changed is contained in the update.

There is no set way of configuring routing protocols for use with every business. This task is performed on a case-by-case basis. However, if you understand how the different routing protocols work, you can make good business decisions.

Both distance-vector and link-state routing protocols are discussed in more detail later in this chapter.

Classful Routing

The basic definition of classful routing is that subnet mask information is not carried within the routine, periodic routing updates. This means that every interface and host on the network must use the same subnet mask. Examples of classful routing protocols are the Routing Information Protocol version 1 (RIPv1) and the Interior Gateway Routing Protocol (IGRP).

RIP version 2 (RIPv2) is an example of a classless routing protocol. Classless routing is discussed later in this chapter.

Devices in an internetwork must know the routing mask associated with any advertised subnets, or those subnets cannot be advertised. If the subnet mask does not match the receiving device, then the receiving device must summarize the received route as a classful boundary and then send the default routing mask in its own advertisements.

Classful routing protocols must exchange routing information using the same subnet mask since subnet mask information is not sent in the periodic updates.

The problem with classful routing protocols is wasted address space. For example, in Figure 2.1, there is a Class C network address of 192.16.10.0, using the subnet mask 255.255.255.240. The subnets would be 16, 32, 48, 64, etc. Each subnet has 14 valid hosts. In the figure, each LAN has a requirement of 10 hosts each, which is fine except for the WAN links connecting the sites. WAN links use only two IP addresses. Since the WAN interfaces must use the same mask, they waste 12 host addresses.

FIGURE 2.1 Classful routing protocol issues

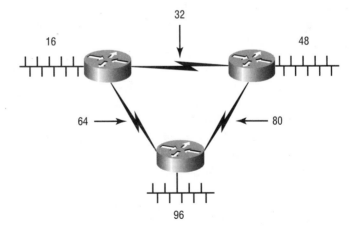

Another problem with classful routing protocols is the periodic routing updates sent out all active interfaces of every router. Distance-vector protocols, which we discuss next, are true classful routing protocols that send complete routing table entries out all active interfaces at periodic time intervals. This can cause congestion on the slower WAN links.

Classless Routing

Classless routing protocols include the subnet mask information when an update is sent. This allows different length subnet masks to be used on the network, called Variable Length Subnet Masks (VLSM). You must use a classless routing protocol if you want to have a network design like the one shown in Figure 2.2.

FIGURE 2.2 Classless network using VLSM

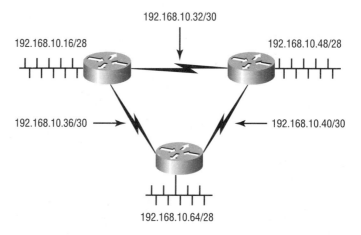

What the classless protocol allows is a subnet mask of 255.255.255.240 on the LANs and a subnet mask of 255.255.255.252 on the WANs, which saves address space.

VLSM is not the only benefit of classless routing protocols. Classless routing protocols allow summarization at non-major network boundaries, unlike classful routing protocols, which allow summarization only at major network boundaries.

Another benefit of classless routing is that less bandwidth is consumed since no periodic updates are sent out the routers' interfaces. Updates are sent only when a change occurs, and then only the change is sent, not the entire routing table as with classful routing protocols. If no changes occur, classless routing protocols send Hello messages to their directly connected neighbors. This ensures that the neighbors are still alive. Only if a router does not receive a Hello message from its neighbor will a convergence of the network take place.

Distance-Vector Protocols

There are four different distance-vector routing algorithms supported by Cisco routers. Table 2.2 shows the different protocols available along with their characteristics. RIP and IGRP use the Bellman-Ford algorithm. EIGRP uses the Diffusing Update-based Algorithm (DUAL).

EIGRP is considered an advanced distance-vector routing algorithm, and Cisco lists it as a distance-vector routing algorithm in their BSCN course. However, since it uses both the characteristics of distance-vector and link-state, it is really considered a hybrid routing protocol. EIGRP will be discussed in detail in Chapter 6, "IGRP and EIGRP."

TABLE 2.2 Distance-Vector Comparisons

Characteristic	RIPv1	RIPv2	IGRP	EIGRP
Count to infinity	X	X	X	
Split horizon with poison reverse	X	X	X	X
Hold-down timer	X	X	X	
Triggered updates with route poisoning	X	X	X	X
Load balancing with equal paths	X	X	X	X

TABLE 2.2 Distance-Vector Comparisons *(continued)*

Characteristic	RIPv1	RIPv2	IGRP	EIGRP
Load balancing with unequal paths			X	X
VLSM support		X		X
Metric	Hops	Hops	Composite	Composite
Hop count limit	16	16	255 (100 by default)	255 (100 by default)
Support for size of network	Medium	Medium	Large	Large

We will discuss RIP and IGRP in detail in the following sections.

RIP

Routing Information Protocol (RIP) is a true distance-vector protocol. It sends the complete routing table out to all active interfaces every 30 seconds. RIP uses only hop count to determine the best way to a remote network, but it has a maximum allowable hop count of 15, meaning that 16 is deemed unreachable. RIP works well in small networks, but it is inefficient on large networks with slow WAN links or on networks with a large number of routers installed.

RIP version 1 uses only classful routing, which means that all devices in the network must use the same subnet mask. This is because RIP version 1 does not send updates with subnet mask information in tow. RIP version 2 provides what is called *prefix routing* and does send subnet mask information with the route updates. RIPv2 uses classless routing.

To keep a network stable, RIP uses timers.

RIP Timers

RIP uses three different kinds of timers to regulate its performance:

Route update timer   Sets the interval (typically 30 seconds) between periodic routing updates in which the router sends a complete copy of its routing table out to all neighbors.

Route invalid timer   Determines the length of time that must expire (90 seconds) before a router determines that a route has become invalid. It will come to this conclusion if it hasn't heard any updates about a particular route for that period. When that happens, the router will send out updates to all its neighbors, letting them know that the route is invalid.

Route flush timer   Sets the time between a route becoming invalid and its removal from the routing table (240 seconds). Before it is removed from the table, the router notifies its neighbors of that route's impending doom. The value of the route invalid timer must be less than that of the route flush timer. This is to provide the router with enough time to tell its neighbors about the invalid route before the routing table is updated.

RIP Updates

The distance-vector routing algorithm passes complete routing tables to neighbor routers. The neighbor routers then combine the received routing table with their own routing tables to complete the internetwork map. This is called *routing by rumor*, as a router receiving an update from a neighbor router believes the information about remote networks without actually finding out for itself.

It is possible to have a network with multiple links to the same remote network. If that is the case, the administrative distance is first checked. If the administrative distance is the same, it will have to use other metrics to determine the best path to use to that remote network.

RIP uses only hop count to determine the best path to an internetwork. If RIP finds more than one link to the same remote network with the same hop count, it will automatically perform a round-robin load balance. RIP can perform load balancing for up to six equal-cost links.

However, a problem with this type of routing metric arises when the two links to a remote network are different bandwidths but the same hop count. Figure 2.3, for example, shows two links to remote network 172.16.50.0.

Since network 172.16.30.0 is a T1 link with a bandwidth of 1.544Mbps, and network 172.16.20.0 is a 56K link, you would want the router to choose the T1 over the 56K link. However, since hop count is the only metric used with RIP routing, they would both be seen as equal-cost links. This is called *pinhole congestion*.

FIGURE 2.3 Pinhole congestion

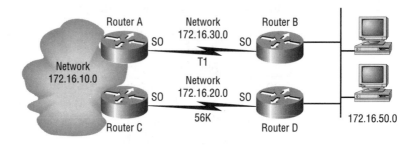

It is important to understand what happens when a distance-vector protocol starts up. In Figure 2.4, the four routers start off with only their directly connected networks in the routing table. After a distance-vector protocol is started on each router, the routing tables are updated with all route information gathered from neighbor routers.

FIGURE 2.4 The internetwork with distance-vector routing

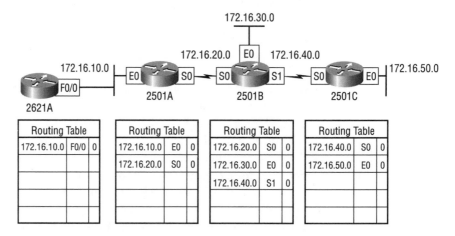

As shown in Figure 2.4, each router has only the directly connected networks in each routing table. Each router sends its complete routing table out to each active interface on the router. The routing table of each router includes the network number, exit interface, and hop count to the network.

In Figure 2.5, the routing tables are complete because they include information about all the networks in the internetwork. They are considered converged. (Converging is discussed later in this chapter.) When the routers are converging, no data is passed. That's why fast convergence time is a plus, and that's one of the problems with RIP: slow convergence time.

FIGURE 2.5 Converged routing tables

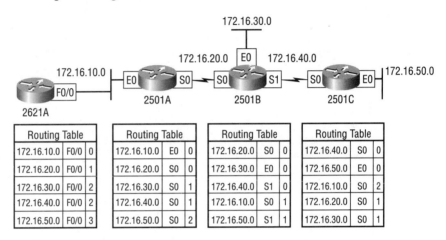

The routing tables in each router keep information regarding the network number, the interface to which the router will send packets out to get to the remote network, and the hop count or metric to the remote network.

Verifying RIP

Each routing table should have the routers' directly connected routes as well as RIP-injected routes received from neighbor routers. The router output below shows the contents of an RIP routing table:

```
2621A#sh ip route
Codes: C - connected, S - static, I - IGRP, R - RIP,
↳M - [output cut]
Gateway of last resort is not set

     172.16.0.0/24 is subnetted, 5 subnets
R       172.16.50.0 [120/3] via 172.16.10.2,
          ↳FastEthernet0/0
```

```
R        172.16.40.0 [120/2] via 172.16.10.2,
         ⤷FastEthernet0/0
R        172.16.30.0 [120/2] via 172.16.10.2,
         ⤷FastEthernet0/0
R        172.16.20.0 [120/1] via 172.16.10.2,
         ⤷FastEthernet0/0
C        172.16.10.0 is directly connected, FastEthernet0/0
2621A#
```

In the above output, notice that the R means that the networks were added dynamically using RIP. The [120/3] is the administrative distance of the route (120) along with the number of hops to that remote network (3).

IGRP

The Interior Gateway Routing Protocol (IGRP) is a Cisco proprietary distance-vector protocol. This means that all of your routers must be Cisco routers in order to be able to use IGRP in your network. Cisco created this routing protocol to overcome the problems associated with RIP.

IGRP has a maximum hop count of 255 with a default of 100. This is helpful in larger networks and solves the problem of there being only 15 hops possible, as is the case in an RIP network. IGRP also uses a different metric than RIP. IGRP uses bandwidth and delay of the line by default as a metric for determining the best route to an internetwork. This is called a *composite metric*. Reliability, load, and maximum transmission unit (MTU) can also be used, although they are not used by default.

IGRP can load balance up to six unequal links to a remote network. RIP networks must have the same hop count to be able to load balance, whereas IGRP uses bandwidth to determine how to load balance. To load balance over unequal-cost links, the `variance` command controls the load balancing between the best metric and the worst acceptable metric.

IGRP Timers

To control performance, IGRP includes timers with default settings for each of the following:

Update timers   These specify how frequently routing update messages should be sent. The default is 90 seconds.

Invalid timers   These specify how long a router should wait before declaring a route invalid if it doesn't receive a specific update about it. The default is three times the update period.

Hold-down timers   These specify the hold-down period. The default is three times the update timer period plus 10 seconds.

Flush timers   These indicate how much time should pass before a route should be flushed from the routing table. The default is seven times the routing update period.

Verifying IGRP

The output below is from an IGRP router:

```
2621A#sh ip route
Codes: C - connected, S - static, I - IGRP, R - RIP,
M - [output cut]
        T - traffic engineered route
Gateway of last resort is not set

        172.16.0.0/24 is subnetted, 5 subnets
I        172.16.50.0 [100/160360] via 172.16.10.2,
         ⮣FastEthernet0/0
I        172.16.40.0 [100/160260] via 172.16.10.2,
         ⮣FastEthernet0/0
I        172.16.30.0 [100/158360] via 172.16.10.2,
         ⮣FastEthernet0/0
I        172.16.20.0 [100/158260] via 172.16.10.2,
         ⮣FastEthernet0/0
C        172.16.10.0 is directly connected, FastEthernet0/0
```

The I means IGRP-injected routes. The [100/160360] is the administrative distance of IGRP and the composite metric. The lower the composite metric, the better the route.

Link-State Routing Protocols

Link-state routing protocols are more advanced than distance-vector protocols because, unlike distance-vector, they do not send periodic routing updates. When a change in the network occurs, the routers send Link State Advertisements (LSAs) about the change that has occurred. The whole routing table is not sent as in distance-vector; only the needed information is sent.

Each device that receives the LSA makes a copy, updates its topological database, and forwards this LSA to all neighbors using multicast addressing. This flooding of the LSA is to make sure that all devices know about the change in the internetwork.

Hierarchical design of the physical network is critical in larger networks to reduce the flooding needed, which reduces the convergence time of the network. This topic will be covered in more detail in Chapters 4 and 5, "Interconnecting OSPF Areas."

Table 2.3 compares the characteristics of the various link-state routing protocols. Enhanced IGRP is called an advanced distance-vector protocol by Cisco, but it has link-state features as well. Intermediate System-to-Intermediate System (IS-IS) is the routing algorithm used by the ISO protocol suite.

TABLE 2.3 Link-State Comparisons

Characteristic	OSPF	IS-IS	EIGRP
Hierarchical topology needed	X	X	
Retains knowledge of all possible routes	X	X	X
Manual route summarization	X	X	X
Automatic route summarization			X
Event-triggered announcements	X	X	X

TABLE 2.3 Link-State Comparisons *(continued)*

Characteristic	OSPF	IS-IS	EIGRP
Load balancing with unequal paths			X
Load balancing with equal paths	X	X	X
VLSM support	X	X	X
Metric	Cost	Cost	Composite
Hop count limit	200	1024	100 by default
Support for size of network	Large	Very Large	Large

Chapters 4 and 5 will discuss OSPF in detail, and Chapter 6 will discuss EIGRP. We will discuss how both EIGRP and OSPF (as well as RIP and IGRP) provide convergence in a network outage situation in the convergence sections below.

Convergence

Convergence is the time it takes for all routers to agree on the network topology after a change in the network. The routers basically synchronize their routing tables.

There are at least two different detection methods used by all routing protocols. The first method is used by the Physical and Data Link layer protocols. When the network interface on the router does not receive three consecutive keepalives, the link will be considered down. The second method is that when the routing protocol at the Network and Transport layers fails to receive three consecutive Hello messages, the link will be considered down.

After the link is considered down is where the routing protocols differ. Routing protocols have timers that are used to stop network loops from occurring on a network when a link failure has been detected. Hold-down timers are used to give the network stability while new route calculations are being performed. Since a network cannot converge during this hold-down period, this can cause a delay in the routing process of the network. Because of this slow convergence time, link-state routing protocols do not use hold-down timers.

The following section will describe the convergence process for both RIP and IGRP when a link failure occurs in a network.

RIP Convergence

Convergence time is one of the problems associated with distance-vector protocols. This section details the convergence process of the RIP protocol. We'll use Figure 2.6 to help describe the RIP convergence process.

FIGURE 2.6 Convergence

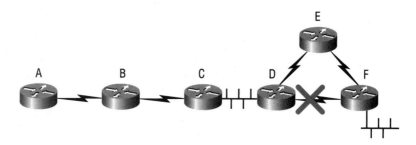

The following list describes the RIP convergence events when a problem occurs. In Figure 2.6, the WAN between Routers D and F goes down. Here is what happens:

1. RouterD sends a poisoned route to Routers E and C. RouterC informs RouterB, which in turn sends the poisoned route to RouterA. RouterC purges the entry for the downed link from the routing table.

2. RouterD sends a query broadcast. RouterC responds with a poison reverse, and RouterE responds with a route to that network. Router D enters this route in the routing table.

3. RouterD does not hold down this route entry since it had just purged a route entry to this link.

4. Router D advertises the new route to RouterC, but RouterC ignores the new route listing because RouterC is in hold-down. RouterC sends another poison reverse to RouterD.

5. The hold-down timers expire on Routers C, B, and A, which cause their routing table entries to be updated.

The time required for RouterA to converge is the detection time, plus the hold-down time, plus two update times, plus another update time. The complete convergence to RouterA could be over 240 seconds.

IGRP Convergence

Using the same Figure 2.6 as an example, let's take a look at IGRP convergence:

1. RouterD detects the failure on the link to RouterF. RouterD sends a poisoned route update to Routers E and C. RouterC sends an update to RouterB, and RouterB sends an update to RouterA. RouterD purges the routing table of a link to the downed route.

2. RouterD sends a query broadcast, and RouterC sends back a poison-reverse response. RouterD sends an update out all interfaces without the failed link entry.

3. RouterE responds to the broadcast with an entry to the downed link. RouterD puts this in the routing table and does not put a hold-down on the link since it does not have an entry for this link. RouterD sends a broadcast out all links, which includes this new entry.

4. RouterC receives this update but ignores the new route since it is in hold-down. It responds again with a poison reverse.

5. Routers C, B, and A hold-down timers expire and their routing tables will then be updated with the new route.

The time it takes for RouterA to converge is the detection time, plus the hold-down time, plus two update times, plus another update time, which is over 490 seconds.

EIGRP Convergence

Let's take a look at the convergence time of Enhanced IGRP (EIGRP). We will again use Figure 2.6 to help describe the convergence process:

1. RouterD detects the link failure between D and F and immediately checks the topology table for a feasible successor. RouterD does not find an alternate route in the topology table and puts the route into active convergence state.

2. RouterD sends a query out all interfaces looking for a route to the failed link. Routers C and E acknowledge the query.

3. RouterC responds with no known link.

4. RouterE responds with a route to the failed link, but it is at a higher cost than the original link.

5. RouterD uses the new link and places it in the topology table, which is then placed in the routing table.

6. RouterD broadcasts this new route out all interfaces, and Routers C and E acknowledge the update back to RouterD, with an update of their own. These updates make sure the routing tables are synchronized.

RouterA convergence time is the total time of detection, plus the query and reply time, plus the update time—about two seconds total. However, the time can be higher.

OSPF Convergence

Using Figure 2.6 as a reference, let's now take a look at the convergence cycle used in OSPF:

1. RouterD detects the link failure between Routers D and F, and a Designated Router (DR) election is held on the E0 interface, but no neighbors respond. The route entry is removed from RouterD. A Link State Advertisement (LSA) is sent out all interfaces on RouterD.

2. Routers C and E receive the LSA and forward the LSA packet out all interfaces except for the interface where the LSA was received.

3. All routers wait five seconds and then run the shortest path first (SPF) algorithm. After the algorithm is run, RouterD adds the route through RouterE, and Routers C, B, and A update the metric in their routing table to that route.

4. After another 30 seconds, RouterF sends an LSA out all interfaces after timing out the link to RouterD. All routers wait five seconds and then run the SPF algorithm, and all routers now know that the route to the failed link is through RouterE.

RouterA convergence time is the time of detection, plus the LSA forwarding time, plus five seconds. This is about six seconds. However, if RouterF's time to converge is considered, then the time is about 36 seconds.

Summary

This chapter described the difference between distance-vector and link-state routing protocols. The idea of this chapter was to provide you with an overview of the different types of routing protocols available, not how to configure routers.

Both link-state and distance-vector routing algorithms were covered, as well as how they create routing tables and regulate performance with timers, and their different convergence methods.

The difference between classful and classless routing protocols is very important to understand before continuing on with the other chapters in this book. We discussed both types of routing protocols in detail.

Key Terms

Before taking the exam, make sure you're familiar with the following terms:

administrative distances

autonomous systems (AS)

composite metric

distance-vector protocol

dynamic routing

framing

hop

link-state routers

packet-switching

pinhole congestion

prefix routing

relay system

routing by rumor

routing table

setting the default route

Written Lab

In this lab, write in the routing protocol that is described. The possibilities are RIP, RIPv2, IGRP, EIGRP, IS-IS, and OSPF. More than one answer may be possible per characteristic.

Protocol   **Characteristic**

Maximum of 15 hops by default

Administrative distance of 120

Administrative distance of 100

Administrative distance of 90

Administrative distance of 110

Uses composite metric to determine the best path to a remote network

Uses only hop count to determine the best path to a remote network

VLSM support

Non-proprietary

Floods network with LSAs to prevent loops

Must have hierarchical network design

Uses only bandwidth as a metric

Uses more than one table to assist in rapid convergence

Route update contains only needed information

Automatic route summarization at major network boundaries

Review Questions

1. What are two benefits of using a link-state routing protocol?

    A. It uses the Hello protocol to establish adjacencies.

    B. It uses several components to calculate the metric of a route.

    C. Updates are sent only when changes occur in the network.

    D. It is a better protocol than the distance-vector protocol.

2. Which protocols do not use a topology table?

    A. EIGRP

    B. IGRP

    C. RIPv1

    D. OSPF

3. RIPv2 provides which of the following benefits over RIPv1?

    A. RIPv2 is link-state.

    B. RIPv2 uses a topology table.

    C. RIPv2 supports VLSM.

    D. RIPv2 uses Hello messages.

4. What is the administrative distance of directly connected routes?

    A. 0

    B. 1

    C. 90

    D. 100

    E. 110

5. Which of the following are considered distance-vector? (Choose all that apply.)

   A. RIP

   B. RIPv2

   C. IGRP

   D. EIGRP

   E. OSPF

   F. IS-IS

6. What is the default administrative distance of OSPF?

   A. 0

   B. 1

   C. 90

   D. 100

   E. 110

7. Which is true regarding classless routing?

   A. It sends periodic subnet mask information.

   B. It sends incremental subnet mask information.

   C. It sends prefix mask information.

   D. All devices on the network must use the same mask.

8. What is the default administrative distance of EIGRP?

   A. 0

   B. 1

   C. 90

   D. 100

   E. 110

9. Which is true regarding classful routing?

   A. It sends periodic subnet mask information.

   B. It sends incremental subnet mask information.

   C. It sends prefix mask information.

   D. All devices on the network must use the same mask.

10. What is the default administrative distance of static routes?

   A. 0

   B. 1

   C. 90

   D. 100

   E. 110

11. Which of the following protocols support VLSM? (Choose all that apply.)

   A. RIP

   B. RIPv2

   C. IGRP

   D. EIGRP

   E. IS-IS

   F. OSPF

12. What is the default administrative distance of IGRP?

   A. 0

   B. 1

   C. 90

   D. 100

   E. 110

13. Which of the following protocols use only hop count to determine the best path to a remote network? (Choose all that apply.)

  A. RIP

  B. RIPv2

  C. IGRP

  D. EIGRP

  E. IS-IS

  F. OSPF

14. What is the default administrative distance of RIP?

  A. 0

  B. 1

  C. 90

  D. 100

  E. 120

15. Which of the following routing protocols use a composite metric? (Choose all that apply.)

  A. RIP

  B. RIPv2

  C. IGRP

  D. EIGRP

  E. IS-IS

  F. OSPF

16. Which of the following consider only bandwidth as a metric? (Choose all that apply.)

    A. RIP

    B. RIPv2

    C. IGRP

    D. EIGRP

    E. IS-IS

    F. OSPF

17. Which of the following must have a hierarchical network design to operate properly? (Choose all that apply.)

    A. RIP

    B. RIPv2

    C. IGRP

    D. EIGRP

    E. IS-IS

    F. OSPF

18. Which of the following routing protocols are non-proprietary? (Choose all that apply.)

    A. RIP

    B. RIPv2

    C. IGRP

    D. EIGRP

    E. IS-IS

    F. OSPF

19. Which of the following are proprietary routing protocols? (Choose all that apply.)

   A. RIP

   B. RIPv2

   C. IGRP

   D. EIGRP

   E. IS-IS

   F. OSPF

20. Which of the following automatically summarize at classful boundaries? (Choose all that apply.)

   A. RIP

   B. RIPv2

   C. IGRP

   D. EIGRP

   E. IS-IS

   F. OSPF

Answer to Written Lab

Protocol	Characteristic
RIP, RIPv2	Maximum of 15 hops by default
RIP, RIPv2	Administrative distance of 120
IGRP	Administrative distance of 100
EIGRP	Administrative distance of 90
OSPF	Administrative distance of 110
IGRP, EIGRP	Uses composite metric to determine the best path to a remote network
RIP, RIPv2	Uses only hop count to determine the best path to a remote network
RIPv2, EIGRP, IS-IS, OSPF	VLSM support
RIP, RIPv2, IS-IS, OSPF	Non-proprietary
OSPF	Floods network with LSAs to prevent loops
IS-IS, OSPF	Must have hierarchical network design
IS-IS, OSPF	Uses only bandwidth as a metric
EIGRP, IS-IS, OSPF	Uses more than one table to assist in rapid convergence
EIGRP, IS-IS, OSPF	Route update contains only needed information
RIP, RIPv2, IGRP, EIGRP	Automatic route summarization at major network boundaries

Answers to Review Questions

1. A, C. Link-state does not send entire routing table updates like distance-vector does. Link-state uses Hello messages to make sure that neighbor routers are still alive, and then when a change in the network does occur, it sends only the necessary information about the change.

2. B, C. IGRP and RIP are distance-vector protocols and do not use a topology table.

3. C. RIPv2 is still distance-vector and acts accordingly. However, it sends prefix routing information in the route updates so that it can support VLSM.

4. A. Directly connected routes have an administrative distance of zero.

5. A, B, C, D. Although EIGRP is really a hybrid routing protocol, it is considered an advanced distance-vector protocol.

6. E. OSPF has an administrative distance of 110.

7. C. Classless routing protocols send prefix routing information with each update.

8. C. EIGRP routes have a default administrative distance of 90.

9. D. Classful routing protocols send no subnet mask information with the routing updates, so all devices on the network must use the same subnet mask.

10. B. Static routes have a default administrative distance of 1.

11. B, D, E, F. RIPv2, EIGRP, IS-IS, and OSPF all send prefix routing information with the route updates.

12. D. IGRP routes have a default administrative distance of 100.

13. A, B. Both RIP and RIPv2 consider only hop count as a metric.

14. E. RIP routes have a default administrative distance of 120.

15. C, D. IGRP and EIGRP use a composite metric of bandwidth and delay of the line.

16. E, F. IS-IS and OSPF use only bandwidth as a metric.

17. E, F. Both IS-IS and OSPF must be run on a hierarchical network design to properly work.

18. A, B, E, F. IGRP and EIGRP are Cisco proprietary routing protocols.

19. C, D. IGRP and EIGRP are Cisco proprietary routing protocols.

20. A, B, C, D. RIP, RIPv2, IGRP, and EIGRP auto-summarize at classful boundaries. EIGRP, OSPF, and IS-IS can be manually configured to summarize at non-classful boundaries.

Chapter 3

IP Addressing

THE CCNP ROUTING EXAM TOPICS COVERED IN THIS CHAPTER ARE AS FOLLOWS:

- ✓ Review the fundamental concepts of IP addressing

- ✓ Gain an understanding of how IP addresses can be depleted if used inefficiently

- ✓ Understand the benefits of VLSM (Variable-Length Subnet Mask)

- ✓ Learn how to calculate VLSM

- ✓ Explain how OSPF supports the use of VLSM

- ✓ Explain how EIGRP supports the use of VLSM

- ✓ Become familiar with CIDR (Classless Interdomain Routing)

- ✓ Recognize the benefits of route summarization

- ✓ Detail how to disable automatic route summarization for classless routing protocols

- ✓ Examine how to use IP unnumbered interfaces

n this chapter, we will discuss IP addressing. However, we will assume a basic understanding of IP addressing and subnetting.

After we review IP addressing, we will provide detailed descriptions and examples of advanced IP addressing techniques that you can use on your production networks. First, we'll discuss Variable-Length Subnet Masks (VLSMs) and provide an example to show how VLSMs can be used to help save precious address space on your network.

After discussing VLSMs, we will provide an understanding of Classless Interdomain Routing (CIDR) as well as summarization techniques.

After you have read the chapter, you can use both the written and hands-on labs to help you better prepare for using the advanced IP addressing techniques found in this chapter. Also, to help you study for the CCNP Routing exam, be sure to read the review questions at the end of this chapter.

Review of IP Addressing

One of the most important topics in any discussion of TCP/IP is IP addressing. An *IP address* is a numeric identifier assigned to each machine on an IP network. It designates the location of a device on the network. An IP address is a software address, not a hardware address. A hardware address is hard-coded on a network interface card (NIC) and used for finding hosts on a local network. IP addressing was designed to allow a host on one network to communicate with a host on a different network, regardless of the type of LANs in which the hosts are participating.

Before we get into the more difficult aspects of IP addressing, let's look at some of the basics.

IP Terminology

In this chapter, we'll introduce you to a number of terms that are fundamental to an understanding of TCP/IP. We'll start by defining a few that are the most important:

Bit   One digit; either a 1 or a 0.

Byte   Seven or eight bits, depending on whether parity is used. For the rest of this chapter, always assume that a byte is eight bits.

Octet   Always eight bits; the Base 8 addressing scheme.

Network address   The designation used in routing to send packets to a remote network; for example, 172.16.0.0 and 10.0.0.0.

Broadcast address   Used by applications and hosts to send information to all nodes on a network; for example, 172.16.255.255 and 10.255.255.255.

The Hierarchical IP Addressing Scheme

An IP address is made up of 32 bits of information. These are divided into four sections, referred to as *octets* or *bytes*, containing one byte (eight bits) each. You can depict an IP address using three methods:

- Dotted-decimal, as in 172.16.30.56

- Binary, as in 10101100.00010000.00011110.00111000

- Hexadecimal, as in AC 10 1E 38

All of these examples represent the same IP address. Although hexadecimal is not used as often as dotted-decimal or binary when IP addressing is discussed, you might find an IP address stored as hexadecimal in some programs. The 32-bit IP address is a structured, or hierarchical, address, as opposed to a flat, or nonhierarchical, address. Although either type of addressing scheme could have been used, the hierarchical variety was chosen for a good reason.

The advantage of the hierarchical scheme is that it can handle a large number of addresses, namely 4.2 billion (a 32-bit address space with two possible values for each position—either 0 or 1—gives you approximately 4.2 billion). The disadvantage of the flat address scheme, and the reason it's not used for IP addressing, relates to routing. If every address were unique, all routers on the Internet would need to store the address of each and every machine on the Internet. This would make efficient routing impossible, even if only a fraction of the possible addresses were used.

The solution to this flat address dilemma is to use a two- or three-level hierarchical addressing scheme that is structured by network and host or by network, subnet, and host. A two- or three-level hierarchy is comparable to the sections of a telephone number. The first section, the area code, designates a very large area. The second section, the prefix, narrows the scope to a local calling area. The final segment, the customer number, zooms in on the specific connection. IP addresses use the same type of layered structure. Rather than all 32 bits being treated as a unique identifier, as in flat addressing, one part of the address is designated as the network address, and the other part is designated as either the subnet or host address. Note that in some literature, the *host address* may be referred to as the *node address*.

In the following sections, we will discuss network addressing and the three different address classes:

- Class A addresses

- Class B addresses

- Class C addresses

Network Addressing

The network address uniquely identifies each network. Every machine on the same network shares that network address as part of its IP address. In the IP address 172.16.30.56, for example, 172.16 is the network address by default.

The host address is assigned to, and uniquely identifies, each machine on a network. This part of the address must be unique because it identifies a particular machine—an individual—as opposed to a network, which is a group.

In the sample IP address 172.16.30.56, .30.56 is the host address by default.

The designers of the Internet decided to create classes of networks based on network size. For the small number of networks possessing a very large number of nodes, they created the rank *Class A network*. At the other extreme is the *Class C network*, reserved for the numerous networks with a small number of nodes. The class distinction for networks between very large and very small is predictably called a *Class B network*. Subdividing an IP address into a network and node address is determined by the class designation of a network. Table 3.1 provides a summary of the three classes of networks, which will be described in much more detail throughout this chapter.

TABLE 3.1 The Three Classes of IP Addresses Used in Networks Today

Class	Leading Bit Pattern	Default Subnet Mask	Address Range	Number of Addresses
A	0	255.0.0.0	1.0.0.0–126.0.0.0	16,777,214
B	10	255.255.0.0	128.1.0.0– 191.254.0.0	65,534
C	110	255.255.255.0	192.0.1.0– 223.255.254.0	254

To ensure efficient routing, Internet designers defined a mandate for the leading bits section of the address for each network class. For example, since a router knows that a Class A network address always starts with 0, the router might be able to speed a packet on its way after reading only the first bit of its address. This is where the address schemes define the difference between a Class A, a Class B, and a Class C address.

Some IP addresses are reserved for special purposes, and network administrators shouldn't assign them to nodes. Table 3.2 lists the members of this exclusive little club and explains why they're included in it.

TABLE 3.2   Reserved IP Addresses

Address	Function
Network address of all zeros	Interpreted to mean "this network or segment."
Network address of all ones	Interpreted to mean "all networks."
Network 127	Reserved for loopback tests. Designates the local node and allows that node to send a test packet to itself without generating network traffic.
Node address of all zeros	Interpreted to mean "this network."
Node address of all ones	Interpreted to mean "all nodes" on the specified network; for example, 128.2.255.255 means "all nodes" on network 128.2 (Class B address).
Entire IP address set to all zeros	Used by Cisco routers to designate the default route.
Entire IP address set to all ones (same as 255.255.255.255)	Broadcast to all nodes on the current network; sometimes called an "all ones broadcast."

We will now take a look at the different network address classes:

- Class A addresses
- Class B addresses
- Class C addresses

Class A Addresses

In a Class A address, the first byte is assigned to the network address, and the three remaining bytes are used for the node addresses. The Class A format is

Network.Node.Node.Node

For example, in the IP address 49.22.102.70, 49 is the network address and 22.102.70 is the node address. Every machine on this particular network would have the distinctive network address of 49.

Class A network addresses are one byte long, with the first bit of that byte reserved and the seven remaining bits available for manipulation. Thus, the maximum number of Class A networks that can be created is 128. Why? Because each of the seven bit positions can either be 0 or 1, thus 2^7 or 128. But to complicate things further, it was also decided that the network address of all zeros (0000 0000) would be reserved to designate the default route (see Table 3.1, earlier in this chapter). Thus, the actual number of usable Class A network addresses is 128 minus 1, or 127. However, the address 127 is reserved for diagnostics, so that can't be used, which means that you can use only numbers 1 through 126 to designate Class A networks.

Each Class A address has three bytes (24-bit positions) for the host address of a machine. Thus, there are 2^{24}—or 16,777,216—unique combinations and, therefore, precisely that many possible unique node addresses for each Class A network. Because addresses with the two patterns of all zeros and all ones are reserved, the actual maximum usable number of nodes for a Class A network is 2^{24} minus 2, which equals 16,777,214.

Here is an example of how to figure out the valid host IDs in a Class A network.

10.0.0.0   All host bits off is the network address.

10.255.255.255   All host bits on is the broadcast address.

The valid hosts are the numbers in between the network address and the broadcast address: 10.0.0.1 through 10.255.255.254. Notice that zeros and 255s are valid host IDs. All you need to remember when trying to find valid host addresses is that the host bits cannot all be turned off or on at the same time.

When you go out to request a network number from the NIC, don't expect to be assigned a Class A address. These have all been taken for quite some time. Big names such as HP and IBM got in the game early enough to have their own Class A network. However, a check of the IANA records shows that several corporations were handed Class A addresses back in 1995 and that Stanford University's Class A was revoked in July 2000. The records also indicate that the IANA has control of many Class A addresses, ones that have not been allocated to regional ISPs. A company can also buy another company to get a Class A network ID. For example, Compaq got the 16 network by acquiring Digital.

Class B Addresses

In a Class B address, the first two bytes are assigned to the network address, and the remaining two bytes are used for host addresses. The format is

Network.Network.Node.Node

For example, in the IP address 172.16.30.56, the network address is 172.16, and the host address is 30.56.

With a network address being two bytes of eight bits each, there would be 65,536 unique combinations. But the Internet designers decided that all Class B addresses should start with the binary digits 1 and 0. This leaves 14 bit positions to manipulate; therefore, there are 16,384 unique Class B addresses.

A Class B address uses two bytes for node addresses. This is 216 minus the two reserved patterns (all zeros and all ones), for a total of 65,534 possible node addresses for each Class B network.

Here is an example of how to find the valid hosts in a Class B network:

172.16.0.0   All host bits turned off is the network address.

172.16.255.255   All host bits turned on is the broadcast address.

The valid hosts would be the numbers in between the network address and the broadcast address: 172.16.0.1 through 172.16.255.254.

Just as we saw with Class A addresses, all Class B addresses have also been assigned. Many universities, which were connected to the Internet in the early '90s, in addition to many big-name organizations such as Microsoft, Cisco, Xerox, Novell, and Sun Microsystems, have all of these addresses consumed. However, they are available under the right circumstances.

Class C Addresses

The first three bytes of a Class C address are dedicated to the network portion of the address, with only one measly byte remaining for the host address. The format is

Network.Network.Network.Node

Using the example IP address 192.168.100.102, the network address is 192.168.100, and the host address is 102.

In a Class C address, the first three bit positions are always the binary 110. The calculation is as follows: 3 bytes, or 24 bits, minus 3 reserved positions, equals 21 positions. There are, therefore, 221, or 2,097,152, possible Class C networks.

Each unique Class C network uses one byte for node addresses. This leads to 28, or 256, minus the two reserved patterns of all zeros and all ones, for a total of 254 node addresses for each Class C network.

Here is an example of how to find a valid host ID in a Class C network:

192.168.100.0   All host bits turned off is the network ID.

192.168.100.1   The first host.

192.168.100.254   The last host.

192.168.100.255   All host bits turned on is the broadcast address.

Extending IP Addresses

In the "old days," when the Network Information Center (NIC) assigned a network number to an organization, it either assigned the first octet (a Class A network), the first two octets (a Class B network), or the first three octets (a Class C network). The organization could take this one network number and further subdivide it into smaller networks through a process called *subnetting*.

To illustrate, let's say that our organization has been assigned the Class B network 172.16.0.0. We have several different network segments, each of which needs a unique network number. So, we decide to subnet our network. We use a *subnet mask* of 255.255.255.0. The subnet mask determines which portion of our IP address belongs to the network portion and which part belongs to the host portion. If we write our subnet mask out in binary, as illustrated in Table 3.3, the ones correspond to the network portion of the address, and the zeros correspond to the node portion of the address.

TABLE 3.3 IP Address Example

Decimal	172	16	0	0
Binary	10101100	00010000	00000000	00000000
Decimal	255	255	255	0
Binary	11111111	11111111	11111111	00000000

So, in our case, instead of having one network (172.16.0.0) with 65,534 available hosts numbers, we have 254 networks (172.16.1.0–172.16.254.0) with 254 available host numbers in each subnet.

We can calculate the number of hosts available on a subnet by using the formula $2^n - 2$ = number of available host IPs, where n is the number of hosts bits (in our example, 8). The minus 2 (–2) represents all host bits on and all hosts bits off, which are reserved.

Similarly, the number of networks (or subnets) can be calculated with nearly the same formula: $2^n - 2$ = number of available networks, where n is the number of subnet bits (in our example, 8). So, with subnetting we have balanced our need for available network and host numbers. However, there may be instances where we need fewer host numbers on a particular subnet and more host numbers on another. The –2 represents all subnet bits on and all subnet bits off.

Let's extend our example to include a serial link between two routers, as shown in Figure 3.1.

FIGURE 3.1 IP address example

Network 172.16.10.0/24

172.16.10.1

172.16.10.2

Since these are routers and not switches, each interface belongs to a different network. The interfaces need to share a network to talk. How many IP numbers do we really need on the network interconnecting the two routers? We only need two IP numbers, one for each serial interface, as shown in

Table 3.3. Unfortunately, we have an eight-bit subnet mask (i.e., 255.255.255.0), so we are wasting 252 of the 254 available numbers on the subnet. One possible solution to this dilemma is to use *Variable-Length Subnet Masks (VLSMs)*.

Variable-Length Subnet Masks

As the name suggests, with Variable-Length Subnet Masks we can have different subnet masks for different subnets. So, for the serial link in our example above, we could have a subnet mask of 255.255.255.252. If we do the math and look at our subnet in binary, we see that we have only two host bits, as shown in Table 3.4.

TABLE 3.4 VLSM Example 1

Decimal	255	255	255	252
Binary	11111111	11111111	11111111	11111100

Therefore, this subnet mask will give us only two host IPs ($2^2 - 2 = 2$), which is exactly what we need for our serial link.

As another example, consider what would happen if we were running out of IP numbers on a particular subnet. Perhaps we have several Web servers on network 172.16.10.0. With our subnet mask of 255.255.255.0 (which we could also write as 172.16.0.0/24, due to the 24 bits in our subnet mask), we have only 254 available host addresses. However, in our Web server implementation, each URL needs its own IP number, and our need for unique IP numbers is about to grow beyond the 254 numbers that we have available. It is possible to support several URLs to an IP address, but for our example we'll use only one address per URL.

Yet again, VLSMs can provide a solution. Instead of making our subnet mask longer, as in the previous example, we can make our subnet mask shorter, sometimes called *supernetting*. In Table 3.5, let's examine what would happen if we backed our subnet mask off from 24 bits to 23 bits.

TABLE 3.5 VLSM Example 2

Decimal	255	255	254	0
Binary	11111111	11111111	11111110	00000000

We now have a network of 172.16.10.0 with a subnet mask of 255.255.254.0, which can also be written as 172.16.10.0/23. Again, by doing the math ($2^9 - 2 = 510$, since we have nine host bits), we see that we now have 510 available IP addresses instead of 254.

Let's work through a VLSM design example, as depicted in Figure 3.2.

FIGURE 3.2 VLSM design example

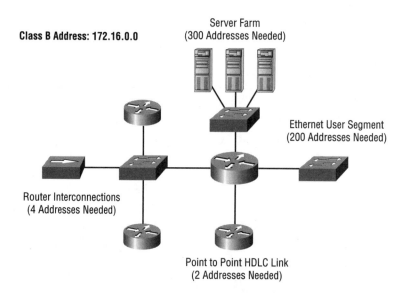

In our example, we have the following set of requirements for our network addressing:

- A server farm requires 300 IP addresses.

- A user segment requires 200 IP addresses.

- A serial link between two routers requires two IP addresses.

- A hub segment interconnecting four routers requires four IP addresses.

- We have been assigned the Class B network of 172.16.0.0.

We will now go through a simple three-step process for efficiently calculating the IP address ranges to be assigned to each segment. We say "efficiently," because we will be using the minimum number of IP addresses required to accomplish our goal.

1. Create a table detailing the segments and the number of hosts required on each segment, as shown in Table 3.6.

TABLE 3.6 Number of IP Addresses Used in Figure 3.2

Description of Segment	Number of IP Addresses Required
Server farm	300
Ethernet user segment	200
Serial link	2
Router interconnection switched segment	4

2. Determine the subnet mask required to support the requirements defined in step 1, and expand the table to list the subnet masks.

We can use our formula 2n − 2 = number of hosts to create a handy reference chart to quickly determine how many hosts can be supported for any given subnet mask, as shown in Table 3.7. The table goes up to only 1022 hosts, because Cisco has a design recommendation that you should not have a non-routed network segment with more than 500 hosts (due to performance problems caused by broadcast traffic). To confuse you further, understand that some Cisco documentation states that the number of hosts on a segment can be up to 800! Just keep in mind the amount of traffic when making this decision.

TABLE 3.7   Number of Hosts Needed in Figure 3.2

Maximum Number of Hosts	Bits in Subnet Mask	Subnet Mask
2	30	255.255.255.252
6	29	255.255.255.248
14	28	255.255.255.240
30	27	255.255.255.224
62	26	255.255.255.192
126	25	255.255.255.128
254	24	255.255.255.0
510	23	255.255.254.0
1022	22	255.255.252.0

Referring to our table, we can easily determine the subnet mask required for each of the segments in our example, as shown in Table 3.8.

TABLE 3.8 Subnet Masks for Figure 3.2

Description of Segment	Number of IP Addresses Required	Subnet Mask (Number of Subnet Bits)
Server farm	300	255.255.254.0 (23)
Ethernet user segment	200	255.255.255.0 (24)
Serial link	2	255.255.255.252 (30)
Router interconnection switched segment	4	255.255.255.248 (29)

3. Starting with the segment requiring the greatest number of subnet bits, begin allocating addresses.

Let's begin with the serial link, which has 30 bits of subnetting. Since all of our addresses are going to start with 172.16, we will examine only the last 16 bits of the IP address. In Table 3.9, we see the subnet mask, in binary and the first and last IP number in the range. Remember that the host portion of the address cannot be all ones (which is the broadcast address) or all zeros (which is the address of the network, or *wire*).

TABLE 3.9 Networks, Hosts, and Subnets for Figure 3.2

	3rd Octet	4th Octet	Decimal IP Address
	128 64 32 16 8 4 2 1	128 64 32 16 8 4 2 1	(Last 16 bits in bold)
Subnet Mask	1 1 1 1 1 1 1 1	1 1 1 1 1 1 0 0	255.255.255.252
Network	0 0 0 0 0 0 0 0	0 0 0 0 0 1 0 0	172.16.0.4
First IP in range	0 0 0 0 0 0 0 0	0 0 0 0 0 1 0 1	172.16.0.5

TABLE 3.9 Networks, Hosts, and Subnets for Figure 3.2 *(continued)*

	3rd Octet	4th Octet	Decimal IP Address
Last IP in range	0 0 0 0 0000	0 0 0 0 0110	172.16.0.6
Broadcast	0 0 0 0 0000	0 0 0 0 0111	172.16.0.7

After picking the first available network number (172.16.0.4) given our 30-bit subnet mask and eliminating host IP addresses that are all ones and all zeros, we have the following range of numbers: 172.16.0.5–172.16.0.6. The broadcast address is all host bits on, or 172.16.0.7. We can take one of these numbers and assign it to one side of the serial link. The other number can be assigned to the other end of the serial link.

Next, we will calculate the range of IP addresses to use for our hub segment, containing four router interfaces. We pick the first available network address given our 29-bit subnet mask. In this case, the first available network is 172.16.0.8, as shown in Table 3.10.

TABLE 3.10 IP Address Range for Switched Segment in Figure 3.2

	3rd Octet	4th Octet	Decimal IP Address
	128 64 32 16 8 4 2 1	**128 64 32 16 8 4 2 1**	(Last 16 bits in bold)
Subnet Mask	1 1 1 1 1111	1 1 1 1 1000	255.255.255.248
Network	0 0 0 0 0000	0 0 0 0 1000	172.16.0.8
First IP in range	0 0 0 0 0000	0 0 0 0 1001	172.16.0.9
Last IP in range	0 0 0 0 0000	0 0 0 0 1110	172.16.0.14
Broadcast	0 0 0 0 0000	0 0 0 0 1111	172.16.0.15

Eliminating host IP addresses that contain all ones and all zeros as before, we discover that our IP address range for this segment is 172.16.0.9–172.16.0.14. The broadcast address is all host bits on, or 172.16.0.15. Now we will perform the same steps on the Ethernet user segment, as shown in Table 3.11, and the server farm segment, as shown in Table 3.12.

TABLE 3.11 Valid Addresses for Ethernet Segment in Figure 3.2

	3rd Octet								4th Octet								Decimal IP Address
	128	64	32	16	8	4	2	1	128	64	32	16	8	4	2	1	(Last 16 bits in bold)
Subnet mask	1	1	1	1	1	1	1	1	0	0	0	0	0	0	0	0	255.255.255.0
Network	0	0	0	0	0	0	0	1	0	0	0	0	0	0	0	0	172.16.1.0
First IP in range	0	0	0	0	0	0	0	1	0	0	0	0	0	0	0	1	172.16.1.1
Last IP in range	0	0	0	0	0	0	0	1	1	1	1	1	1	1	1	0	172.16.1.254
Broadcast	0	0	0	0	0	0	0	1	1	1	1	1	1	1	1	1	172.16.1.255

TABLE 3.12 Valid Addresses for Server Farm Segment in Figure 3.2

	3rd Octet								4th Octet								Decimal IP Address
	128	64	32	16	8	4	2	1	128	64	32	16	8	4	2	1	(Last 16 bits in bold)
Subnet mask	1	1	1	1	1	1	1	0	0	0	0	0	0	0	0	0	255.255.254.0
Network	0	0	0	0	0	0	1	0	0	0	0	0	0	0	0	0	172.16.2.0
First IP in range	0	0	0	0	0	0	1	0	0	0	0	0	0	0	0	1	172.16.2.1
Last IP in range	0	0	0	0	0	0	1	1	1	1	1	1	1	1	1	0	172.16.3.254
Broadcast	0	0	0	0	0	0	1	1	1	1	1	1	1	1	1	1	172.16.3.255

From these tables, we see that our IP address range for the Ethernet user segment is 172.16.1.1–172.16.1.254. Also, we see that the IP address range for the server farm segment is 172.16.2.1–172.16.3.254.

In summary, we have defined the following address ranges for our four segments, as detailed in Table 3.13.

TABLE 3.13 Valid IP Addresses for All Four Segments Used in Figure 3.2

Description of Segment	Address Range
Server farm	172.16.2.1–172.16.3.254
Ethernet user segment	172.16.1.1–172.16.1.254
Serial link	172.16.0.5–172.16.0.6
Router interconnection switched segment	172.16.0.9–172.16.0.14

We can now take our VLSM address ranges and apply them to our network diagram, as shown in Figure 3.3.

FIGURE 3.3 VLSM example with IP addresses

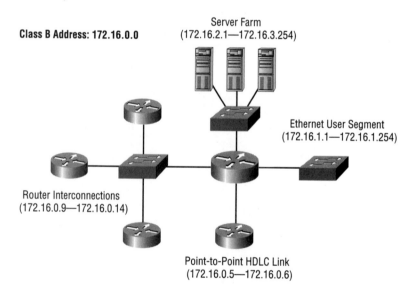

Design Considerations with VLSM

Now that we have seen how valuable VLSMs can be in preserving those precious IP addresses, be aware that there is a catch. Specifically, if you use a classful routing protocol (a protocol that advertises routes at the Class A, Class B, and Class C boundaries) such as RIPv1 or IGRP, then VLSMs are not going to work.

RIPv1 and IGRP routing protocols do not have a field for subnet information. Therefore, the subnet information gets dropped. This means that if a router running RIP has a subnet mask of a certain value, it assumes that *all* interfaces within the classful address space have the same subnet mask. Classless routing protocols, however, do support the advertisement of subnet information. So, you can use VLSM with routing protocols such as RIPv2, EIGRP, or OSPF.

Another important point to consider when assigning addresses is to not have discontiguous networks. Specifically, if you have two subnets of the same network separated by a different network, some of your hosts could become unreachable. Consider the network shown in Figure 3.4.

FIGURE 3.4   Discontiguous networking example

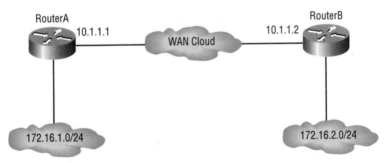

If routes are being summarized—a technique called *route summarization*—then both RouterA and RouterB will be advertising to the WAN cloud that they are the route to network 172.16.0.0/16. While there are techniques to overcome this behavior, which will be discussed in the "Route Summarization" section later in this chapter, it makes for better network design to not separate a network's subnets by another network.

Classless Interdomain Routing

Classless Interdomain Routing (CIDR) is an industry standard for displaying the number of subnet bits used with the IP address of a host or a network. Let's say you have a 172.16.10.1 address with a 255.255.255.0 mask. Instead of writing the IP address and subnet mask separately, you can combine them. For example, 172.16.10.1/24 means that the subnet mask has 24 out of 32 bits on.

The following list shows all the possible CIDRs:

255.0.0.0 = /8

255.128.0.0 = /9

255.192.0.0 = /10

255.224.0.0 = /11

255.240.0.0 = /12

255.248.0.0 = /13

255.252.0.0 = /14

255.254.0.0 = /15

255.255.0.0 = /16

255.255.128.0 = /17

255.255.192.0 = /18

255.255.224.0 = /19

255.255.240.0 = /20

255.255.248.0 = /21

255.255.252.0 = /22

255.255.254.0 = /23

255.255.255.0 = /24

255.255.255.128 = /25

255.255.255.192 = /26

255.255.255.224 = /27

$$255.255.255.240 = /28$$

$$255.255.255.248 = /29$$

$$255.255.255.252 = /30$$

Notice that the CIDR list starts at a minimum of /8 and can't go higher than /30. This is because the mask must at least be a Class A default, and you must leave two hosts at a minimum.

Let's now take a look at how Cisco handles CIDR.

Cisco and CIDR

Cisco has not always followed the CIDR standard. Take a look at the way a Cisco 2500 series router asks you to put the subnet mask in the configuration when using the Setup mode:

```
Configuring interface Ethernet0:
  Is this interface in use? [yes]: return
  Configure IP on this interface? [yes]: return
    IP address for this interface: 1.1.1.1
    Number of bits in subnet field [0]: 8
    Class A network is 1.0.0.0, 8 subnet bits; mask is /16
```

Notice that the router asks for the number of bits used only for subnetting, which does not include the default mask. When dealing with these questions, remember that your answers involve the number of bits used for creating subnets, not the number of bits in the subnet mask. The industry standard is that you count all bits used in the subnet mask and then display that number as a CIDR, for example, /25 is 25 bits.

The newer IOS that runs on Cisco routers, however, runs a Setup script that no longer asks you to enter the number of bits used only for subnetting. Here is an example of a new 1700 series router in Setup mode:

```
Configure IP on this interface? [no]: y
IP address for this interface: 1.1.1.1
Subnet mask for this interface [255.0.0.0]: 255.255.0.0
Class A network is 1.0.0.0, 16 subnet bits; mask is /16
```

Notice that the Setup mode asks you to enter the subnet mask address. It then displays the mask using the slash notation format. Much better.

Route Summarization

In the "Design Considerations with VLSM" section, we briefly mentioned the concept of route summarization. So, what is it, and why do we need it? On very large networks, there may be hundreds or even thousands of individual networks and subnetworks being advertised. All these routes can be very taxing on a router's memory and processor.

In many cases, the router doesn't even need specific routes to each and every subnet (e.g., 172.16.1.0/24). It would be just as happy if it knew how to get to the major network (e.g., 172.16.0.0/16) and let another router take it from there. A router's ability to take a group of subnetworks and summarize them as one network (i.e., one advertisement) is called *route summarization*, as shown in Figure 3.5.

In some of the literature, you may find route summarization referred to as *route aggregation*.

FIGURE 3.5   Route summarization

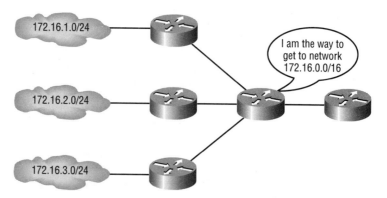

Besides reducing the number of routing entries that a router must keep track of, route summarization can also help protect an external router from making multiple changes to its routing table, due to instability within a particular subnet. For example, let's say that we were working on a router that connected to 172.16.2.0/24. As we were working on the router, we rebooted it several times. If we were not summarizing our routes, an external router would see each time 172.16.2.0/24 went away and came back. Each time, it would have to modify its own routing table. However, if our external router were receiving only a summary route (i.e., 172.16.0.0/16), then it wouldn't have to be concerned with our work on one particular subnet.

We will get the most benefit from route summarization when the networks or subnetworks that we are summarizing are contiguous. To illustrate this point, let's look at an example.

Route Summarization Example 1

We have the following networks that we want to advertise as a single summary route:

> 172.16.100.0/24
>
> 172.16.101.0/24
>
> 172.16.102.0/24
>
> 172.16.103.0/24
>
> 172.16.104.0/24
>
> 172.16.105.0/24
>
> 172.16.106.0/24

To determine what the summary route would be for these networks, we can follow a simple two-step process.

1. Write out each of the numbers in binary, as shown in Table 3.14.

TABLE 3.14   Summary Example

IP Network Address	Binary Equivalent
172.16.100.0	**10101100.0001000.01100**100.0
172.16.101.0	**10101100.0001000.01100**101.0
172.16.102.0	**10101100.0001000.01100**110.0
172.16.103.0	**10101100.0001000.01100**111.0
172.16.104.0	**10101100.0001000.01101**000.0
172.16.105.0	**10101100.0001000.01101**001.0
172.16.106.0	**10101100.0001000.01101**010.0

2. Examine the table to determine the maximum number of bits (starting from the left) that all of the addresses have in common (where they stop lining up; we bolded them to make them easier for you to see). The number of common bits is the subnet mask for the summarized address (/20).

In our example, we can see from the table that all of the addresses have the first 20 bits in common. The decimal equivalent of these first 20 bits is 172.16.96.0. So, we can write our new summarized address as 172.16.96.0/20. If we were to later add a network 172.16.98.0, it would need to come off the router summarizing this address space. If we didn't, it could cause problems. Okay, this is confusing, we know. This is why we're going to give you three more examples.

Route Summarization Example 2

In this example, we will summarize 10.1.0.0 through 10.7.0.0. First, put everything into binary, and then follow the bits, starting on the left and stopping when the bits do not line up. Notice where we stopped boldfacing the following:

10.1.0.0	**00001010.00000**001.00000000.00000000
10.2.0.0	**00001010.00000**010.00000000.00000000
10.3.0.0	**00001010.00000**011.00000000.00000000
10.4.0.0	**00001010.00000**100.00000000.00000000
10.5.0.0	**00001010.00000**101.00000000.00000000
10.6.0.0	**00001010.00000**110.00000000.00000000
10.7.0.0	**00001010.00000**111.00000000.00000000

Now, create the network number using only the boldfaced bits. Do not count the bits that are not in boldface. The second octet has no bits on (bits in the bolded section), so we get this:

10.0.0.0

To come up with the summary mask, count all the bolded bits as ones. Because eight bits are boldface in the first octet and five bits in the second, we'll get this:

255.248.0.0

Route Summarization Example 3

This example will show you how to summarize 172.16.16.0 through 172.16.31.0. First, let's put the network addresses into binary and then line up the bits.

172.16.16.0	10101100.0001000.00010000.00000000
172.16.17.0	10101100.0001000.00010001.00000000
172.16.18.0	10101100.0001000.00010010.00000000
172.16.19.0	10101100.0001000.00010011.00000000
172.16.20.0	10101100.0001000.00010100.00000000
172.16.21.0	10101100.0001000.00010101.00000000
172.16.22.0	10101100.0001000.00010110.00000000
172.16.23.0	10101100.0001000.00010111.00000000
172.16.24.0	10101100.0001000.00011000.00000000
172.16.25.0	10101100.0001000.00011001.00000000
172.16.26.0	10101100.0001000.00011010.00000000
172.16.27.0	10101100.0001000.00011011.00000000
172.16.28.0	10101100.0001000.00011100.00000000
172.16.29.0	10101100.0001000.00011101.00000000
172.16.30.0	10101100.0001000.00011110.00000000
172.16.31.0	10101100.0001000.00011111.00000000

Notice where the bits stop lining up (in boldface). Count only the bits that are on (ones) to get the network address:

172.16.0.0

Now, create the summary mask by counting all the bits that are in boldface up to the point where they stop lining up. We have eight bits in the first octet, eight bits in the second octet, and four bits in the third octet. That is a /20 or

255.255.240.0

Boy, that sure seems like a pain in the pencil, huh? Try this shortcut. Take the first number and the very last number, and put them into binary:

172.16.16.0	**10101100.0001000.0001**0000.00000000
172.16.31.0	**10101100.0001000.0001**1111.00000000

Can you see that we actually came up with the same numbers? It is a lot easier than writing out possibly dozens of addresses. Let's do another example, but let's use our shortcut.

Route Summarization Example 4

In this example, we will show you how to summarize 192.168.32.0 through 192.168.63.0. By using only the first network number and the last, we'll save a lot of time and come up with the same network address and subnet mask:

First number: 192.168.32.0 =
11000000.10101000.00100000.00000000

Last number: 192.168.63.0 =
11000000.10101000.00111111.00000000

Network address: 192.168.32.0

Subnet mask: 255.255.224.0

Design Considerations for Route Summarization

Keep the following information in mind when designing your network summarization points:

- Only classless routing protocols support route summarization. Examples of classless routing protocols include RIPv2, EIGRP, and OSPF. Therefore, if you are working in a RIPv1 or IGRP environment, route summarization is not going to work for you.

Classless and classful protocols were discussed in Chapter 2, "Routing Principles."

- Route summarization is most effective when the addresses have been organized in a hierarchy (i.e., "hierarchical addressing"). When we speak of addresses being hierarchical, we mean that the IP subnets at the "bottom of the tree" (i.e., the ones with the longest subnet masks) are subsets of the subnets at the "top of the tree" (i.e., the ones with the shortest subnet masks). Figure 3.6 will be used to illustrate hierarchical versus non-hierarchical addressing.

FIGURE 3.6 Discontiguous networking example

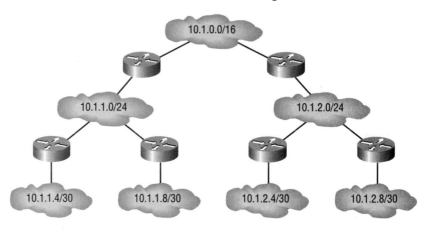

Hierarchical Adressing

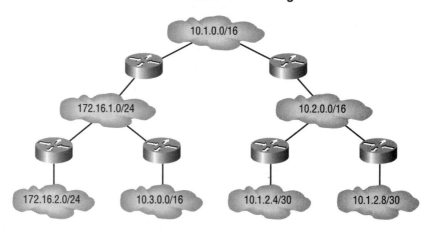

Non-Hierarchical Adressing

In the VLSM section of this chapter, we discussed how route summarization in discontiguous networks could cause some hosts to become unreachable, as we saw in Figure 3.4. If both RouterA and RouterB are sending out advertisements to the WAN cloud advertising that they are the path to network 172.16.0.0/16, then devices in the WAN cloud will not know which advertisement to believe.

Remember that you can avoid this situation by proper address planning ahead of time. However, you may find yourself in a situation where you are dealing with a legacy installation, and you need to overcome this issue of discontiguous networks.

One solution is to turn off route summarization on the routers. To keep routing protocols such as RIPv2 and EIGRP from automatically summarizing routes, we can explicitly disable route summarization in the Cisco IOS. Following are examples of IOS configurations, where we are disabling automatic route summarization. As the OSPF chapters will show, OSPF does not automatically summarize.

To turn off auto-summarization for RIP version 2 routed networks, use the following router configuration:

```
router rip
 version 2
 network 10.0.0.0
 network 172.16.0.0
 no auto-summary
```

To turn off auto-summarization for EIGRP routed networks, use the following router configuration:

```
router eigrp 100
 network 10.0.0.0
 network 172.16.0.0
 no auto-summary
```

Another way to allow discontiguous networks to be interconnected over a serial link is to use Cisco's IOS feature called *IP unnumbered*. We'll look at this next.

IP Unnumbered

With IP unnumbered, a serial interface is not on a separate network, as all router interfaces tend to be. Instead, the serial port "borrows" an IP address from another interface. In the following router configuration example, interface Serial 0 is using a borrowed IP address from interface Ethernet 0:

```
interface serial 0
ip unnumbered ethernet 0
```

Therefore, by using IP unnumbered, the apparently discontiguous subnets, shown in Figure 3.4, are actually supported. Understand that both sides of the network must be the same address class. In other words, you can't borrow an IP address on one side from a 10.0.0.0 network and then from 172.16.0.0 on the other side of the point-to-point link.

There are a few things to be aware of before using IP unnumbered interfaces. For example, IP unnumbered is not supported on X.25 or SMDS networks. Also, since the serial interface has no IP number, you will not be able to ping the interface to see if it is up, although you can determine the interface status with SNMP. In addition, IP security options are not supported on an IP unnumbered interface.

Decimal-to-Binary Conversion Chart

For your convenience, Table 3.15 provides a decimal-to-binary chart to help you with your IP addressing.

TABLE 3.15 Decimal-to-Binary Chart

Decimal	Binary	Decimal	Binary	Decimal	Binary	Decimal	Binary
0	00000000	16	00010000	32	00100000	48	00110000
1	00000001	17	00010001	33	00100001	49	00110001
2	00000010	18	00010010	34	00100010	50	00110010
3	00000011	19	00010011	35	00100011	51	00110011
4	00000100	20	00010100	36	00100100	52	00110100
5	00000101	21	00010101	37	00100101	53	00110101
6	00000110	22	00010110	38	00100110	54	00110110

TABLE 3.15   Decimal-to-Binary Chart *(continued)*

Decimal	Binary	Decimal	Binary	Decimal	Binary	Decimal	Binary
7	00000111	23	00010111	39	00100111	55	00110111
8	00001000	24	00011000	40	00101000	56	00111000
9	00001001	25	00011001	41	00101001	57	00111001
10	00001010	26	00011010	42	00101010	58	00111010
11	00001011	27	00011011	43	00101011	59	00111011
12	00001100	28	00011100	44	00101100	60	00111100
13	00001101	29	00011101	45	00101101	61	00111101
14	00001110	30	00011110	46	00101110	62	00111110
15	00001111	31	00011111	47	00101111	63	00111111
64	01000000	80	01010000	96	01100000	112	01110000
65	01000001	81	01010001	97	01100001	113	01110001
66	01000010	82	01010010	98	01100010	114	01110010
67	01000011	83	01010011	99	01100011	115	01110011
68	01000100	84	01010100	100	01100100	116	01110100
69	01000101	85	01010101	101	01100101	117	01110101
70	01000110	86	01010110	102	01100110	118	01110110
71	01000111	87	01010111	103	01100111	119	01110111
72	01001000	88	01011000	104	01101000	120	01111000
73	01001001	89	01011001	105	01101001	121	01111001
74	01001010	90	01011010	106	01101010	122	01111010

TABLE 3.15 Decimal-to-Binary Chart *(continued)*

Decimal	Binary	Decimal	Binary	Decimal	Binary	Decimal	Binary
75	01001011	91	01011011	107	01101011	123	01111011
76	01001100	92	01011100	108	01101100	124	01111100
77	01001101	93	01011101	109	01101101	125	01111101
78	01001110	94	01011110	110	01101110	126	01111110
79	01001111	95	01011111	111	01101111	127	01111111
128	10000000	144	10010000	160	10100000	176	10110000
129	10000001	145	10010001	161	10100001	177	10110001
130	10000010	146	10010010	162	10100010	178	10110010
131	10000011	147	10010011	163	10100011	179	10110011
132	10000100	148	10010100	164	10100100	180	10110100
133	10000101	149	10010101	165	10100101	181	10110101
134	10000110	150	10010110	166	10100110	182	10110110
135	10000111	151	10010111	167	10100111	183	10110111
136	10001000	152	10011000	168	10101000	184	10111000
137	10001001	153	10011001	169	10101001	185	10111001
138	10001010	154	10011010	170	10101010	186	10111010
139	10001011	155	10011011	171	10101011	187	10111011
140	10001100	156	10011100	172	10101100	188	10111100
141	10001101	157	10011101	173	10101101	189	10111101
142	10001110	158	10011110	174	10101110	190	10111110

TABLE 3.15 Decimal-to-Binary Chart *(continued)*

Decimal	Binary	Decimal	Binary	Decimal	Binary	Decimal	Binary
143	10001111	159	10011111	175	10101111	191	10111111
192	11000000	208	11010000	224	11100000	240	11110000
193	11000001	209	11010001	225	11100001	241	11110001
194	11000010	210	11010010	226	11100010	242	11110010
195	11000011	211	11010011	227	11100011	243	11110011
196	11000100	212	11010100	228	11100100	244	11110100
197	11000101	213	11010101	229	11100101	245	11110101
198	11000110	214	11010110	230	11100110	246	11110110
199	11000111	215	11010111	231	11100111	247	11110111
200	11001000	216	11011000	232	11101000	248	11111000
201	11001001	217	11011001	233	11101001	249	11111001
202	11001010	218	11011010	234	11101010	250	11111010
203	11001011	219	11011011	235	11101011	251	11111011
204	11001100	220	11011100	236	11101100	252	11111100
205	11001101	221	11011101	237	11101101	253	11111101
206	11001110	222	11011110	238	11101110	254	11111110
207	11001111	223	11011111	239	11101111	255	11111111

Summary

After a review of fundamental IP addressing concepts, which detailed the various classes of IP numbers in addition to the concepts of subnetting and CIDR, this chapter discussed how to preserve IP addresses by using VLSMs (Variable-Length Subnet Masks). It also examined various design considerations, such as using contiguous network addressing and using classless routing protocols (e.g., RIPv2 and EIGRP).

Next, we introduced the concept of route summarization. We saw how router resources, such as memory and processor cycles, could be preserved by representing contiguous network address space by a single route advertisement. We also showed how to overcome the caveat of having discontiguous address space by using such methods as disabling automatic summarization on our routers and by using IP unnumbered.

Key Terms

Before you take the exam, be sure you are familiar with the following terms:

bytes

Classless Interdomain Routing (CIDR)

IP address

IP unnumbered

octets

route summarization

subnet mask

Variable-Length Subnet Mask (VLSM)

Commands Used in This Chapter

Here is the list of commands used in this chapter:

Command	Description
no auto-summary	Used to disable the automatic route summarization performed by various classless routing protocols, such as RIPv2 and EIGRP.
ip unnumbered	Allows serial interfaces to borrow an IP number from another router interface (which may or may not be specified), so that it can join two contiguous address spaces.

Written Lab

Given the following set of address requirements, the available Class B network address, and the topology map shown in the graphic below, use VLSM to efficiently assign addresses to each of the four network segments.

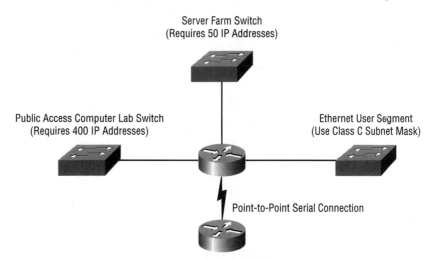

Server Farm Switch
(Requires 50 IP Addresses)

Public Access Computer Lab Switch
(Requires 400 IP Addresses)

Ethernet User Segment
(Use Class C Subnet Mask)

Point-to-Point Serial Connection

Design Requirements

- You have been given the Class B address of 172.16.0.0/16 to use.

- The first segment connects to a server farm requiring no more than 50 IP addresses.

- The second segment is a serial connection to a remote router. Due to security concerns, you should not use IP unnumbered.

- The third segment is a large publicly accessible computer laboratory containing 400 PCs, each of which requires its own unique IP address.

- The forth segment is an Ethernet user LAN. To simplify management, the network administrator has requested that the LAN have a Class C subnet mask.

Solution to Written Exercise

Although there are multiple ways that the given address space (172.16.0.0/16) could be divided up, here is one possible solution based on the methodology presented in this chapter.

1. Create a table detailing the segments and the number of hosts required on each segment, as shown in the following table:

Description of Segment	Number of IP Addresses Required
Server farm	50 (Because the maximum number of servers is 50)
Ethernet user segment	254 (Because a Class C subnet was specified)
Serial link	2 (Because each of the two routers needs one IP address)
Computer lab	400 (Because each PC needs its own IP address)

2. Determine the subnet mask required to support the requirements defined in step 1, and expand the table to list the subnet masks. We will use the table listed earlier in the chapter (Table 3.7), which tells the maximum number of hosts permitted by each subnet mask. The

following table shows the number of IP addresses required and the subnet masks needed to support the network.

Description of Segment	Number of IP Addresses Required	Subnet Mask (Number of Bits in Subnet)
Server farm	50 (Because the maximum number of servers is 50)	255.255.255.192 (26)
Ethernet user segment	254 (Because a Class C subnet was specified)	255.255.255.0 (24)
Description of Segment	**Number of IP Addresses Required**	**Subnet Mask (Number of Bits in Subnet)**
Serial link	2 (Because each of the two routers needs one IP address)	255.255.255.252 (30)
Computer lab	400 (Because each PC needs its own IP address)	255.255.254 (23)

3. Beginning with the segment requiring the greatest number of subnet bits, begin allocating addresses.

We'll do the serial link first, since it has 30 bits of subnetting. Since all of our addresses begin with 172.16, we will examine only the last 16 bits of the IP address. In the following table, we show the subnet mask, in binary, and the first and last IP number in the range. Remember that the host portion of the address cannot be all ones or all zeros.

	3rd Octet	4th Octet	Decimal IP Address
	128 64 32 16 8 4 2 1	128 64 32 16 8 4 2 1	(Last 16 bits in bold)
Subnet mask	1 1 1 1 1 1 1 1	1 1 1 1 1 1 0 0	255.255.255.252
Network	0 0 0 0 0 0 0 0	0 0 0 0 0 1 0 0	172.16.0.4
First IP in range	0 0 0 0 0 0 0 0	0 0 0 0 0 1 0 1	172.16.0.5
Last IP in range	0 0 0 0 0 0 0 0	0 0 0 0 0 1 1 0	172.16.0.6

After picking the first available network number (172.16.0.4) given our 30-bit subnet mask and eliminating host IP addresses that are all ones and all zeros, we have the following range of numbers: 172.16.0.5–172.16.0.6. Each of these numbers in the range can be assigned to one side of the serial link.

Next, as shown in the following table, we will calculate the range of IP addresses to use for our server farm segment, which needs 50 IP addresses. We pick the first available network address, given our 26-bit subnet mask. In this case, the first available network is 172.16.0.64.

	3rd Octet 128 64 32 16 8 4 2 1	4th Octet 128 64 32 16 8 4 2 1	Decimal IP Address (Last 16 bits in bold)
Subnet mask	1 1 1 1 1111	1 1 0 0 0000	255.255.255.248
Network	0 0 0 0 0000	0 1 0 0 0000	172.16.0.64
First IP in range	0 0 0 0 0000	0 1 0 0 0001	172.16.0.65
Last IP in range	0 0 0 0 0000	0 1 1 1 1110	172.16.0.126

Eliminating host IP addresses that contain all ones and all zeros, as before, we discover that our IP address range for this segment is: 172.16.0.65–172.16.0.126.

We now perform the same steps for the Ethernet user segment, as shown in the table below:

	3rd Octet 128 64 32 16 8 4 2 1	4th Octet 128 64 32 16 8 4 2 1	Decimal IP Address (Last 16 bits in bold)
Subnet mask	1 1 1 1 1111	0 0 0 0 0000	255.255.255.0
Network	0 0 0 0 0001	0 0 0 0 0000	172.16.1.0
First IP in range	0 0 0 0 0001	0 0 0 0 0001	172.16.1.1
Last IP in range	0 0 0 0 0001	1 1 1 1 1110	172.16.1.254

We now perform the same steps for the public lab segment, as shown in the following table:

	3rd Octet								4th Octet								Decimal IP Address
	128	64	32	16	8	4	2	1	128	64	32	16	8	4	2	1	(Last 16 bits in bold)
Subnet mask	1	1	1	1	1	1	1	0	0	0	0	0	0	0	0	0	255.255.254.0
Network	0	0	0	0	0	0	1	0	0	0	0	0	0	0	0	0	172.16.2.0
First IP in range	0	0	0	0	0	0	1	0	0	0	0	0	0	0	0	1	172.16.2.1
Last IP in range	0	0	0	0	0	0	1	1	1	1	1	1	1	1	1	0	172.16.3.254

In summary, we have defined the address ranges for our four segments shown in the following table:

Description of Segment	Address Range
Server farm	172.16.0.65–172.16.0.126
Ethernet user segment	172.16.1.1–172.16.1.254
Serial link	172.16.0.5–172.16.0.6
Computer lab	172.16.2.1–172.16.3.254

We can now take our VLSM address ranges and apply them to our network diagram, as shown in the following graphic.

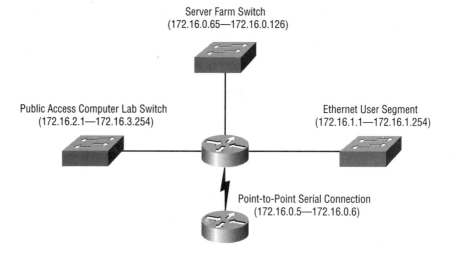

Server Farm Switch
(172.16.0.65—172.16.0.126)

Public Access Computer Lab Switch
(172.16.2.1—172.16.3.254)

Ethernet User Segment
(172.16.1.1—172.16.1.254)

Point-to-Point Serial Connection
(172.16.0.5—172.16.0.6)

Hands-on Lab

For this lab, you will need the following:

- Two Cisco routers running IOS 11.2 or later, each with at least one serial interface

- A serial crossover cable (or connect a DTE cable to a DCE cable to make your own crossover cable)

- A terminal (or a PC running terminal emulation software) with the appropriate console connection hardware for the routers

Using IP Unnumbered

Following are the steps required to complete the lab:

1. Physically connect the routers, as shown in the diagram.

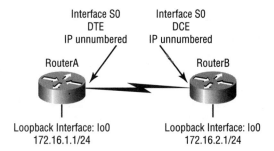

2. Configure a loopback interface on RouterA with an IP number of 172.16.1.1 and a 24-bit subnet mask:

```
hostname RouterA
interface lo0
   ip address 172.16.1.1 255.255.255.0
   no shut
```

3. Configure a loopback interface on RouterB with an IP number of 172.16.2.1 and a 24-bit subnet mask:

```
hostname RouterB
interface lo0
   ip address 172.16.2.1 255.255.255.0
   no shut
```

4. Interconnect the serial ports on the routers with a serial crossover cable (RouterA connected to the DTE side of the cable and RouterB connected to the DCE side of the cable).

5. For RouterA, configure for RIPv2:

```
router rip
   version 2
   network 172.16.0.0
```

6. For RouterB, configure for RIPv2:

```
router rip
  version 2
  network 172.16.0.0
```

7. Configure the serial interfaces on RouterA for IP unnumbered:

```
interface s0
  ip unnumbered lo0
  no shut
```

8. Configure the serial interfaces on RouterB for IP unnumbered:

```
interface s0
  ip unnumbered lo0
  clockrate 56000
  no shut
```

9. To test your configuration, from RouterA, ping 172.16.2.1.

10. To further test your configuration, from RouterB, ping 172.16.1.1.

Review Questions

1. A router can determine that an IP address is part of a Class B network by examining the first two bits in the IP address. What are the first two bits for a Class B network?

   A. 00

   B. 01

   C. 10

   D. 11

2. What does an IP address of 127.0.0.1 indicate?

   A. A local broadcast

   B. A directed multicast

   C. The local network

   D. A local loopback

3. Which of the following subnet masks will support 50 IP addresses? (Choose all that apply.)

   A. 255.255.255.240

   B. 255.255.255.0

   C. 255.255.255.192

   D. 255.255.255.224

4. VLSM is compatible with which of the following routing protocols? (Choose all that apply.)

   A. RIPv1

   B. RIPv2

   C. IGRP

   D. EIGRP

5. Which of the following best describes route summarization?

   A. A router's ability to take a group of subnetworks and summarize them as one network advertisement

   B. The Cisco IOS feature that permits serial interfaces to borrow an IP address from another specified interface

   C. The ability to tunnel IP address information inside an AURP encapsulated frame

   D. EIGRP's ability to isolate discontiguous route advertisements from one AS to another

6. Which of the following best summarizes the networks 172.16.100.0/24 and 172.16.106.0/24?

   A. 172.16.0.0/24

   B. 172.16.100.0/20

   C. 172.16.106.0/20

   D. 172.16.96.0/20

7. Which of the following is a good design practice for implementing route summarization?

   A. Use primarily with discontiguous networks.

   B. Use primarily with contiguous networks.

   C. Do not use with VLSM.

   D. Use with non-hierarchical addressing.

8. Which of the following router-configuration commands would you use to disable automatic route summarization in an EIGRP environment?

   A. no summary

   B. no auto-summary

   C. no summary stub

   D. no route-summary

9. Which of the following are caveats of Cisco's IP unnumbered IOS feature? (Choose all that apply.)

A. Does not work over HDLC networks.

B. Is not compatible with SNMP.

C. Does not work over X.25 networks.

D. You cannot ping an unnumbered interface.

10. If you have a subnet mask of 255.255.255.248, what is another way of displaying this mask?

A. /17

B. /23

C. /27

D. /29

11. Given the VLSM address 172.16.1.8/30, what are the two IP addresses in the range that may be assigned to hosts?

A. 172.16.1.8

B. 172.16.1.9

C. 172.16.1.10

D. 172.16.1.11

12. Given an IP address of 172.16.0.10/29, what is the network address?

A. 172.16.0.8

B. 172.16.0.9

C. 172.16.0.11

D. 172.16.0.12

13. Which of the following may be done to overcome problems associated with discontiguous networks?

   A. Use route summarization.

   B. Use VLSM.

   C. Use IP unnumbered.

   D. Disable route summarization.

14. Which of the following IP addresses do Cisco routers use to designate the default route?

   A. 1.1.1.1

   B. 0.0.0.0

   C. 255.255.255.255

   D. 127.0.0.1

15. If you decide not to use IP unnumbered on a serial link, to best preserve IP addresses, what should your subnet mask be?

   A. 255.255.255.255

   B. 255.255.255.0

   C. 255.255.255.252

   D. 255.255.252.0

16. What are the two methods that are most commonly used to represent an IP address?

   A. Dotted-decimal

   B. Octal

   C. Binary

   D. Hexadecimal

17. An IP address is made up of what? (Choose all that apply.)

A. four octets

B. 32 bits

C. four bytes

D. eight bits

18. Route summarization is particularly effective in which of the following environments? (Choose all that apply.)

A. When a large number of contiguous network numbers are being advertised

B. When IGRP is being used as the routing protocol

C. When EIGRP is being used as the routing protocol

D. When VLSMs are in use

19. If you have an IP address of 172.16.1.10/25, what is the broadcast address that the host will use?

A. 172.16.255.255

B. 172.16.1.255

C. 172.16.1.0

D. 172.16.1.127

20. How many hosts will the 255.255.255.224 subnet mask support?

A. 6

B. 14

C. 30

D. 62

Answers to Review Questions

1. C. A leading bit pattern of 0 indicates a Class A network. A leading bit pattern of 10 indicates a Class B network. A leading bit pattern of 110 indicates a Class C network.

2. D. Network 127 is reserved for loopback purposes (e.g., for trouble-shooting diagnostics). With a local loopback address, a host can send a test packet to itself without generating network traffic.

3. B, C. The formula $2^n - 2$ = number of hosts (where n is the number of host bits in the subnet mask) tells us how many hosts can be supported for a particular subnet. Here are some examples:

    255.255.255.240 => 4 host bits => 14 hosts

    255.255.255.0 => 8 host bits => 254 hosts

    255.255.255.192 => 6 host bits => 62 hosts

    255.255.255.224 => 5 host bits => 30 hosts

4. B, D. VLSM is compatible only with classless routing protocols. Classless routing protocols have the ability to carry subnet information in their route advertisements. RIPv1 and IGRP are classful, whereas RIPv2 and EIGRP are classless.

5. A. Route summarization, which works best with contiguous address space, reduces the memory and processor burden on routers by representing multiple subnets in a single route advertisement.

6. D. If you write out the networks 172.16.100.0/24 and 172.16.106.0/24 in binary and see how many leading bits they have in common, you will find that the first 20 bits are the same for both networks. If you then convert these 20 bits back into decimal, you will have the address of the summarized route.

7. B. Route summarization is most effective when used with contiguous address space, because contiguous address space tends to have the most higher-order bits in common.

8. B. The command `no auto-summary` is a router-configuration command that disables the automatic summarization of routes.

9. C, D. IP unnumbered is not supported on X.25 or SMDS networks. Since the serial interface has no IP number, you will not be able to ping the interface to see if it is up. However, you can determine the interface status with SNMP. Also, IP security options are not supported on an IP unnumbered interface.

10. D. If you write out 255.255.255.248 in binary, you will find that the first 29 bits are ones, and the remaining three bits are zeros. Therefore, we say that it is a /29.

11. B, C. If we look at each of these IP addresses and the subnet mask in binary, we see that the host portion of the address for 172.16.1.8 is all zeros, which refers to the network. The host portion of 172.16.1.9 is 01, which is valid for a host address. The host portion of 172.16.1.10 is 10, which is also valid for a host address. The host portion of 172.16.1.11 is 11, which refers to the broadcast address.

12. A. If you write out the last octet in binary, you have 00001010. Since we are using a 29-bit subnet mask, the last three bits are not part of the network address, which leaves us with a network address of 00001000. If we convert this number back to decimal, we get 8. Therefore, the network address is 172.16.0.8.

13. C and D. IP unnumbered can, in some cases, make a discontiguous network appear as contiguous across a serial link. Also, if you disable route summarization, then a router will advertise each individual subnet. However, answer D only works with routing protocols that can carry subnet information, otherwise you still end up with a discontiguous network, for example EIGRP and RIP V2.

14. B. The command to set a default route in Cisco IOS is `set ip route 0.0.0.0 0.0.0.0 next_hop` (where `next_hop` can be a local interface or the IP of an adjacent router interface).

15. C. On a serial link, we need only two IP addresses, one for each side of the link. A subnet mask of 255.255.255.252 has only two host bits, which gives us a maximum of two host IP addresses ($2^2 - 2 = 2$), which is exactly what we need for our serial link.

16. A, C. Although an IP number can be represented in practically any base of numbering system, dotted-decimal and binary are the most common representations.

17. A, B, C. An IP address is 32 bits in length. An octet is eight bits in length. Therefore, four octets equal 32 bits. Since a byte is eight bits, four bytes also equal 32 bits.

18. A, C, D. Route summarization is not compatible with IGRP, because IGRP is a classful routing protocol, meaning that it does not carry subnet information in its routing updates.

19. D. With 25 bits of subnetting, we have the last seven bits to use as the host address. If we set each of these last seven bits to 1 (the definition of a broadcast address), then we get 172.16.1.127.

20. C. If you convert 224 to binary, you get 11100000. With five host bits (i.e., bits set to 0 in the subnet mask), you can support 30 host addresses ($2^5 - 2 = 30$, where 5 is the number of host bits).

Chapter

4

OSPF Areas

THE CCNP ROUTING TOPICS COVERED IN THIS CHAPTER ARE AS FOLLOWS:

- ✓ Introduction to OSPF terminology

- ✓ Introduction to OSPF functionality

- ✓ Discussion of OSPF areas, routers, and link-state advertisements

- ✓ Discussion of choosing and maintaining routes, in particular in multi-access, PPP, and non-broadcast multi-access networks

- ✓ Configuration and verification of OSPF operation

his chapter is the introduction to Open Shortest Path First (OSPF) areas. It will introduce the term *OSPF areas* and discuss their role in OSPF routing. It is very important that you take the time to learn the terminology used in OSPF. Without this knowledge, the remaining sections of the chapter will be difficult to follow.

Open Shortest Path First

Open Shortest Path First (OSPF) is an open standards routing protocol. It is important to recognize that Cisco's implementation of OSPF is a standards-based version. This means that Cisco based its version of OSPF on the open standards. While doing so, Cisco also has added features to its version of OSPF that may not be found in other implementations of OSPF. This becomes important when interoperability is needed.

John Moy heads up the working group of OSPF. Two RFCs define OSPF: Version 1 is defined by RFC 1131, and Version 2 is defined by RFC 2328. Version 2 is the only version to make it to an operational status. However, many vendors modify OSPF. OSPF is known as a link-state routing protocol (link-state routing protocols were discussed in Chapter 2, "Routing Principles"). The Dijkstra algorithm is used to calculate the shortest path through the network. Within OSPF, links become synonymous with interfaces.

OSPF is a robust protocol, and due to the robustness, you must learn many terms in order to understand the operation of OSPF. The next section covers the terminology necessary to enable you to understand the many operations and procedures performed by the OSPF process.

OSPF Terminology

The most basic of terms that are related to OSPF are related to many routing protocols. We begin by defining relationships among routers. From there, we will move on to defining terms relating to OSPF operations.

Neighbor   A neighbor refers to a connected (adjacent) router that is running an OSPF process with the adjacent interface assigned to the same area. Neighbors are found via Hello packets. No routing information is exchanged with neighbors unless adjacencies are formed.

Adjacency   An adjacency refers to the logical connection between a router and its corresponding designated routers and backup designated routers. The formation of this type of relationship depends heavily on the type of network that connects the OSPF routers.

Link   In OSPF, a link refers to a network or router interface assigned to any given network. Within OSPF, link is synonymous with interface.

Interface   An interface is the physical interface on a router. When an interface is added to the OSPF process, it is considered by OSPF as a link. If the interface is up, then the link is up. OSPF uses this association to build its link database.

Link State Advertisement   *Link State Advertisement (LSA)* is an OSPF data packet containing link-state and routing information that is shared among OSPF routers.

Designated router   A *designated router (DR)* is used only when the OSPF router is connected to a broadcast (multi-access) network. To minimize the number of adjacencies formed, a DR is chosen to disseminate/receive routing information to/from the remaining routers on the broadcast network or link.

Backup designated router   A *backup designated router (BDR)* is a hot standby for the DR on broadcast (multi-access) links. The BDR receives all routing updates from OSPF adjacent routers but does not flood LSA updates.

OSPF areas   *OSPF areas* are similar to EIGRP Autonomous Systems. Areas are used to establish a hierarchical network. OSPF uses four types of areas, all of which will be discussed later in this chapter.

Area border router   An *area border router (ABR)* is a router that has multiple area assignments. An interface may belong to only one area. If a router has multiple interfaces and if any of these interfaces belong to different areas, the router is considered an ABR.

Autonomous system boundary router   An *autonomous system boundary router (ASBR)* is a router with an interface connected to an external network or a different AS. An external network or autonomous system refers to an interface belonging to a different routing protocol, such as EIGRP. An ASBR is responsible for injecting route information learned by other Interior Gateway Protocols (IGPs) into OSPF.

Non-broadcast multi-access   *Non-broadcast multi-access (NMBA)* networks are networks such as Frame Relay, X.25, and ATM. This type of network allows for multi-access but has no broadcast ability like Ethernet. NBMA networks require special OSPF configuration to function properly.

Broadcast (multi-access)   Networks such as Ethernet allow multiple access as well as provide broadcast ability. A DR and BDR must be elected for multi-access broadcast networks.

Point-to-point   This type of network connection consists of a unique NMBA configuration. The network can be configured using Frame Relay and ATM to allow point-to-point connectivity. This configuration eliminates the need for DRs or BDRs.

Router ID   The Router ID is an IP address that is used to identify the router. Cisco chooses the Router ID by using the highest IP address of all configured loopback interfaces. If no loopback addresses are configured, OSPF will choose the highest IP address of the functional physical interfaces.

All of these terms play an important part in understanding the operation of OSPF. You must come to know and understand each of these terms. As you read through the chapter, you will be able to place the terms in their proper context.

OSPF Operation

OSPF operation can be divided into three categories:

- Neighbor and adjacency initialization
- LSA flooding
- SPF tree calculation

We will discuss each in the following sections.

Neighbor and Adjacency Initialization

We begin with neighbor/adjacency formation. This is a very big part of OSPF operation. These relationships are often easily formed over point-to-point connections, but much more complex procedures are required when multiple OSPF routers are connected via a broadcast multi-access media.

The Hello protocol is used to discover neighbors and establish adjacencies. Hello packets contain a great deal of information regarding the originating router. Hello packets are multicast out every interface on a 10-second interval by default. The data contained in the Hello packet can be seen in Table 4.1. It is important to remember that the Router ID, Area ID, and authentication information are carried in the common OSPF header. The Hello packet uses the common OSPF header.

TABLE 4.1 OSPF Hello Packet Information

Originating Router Characteristic	Description
Router ID	The highest active IP address on the router. (Loopback addresses are used first. If no loopback interfaces are configured, OSPF will choose from physical interfaces.)
Area ID	The area to which the originating router interface belongs.
Authentication information	The authentication type and corresponding information.
Network mask	The IP mask of the originating router's interface IP address.

TABLE 4.1 OSPF Hello Packet Information *(continued)*

Originating Router Characteristic	Description
Hello interval	The period between Hello packets.
Options	OSPF options for neighbor formation.
Router priority	An 8-bit value used to aid in the election of the DR and BDR. (Not set on point-to-point links.)
Router dead interval	The length of time allotted for which a Hello packet must be received before considering the neighbor down—four times the Hello interval, unless otherwise configured.
DR	The Router ID of the current DR.
BDR	The Router ID of the current BDR.
Neighbor router IDs	A list of the Router IDs for all the originating router's neighbors.

Neighbor States

There are a total of eight states for OSPF neighbors:

Down   No Hello packets have been received on the interface.

Attempt   Neighbors must be configured manually for this state. It applies only to NBMA network connections. (Note: This state is not represented in Figure 4.1)

Init   Hello packets have been received from other routers.

2Way   Hello packets have been received that include their own Router ID in the Neighbor field.

ExStart   Master/Slave relationship is established in order to form an adjacency by exchanging Database Description (DD) packets. (The router with the highest Router ID becomes the Master.)

Exchange   Routing information is exchanged using DD and LSR packets.

Loading   Link State Request packets are sent to neighbors to request any new LSAs that were found while in the Exchange state.

Full   All LSA information is synchronized among adjacent neighbors.

To gain a better understanding of how an adjacency is formed, let's consider the formation of an adjacency in a broadcast multi-access environment. Figure 4.1 displays a flow chart that depicts each step of the initialization process. The process starts by sending out Hello packets. Every listening router will then add the originating router to the neighbor database. The responding routers will reply with all of their Hello information so that the originating router can add them to its own neighbor table.

FIGURE 4.1   OSPF peer initialization

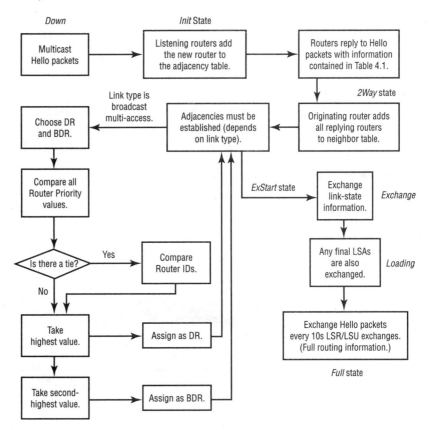

Adjacency Requirements

Once neighbors have been identified, adjacencies must be established so that routing (LSA) information can be exchanged. There are two steps required to change a neighboring OSPF router into an adjacent OSPF router:

- Two-way communication (achieved via the Hello protocol)

- Database synchronization—this consists of three packet types being exchanged between routers:

  - Database Description (DD) packets

  - Link State Request (LSR) packets

  - Link State Update (LSU) packets

Once the database synchronization has taken place, the two routers are considered adjacent. This is how adjacency is achieved, but you must also know when an adjacency will occur.

When adjacencies form depends on the network type. If the link is point-to-point, the two neighbors will become adjacent if the Hello packet information for both routers is configured properly.

On broadcast multi-access networks, adjacencies are formed only between the OSPF routers on the network and the DR and BDR. Figure 4.2 gives an example. Three types of routers are pictured: DR, BDR, and DROther. DROther routers are routers that belong to the same network as the DR and BDR but do not represent the network via LSAs.

FIGURE 4.2 OSPF adjacencies for multi-access networks

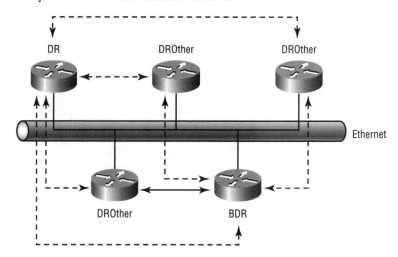

You will notice the dotted lines connecting the DROther routers to the DR and BDR routers. Notice also that there are no dotted lines between any of the DROther routers. The dotted lines represent the formation of adjacencies. DROther routers form only two adjacencies on a broadcast multi-access network—one with the DR and the other with the BDR. The following router output indicates the assignments of routers connected via a broadcast multi-access network as well as two Frame Relay (non-broadcast multi-access, or NBMA) network connections.

Note that the Frame Relay connections displayed below do not have DR/BDR assignments. DR/BDR roles and election will be covered more fully in the following section, "DR and BDR Election Procedure."

RouterA>**sho ip ospf neighbor**

```
Neighbor ID     Pri   State         Dead Time   Address        Interface
172.16.22.101   1     FULL/DROTHER  00:00:32    172.16.22.101  FastEthernet0/0
172.16.247.1    1     FULL/DR       00:00:34    172.16.22.9    FastEthernet0/0
172.16.245.1    1     2WAY/DROTHER  00:00:32    172.16.12.8    FastEthernet1/0
172.16.244.1    1     2WAY/DROTHER  00:00:37    172.16.12.13   FastEthernet1/0
172.16.247.1    1     FULL/BDR      00:00:34    172.16.12.9    FastEthernet1/0
172.16.249.1    1     FULL/DR       00:00:34    172.16.12.15   FastEthernet1/0
172.16.248.1    1     2WAY/DROTHER  00:00:36    172.16.12.12   FastEthernet1/0
172.16.245.1    1     FULL/ -       00:00:34    172.16.1.105   Serial3/0.1
172.16.241.1    1     FULL/ -       00:00:34    172.16.202.2   Serial3/1
172.16.248.1    1     FULL/ -       00:00:35    172.16.1.41    Serial3/3.1
RouterA>
```

We need to bring up a few important points about this output. Notice that four different interfaces are configured to use OSPF.

Interface Fast Ethernet 0/0 shows only a DROther and a DR. You know that there must always be a DR and a BDR for each multi-access segment. Deductively, you can ascertain that RouterA must be the BDR for this segment.

It is also important to recognize that this command displays OSPF neighbors and not adjacencies. To learn adjacency formations, study the following summarization:

- Point-to-point valid neighbors form adjacencies.

- NBMA neighbors require special configuration (e.g., point-to-point subinterfaces) for adjacency formation.

- Broadcast multi-access neighbors require the election of a DR and a BDR. All other routers form adjacencies with only the DR and BDR.

DR and BDR Election Procedure

Each OSPF interface (multi-access only) possesses a configurable Router Priority. The Cisco default is 1. If you don't want a router interface to participate in the DR/BDR election, set the Priority to 0 using the `ip ospf priority` command in Interface Configuration mode. Here is a sample (the Priority field is bolded for ease of identification):

```
RouterA>show ip ospf interface
FastEthernet0/0 is up, line protocol is up
  Internet Address 172.16.22.14/24, Area 0
  Process ID 100, Router ID 172.16.246.1, Network Type
  ⤷BROADCAST, Cost: 1
  Transmit Delay is 1 sec, State BDR, Priority 1
  Designated Router (ID) 172.16.247.1, Interface address
  ⤷172.16.22.9
  Backup Designated router (ID) 172.16.246.1, Interface
  ⤷address 172.16.22.14
  Timer intervals configured, Hello 10, Dead 40, Wait 40,
  ⤷Retransmit 5
    Hello due in 00:00:08
  Neighbor Count is 2, Adjacent neighbor count is 2
    Adjacent with neighbor 172.16.22.101
    Adjacent with neighbor 172.16.247.1  (Designated
    ⤷Router)
  Suppress hello for 0 neighbor(s)
  Message digest authentication enabled
    Youngest key id is 10
RouterA>
```

This value is key when electing the DR and BDR. Let's go through the steps that occur when the DR and BDR are elected.

1. A list of eligible routers is created. The criteria for eligible routers are:

   - Priority ≥ 1.

   - OSPF state of 2Way.

   - DR or BDR IP address is the same as the participating interface's IP address.

2. A list of all routers not claming to be the DR (the DR IP address is the same as the participating interface's IP address) is compiled from the list of eligible routers.

3. The BDR is chosen from the list in Step 2 based on the following criteria:

   - The BDR IP address is the same as the participating interface's IP address.

   - The router with the highest Router Priority becomes the BDR.

   - If all Router Priorities are equal, the router with the highest Router ID becomes the BDR.

   or

   - If none of the above criteria hold true, the router with the highest Router Priority is chosen, and in case of a tie, the router with the highest Router ID is chosen as BDR.

4. The DR is chosen from the remaining eligible routers based on the following criteria:

   - The DR field is set with the router's interface IP address.

   - The router with the highest Router Priority is chosen DR. If all Router Priorities are equal, the router with the highest Router ID is chosen.

   or

   - If none of the remaining eligible routers claim to be the DR, the BDR that was chosen in Step 3 becomes the DR. Step 3 would then be repeated to choose another BDR.

You should remember that the previous process occurs when multiple routers become active at the same time on a segment. If a DR and BDR already exist on the segment, any new interfaces accept the DR and BDR regardless of their own Router ID or Router Priority.

To further the example, if initially there is only one OSPF router interface active on the segment, it becomes the DR. The next router would become the BDR. Subsequent routers would all accept the existing DR and BDR and form adjacencies with them.

LSA Flooding

LSA flooding is the method by which OSPF shares routing information. Via LSU packets, LSA information containing link-state data is shared with all OSPF routers. The network topology is created from the LSA updates. Flooding is used so that all OSPF routers have the topology map from which SPF calculations may be made.

Efficient flooding is achieved through the use of a reserved multicast address, 224.0.0.5 (AllSPFRouters). LSA updates (indicating that something in the topology changed) are handled somewhat differently. The network type determines the multicast address used for sending updates. Table 4.2 contains the multicast address associated with LSA flooding. Point-to-multipoint networks use the adjacent router's unicast IP address. Figure 4.3 depicts a simple update and flood scenario on a broadcast multi-access network.

TABLE 4.2 LSA Update Multicast Addresses

Network Type	Multicast Address	Description
Point-to-point	224.0.0.5	AllSPFRouters
Broadcast	224.0.0.6	AllDR
Point-to-multipoint	NA	NA

FIGURE 4.3   LSA updates and flooding

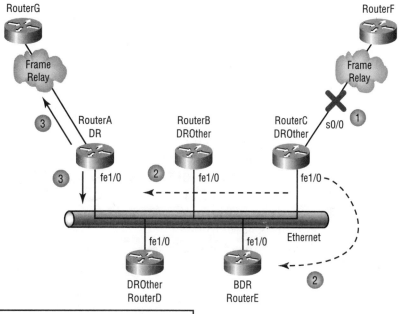

1. Link s0/0 goes down.
2. RouterC sends LSU containing the LSA for int s0/0 on multicast AllDRouters (224.0.0.6) to the DR and BDR.
3. RouterA floods the LSA to AllSPFRouters (224.0.0.5) out all interfaces.

Once the LSA updates have been flooded throughout the network, each recipient must acknowledge that the flooded update was received. It is also important that the recipient validate the LSA update.

LSA Acknowledgement and Validation

Routers receiving LSA updates must acknowledge the receipt of the LSA, but they can do it using two forms:

Explicit acknowledgement   The recipient sends a Link State Acknowledgement packet to the originating interface.

Implicit acknowledgement   A duplicate of the flooded LSA is sent back to the originator.

Here is a packet decode of an Explicit acknowledgement:

```
IP Header - Internet Protocol Datagram
    Version:               4
    Header Length:         5
    Precedence:            6
    Type of Service:       %000
    Unused:                %00
    Total Length:          84
    Identifier:            1285
    Fragmentation Flags:   %000
    Fragment Offset:       0
    Time To Live:          1
IP Type:                   0x59  OSPF (Hex value for protocol
⮑number)
    Header Checksum:       0x8dda
    Source IP Address:     131.31.194.140
    Dest. IP Address:      224.0.0.6
    No Internet Datagram Options
OSPF - Open Shortest Path First Routing Protocol
    Version:               2
    Type:                  5  Link State Acknowledgement
    Packet Length:         64
    Router IP Address:     142.42.193.1
    Area ID:               1
    Checksum:              0x6699
    Authentication Type:   0  No Authentication
    Authentication Data:
    ........               00 00 00 00 00 00 00 00
Link State Advertisement Header
    Age:                   3600  seconds
    Options:               %00100010
          No AS External Link State Advertisements
    Type:                  3  Summary Link (IP Network)
    ID:                    0x90fb6400
    Advertising Router:    153.53.193.1
```

```
Sequence Number:        2147483708
Checksum:               0x3946
Link State Length:      28
Link State Advertisement Header
Age:                    3600   seconds
Options:                %00100010
        No AS External Link State Advertisements
Type:                   3  Summary Link (IP Network)
ID:                     0x90fb6400
Advertising Router:     131.31.193.1
Sequence Number:        2147483650
Checksum:               0x25c0
Link State Length:      28
Frame Check Sequence:   0x00000000
```

You can tell that this is a Link State Acknowledgement packet based on the OSPF header information. You will see that it is a type 5 OSPF packet, or a Link State Acknowledgement packet.

There are two methods by which an implicit acknowledgement may be made:

Direct method   The acknowledgement, either explicit or implicit, is sent immediately. The following criteria must be met before the Direct method is used:

- A duplicate flooded LSA is received.

- LSA age equals MaxAge (one hour).

Delayed method   The recipient waits to send the *LSA acknowledgement* with other LSA acknowledgements that need to be sent.

Validation occurs through the use of the sequencing, checksum, and aging data contained in the LSA update packet. This information is used to make sure that the router possesses the most recent copy of the link-state database.

SPF Tree Calculation

Shortest Path First (SPF) trees are paths through the network to any given destination. A separate path exists for each known destination. There are two destination types recognized by OSPF: network and router. Router destinations are specifically for area border routers (ABRs) and autonomous system boundary routers (ASBRs).

Once all of the OSPF routers have synchronized link-state databases, each router is responsible for calculating the SPF tree for each known destination. This calculation is done using the Dijkstra algorithm. In order to do calculations, metrics for each link are required.

OSPF Metrics

OSPF uses a metric referred to as *cost*. A cost is associated with every outgoing interface along an SPF tree. The cost of the entire path is the sum of costs of the outgoing interfaces along the path. Since cost is an arbitrary value as defined in RFC 2338, Cisco had to implement its own method of calculating the cost for each OSPF-enabled interface. Cisco uses a simple equation of 10^8 /bandwidth. The bandwidth is the configured bandwidth for the interface.

This value may be overridden by using the ip ospf cost command. The cost is manipulated by changing the value to a number within the range of 1 to 65,535. Since the cost is assigned to each link, the value must be changed on each interface.

Cisco bases link cost on bandwidth. Other vendors may use other metrics to calculate the link's cost. When connecting links between routers from different vendors, you may have to adjust the cost to match the other router. Both routers must assign the same cost to the link for OSPF to work.

NBMA Overview

Non-broadcast multi-access networks (e.g., Frame Relay and ATM) present a special challenge for OSPF. As you know, multi-access networks use an election process to select a DR and a BDR to represent all OSPF routers on the network. This election process requires the participation of all routers on the multi-access network. However, Hello packets are used to facilitate the communication for the election process. This works fine on broadcast multi-access because the connected devices on the network can hear the AllSPFRouters multicast address for the subnet.

When you move to a non-broadcast form of multi-access network, you lose the assurance that all connected devices are receiving the Hello packets and are participating in the DR/BDR election.

Because of the difficulty in running OPSF on NBMA networks, it is important to know which configuration, or environment, will be the most effective solution. The following section, "NBMA Environments," discusses some possible solutions for implementing OSPF over NBMA networks.

NBMA Environments

Earlier, we mentioned that there are three types of networks: broadcast multi-access, non-broadcast multi-access, and point-to-point. Although NBMA requires somewhat more configuration to make OSPF operational, it also gives you the option of deciding how you want it to behave.

With extended configurations on NBMA interfaces, an administrator can cause OSPF to behave as if it were running on one of the following four network types:

- Broadcast
- Non-broadcast
- Point-to-point
- Point-to-multipoint

Broadcast

In order to achieve a broadcast implementation of OSPF on an NBMA network, a full mesh must exist among the routers. Figure 4.4 depicts what the NBMA network would have to look like. You can see that each router has a permanent virtual circuit (PVC) configured with all of the other routers.

FIGURE 4.4 NBMA broadcast implementation

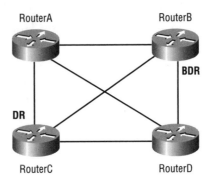

This configuration guarantees that all routers have connectivity and that all will be able to participate in the DR/BDR election process. Once the DR and BDR have been chosen, the meshed networks act as a broadcast network. All LSA updates are sent to the DR and BDR, and the DR floods the updates out every interface.

One of the major weaknesses with this configuration is that if one of the PVCs fails (especially if it is a PVC between a DROther and the DR), then communication is also halted between the two adjacent peers.

Non-broadcast

This environment requires that all OSPF neighbors be manually configured. This is the default setting for the router. By manually configuring each neighbor, OSPF knows exactly which neighbors need to participate and which neighbor is identified as the DR. Also, communication between neighbors is done via unicast instead of multicast. This configuration also requires a full mesh and has the same weakness as the broadcast environment.

Point-to-Point

This environment uses subinterfaces on the physical interface to create point-to-point connections with other OSPF neighbors. No DR or BDR is elected since the link is treated as a point-to-point circuit. This allows for faster convergence.

A full mesh is not required when implementing this environment. PVCs on the subinterface may fail, but there is still OSPF connectivity to other PVCs on the same physical interface.

The drawback of this environment is inefficient flooding. Because of multiple PVCs per interface and depending on the mesh of the PVCs, one LSA update can be flooded multiple times.

Point-to-Multipoint

This environment is very similar to the point-to-point environment. No DR or BDR is chosen. All PVCs are treated as point-to-point links. The only difference is that all the PVCs go back to a single router. Figure 4.5 depicts the difference between a true point-to-point environment and a point-to-multipoint deployment.

FIGURE 4.5 Point-to-point vs. point-to-multipoint

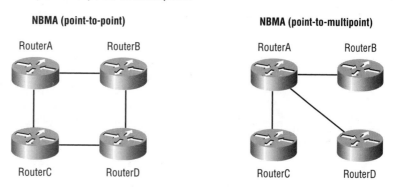

Configuring OSPF

Configuring OSPF is a simple task. There are many options that are allowed within OSPF, such as statically configuring neighbors, creating a virtual link between an area that is not physically connected to Area 0, neighbor/adjacency encryption, and many more. The following sections describe how to configure OSPF in different environments.

Enabling OSPF is common for all implementations of OSPF; the difference comes when you configure parameters to make OSPF behave in the desired fashion. We'll cover parameters for NBMA as well.

The basic elements of OSPF configuration are:

- Enabling OSPF

- Configuring OSPF for different network types

- Configuring the OSPF area

- Route summarization

- Route redistribution (covered in detail in Chapter 10, "Route Optimization")

- Interface parameters

We will start with basic configuration of OSPF, then introduce commands relating to NBMA, as well as the methods and commands used to verify proper configuration and operation of OSPF.

Discovering the Network with OSPF

The moment OSPF is enabled on a router and networks are added to the OSPF process, the router will try to discover the OSPF neighbors on the connected links. Here is a sample of what OSPF events transpire when the interface is added to an OSPF process:

```
RouterA(config-router)#network 172.16.10.5 0.0.0.0 area 0
RouterA(config-router)#
OSPF: Interface Serial0 going Up
OSPF: Tried to build Router LSA within MinLSInterval
OSPF: Tried to build Router LSA within MinLSInterval^Z
RouterA#
OSPF: rcv. v:2 t:1 1:44 rid:172.16.20.1
      aid:0.0.0.0 chk:3B91 aut:0 auk: from Serial0
OSPF: rcv. v:2 t:2 1:32 rid:172.16.20.1
      aid:0.0.0.0 chk:2ECF aut:0 auk: from Serial0
OSPF: Rcv DBD from 172.16.20.1 on Serial0 seq 0x71A opt
↳0x2 flag 0x7 len 32 state INIT
```

```
OSPF: 2 Way Communication to 172.16.20.1 on Serial0, state
↳2WAY
OSPF: Send DBD to 172.16.20.1 on Serial0 seq 0x2E opt 0x2
↳flag 0x7 len 32
OSPF: First DBD and we are not SLAVE
OSPF: rcv. v:2 t:2 1:52 rid:172.16.20.1
       aid:0.0.0.0 chk:A641 aut:0 auk: from Serial0
OSPF: Rcv DBD from 172.16.20.1 on Serial0 seq 0x2E opt 0x2
↳flag 0x2 len 52 state EXSTART
OSPF: NBR Negotiation Done. We are the MASTER
OSPF: Send DBD to 172.16.20.1 on Serial0 seq 0x2F opt 0x2
↳flag 0x3 len 52
OSPF: Database request to 172.16.20.1
OSPF: sent LS REQ packet to 172.16.10.6, length 12
OSPF: rcv. v:2 t:2 1:32 rid:172.16.20.1
       aid:0.0.0.0 chk:35C1 aut:0 auk: from Serial0
OSPF: rcv. v:2 t:3 1:36 rid:172.16.20.1
       aid:0.0.0.0 chk:5A1 aut:0 auk: from Serial0
OSPF: Rcv DBD from 172.16.20.1 on Serial0 seq 0x2F opt 0x2
↳flag 0x0 len 32 state EXCHANGE
OSPF: Send DBD to 172.16.20.1 on Serial0 seq 0x30 opt 0x2
↳flag 0x1 len 32
OSPF: rcv. v:2 t:4 1:64 rid:172.16.20.1
       aid:0.0.0.0 chk:F4EA aut:0 auk: from Serial0
OSPF: rcv. v:2 t:2 1:32 rid:172.16.20.1
       aid:0.0.0.0 chk:35C0 aut:0 auk: from Serial0
OSPF: Rcv DBD from 172.16.20.1 on Serial0 seq 0x30 opt 0x2
↳flag 0x0 len 32 state EXCHANGE
OSPF: Exchange Done with 172.16.20.1 on Serial0
OSPF: Synchronized with 172.16.20.1 on Serial0, state FULL
```

This simple debug output describes exactly what we talked about earlier in this chapter regarding LSA exchanges and the state of adjacent OSPF neighbors. We bolded the state information for your convenience.

We used the OSPF debugging commands to produce this output. The configuration commands consisted of two simple OSPF commands:

router ospf 1   This command starts the OSPF process on RouterA. The number 1 indicates the OSPF process ID.

network 172.16.10.5 0.0.0.0 area 0   This command adds the network (link) 172.16.10.5. The wildcard mask indicates that only this single IP address is going to be part of the link. Area 0 indicates that the interface with the address 172.16.10.5 is assigned to Area 0.

The generic IOS syntax for the commands is router ospf *process-id* and network *ip-address* wildcard-mask area *area-id*, respectively.

Point-to-Point

Since the link described by the previous output is point-to-point, no DR/BDR election occurred; instead, each router decided which would be the Master and which would be the Slave. Once the Master/Slave roles had been established, DBD packets containing LSA information for each router were exchanged.

LSA exchanges continue until the link-state databases for each router are identical (synchronized). Once that happens, the OSPF state changes to Full.

Broadcast

Discovering the neighbors on a broadcast network is done somewhat differently. Here you will see what happens on a broadcast multi-access network:

```
RouterA(config-if)#router ospf 1
RouterA(config-router)#network 172.16.230.0 0.0.0.255
↳area 0
OSPF: Interface Ethernet0 going Up
OSPF: Tried to build Router LSA within MinLSInterval
OSPF: Tried to build Router LSA within MinLSInterval
RouterA(config-router)#
OSPF: end of Wait on interface Ethernet0
OSPF: DR/BDR election on Ethernet0
OSPF: Elect BDR 172.16.240.1
OSPF: Elect DR 172.16.240.1
OSPF: Elect BDR 0.0.0.0
```

```
OSPF: Elect DR 172.16.240.1
      DR: 172.16.240.1 (Id)    BDR: none
OSPF: Build router LSA for area 0, router ID 172.16.240.1
```

We end the output here, because we know that once adjacencies have been established, the link-state databases must synchronize during the Exchange state and the transfer of DBD packets containing LSA updates.

Of interest in this output is the election of the DR and BDR. Initially, the value for the BDR was 0.0.0.0. This was the first router on the network to become active. Therefore, the first election to take place is that of BDR, because Ethernet 0 is the only active OSPF interface at the moment, and the Router ID of 172.16.240.1 (the loopback 0 IP address) is chosen to be the BDR.

When the process goes on to elect the DR, the only router capable is itself. The role of DR is taken by 172.16.240.1, and the BDR is reset to 0.0.0.0 because there are no other routers active on this multi-access network.

No new commands were used to create this output. The only difference was that the network 172.16.230.0 was configured on a broadcast multi-access network.

Configuring OSPF—Single Area

The easiest (and least scalable) way to configure OSPF is to simply use Area 0. If all you want to configure is one area, it must be Area 0. Creating a single backbone area makes it easy to understand what OSPF is doing, but once you get a number of routers in the area with all the interfaces assigned to Area 0, processing time is going to be much greater and convergence slower.

To start learning, however, a single area is the perfect place to start. You have already seen the command that is used for assigning an interface to an area. Let's look at the configuration of a few routers to get a good feeling for how it is done. Figure 4.6 depicts the physical layout of a test network.

FIGURE 4.6 OSPF area topology

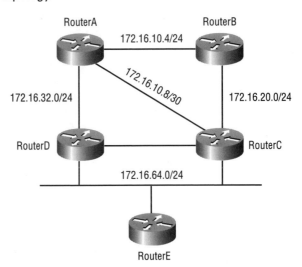

Only two of the five configurations are shown—otherwise you would just see a lot of redundant information. Notice the very specific wildcard masks in the network statements. These facilitate the removal or addition of specific links when troubleshooting. If you have a link that is flapping, you can easily remove it so that it does not cause LSA flooding within the area. After the link has stabilized, it will be very easy to add the interface back in.

For example, if all of the router's interfaces could be summarized by a network statement of 172.16.0.0 0.0.255.255, then you would need only one network statement to add all interfaces to the OSPF process. However, if one out of the many interfaces was flapping, you could not easily isolate that interface so that it would not cause unnecessary LSA flooding. Let's examine the IOS configuration for this topology:

```
RouterA#show running-config
Building configuration...

Current configuration:
!
version 11.2
no service password-encryption
no service udp-small-servers
```

```
no service tcp-small-servers
!
hostname RouterA
!
enable password cisco
!
!
interface Loopback0
 ip address 172.16.240.1 255.255.255.0
!
interface Ethernet0
 ip address 172.16.230.20 255.255.255.0
!
interface Serial0
 ip address 172.16.10.5 255.255.255.252
 clockrate 2000000
 dce-terminal-timing-enable
!
interface Serial1
 ip address 172.16.10.9 255.255.255.252
 clockrate 2000000
 dce-terminal-timing-enable
!
interface Serial2
 no ip address
 shutdown
!
interface Serial3
 no ip address
 shutdown
!
interface BRI0
 no ip address
 shutdown
!
router ospf 1
```

```
 network 172.16.230.0 0.0.0.255 area 0
 network 172.16.10.5 0.0.0.0 area 0
 network 172.16.10.9 0.0.0.0 area 0
!

RouterB#wr t
Building configuration...

Current configuration:
!
version 12.0
service timestamps debug uptime
service timestamps log uptime
no service password-encryption
!
hostname RouterB
!
enable password cisco
!
ip subnet-zero
!
!
!
interface Loopback0
 ip address 172.16.241.1 255.255.255.0
 no ip directed-broadcast
!
interface Ethernet0
 no ip address
 no ip directed-broadcast
 shutdown
!
interface Serial0
 ip address 172.16.10.6 255.255.255.252
 no ip directed-broadcast
 no ip mroute-cache
```

```
 no fair-queue
!
interface Serial1
 ip address 172.16.20.1 255.255.255.0
 no ip directed-broadcast
 clockrate 2000000
 dce-terminal-timing-enable
!
interface Serial2
 no ip address
 no ip directed-broadcast
 shutdown
!
interface Serial3
 no ip address
 no ip directed-broadcast
 shutdown
!
interface BRI0
 no ip address
 no ip directed-broadcast
 shutdown
!
router ospf 1
 network 172.16.10.6 0.0.0.0 area 0
 network 172.16.20.0 0.0.0.255 area 0
!
```

As you can see, these are very simple, straightforward configurations. All interfaces are assigned to Area 0. Another interesting fact about creating a single area is that there are no ABRs or ASBRs. It is possible to have an ASBR without having an ABR. If external routes are injected into the area, the router injecting them will be considered an ASBR. In order to activate an ABR, any interface on the router must be assigned to a different area.

It is also important to recognize that the neighbor discovery was automatic in this single-area configuration. Now let's move on to an environment where sometimes neighbors must be configured manually.

Configuring OSPF—Single Area (NBMA Environment)

Previously, we mentioned three different possible ways to configure NBMA network interfaces. They are:

- Broadcast
- Non-broadcast
- Point-to-multipoint (a version of point-to-point)

We'll outline all three methods in this section. The key configuration statement that is common to all configuration methods is the `ip ospf network` command.

The command has the options of specifying broadcast, non-broadcast, and point-to-multipoint network types. The IOS senses the media type for all interfaces and assigns the default network type accordingly. If you wish to change that assignment, you would do so via the `ip ospf network` command.

Broadcast Configuration

A full mesh among all OSPF routers is required for this environment to be configured and work properly. A full explanation of the PVC configuration is beyond the scope of this chapter, but here is a sample configuration:

```
RouterA#conf t
Enter configuration commands, one per line.  End with
↳CNTL/Z.
RouterA(config)#int serial 1
RouterA(config-if)#ip ospf network broadcast
RouterA(config-if)#encapsulation frame-relay
RouterA(config-if)#frame-relay map ip 172.16.11.2 102
↳broadcast
RouterA(config-if)#frame-relay map ip 172.16.11.3 103
↳broadcast
RouterA(config-if)#frame-relay map ip 172.16.11.4 104
↳broadcast
RouterA(config-if)#router ospf 1
RouterA(config-router)#network 172.16.11.0 0.0.0.255
↳area 0
RouterA(config-router)#^Z
```

```
RouterA#show running-config
Building configuration...

Current configuration:
!
version 11.2
no service password-encryption
no service udp-small-servers
no service tcp-small-servers
!
hostname RouterA
!
enable password cisco
!
!
interface Loopback0
 ip address 172.16.240.1 255.255.255.0
!
interface Ethernet0
 ip address 172.16.230.20 255.255.255.0
!
interface Serial0
 ip address 172.16.10.5 255.255.255.252
 clockrate 2000000
 dce-terminal-timing-enable
!
interface Serial1
 no ip address
 encapsulation frame-relay
 ip ospf network broadcast
 frame-relay map ip 172.16.11.2 102 broadcast
 frame-relay map ip 172.16.11.3 103 broadcast
 frame-relay map ip 172.16.11.4 104 broadcast
!
interface Serial2
 no ip address
```

```
    shutdown
    !
    interface Serial3
     no ip address
     shutdown
    !
    interface BRIO
     no ip address
     shutdown
    !
    router ospf 1
     network 172.16.10.5 0.0.0.0 area 0
     network 172.16.11.0 0.0.0.255 area 0
    !
```

Connected routers would have similar configurations. The key to this configuration is to override the default network type by using the ip ospf network broadcast command.

Non-broadcast Configuration

This environment requires all neighbors to be statically configured so that a DR may be chosen from the attached routers on the network segment. We use the same commands as for the configuration of a broadcast network, with the exception of the neighbor statements used under the OSPF routing process. Here is a sample configuration:

RouterB#**conf t**

Enter configuration commands, one per line. End with ⮑CNTL/Z.

RouterB(config)#**interface serial1**

RouterB(config-if)#**ip ospf network non-broadcast**

RouterB(config-if)#**encapsulation frame-relay ietf**

RouterB(config-if)#**frame-relay map ip 172.16.25.10 210** ⮑**broadcast**

RouterB(config-if)#**frame-relay map ip 172.16.25.11 211** ⮑**broadcast**

RouterB(config-if)#**frame-relay map ip 172.16.25.12 212** ⮑**broadcast**

```
RouterB(config-if)#router ospf 1
RouterB(config-router)#neighbor 172.16.25.10 priority 1
RouterB(config-router)#neighbor 172.16.25.11 priority 1
RouterB(config-router)#neighbor 172.16.25.12 priority 1
RouterB(config-router)#network 172.16.25.0 0.0.0.255 area
↳0
RouterB(config-router)#^Z
RouterB#
```

Point-to-Multipoint

This configuration does away with the assumption that there are PVCs configured for all routers creating a full mesh. The same ip ospf network broadcast command is used to specify that the network type is point-to-multipoint non-broadcast. This tells the router that no DR/BDR needs to be elected and that the interfaces are treated as individual point-to-point links. Here is a sample configuration:

```
RouterC#conf t
Enter configuration commands, one per line.  End with
↳CNTL/Z.
RouterC(config)#interface serial2
RouterC(config-if)#ip ospf network point-to-multipoint
↳non-broadcast
RouterC(config-if)#encapsulation frame-relay ietf
RouterC(config-if)#frame-relay local dlci 300
RouterC(config-if)#frame-relay map ip 172.16.26.12 312
↳broadcast
RouterC(config-if)#frame-relay map ip 172.16.26.13 313
↳broadcast
RouterC(config-if)#router ospf 1
RouterC(config-router)#neighbor 172.16.26.12 priority 1
RouterC(config-router)#neighbor 172.16.26.13 priority 1
RouterC(config-router)#network 172.16.25.0 0.0.0.255
↳area 0
RouterC(config-router)#^Z
RouterC#
```

Once the configuration has been created, it is time to test it and make sure it works. There are several **show** commands that facilitate this task, and we discuss them in the following section.

Verifying OSPF Configuration

This section describes several ways in which to verify proper OSPF configuration and operation. Table 4.5 contains a list of OSPF **show** commands.

TABLE 4.3 OSPF Show Commands

Command	Description
show ip ospf	Summarizes all relative OSPF information, such as OSPF processes, Router ID, area assignments, authentication, and SPF statistics.
show ip ospf process-id	Shows the same information as the show ip ospf command, but only for the specified process.
show ip ospf border-routers	Displays the Router IDs of all ABRs and ASBRs within the autonomous system.
show ip ospf database	Displays the link-state database.
show ip ospf interface	Displays interface OSPF parameters and other OSPF information specific to the interface.
show ip ospf neighbor	Displays each OSPF neighbor and adjacency status.

show ip ospf

This command is used to display OSPF information for one or all OSPF processes running on the router. Information contained therein includes the Router ID, area information, SPF statistics, and LSA timer information. Here is a sample output:

```
RouterA#sho ip ospf
  Routing Process "ospf 1" with ID 172.16.240.1
  Supports only single TOS(TOS0) routes
```

```
    SPF schedule delay 5 secs, Hold time between two SPFs 10
↳secs
  Number of DCbitless external LSA 0
  Number of DoNotAge external LSA 0
  Number of areas in this router is 1. 1 normal 0 stub 0
↳nssa
    Area BACKBONE(0)
        Number of interfaces in this area is 3
        Area has no authentication
        SPF algorithm executed 17 times
        Area ranges are
        Link State Update Interval is 00:30:00 and due in
↳00:17:52
        Link State Age Interval is 00:20:00 and due in
↳00:07:52
        Number of DCbitless LSA 0
        Number of indication LSA 0
        Number of DoNotAge LSA 0


RouterA#
```

show ip ospf border-routers

This command displays the process ID on the router, the route to the ABR or ASBR, and the SPF information. Here is a sample output:

```
RouterC#show ip ospf border-routers

OSPF Process 1 internal Routing Table

Codes: i - Intra-area route, I - Inter-area route

i 172.16.240.1 [65] via 172.16.1.106, Serial1, ABR,
↳Area 0, SPF 582
i 172.16.241.1 [65] via 172.16.1.94, Serial11, ASBR,
↳Area 0, SPF 582
RouterC#
```

This is a simple output that shows only one ABR and one ASBR. In order to have an ABR, you must have multiple areas configured. In order to have an ASBR, external routes on an external autonomous system must be connected to the router.

show ip ospf database

The information displayed by this command indicates the number of links and the neighboring Router ID. The output is broken down by area. Here is a sample output:

```
RouterA#show ip ospf database

    OSPF Router with ID (172.16.240.1) (Process ID 1)


                Router Link States (Area 0)

Link ID         ADV Router      Age    Seq#          Checksum   Link count
172.16.240.1    172.16.240.1    1530   0x80000016    0x9C7C     4
172.16.241.1    172.16.241.1    667    0x80000008    0x3AFF     3
RouterA#
```

show ip ospf interface

This command displays all interface-related OSPF information. Data is displayed about OSPF information for all interfaces or for specified interfaces. Information includes the interface IP address, area assignment, Process ID, Router ID, network type, cost, priority, DR/BDR (if applicable), timer intervals, and adjacent neighbor information. Here is a sample output:

```
RouterA#show ip ospf interface
BRI0 is administratively down, line protocol is down
   OSPF not enabled on this interface
BRI0:1 is administratively down, line protocol is down
   OSPF not enabled on this interface
BRI0:2 is administratively down, line protocol is down
   OSPF not enabled on this interface
Ethernet0 is up, line protocol is up
```

```
   Internet Address 10.11.230.20/24, Area 0
   Process ID 1, Router ID 172.16.240.1, Network Type
↳BROADCAST, Cost: 10
   Transmit Delay is 1 sec, State DR, Priority 1
   Designated Router (ID) 172.16.240.1, Interface address
   ↳10.11.230.20
   No backup designated router on this network
   Timer intervals configured, Hello 10, Dead 40, Wait 40,
↳Retransmit 5
      Hello due in 00:00:08
   Neighbor Count is 0, Adjacent neighbor count is 0
   Suppress hello for 0 neighbor(s)
Loopback0 is up, line protocol is up
   Internet Address 172.16.240.1/24, Area 0
   Process ID 1, Router ID 172.16.240.1, Network Type
↳LOOPBACK, Cost: 1
   Loopback interface is treated as a stub Host
Serial0 is up, line protocol is up
   Internet Address 172.16.10.5/30, Area 0
   Process ID 1, Router ID 172.16.240.1, Network Type
↳POINT_TO_POINT, Cost: 64
   Transmit Delay is 1 sec, State POINT_TO_POINT,
   Timer intervals configured, Hello 10, Dead 40, Wait 40,
↳Retransmit 5
      Hello due in 00:00:02
   Neighbor Count is 1, Adjacent neighbor count is 1
      Adjacent with neighbor 172.16.241.1
   Suppress hello for 0 neighbor(s)
Serial1 is administratively down, line protocol is down
      OSPF not enabled on this interface
```

show ip ospf neighbor

This is a very useful command. It summarizes the pertinent OSPF information regarding neighbors and the adjacency state. If a DR or BDR exists, that information is also displayed. Here is a sample:

```
RouterA#show ip ospf neighbor
```

```
Neighbor ID  Pri  State    Dead Time  Address      Interface
172.16.241.1  1   FULL/  - 00:00:39   172.16.10.6  Serial0
RouterA#
```

Summary

This chapter contains a great deal of information about OSPF. It is difficult to include everything about OSPF because so much of it falls outside the scope of this chapter and book.

We have discussed the following topics:

- OSPF terminology

- OSPF operation

- OSPF configuration

Of course, each of the preceding bullet points encompasses quite a bit of information. We also explained all of the important and pertinent terms required to fully understand OSPF's operation. Several processes fall under OSPF operation, such as DR/BDR election, adjacency formation, etc. OSPF configuration is actually very simple. Once you understand how OSPF works, it is easy to configure it.

Key Terms

Before taking the exam, make sure you are familiar with the following terms:

area border router (ABR)

autonomous system boundary router (ASBR)

backup designated router (BDR)

designated router (DR)

Link State Advertisement (LSA)

LSA acknowledgement

LSA flooding

non-broadcast multi-access (NMBA)

Open Shortest Path First (OSPF)

OSPF areas

Shortest Path First (SPF) trees

Written Lab

1. Write the command that will enable OSPF process 101 on a router.

2. Write the command that will display details of all OSPF routing processes enabled on a router.

3. Write the command that enables OSPF on an NBMA network for a non-broadcast configuration.

4. Write the command that enables OSPF on an NBMA network for a broadcast configuration.

5. Write the command that will display interface-specific OSPF information.

6. Write the command that will display all OSPF neighbors.

7. Write the command that will display the SPF information to the ABR and ASBR.

8. Write the command that will display all different OSPF route types that are currently known by the router.

Hands-on Lab

Due to the content of this chapter, you will only be asked to enable OSPF routing on three routers. The following graphic depicts the physical layout of the network. It also includes IP assignments and hostnames.

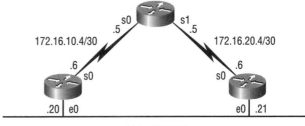

This section includes the following lab exercises:

- Lab 4.1: Enabling the OSPF Process
- Lab 4.2: Configuring OSPF Neighbors
- Lab 4.3: Verifying OSPF Operation

LAB 4.1

Enabling the OSPF Process

1. Enable OSPF process 100 on RouterA.

2. Enable OSPF process 101 on RouterB.

3. Enable OSPF process 102 on RouterC.

LAB 4.2

Configuring OSPF Neighbors

1. Configure the network between RouterA and RouterB. Assign it to Area 0.

2. Configure the network between RouterA and RouterC. Assign it to Area 0.

3. Configure the network between RouterB and RouterC. Assign it to Area 0.

LAB 4.3

Verifying OSPF Operation

1. Execute a show ip ospf neighbors command from each router. What are the results?

2. Execute a show ip route command to verify that all other routers are learning all routes.

Answer to Lab 4.1

```
RouterA#conf t
Enter configuration commands, one per line.  End with
↳CNTL/Z.
RouterA(config)#router ospf 100
RouterA(config-router)#^Z


RouterB#conf t
Enter configuration commands, one per line.  End with
↳CNTL/Z.
RouterB(config)#router ospf 101
RouterB(config-router)#^Z
RouterB#


RouterC#conf t
Enter configuration commands, one per line.  End with
↳CNTL/Z.
Router(config)#router ospf 102
RouterC(config-router)#^Z
RouterC#
```

Answer to Lab 4.2

```
RouterA#conf t
Enter configuration commands, one per line.  End with
↳CNTL/Z.
RouterA(config)#router ospf 100
```

```
RouterA(config-router)#network 172.16.10.5 0.0.0.0 area 0
RouterA(config-router)#network 172.16.20.5 0.0.0.0 area 0
RouterA(config-router)#^Z
RouterA#

RouterB#conf t
Enter configuration commands, one per line.  End with
↳CNTL/Z.
RouterB(config)#router ospf 101
RouterB(config-router)#network 172.16.10.6 0.0.0.0 area 0
RouterB(config-router)#network 10.11.230.0 0.0.0.255
↳area 1
RouterB(config-router)#^Z
RouterB#exit

RouterC#conf t
Enter configuration commands, one per line.  End with
↳CNTL/Z.
RouterC(config)#router ospf 102
RouterC(config-router)#network 172.16.20.6 0.0.0.0 area 0
RouterC(config-router)#network 10.11.230.0 0.0.0.255
↳area 1
RouterC(config-router)#^Z
RouterC#
```

Answer to Lab 4.3

```
RouterA#sho ip ospf neig

Neighbor ID     Pri   State         Dead Time   Address        Interface
172.16.241.1      1   FULL/   -     00:00:31    172.16.10.6    Serial0
172.16.20.6       1   FULL/   -     00:00:38    172.16.20.6    Serial1

RouterA#sho ip route
Codes: C - connected, S - static, I - IGRP, R - RIP,
↳M - mobile, B - BGP
```

```
        D - EIGRP, EX - EIGRP external, O - OSPF, IA - OSPF
↳inter area
        N1 - OSPF NSSA external type 1, N2 - OSPF NSSA
↳external type 2
        E1 - OSPF external type 1, E2 - OSPF external
↳type 2, E - EGP
        i - IS-IS, L1 - IS-IS level-1, L2 - IS-IS level-2,
↳* - candidate default
        U - per-user static route, o - ODR

Gateway of last resort is not set

     10.0.0.0/24 is subnetted, 1 subnets
O IA    10.11.230.0 [110/74] via 172.16.20.6, 00:00:24,
↳Serial1
     172.16.0.0/16 is variably subnetted, 4 subnets, 3
↳masks
O       172.16.241.1/32 [110/65] via 172.16.10.6,
↳00:01:28, Serial0
C       172.16.240.0/24 is directly connected, Loopback0
C       172.16.20.4/30 is directly connected, Serial1
C       172.16.10.4/30 is directly connected, Serial0
RouterA#
```

RouterB#**sho ip ospf neig**

Neighbor ID	Pri	State	Dead Time	Address	Interface
172.16.20.6	1	FULL/DR	00:00:33	10.11.230.21	Ethernet0
172.16.240.1	1	FULL/ -	00:00:32	172.16.10.5	Serial0

RouterB#**sho ip route**

```
Codes: C - connected, S - static, I - IGRP, R - RIP,
↳M - mobile, B - BGP
        D - EIGRP, EX - EIGRP external, O - OSPF, IA - OSPF
↳inter area
        N1 - OSPF NSSA external type 1, N2 - OSPF NSSA
↳external type 2
        E1 - OSPF external type 1, E2 - OSPF external
↳type 2, E - EGP
```

      i - IS-IS, L1 - IS-IS level-1, L2 - IS-IS level-2,
↳* - candidate default
      U - per-user static route, o - ODR

Gateway of last resort is not set

      172.16.0.0/16 is variably subnetted, 3 subnets, 2
↳masks
C   172.16.241.0/24 is directly connected, Loopback0
O IA   172.16.20.4/30 [110/74] via 10.11.230.21,
↳00:00:48, Ethernet0
C   172.16.10.4/30 is directly connected, Serial0
      10.0.0.0/24 is subnetted, 1 subnets
C   10.11.230.0 is directly connected, Ethernet0
RouterB#

RouterC#**sho ip ospf neigh**

Neighbor ID	Pri	State	Dead Time	Address	Interface
172.16.10.6	1	FULL/BDR	00:00:34	10.11.230.20	Ethernet0
172.16.240.1	1	FULL/ -	00:00:36	172.16.20.5	Serial0

RouterC#**sho ip route**
Codes: C - connected, S - static, I - IGRP, R - RIP,
↳M - mobile, B - BGP
      D - EIGRP, EX - EIGRP external, O - OSPF, IA - OSPF
↳inter area
      N1 - OSPF NSSA external type 1, N2 - OSPF NSSA
↳external type 2
      E1 - OSPF external type 1, E2 - OSPF external
↳type 2, E - EGP
      i - IS-IS, L1 - IS-IS level-1, L2 - IS-IS level-2,
↳* - candidate default
      U - per-user static route, o - ODR

Gateway of last resort is not set

      172.16.0.0/16 is variably subnetted, 3 subnets, 2
↳masks

```
O       172.16.241.1/32 [110/129] via 172.16.20.5,
↳00:03:04, Serial0
C       172.16.20.4/30 is directly connected, Serial0
O       172.16.10.4/30 [110/128] via 172.16.20.5,
↳00:03:04, Serial0
     10.0.0.0/24 is subnetted, 1 subnets
C       10.11.230.0 is directly connected, Ethernet0
RouterC#
```

Review Questions

1. A router chooses the Router ID based on which of the following?

    A. Lowest IP address from any interface

    B. Highest IP address from any interface

    C. Lowest IP address from any loopback interface

    D. Highest IP Address from any loopback interface

2. What are the three areas of OSPF operation? (Choose three.)

    A. Link-state routing

    B. SPF calculation

    C. LSA flooding

    D. Neighbor discover and adjacency formation

3. Which of the following is the IOS command to set the cost on an OSPF interface?

    A. `ip ospf no-default cost`

    B. `ip ospf no-summary cost`

    C. `ip ospf cost cost`

    D. `ip ospf-cost cost`

4. In what type of topology do all routers have a virtual connection to all other routers?

    A. Full-mesh

    B. Star

    C. Hub-and-spoke

    D. Bus

5. What does an OSPF neighbor status of *down* mean?

   A. The connected interfaces are in a "line down, line protocol down" state.

   B. No Hello packets have been transmitted from the interface.

   C. The interface is administratively shut down.

   D. No Hello packets have been received on the interface.

6. What does the OSPF neighbor status *init* mean?

   A. Hello packets have been received from the OSPF neighbor.

   B. The router is going to exchange LSA information.

   C. The interface has been assigned to an area.

   D. Adjacency information has been exchanged between neighbors.

7. What does the OSPF neighbor status *2Way* mean?

   A. That a router has received a Hello packet with its own Router ID listed as a neighbor.

   B. That a router has received a Hello packet from the DR.

   C. That a router is exchanging LSU packets.

   D. That a router is waiting for the LSU from the DR.

8. What does the OSPF neighbor status *ExStart* mean?

   A. The OSPF process is starting on the interface.

   B. The router is establishing the Master/Slave roles for Database Description packet exchange.

   C. All routing information is beginning to be exchanged between routers.

   D. An LSA flood is about to start.

9. What does the OSPF neighbor status *Loading* mean?

   A. Routers are loading (exchanging) full DD and LSR packets.

   B. Routers are loading the topology database.

   C. Routers are loading the link-state database.

   D. Routers are sending LSR packets to request new LSA information.

10. What does the OSPF neighbor status *Exchange* mean?

   A. Exchange of Hello packets

   B. Exchange of routing updates

   C. Exchange of full route information via LSR and Database Description packets

   D. Exchange of ABR and ASBR information

11. What does the OSPF neighbor status *Full* indicate?

   A. The OSPF topology database has been filled.

   B. The OSPF topology databases are synchronized.

   C. The neighbor database is synchronized.

   D. The OSPF link-state table is full.

12. Which of the following network types have a DR and a BDR assigned? (Choose all that apply.)

   A. Broadcast

   B. Point-to-point

   C. NBMA broadcast

   D. NBMA point-to-point

   E. NBMA point-to-multipoint

13. Which routers form adjacencies with routers designated as DROther on a broadcast multi-access network? (Choose all that apply.)

A. DROther

B. BDR

C. DR

D. RP

14. Which IP multicast address corresponds with AllSPFRouters?

A. 224.0.0.4

B. 224.0.0.5

C. 224.0.0.6

D. 224.0.0.7

15. Which of the following OSPF terms refers to a connected (or adjacent) router that is running an OSPF process, with the adjacent interface assigned to the same area?

A. Link

B. Neighbor

C. LSA

D. STP

16. What is the valid range for the cost metric for OSPF interfaces?

A. 1–255

B. 1–2046

C. 1–63,535

D. 1–65,535

17. Which method does Cisco use to calculate the cost of a link?

   A. 1 x 10^8 / bandwidth

   B. bandwidth / 1 x 10^8

   C. Dijkstra's Algorithm

   D. 1 / bandwidth

18. What OSPF term refers to a network or router interface assigned to any given interface?

   A. Link

   B. Area

   C. LSA

   D. STP

19. All OSPF networks must contain which of the following?

   A. Route redistribution configuration

   B. Area 0

   C. A designated controller

   D. A manually defined interface cost

20. Which of the following are advantages of OSPF over RIP? (Choose all that apply.)

   A. Speed of convergence

   B. Simplicity to configure

   C. Support for VLSMs

   D. Scalability

Answers to Written Lab

1. Write the command that will enable OSPF process 101 on a router.

2. Write the command that will display details of all OSPF routing processes enabled on a router.

3. Write the command that enables OSPF on an NBMA network for a non-broadcast configuration.

4. Write the command that enables OSPF on an NBMA network for a broadcast configuration.

5. Write the command that will display interface-specific OSPF information.

6. Write the command that will display all OSPF neighbors.

7. Write the command that will display the SPF information to the ABR and ASBR.

8. Write the command that will display all different OSPF route types that are currently known by the router.

Answers to Review Questions

1. D. The Router ID is determined by the highest IP address configured on a loopback interface. If a router does not have a loopback interface, then the Router ID is determined by the highest IP address configured on the router.

2. B, C, D. Link-state routing is the type of routing performed by OSPF; however, it is not an area of operation.

3. C. The IOS command to set the cost of an OSPF interface is `ip ospf cost cost`, where `cost` is a number from 1 to 65,535.

4. A. In a full-mesh topology, all routers have a virtual connection to all other routers. The configuration of a fully meshed network can quickly become administratively prohibitive, because as the number of full-meshed routers grows, the number of required virtual links grows exponentially.

5. D. This status could result from an interface being down, but the specific OSPF definition is the lack of Hello packets received from the neighbor.

6. A. The init state is simply the state of receiving Hello packets on the interface; no adjacencies or other information have been exchanged at this point.

7. A. Hello packets contain Router ID information. Once a router sees its own Router ID, it is in a 2Way state.

8. B. ExStart is the step prior to exchanging all route information. LSA floods occur for routing updates after adjacencies have been formed.

9. D. This process follows the Exchange state and verifies that no new LSA information became available during the exchange process.

10. C. Although there are continuous route exchanges, the Exchange state occurs at the time adjacencies are established.

11. B. When a neighbor reaches Full status, it has synchronized its database with all of the adjacent routers.

12. A, C. No DR is assigned on any type of point-to-point link. No DR/BDR is assigned on the NBMA point-to-multipoint due to the hub/spoke topology.

13. B, C. DROther routers form adjacencies only with the DR and BDR. An RP is a rendezvous point for multicast routing.

14. B. 224.0.0.6 is used for AllDRs.

15. B. Found via Hello packets, a neighbor is an adjacent OSPF router. Note that no routing information is exchanged with neighbors unless adjacencies are formed.

16. D. The 1–255 range often describes the load or reliability metric for distance-vector algorithms.

17. A. The correct equation gives values for Cisco-derived metrics, although this can be modified.

18. A. Within OSPF, link is synonymous with interface.

19. B. Every OSPF network must contain a backbone area, which is numbered as Area 0.

20. A, C, and D. While OSPF has more configuration complexity than RIP, OSPF does offer far speedier convergence, the support of Variable Length Subnet Masks, and greater scalability (overcoming RIP's 15 hop-count limitation).

Chapter 5

Interconnecting OSPF Areas

THE CCNP ROUTING EXAM TOPICS COVERED IN THIS CHAPTER ARE AS FOLLOWS:

- ✓ OSPF scalability considerations

- ✓ Definitions of multi-area components (e.g., classifications of routers, Link State Advertisements, and areas)

- ✓ Step-by-step guide to multi-area OSPF configuration

- ✓ Guidelines for establishing stub, totally stubby, and not-so-stubby areas

- ✓ Virtual link configuration

- ✓ Strategies for monitoring and troubleshooting multi-area OSPF networks

n this chapter, we will illustrate the scalability constraints of an OSPF network with a single area. The concept of multi-area OSPF will be introduced as a solution to these scalability limitations. This chapter will also identify the various categories of routers used in multi-area configurations. These router categories include a backbone router, internal router, area border router (ABR), and autonomous system boundary router (ASBR). We'll explore how these routers can use summarization and default routes to reduce the amount of route information that is injected into an area, thus reducing a router's memory and processor overhead.

The functions of different OSPF Link State Advertisements (LSAs) are very important to understand for the Routing exam, and we will detail the types of LSAs used by OSPF. We will see how these LSAs can be minimized through the effective implementation of specific OSPF area types.

Specifically, we will examine stub areas, totally stubby areas, and not-so-stubby areas and show how these areas can be used to minimize the number of LSAs advertised into an area. We'll also provide a set of design guidelines and configuration examples as well as the syntax required to configure route summarization at both area border routers and autonomous system boundary routers.

You'll learn that all areas need to have a link to Area 0. If an area is not attached to Area 0, *virtual links* can be used to span *transit areas* in OSPF networks where all areas are not physically adjacent to the backbone area. We then will conclude with a collection of debug and show commands that can be used to effectively monitor and troubleshoot a multi-area OSPF implementation.

OSPF Scalability

In the previous chapter, we examined the configuration of OSPF networks that contained a single area. We saw that OSPF had significant advantages over distance-vector protocols, such as RIP, due to OSPF's ability to represent an entire network within its link state database, thus vastly reducing the time required for convergence.

However, let's consider what the router does in order to give us such great performance. Each router recalculates its database every time there is a topology change, requiring CPU overhead. Each router has to hold the entire link state database, which represents the topology of the entire network, requiring memory overhead. Furthermore, each router contains a complete copy of the routing table, requiring more memory overhead. Keep in mind that the number of entries in the routing table may be significantly greater than the number of networks in the routing table because we may have multiple routes to multiple networks.

With these OSPF behavioral characteristics in mind, it becomes obvious that in very large networks, single area OSPF has some serious scalability considerations. Fortunately, OSPF gives us the ability to take a large OSPF topology and break it down into multiple, more manageable areas, as illustrated in Figure 5.1.

FIGURE 5.1 OSPF areas

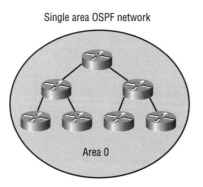
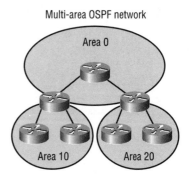

Consider the advantages of this hierarchical approach. First of all, routers that are internal to a defined area need not worry about having a link state database for the entire network, only their own areas, thus reducing memory overhead. Second, routers that are internal to a defined area now only have to recalculate their link state database when there is a topology change within their particular area. Topology changes in one area will not cause global OSPF recalculations, thus reducing processor overhead. Finally, since routes can be summarized at area boundaries, the routing tables on each router need not be as large as they would be in a single area environment.

Of course, as we start subdividing our OSPF topology into multiple areas, we introduce some complexity into our configuration. Therefore, in this chapter we will examine these various configuration subtleties, in addition to strategies for effectively troubleshooting multi-area OSPF networks.

Categories of Multi-area Components

This section covers the various roles that routers play in an OSPF large network. These include backbone routers, internal routers, area border routers, and autonomous system boundary routers. We'll also discuss the different types of advertisements that are used in an OSPF network and the different types of areas that can be configured.

OSPF Router Roles

As we alluded to earlier, routers within a multi-area OSPF network fall into different categories. To gain an understanding of the various roles that our routers can play, let's consider Figure 5.2.

FIGURE 5.2 Router roles

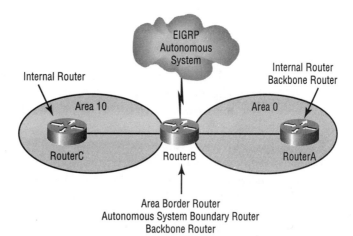

Starting at the core of the given network and working our way outward, consider RouterA. Notice that RouterA is part of Area 0. As we learned in the previous chapter, Area 0 is referred to as the *backbone area*. Therefore, we can make the following definition:

Backbone router A backbone router is any router that exists (wholly or in part) in OSPF Area 0.

Another distinction that we can make about RouterA is that it is contained completely within a single area, in this case Area 0. Since all of RouterA's interfaces are internal to a single area, we can make the following definition:

Internal router An internal router is any router that has all of its interfaces as members of the same area.

Remember that a router can play more than one role. In our example, RouterA is both a backbone router and an internal router.

Now consider RouterB. Notice that RouterB meets the requirement to be classified as a backbone router (i.e., RouterB has one or more interfaces that are part of Area 0). However, unlike RouterA, RouterB is partially in Area 0 and partially in Area 10. There is yet another term to define routers that have interfaces in more than one area:

Area border router   An area border router is any router that is connected to multiple OSPF areas.

Recall that the topology of an OSPF area is contained in a link state database. Therefore, if a router is connected to multiple areas, it will contain multiple link state databases. This should be a design consideration when sizing a router that will function as an area border router.

Also notice that RouterB is connected to an EIGRP network. Whether an OSPF network is connected to an EIGRP network, a BGP network, an OSPF network with a different Process ID, or a network running any other such external routing process, this external network may be referred to as an *autonomous system*. The scenario of an OSPF router sitting at the boundary of an external routing process leads us to a fourth category of OSPF router:

Autonomous system boundary router   An autonomous system boundary router is any OSPF router that is connected to an external routing process.

The ability of an ASBR to exchange routing information between its OSPF routing process and the external routing process to which the router is connected is not an automatic process. Such routes are exchanged through a process called *route redistribution*, which is the focus of Chapter 10, "Route Optimization."

Link State Advertisements

Recall that a router's link state database is made up of Link State Advertisements (LSAs). However, just as we had multiple OSPF router categories to consider, we also have multiple types of LSAs to consider. Specifically, there are five types of LSAs that we need to be concerned with. While the importance of LSA classification may not be immediately apparent, we will see its application when we examine the various types of OSPF areas. Let's examine the function of the various LSA types:

Type 1 LSA   Referred to as a *Router Link Advertisement (RLA)*, the Type 1 LSA is an advertisement sent by a router to other routers in its area. The advertisement contains the status of a router's link to the area it is connected to. If a router is connected to multiple areas, then it will send a Type 1 LSA for each of the areas it is connected to.

Type 2 LSA   Referred to as a *Network Link Advertisement (NLA)*, the Type 2 LSA is generated by designated routers (DRs). Recall that a designated router is elected to represent other routers in its network, and it has established adjacencies with each of the routers within its network. The DR uses the Type 2 LSA to send out information about the state of other routers that are part of the same network. Note that the Type 2 LSA is only sent to routers that are in the area containing the specific network.

Type 3 and Type 4 LSAs   Referred to as *Summary Link Advertisements (SLAs)*, the Type 3 and Type 4 LSAs are generated by area border routers. These ABRs send Type 3 and Type 4 LSAs to all routers within an area. These LSAs advertise intra-area routes to the backbone area (Area 0) and both intra-area and inter-area routes to non-backbone areas.

Type 5 LSA   Referred to as *AS External Link Advertisements*, Type 5 LSAs are sent by autonomous system boundary routers (ASBRs). These ASBRs use Type 5 LSAs to advertise routes that are external to the OSPF autonomous system.

OSPF Area Types

One of our main motivations for subdividing a single OSPF area into multiple areas was to reduce router overhead. We decided that all routers didn't need to have the entire network topology in their link state databases. Let's now examine the types of non-standard areas we can use to reduce router overhead:

Stub area   Routers in a stub area do not receive Type 5 LSAs. Instead, they receive a default route that is used to reach external networks. Therefore, stub area routers have reduced overhead since they do not have to process Type 5 LSAs.

Totally stubby area   To further reduce the number of LSAs that an internal router will need to process, the router can be configured as a totally stubby area. In addition to not receiving Type 5 LSAs, a totally stubby area does not receive summary LSAs. The function of a totally stubby area is Cisco-specific, which is an important concept to remember when designing an OSPF network in a multi-vendor routing environment.

Not-so-stubby area (NSSA)   Like a stub area, a not-so-stubby area does not receive Type 5 LSAs. However, sometimes there is a need, on a limited basis, to import external routes. Such a situation is where NSSAs are useful. The NSSA imports external routes (Type 7 LSAs), via route redistribution, and then translates these Type 7 LSAs into Type 5 LSAs.

Basic Multi-area Configuration

Consider the multi-area OSPF network shown in Figure 5.3. To review some of the router classifications that we previously discussed, notice that RouterA would be classified as both an internal router and a backbone router. Also, RouterB would be classified as both a backbone router and an area border router. Finally, RouterC would be classified as an internal router.

FIGURE 5.3   Sample multi-area configuration

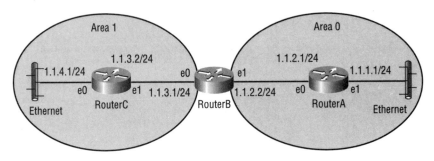

RouterA

```
interface Ethernet0
  ip address 1.1.1.1 255.255.255.0
!
interface Ethernet1
  ip address 1.1.2.1 255.255.255.0
!
router ospf 70
  network 1.1.1.0 0.0.0.255 area 0
  network 1.1.2.0 0.0.0.255 area 0
```

RouterB

```
interface Ethernet0
  ip address 1.1.3.1 255.255.255.0
!
interface Ethernet1
  ip address 1.1.2.2 255.255.255.0
!
router ospf 70
  network 1.1.2.0 0.0.0.255 area 0
  network 1.1.3.0 0.0.0.255 area 1
```

RouterC

```
interface Ethernet0
  ip address 1.1.4.1 255.255.255.0
!
interface Ethernet1
  ip address 1.1.3.2 255.255.255.0
!
router ospf 70
  network 1.1.3.0 0.0.0.255 area 1
  network 1.1.4.0 0.0.0.255 area 1
```

Let's examine the syntax to configure OSPF on RouterA. First, we need to enable the OSPF process on the router:

RouterA (config)#**router ospf 70**

where 70 is the Process ID.

Next, we need to identify each of the networks connected to the router that we want to participate in the OSPF process. In this example, we have two networks connected to RouterA (1.1.1.0/24 and 1.1.2.0/24):

RouterA(config-router)#**network 1.1.1.0 0.0.0.255 area 0**

where 1.1.1.0 0.0.0.255 is the network and wildcard mask of a network connected to RouterA and where 0 is the area that network 1.1.1.0/24 is a member of.

RouterA(config-router)#**network 1.1.2.0 0.0.0.255 area 0**

The syntax for RouterB is similar to that used for RouterA. The primary difference is that RouterB is connected to two areas:

```
RouterB(config)#router ospf 70
RouterB(config-router)#network 1.1.2.0 0.0.0.255 area 0
RouterB(config-router)#network 1.1.3.0 0.0.0.255 area 1
```

The syntax for RouterC is very similar to that of RouterA. The difference is that RouterA is internal to Area 0, thereby classifying it as a backbone router:

```
RouterC(config)#router ospf 70
RouterC(config-router)#network 1.1.3.0 0.0.0.255 area 1
RouterC(config-router)#network 1.1.4.0 0.0.0.255 area 1
```

Stub Area Configuration

Since the main purpose of having stub areas (and totally stubby areas) is to keep such areas from carrying external routes, we need to review some design guidelines before configuring a stub area or a totally stubby area:

- Do not make the backbone area (Area 0) a stub area.

- Since external routes are injected by autonomous system boundary routers, do not make any area containing an ASBR a stub area.

- Since routers within a stub area use a default route to get out of the stub area, typically there is only one route out of the stub area. Therefore, a stub area should usually only contain a single area border router. Keep in mind that since a default route is being used, if a stub area contains more than one ABR, a non-optimal path may be used.

- If you decide to make a particular area a stub area, be sure to configure *all* the routers in the area as stubby. If a router within a stub area has not been configured as stubby, it will not be able to correctly form adjacencies and exchange OSPF routes.

With these guidelines in mind, let's examine a sample configuration for a stub area. Consider the network shown in Figure 5.4. We're going to make Area 25 a stub area. In this example, we won't be concerned with the configuration of RouterA, since it does not participate in Area 25. We will then examine the syntax for RouterB, RouterC, and RouterD.

FIGURE 5.4 OPSF configuration example continued—stub area configuration

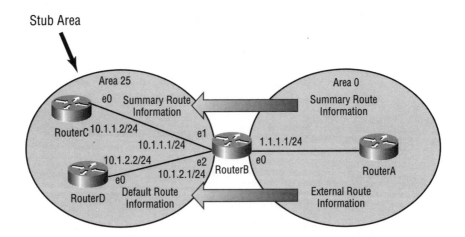

RouterB

```
interface Ethernet0
  ip address 1.1.1.1 255.255.255.0
!
interface Ethernet1
  ip address 10.1.1.1 255.255.255.0
!
interface Ethernet2
  ip address 10.1.2.1 255.255.255.0
!
router ospf 10
  network 1.0.0.0 0.255.255.255 area 0
  network 10.0.0.0 0.255.255.255 area 25
  area 25 stub
```

RouterC

```
interface Ethernet0
  ip address 10.1.2.2 255.255.255.0
!
router ospf 10
  network 10.0.0.0.0 255.255.255 area 25
  area 25 stub
```

RouterD

```
interface Ethernet0
  ip adress 10.1.1.2 255.255.255.0
!
router ospf 10
  network 10.0.0.0 0.255.255.255 area 25
  area 25 stub
```

First, we'll configure RouterB. Notice that RouterB is an ABR and that it is the only ABR in Area 25, as recommended in our stub area design guidelines. When configuring an ABR that is a member of a stub area, be cautious to only configure the stub area as stubby:

RouterB(config)#**router ospf 10**

where 10 is the Process ID.

RouterB(config-router)#**network 1.0.0.0 0.255.255.255 area 0**

where 1.0.0.0 0.255.255.255 is the network and wildcard mask of a network connected to RouterB and where 0 is the area that network 1.1.1.0/24 is a member of.

RouterB(config-router)#**network 10.0.0.0 0.255.255.255 area 25**

where 10.0.0.0 0.255.255.255 is a summary network and wildcard mask of networks connected to RouterB and where 25 is the area that networks 10.1.1.0/24 and 10.1.2.0/24 are members of.

RouterB(config-router)#**area 25 stub**

where 25 is the area that we have designated as stubby.

Notice that instead of using two network statements to represent networks 10.1.1.0/24 and 10.1.2.0/24, we used a single network statement specifying network 10.0.0.0/8, which includes, or summarizes, these two networks. By using these summary routes where possible, we can reduce the size of a router's routing tables, thus lowering memory and processor overhead.

We will also use the 10.0.0.0/8 summary when we configure RouterC and RouterD. Remember that it is critical that all routers that are members of a stub area be configured as stubby for that area. Therefore, RouterC and RouterD will have identical OSPF configurations:

```
RouterC(config)#router ospf 10
RouterC(config-router)#network 10.0.0.0 0.255.255.255 area
↳25
RouterC(config-router)#area 25 stub

RouterD(config)#router ospf 10
RouterD(config-router)#network 10.0.0.0 0.255.255.255 area
↳25
RouterD(config-router)#area 25 stub
```

Let's review some key elements of our stub area configuration example:

- The syntax to make a router stubby is `area area-id stub`.

- All routers that are part of Area 25 are configured as stubby.

- Area 25 has only one ABR (i.e., only one path out of the area).

- The ABR used the `area area-id stub` command only for Area 25, not for Area 0, which is not stubby.

Totally Stubby Area Configuration

Using the same network topology as we had for the stub area configuration, let's examine how to make Area 25 a totally stubby area. Remembering that the difference between a stub area and a totally stubby area is that a totally stubby area doesn't have summary routes injected into it, we only need to change the configuration of RouterB. Since RouterB is the ABR, it is the router that will have the responsibility for blocking summary routes from entering the stub area. So, again consider our network, as illustrated in Figure 5.5.

FIGURE 5.5 OPSF configuration example continued—totally stubby area configuration

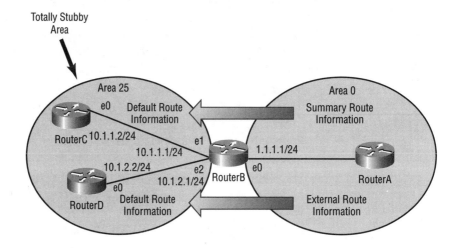

RouterB

```
interface Ethernet0
  ip address 1.1.1.1 255.255.255.0
!
interface Ethernet1
  ip address 10.1.1.1 255.255.255.0
!
interface Ethernet2
  ip address 10.1.2.1 255.255.255.0
!
router ospf 10
  network 1.0.0.0 0.255.255.255 area 0
  network 10.0.0.0 0.255.255.255 area 25
  area 25 stub no-summary
```

RouterC

```
interface Ethernet0
  ip address 10.1.2.2 255.255.255.0
!
router ospf 10
  network 10.0.0.0 0.255.255.255 area 25
  area 25 stub
```

RouterD

```
interface Ethernet0
  ip address 10.1.1.2 255.255.255.0
!
router ospf 10
  network 10.0.0.0 0.255.255.255 area 25
  area 25 stub
```

Notice that we only have to change, from the previous example, the configuration of RouterB. We simply add the no-summary argument to the area area-id stub command:

RouterB(config)#**router ospf 10**
where 10 is the Process ID.

RouterB(config-router)#**network 1.0.0.0 0.255.255.255 area 0**
where 1.0.0.0 0.255.255.255 is the network and wildcard mask of a network connected to RouterB and where 0 is the area that network 1.1.1.0/24 is a member of.

RouterB(config-router)#**network 10.0.0.0 0.255.255.255 area 25**
where 10.0.0.0 0.255.255.255 is a summary network and wildcard mask of networks connected to RouterB and where 25 is the area that networks 10.1.1.0/24 and 10.1.2.0/24 are members of.

RouterB(config-router)#**area 25 stub no-summary**
where the no-summary argument makes Area 25 totally stubby.

Not-So-Stubby Area Configuration

Recall that a not-so-stubby area (NSSA) is useful when we have an area that requires the injection of external routes, although we still want to eliminate the injection of Type 5 LSAs. Figure 5.6 presents such a scenario. In Area 1, we want to prevent Area 0 from injecting Type 5 LSAs, yet we still need external routes from the RIP routing process to be injected into Area 1. The solution to these requirements is to make Area 1 an NSSA.

FIGURE 5.6 OPSF configuration example continued—not-so-stubby area configuration

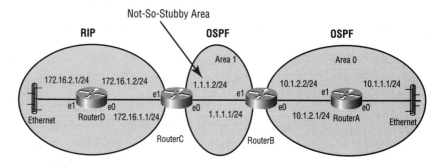

RouterA

```
interface Ethernet0
  ip address 10.1.1.1 255.255.255.0
!
interface Ethernet1
  ip address 10.1.2.1 255.255.255.0
!
router ospf 24
  network 10.0.0.0 0.255.255.255 area 0
```

RouterB

```
interface Ethernet0
  ip address 10.1.2.2 255.255.255.0
!
```

```
interface Ethernet1
  ip address 1.1.1.1 255.255.255.0
!
router ospf 24
  network 10.0.0.0 0.255.255.255 area 0
  network 1.0.0.0 0.255.255.255 area 1
  area 0 range 10.0.0.0 255.255.0.0
  area 1 nssa
```

RouterC

```
interface Ethernet0
  ip address 1.1.1.2 255.255.255.0
!
interface Ethernet1
  ip address 172.16.1.1 255.255.255.0
!
router ospf 24
  redistribute rip
  network 1.0.0.0 0.255.255.255 area 1
  default-metric 128
  area 1 nssa
!
router rip
  redistribute ospf 24
  network 172.16.0.0
  default-metric 3
```

RouterD

```
interface Ethernet0
  ip address 172.16.1.2 255.255.255.0
!
interface Ethernet1
  ip address 172.16.2.1 255.255.255.0
!
router rip
  network 172.16.0.0
```

Let's examine the configuration of each of these routers, beginning with RouterA. RouterA is a backbone router (and an internal router), which does not participate in our NSSA (Area 1). Therefore, RouterA doesn't need any special NSSA configuration. However, by way of review, we will still examine its syntax:

RouterA(config)#**router ospf 24**

where 24 is the Process ID.

RouterA(config-router)#**network 10.0.0.0 0.255.255.255**
↳**area 0**

where 10.0.0.0 0.255.255.255 is a network and wildcard mask summarization of the networks connected to RouterA and where 0 is the area that networks 10.1.1.0/24 and 10.1.2.0/24 are members of.

RouterB does participate in the NSSA. Therefore, it will require a special configuration:

RouterB(config)#**router ospf 24**

RouterB(config-router)#**network 10.0.0.0 0.255.255.255**
↳**area 0**

RouterB(config-router)#**network 1.0.0.0 0.255.255.255**
↳**area 1**

RouterB(config-router)#**area 0 range 10.0.0.0 255.0.0.0**

where 10.0.0.0 255.0.0.0 is the network number and subnet mask of a network that summarizes the individual networks within Area 0, thus reducing the number of a router's routing table entries.

RouterB(config-router)#**area 1 nssa**

where 1 is the area that is being designated as a not-so-stubby area.

Notice that the configuration for RouterB included the command area area-id range network_address network_mask, which can be used on area border routers to summarize the IP address space being used by routers within a given area. Also notice the area area-id nssa command. This command tells the router that the specified area the router is connected to is a not-so-stubby area. As we saw when configuring stub areas, all routers within a not-so-stubby area must agree that they are connected to a NSSA (i.e., be configured with the area area-id nssa command).

To expand upon the idea of advertising summarized routes, the area area-id range network_address network_mask command is used to summarize intra-area routes on an ABR. Similarly, we can summarize external routes on an autonomous system boundary router (ASBR) with the command summary-address network_address network_mask. Proper use of these summarization tools can greatly reduce the number of routes that have to be maintained by a router, thus reducing memory and processor overhead.

RouterC will be an even more complex configuration. Not only is RouterC part of an NSSA, it also participates in a RIP routing process. In order to exchange its OSPF and RIP routes, RouterC must perform route redistribution (route redistribution is the focus of Chapter 10):

```
RouterC(config)#router ospf 24
RouterC(config-router)#redistribute rip
```

where rip is the routing protocol whose routes are being injected into the OSPF routing process.

```
RouterC(config-router)#network 1.0.0.0 0.255.255.255 area 1
RouterC(config-router)#default-metric 128
```

where 128 is the OSPF metric value to be assigned to routes being redistributed into the OSPF routing process.

```
RouterC(config-router)#area 1 nssa
RouterC(config-router)#router rip
```

This enables the RIP routing process on the router.

```
RouterC(config-router)#redistribute ospf 24
```

where ospf 24 is the routing process whose routes are being injected into the RIP routing process.

```
RouterC(config-router)#network 172.16.0.0
RouterC(config-router)#default-metric 3
```

where 3 is the RIP metric value (hop count) to be assigned to routes being redistributed into the RIP routing process.

RouterD is internal to the RIP routing process. Therefore, RouterD does not require any NSSA-specific configuration:

```
RouterD(config)#router rip
RouterD(config-router)#network 172.16.0.0
```

OSPF Virtual Links

When designing a multi-area OSPF network, all areas should be connected to the backbone area. However, there may be instances when an area has to cross another area to reach the backbone area, as shown in Figure 5.7. Since, in this example, Area 20 does not have a direct link to Area 0, we need to create a virtual link.

FIGURE 5.7   OSPF virtual link

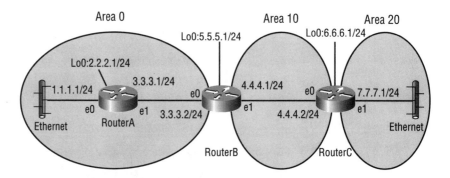

The syntax for creating a virtual link across an area is

area *area-id* virtual-link *router-id*

where *area-id* is the number of the transit area, in this example, Area 10, and *router-id* is the IP address of the highest loopback interface configured on a router. If a loopback interface has not been configured on the router, then the *router-id* is the highest IP address configured on the router. Note that a virtual link has area border routers as the endpoints of the link.

As shown in Figure 5.8, we are going to create a virtual link from Area 20 to Area 0, with Area 10 acting as the transit area. Let's examine the configuration of RouterB and RouterC, since RouterA does not have any virtual-link-specific configuration.

FIGURE 5.8 OSPF virtual link

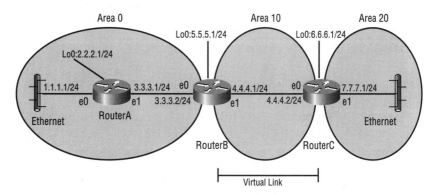

Here is the configuration of RouterB and RouterC:

```
RouterB(config)#router ospf 10
RouterB(config-router)#network 3.0.0.0 0.255.255.255
↳area 0
RouterB(config-router)#network 4.0.0.0 0.255.255.255
↳area 10
RouterB(config-router)#area 10 virtual-link 6.6.6.1
```

where 10 is the Area ID of the transit area and where 6.6.6.1 is the highest loopback address of the ABR joining the transit area to Area 20.

```
RouterC(config)#router ospf 10
RouterC(config-router)#network 4.0.0.0 0.255.255.255
↳area 10
RouterC(config-router)#network 7.0.0.0 0.255.255.255
↳area 20
RouterC(config-router)#area 10 virtual-link 5.5.5.1
```

where 10 is the Area ID of the transit area and where 5.5.5.1 is the highest loopback address of the ABR joining the transit area to the backbone area.

RouterA

```
interface Loopback0
  ip address 2.2.2.1 255.255.255.0
!
internet Ethernet0
  ip address 1.1.1.1 255.255.255.0
!
```

```
interface Ethernet1
  ip address 3.3.3.1 255.255.255.0
!
router ospf 10
  network 1.0.0.0 0.255.255.255 area 0
  network 3.0.0.0 0.255.255.255 area 0
```

RouterB

```
interface Loopback0
  ip address 5.5.5.1 255.255.255.0
!
interface Ethernet0
  ip address 3.3.3.2 255.255.255.0
!
interface Ethernet1
  ip address 4.4.4.1 255.255.255.0
!
router ospf 10
  network 3.0.0.0 0.255.255.255 area 0
  network 4.0.0.0 0.255.255.255 area 10
  area 10 virtual-link 6.6.6.1
```

RouterC

```
interface Loopback0
  ip address 6.6.6.1 255.255.255.0
!
interface Ethernet0
  ip address 4.4.4.2 255.255.255.0
!
interface Ethernet1
  ip address 7.7.7.1 255.255.255.0
!
router ospf 10
  network 4.0.0.0 0.255.255.255 area 10
  network 7.0.0.0 0.255.255.255 area 20
  area 10 virtual-link 5.5.5.1
```

Monitoring and Troubleshooting Multi-area OSPF Networks

Cisco's IOS has several debug and show commands that can be useful in monitoring and troubleshooting OSPF networks. Following is a sampling of these commands, which can be used to gain information about various OSPF characteristics:

debug ip ospf events   Shows information concerning OSPF events, such as the selection of a designated router and the formation of router adjacencies.

debug ip ospf packet   Shows information contained in each OSPF packet, such as Router ID and Area ID.

show ip ospf border-routers   Shows an ABR's internal routing table.

show ip ospf virtual-links   Shows the status of a router's virtual link.

show ip ospf neighbor   Shows neighbor router information, such as Neighbor ID and the state of adjacency with the neighboring router.

show ip ospf process-id   Shows area information, such as identifying the area's area border router or autonomous system boundary router.

show ip ospf database   Shows information about a router's OSPF database, such as a router's router link states and network link states.

Summary

In this chapter, we illustrated the scalability constraints of an OSPF network with a single area. We introduced the concept of multi-area OSPF as a solution to these scalability limitations.

We identified the different categories of routers used in multi-area configurations. These router categories include backbone router, internal router, area border router, and autonomous system boundary router. We explored how these routers can use summarization and default routes to reduce the amount of route information that is injected into an area, thus reducing a router's memory and processor overhead.

We detailed the function of different OSPF Link State Advertisements (LSAs). We saw how these LSAs could be minimized through the effective implementation of specific OSPF area types.

Specifically, we examined stub areas, totally stubby areas, and not-so-stubby areas and showed how these areas can be used to minimize LSAs advertised into an area. We provided a set of design guidelines and configuration examples. We also showed the syntax required to configure route summarization at both area border routers and autonomous system boundary routers.

Since all areas need to have a link to the backbone area, we explained how virtual links could be used to span transit areas in OSPF networks where all areas are not physically adjacent to the backbone area. We then concluded with a collection of debug and show commands that can be used to effectively monitor and troubleshoot a multi-area OSPF implementation.

Key Terms

Before taking the exam, make sure you're familiar with the following terms:

transit area

virtual link

Written Lab

Given the network diagram in the following graphic, write out the OSPF-specific configuration to create the virtual link that would be required for this topology.

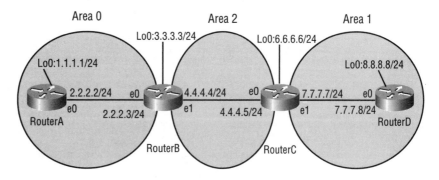

Solution

Recall that all areas need a link back to the backbone area. If an area is not physically adjacent to the backbone area, then a virtual link can be used to span the transit area that separates the area from the backbone area. In this exercise, since Area 1 does not attach directly to Area 0, we need to create a virtual link across the transit area (Area 2).

Since a virtual link requires that only the ABRs on each side of the transit area be configured, we will examine only the configuration of RouterB and RouterC.

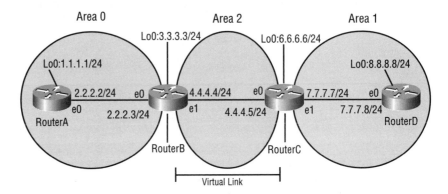

As shown in the above graphic, RouterB uses the following command to create its side of the virtual link:

```
area 2 virtual-link 6.6.6.6
```

where 2 is the transit area and where 6.6.6.6 is the Router ID (the highest loopback IP address) of the ABR at the other side of the transit area.

Similarly, RouterC uses the following command to create its side of the virtual link:

```
area 2 virtual-link 3.3.3.3
```

where 2 is the transit area and where 3.3.3.3 is the Router ID (the highest loopback IP address) of the ABR at the other side of the transit area.

RouterB

```
interface Loopback0
  ip address 3.3.3.3 255.255.255.0
!
internet Ethernet0
  ip address 2.2.2.3 255.255.255.0
!
interface Ethernet1
  ip address 4.4.4.4 255.255.255.0
!
router ospf 20
```

```
network 2.0.0.0 0.255.255.255 area 0
network 4.0.0.0 0.255.255.255 area 2
area 2 virtual-link 6.6.6.6
```

RouterC

```
interface Loopback0
  ip address 6.6.6.6 255.255.255.0
!
interface Ethernet0
  ip address 4.4.4.5 255.255.255.0
!
interface Ethernet1
  ip address 7.7.7.7 255.255.255.0
!
router ospf 20
  network 4.0.0.0 0.255.255.255 area 2
  network 7.0.0.0 0.255.255.255 area 1
  area 2 virtual-link 3.3.3.3
```

Hands-on Lab

Interconnect three routers, as shown in the graphic below. Configure Area 10 as a stub area, and configure Area 20 as a totally stubby area.

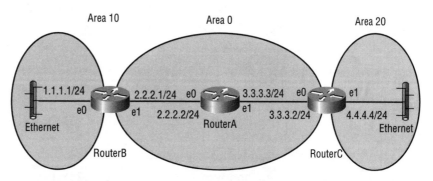

Solution

The configuration given below is a suggested solution to the lab. Notice that RouterB uses the command `area 10 stub` to specify that Area 10 is a stub area. Also notice that RouterC uses the command `area 20 stub no-summary` to specify that Area 20 is a totally stubby area. Recall that the difference between a stub area and a totally stubby area is that a totally stubby area does not receive summary Link State Advertisements. Another important design distinction is that the concept of a totally stubby area is specific to Cisco routers.

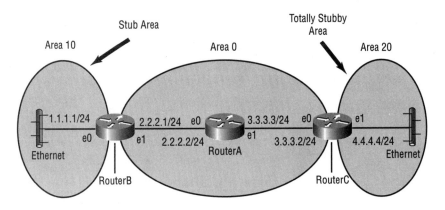

RouterA

```
!
version 11.2
no services udp-small-servers
no services tcp-small-servers
!
hostname RouterA
!
interface Ethernet0
  ip address 2.2.2.2 255.255.255.0
!
interface Ethernet1
  ip address 3.3.3.3 255.255.255.0
!
```

```
!
router ospf 50
  network 2.0.0.0 0.255.255.255 area 0
  network 3.0.0.0 0.255.255.255 area 0
!
no ip classless
!
!
line con 0
line aux 0
line vty 0 4
  login
!
end
```

RouterB

```
!
version 11.2
no services udp-small-servers
no services tcp-small-servers
!
hostname RouterB
!
interface Ethernet0
  ip address 1.1.1.1 255.255.255.0
!
interface Ethernet1
  ip address 2.2.2.1 255.255.255.0
!
!
router ospf 50
  network 1.0.0.0 0.255.255.255 area 10
  network 2.0.0.0 0.255.255.255 area 0
  area 10 stub
!
no ip classless
```

```
!
!
line con 0
line aux 0
line vty 0 4
  login
!
end
```

RouterC

```
!
version 11.2
no services udp-small-servers
no services tcp-small-servers
!
hostname RouterC
!
interface Ethernet0
  ip address 3.3.3.2 255.255.255.0
!
interface Ethernet1
  ip address 4.4.4.4 255.255.255.0
!
!
router ospf 50
  network 3.0.0.0 0.255.255.255 area 0
  network 4.0.0.0 0.255.255.255 area 20
  area 20 stub no-summary
!
no ip classless
!
!
line con 0
line aux 0
line vty 0 4
  login
!
end
```

Review Questions

1. Which of the following are scalability issues with single area OSPF networks? (Choose all that apply.)

   A. Size of the routing table

   B. Size of the OSPF database

   C. Maximum hop count limitation

   D. Recalculation of the OSPF database

2. Which of the following describes a router that connects to an external routing process (e.g., EIGRP)?

   A. ABR

   B. ASBR

   C. Type 2 LSA

   D. Stub router

3. Which of the following makes use of route redistribution?

   A. Stub area

   B. Totally stubby area

   C. ABR

   D. NSSA

4. Which of the following describes the syntax used to summarize intra-area routes on an ABR?

   A. `ip route summarize area-id network-address network-mask`

   B. `summary-address network-address network-mask`

   C. `area area-id range network-address network-mask`

   D. `summary area-id network-address network-mask`

5. Which IOS command shows information about a router's OSPF database, such as router link states and network link states?

   A. debug ospf events

   B. show ip ospf border-routers

   C. show ip ospf neighbor

   D. show ip ospf database

6. What is the term given to describe a router connected to multiple OSPF areas?

   A. ABR

   B. ASBR

   C. Type 2 LSA

   D. Stub router

7. As compared to a standard OSPF area, what is unique about a stub area?

   A. It does not receive Summary Link Advertisements.

   B. It does not receive Type 5 LSAs.

   C. It makes use of route redistribution.

   D. It is a concept specific to Cisco routers.

8. What is the IOS syntax to designate an area as a not-so-stubby area?

   A. area area-id nssa

   B. area area-id stub

   C. area area-id no-summary

   D. area area-id stub no-summary

9. What is an autonomous system boundary router (ASBR)?

   A. Any OSPF router that is connected to an external routing process

   B. Any OSPF router that is connected to an internal routing process

   C. Any router that is connected to multiple OSPF areas

   D. Any router that is connected to single OSPF areas

10. Which of the following can be described as a router that has all of its interfaces in the same area?

    A. Area border router

    B. Internal router

    C. Autonomous System Boundary Router

    D. Designated router

11. Which of the following IOS commands shows an ABR's internal router routing table?

    A. debug ospf events

    B. show ip ospf border-routers

    C. show ip ospf neighbor

    D. show ip ospf database

12. As compared to an OSPF stub area, what is unique about an OSPF totally stubby area? (Choose all that apply.)

    A. It does not receive Type 5 LSAs.

    B. It is a Cisco-specific feature.

    C. It does not receive summary Link State Advertisements.

    D. It makes use of route redistribution.

13. Which of the following are design guidelines for setting up stub areas? (Choose all that apply.)

   A. Use only when a router within an area connects to an external routing process (e.g., EIGRP).

   B. Do not make the backbone area a stub area.

   C. If you decide to make a particular area a stub area, be sure to configure all the routers in the area as stubby.

   D. Configure only the area's ABR as stubby.

14. What is the IOS syntax to create a virtual link?

   A. `area source-area-id virtual-link destination-area-id`

   B. `link area-id router-id`

   C. `ospf map area-id router-id`

   D. `area area-id virtual-link router-id`

15. Which of the following IOS commands shows the state of adjacency with neighbor routers?

   A. `debug ospf events`

   B. `show ip ospf border-routers`

   C. `show ip ospf neighbor`

   D. `show ip ospf database`

16. Which of the following statements are true regarding Summary Link Advertisements (SLAs)? (Choose all that apply.)

   A. Type 3 LSAs are Summary Link Advertisements.

   B. Totally stubby areas do not receive Summary Link Advertisements.

   C. Type 4 LSAs are Summary Link Advertisements.

   D. Stub areas do not receive Summary Link Advertisements.

17. Which of the following can be defined as a router that exists (wholly or in part) in OSPF Area 0?

A. Backbone router

B. Autonomous system boundary router

C. Designated router

D. Area border router

18. Which of the following describes the syntax used to summarize external routes on an ASBR?

A. `ip route summarize area-id network-address network-mask`

B. `summary-address network-address network-mask`

C. `area area-id range network-address network-mask`

D. `summary area-id network-address network-mask`

19. Which of the following IOS commands shows the formation of router adjacencies?

A. `debug ospf events`

B. `debug ip ospf border-routers`

C. `debug ip ospf neighbor`

D. `debug ip ospf database`

20. Which of the following LSA types is referred to as an AS External Link Advertisement?

A. Type 1 LSA

B. Type 2 LSA

C. Type 3 or Type 4 LSA

D. Type 5 LSA

Answers to Review Questions

1. A, B, and D.   As the size of a single area OSPF network grows, so does the size of the routing table and OSPF database that has to be maintained. Also, if there is a change in network topology, the OSPF algorithm has to be rerun for the entire network.

2. B.   An autonomous system boundary router (ASBR) is any OSPF router that is connected to an external routing process.

3. D.   A not-so-stubby area (NSSA) imports external routes (Type 7 LSAs) via route redistribution and then translates these Type 7 LSAs into Type 5 LSAs.

4. C.   The command `area area-id range network-address network-mask` is used on an ABR to summarize routes before they are injected into an area.

5. D.   The IOS command `show ip ospf database` shows details about a router's OSPF database. Some of these details include router link states and network link states.

6. A.   An area border router (ABR) is any OSPF router that is connected to more than one OSPF area.

7. B.   Routers in a stub area do not receive Type 5 LSAs (referred to as AS External Link Advertisements). Instead, they use a default route to reach external networks.

8. A.   The router configuration command `area area-id nssa` is used to designate an area as a not-so-stubby area (NSSA).

9. A.   An autonomous system boundary router (ASBR) is any OSPF router that is connected to an external routing process.

10. B. The definition of an internal router is a router that has all of its interfaces within the same OSPF area. Keep in mind that a router can fall into multiple categories. For example, if an internal router is in Area 0, it would also be considered a backbone router.

11. B. The routing table of area border routers can be shown using the IOS command `show ip ospf border-routers`. This table shows which border router will get a packet to the network.

12. B and C. The concept of an OSPF totally stubby area is specific to Cisco routers. In addition to not receiving Type 5 LSAs as a stub area does, a totally stubby area does not receive summary Link State Advertisements.

13. B and C. The backbone area cannot be a stub area. Also, only routers configured as stubby will be able to form adjacencies within a stubby area.

14. D. The syntax for creating a virtual link is `area area-id virtual-link router-id`, where `area-id` is the number of the transit area and where `router-id` is the IP address of the highest loopback interface configured on a router. If a loopback is not configured, then the `router-id` is the highest IP address configured on the router.

15. C. The IOS command `show ip ospf neighbor` shows neighbor router information, such as Neighbor ID and the state of adjacency with the neighboring router.

16. A, B, and C. Both Type 3 LSAs and Type 4 LSAs are considered to be Summary Link Advertisements. While totally stubby areas do not receive Summary Link Advertisements, stub areas do.

17. A. A backbone router has at least one of its interfaces connected to OSPF Area 0.

18. B. The command `summary-address network-address network-mask` is used on an autonomous system boundary router (ASBR) to summarize external routes before they are injected into OSPF.

19. A. The IOS command `debug ospf events` shows such events as the selection of a designated router and the formation of router adjacencies.

20. D. Type 5 LSAs are referred to as AS External Link Advertisements. Type 5 LSAs are blocked by stub areas, totally stubby areas, and not-so-stubby areas.

Chapter

6

IGRP and EIGRP

THE CCNP ROUTING EXAM TOPICS COVERED IN THIS CHAPTER ARE AS FOLLOWS:

- ✓ Describe IGRP features and operation
- ✓ Configure IGRP
- ✓ Verify IGRP operation
- ✓ Describe Enhanced IGRP features and operation
- ✓ Explain how metrics are used with EIGRP
- ✓ Explain how DUAL is used with EIGRP
- ✓ Explain the features supported by EIGRP
- ✓ Learn how EIGRP discovers, decides, and maintains routes
- ✓ Explain EIGRP process identifiers
- ✓ Explain EIGRP troubleshooting commands
- ✓ Configure EIGRP and verify its operation
- ✓ Verify route redistribution

So far in this book, we have taken an in-depth look at the routing protocol OSPF and shown how a routing protocol is used to find routes through the network. We also learned how routing protocols are used to exchange IP address information between routers in an enterprise network. IP addressing schemes establish a hierarchy that makes path information both distinct and efficient. A router receives this routing information via a given interface. It then advertises the information it knows out the other physical interfaces. This routing process occurs at Layer 3 of the OSI model. In this chapter, in order to decide on the best routing protocol or protocols to use, we'll take a look at both the Interior Gateway Routing Protocol (IGRP) and its big brother, the Enhanced Interior Gateway Routing Protocol (EIGRP).

Unlike OSPF, IGRP and EIGRP are proprietary Cisco protocols and run on Cisco routers and internal route processors found in the Cisco Distribution and Core layer switches. (I need to note here that Cisco has licensed IGRP to be used on other vendors' equipment, such as Compaq.) Each of these routing protocols also has its own identifiable functions, so we'll discuss each routing protocol's features and differences. Once you understand how these protocols differ from OSPF and how they calculate routes, you will learn how to configure these protocols and fine-tune them with configuration changes to make each perform at peak efficiency.

Scalability Features of Routing Protocols

Several times in this book, as we look at the different routing protocols—OSPF, IGRP, EIGRP, and BGP—we will refer back to distance-vector and link-state routing protocol differences. It is important to identify how these protocols differ from one another.

As networks grow and administrators implement or use Cisco-powered networks, OSPF might not be the most efficient or recommended protocol to use. OSPF does have some advantages of IGRP, EIGRP, and BGP, including:

- It is versatile.

- It uses a very scalable routing algorithm.

- It allows the use of a routing protocol that is compatible with non-Cisco routers.

BGP will be discussed in Chapters 7 through 9.

Cisco provides two other proprietary solutions that allow better scaling and convergence, which can be very critical issues. These are the *Interior Gateway Routing Protocol (IGRP)* and *Enhanced IGRP (EIGRP)*. Network growth imposes a great number of changes on the network environment and takes into consideration the following factors:

- The number of hops between end systems

- The number of routes in the routing table

- The different ways a route was learned

- Route convergence

IGRP and EIGRP can be used to maintain a very stable routing environment, which is absolutely crucial in larger networks.

As the effects of network growth start to manifest themselves, whether or not your network's routers can meet the challenges faced in a larger scaled network is completely up to the routing protocol the routers are running. If you use a protocol that's limited by the number of hops it can traverse, the number of routes it can store in its table, or even the inability to communicate with other protocols, then you have a protocol that will likely hinder the growth of your network.

All the issues we've brought up so far are general scalability considerations. Before we look at IGRP and EIGRP, let's take another look at the differences between link-state routing protocols and distance-vector protocols and the scalability issues of each.

Link-state routing and distance-vector protocols are discussed in detail in Chapter 2, and are discussed in Chapter 7 as they relate to BGP.

Distance-Vector Protocol Scalability Issues

In small networks—meaning those with fewer than 100 routers and an environment that's much more forgiving of routing updates and calculations—distance-vector protocols perform fairly well. However, you'll run into several problems when attempting to scale a distance-vector protocol to a larger network—convergence time, router overhead (CPU utilization), and bandwidth utilization all become factors that hinder scalability.

A network's convergence time is determined by the ability of the protocol to propagate changes within the network topology. Distance-vector protocols don't use formal neighbor relationships between routers. A router using distance-vector algorithms becomes aware of a topology change in two ways:

- When a router fails to receive a routing update from a directly connected router

- When a router receives an update from a neighbor notifying it of a topology change somewhere in the network

Routing updates are sent out on a default or specified time interval. So when a topology change occurs, it could take up to 90 seconds before a neighboring router realizes what's happened. When the router finally recognizes the change, it recalculates its routing table and sends the whole thing out to all its neighbors.

Not only does this cause significant network convergence delay, it also devours bandwidth—just think about 100 routers all sending out their entire routing table and imagine the impact on your bandwidth. It's not exactly a sweet scenario, and the larger the network, the worse it gets, because a greater percentage of bandwidth is needed for routing updates.

As the size of the routing table increases, so does CPU utilization, because it takes more processing power to calculate the effects of topology changes and then converge using the new information. Also, as more routes populate a routing table, it becomes increasingly complex to determine the best path and next hop for a given destination. The following list summarizes the scalability limitations inherent in distance-vector algorithms:

- Network convergence delay

- Increased CPU utilization

- Increased bandwidth utilization

Scalability Limitations of Link-State Routing Protocols

Link-state routing protocols assuage the scalability issues faced by distance-vector protocols because the algorithm uses a different procedure for route calculation and advertisement. This enables them to scale along with the growth of the network.

Addressing distance-vector protocols' problem with network convergence, link-state routing protocols maintain a formal neighbor relationship with directly connected routers that allows for faster route convergence. They establish peering by exchanging Hello packets during a session, which cements the neighbor relationship between two directly connected routers. This relationship expedites network convergence because neighbors are immediately notified of topology changes. Hello packets are sent at short intervals (typically every 10 seconds), and if an interface fails to receive Hello packets from a neighbor within a predetermined hold time, the neighbor is considered down, and the router will then flood the update out all physical interfaces. This occurs before the new routing table is calculated, so it saves time. Neighbors receive the update, copy it, flood it out their interfaces, and *then* calculate the new routing table. The procedure is followed until the topology change has been propagated throughout the network.

It's noteworthy that the router sends an update concerning only the *new* information—not the entire routing table. So the update is a lot smaller, which saves both bandwidth and CPU utilization. Plus, if there aren't any network changes, updates are sent out only at specified, or default, intervals, which differ among specific routing protocols and can range from 30 minutes to two hours.

These are key differences that permit link-state routing protocols to function well in large networks—they really have no limitations when it comes to scaling, other than the fact that they're a bit more complex to configure than distance-vector protocols.

Interior Gateway Routing Protocol

Interior Gateway Routing Protocol (IGRP) is a Cisco proprietary routing protocol that uses a distance-vector algorithm. It uses this algorithm because it uses a vector (a one-dimensional array) of information to calculate the best path. This vector consists of four elements:

- Bandwidth
- Delay
- Load
- Reliability

We'll describe each element in detail shortly.

NOTE Maximum transfer unit (MTU) information is included in the final route information, but it's used as part of the vector of metrics.

IGRP is intended to replace RIP and create a stable, quickly converging protocol that will scale with increased network growth. As we mentioned, it's preferable to implement a link-state routing protocol in large networks because of the overhead and delay that results from using a distance-vector protocol.

In the next few sections, we will quickly take you through the features of IGRP and show how to implement this routing protocol in your network. We will also cover the types of metrics, unequal-cost load balancing, and the limitations of redistribution.

IGRP Features and Operation

IGRP has several features included in the algorithm—these features and a brief description can be found below in Table 6.1. Most of these features were added to make IGRP more stable, and a few were created to deal with routing updates and make network convergence happen faster.

TABLE 6.1 IGRP Features

Feature	Description
Configurable metrics	The user can configure metrics involved in the algorithm responsible for calculating route information.
Flash update	Updates are sent out prior to the default time setting. This occurs when the metrics for a route change.
Poison reverse updates	Implemented to prevent routing loops, these updates place a route in *hold-down.* Hold-down means that the router won't accept any new route information on a given route for a certain period of time.
Unequal-cost load balancing	Allows packets to be shared or distributed across multiple paths.

IGRP is a classful protocol, which means it doesn't include any subnet information about the network with route information.

Classful protocols are discussed in Chapter 2.

IGRP recognizes three types of routes:

Interior Networks directly connected to a router interface.

System Routes advertised by other IGRP neighbors within the same autonomous system (AS). The AS number (ASN) identifies the IGRP session, because it's possible for a router to have multiple IGRP sessions.

Exterior Routes learned via IGRP from a different ASN, which provide information used by the router to set the *gateway of last resort*. The gateway of last resort is the path a packet will take if a specific route isn't found on the router.

When we talked about the scalability of distance-vector protocols, we told you that they don't establish a formal neighbor relationship with directly connected routers and that routing updates are sent at designated intervals. IGRP's interval is 90 seconds, which means that every 90 seconds IGRP will broadcast its entire routing table to all directly connected IGRP neighbors.

IGRP Metrics

Metrics are the mathematics used to select a route. The higher the metric associated with a route, the less desirable it is. The overall metric assigned to a route is created by the Bellman-Ford algorithm, using the following equation:

metric = [K1 × Bw + (K2 × Bw) / (256 − Load) + K3 × Delay] × [K5 / (Rel + K4)]

- By default: K1 = 1, K2 = 0, K3 = 1, K4 = 0, K5 = 0.
- Delay is the sum of all the delays of the links along the paths.
- Delay = [Delay in 10s of microseconds] × 256.
- BW is the lowest bandwidth of the links along the paths.
- BW = [10000000 / (bandwidth in Kbps)] × 256.
- By default, metric = bandwidth + delay.

The formula above is used for the non-default setting, when K5 does not equal 0. If K5 equals the default value of 0, then this formula is used: metric = K1 × bandwidth + (K2 × bandwidth) / (256 − Load) + K3 × Delay].

If necessary, you can adjust metrics within the router configuration interface. Metrics are tuned to change the manner in which routes are calculated.

After you enable IGRP on a router, metric weights can be changed using the following command:

```
metric weights tos K1 K2 K3 K4 K5
```

Table 6.2 shows the relationship between the constant and the metric it affects.

TABLE 6.2 Metric Association of K Values

Constant	Metric
K1	Bandwidth (B_e)
K2	Delay (D_c)
K3	Reliability (r)
K4	Load (utilization on path)
K5	MTU

Each constant is used to assign a weight to a specific variable. This means that when the metric is calculated, the algorithm will assign a greater importance to the specified metric. By assigning a weight, you are able to specify what is most important. If bandwidth is of greatest concern to a network administrator, then a greater weight would be assigned to *K1*. If delay is unacceptable, then the *K2* constant should be assigned a greater weight. The *tos* variable is the type of service.

As well as tuning the actual metric weights, you can do other tunings. All routing protocols have an administrative distance associated with the protocol type. If multiple protocols are running on one router, the administrative distance value helps the router decide which path is best. The protocol with the lowest administrative distance will be chosen. IGRP has a default administrative distance of 100. The tuning of this value is accomplished with the `distance` command, like this:

```
distance 1-255
```

Valid values for the administrative distance range from 1 to 255. Again, the lower the value, the better.

When redistributing static routes or other protocol types within IGRP, metrics may be set for these routes as well by using the `default-metric` command:

```
default-metric bandwidth delay reliability load MTU
```

The words in italics in the command above are just placeholders for variables and should be replaced with numbers.

Bandwidth and *delay* have a range of values from 0 to 4,294,967,295 (in Kbps) and 0 to 4,294,967,295 (in 10-microsecond units), respectively. *Reliability* ranges from 0 to 255, with 255 being the most reliable. *Load* ranges from 0 to 255; however, a value of 255 means that the link is completely loaded. Finally, the value of *MTU* has the same range as the *bandwidth* variable: 0 to 4,294,967,295.

When a router receives multiple routes for a specific network, one of the routes must be chosen as the best route from all of the advertisements. The router still knows that it is possible to get to a given network over multiple interfaces, yet all data default to the best route.

IGRP provides the ability of unequal-cost load balancing. The `variance` command is used to assign a weight to each feasible successor. A feasible successor is a predetermined route to use should the most optimal path be lost. The feasible successor can also be used as long as the secondary route conforms to the following three criteria, and an unequal-cost load balancing session may be established:

- A limit of four feasible successors may be used for load balancing. Four is the default; the maximum number of feasible successors is six for IOS version 11.0 and later.

- The feasible successor's metric must fall within the specified variance of the local metric.

- The local metric must be greater than the metric for the next-hop router.

A lower metric signifies a better route.

Redistribution Limitations

As an enterprise network grows, there is a possibility that more than one protocol will run on the router. An example is when a company acquires another company and needs to merge the two existing networks. The problem surfaces when the routes of the purchasing company need to be advertised to the newly acquired company. IGRP solves the problem with route redistribution.

When multiple protocols run on a router, you can configure IGRP to redistribute routes from specified protocols. Since different protocols calculate metrics distinctly, adjustments must be made when redistributing protocols. These adjustments cause some limitations in how the redistribution works. The adjustments are made by using the `default-metric` command, as shown previously.

IGRP may also be redistributed to other routing protocols such as RIP, other IGRP sessions, EIGRP, and OSPF. Metrics are also configured using the `default-metric` command.

Enhanced Interior Gateway Routing Protocol

Enhanced Interior Gateway Routing Protocol (EIGRP) is better than its little brother, IGRP. EIGRP allows for equal-cost load balancing, incremental routing updates, and formal neighbor relationships, which overcome the limitations of IGRP. The enhanced version uses the same distance-vector information as IGRP, yet with a different algorithm. EIGRP uses DUAL (Diffusing Update Algorithm) for metric calculation, which permits rapid convergence. This algorithm allows for the following:

- Backup route determination if one is available

- Support of Variable-Length Subnet Masks (VLSM)

- Dynamic route recoveries

- Querying neighbors for unknown alternate routes

- Sending out queries for an alternate route if no route can be found

EIGRP fixes many of the problems associated with IGRP, such as the propagation of the entire routing table, which is sent when changes occur in the network topology. One unique characteristic of EIGRP is that it is both a link-state routing and a distance-vector protocol. How can this be? Let's look at how this protocol combines the best from both routing protocol types.

Along with rapid convergence discussed above, EIGRP reduces bandwidth usage. It does this by not making scheduled updates but sending updates only when topology changes occur. When EIGRP does send an update, the update contains information only on the change in the topology, which requires a path or metric change. Another plus is the fact that only the routers that need to know about the change receive the update.

One of the best features is that the routing protocol supports all of the major Layer 3 routed protocols using protocol-dependent modules (PDMs), those being IP, IPX, and AppleTalk. At the same time, EIGRP can maintain a completely loop-free routing topology and very predictable behavior, even when using all three routed protocols over multiple redundant links.

With all these features, EIGRP must be hard to configure, right? Guess again. Cisco has made this part easy as well and allows you to implement load balancing over equal-cost links. So why would you use anything else? Well, I guess you might if all your routers weren't Cisco routers. Remember, EIGRP is proprietary and only runs over Cisco routers and internal route processors.

Now that we have mentioned all this, we've sold you on EIGRP, right? Well, if we stopped right here, you would miss out on many other important details of the route-tagging process, neighbor relationships, route calculation, and the metrics used by EIGRP, which will be discussed in the next few sections. Following that discussion, we will look at how to configure EIGRP, tune EIGRP, load balance, redistribute routes, and troubleshoot.

Route Tagging

Route tagging is used to distinguish routes learned by the different EIGRP sessions. By defining a different AS number, EIGRP can run multiple sessions on a single router. Routers using the same ASN speak to each other and share routing information, which includes the routes learned and the advertisement of topology changes.

Route redistribution, which will be covered in its own section later in this chapter, allows routes learned by one AS EIGRP session to be shared with another session. When route distribution occurs, the routes are tagged as being learned from an external EIGRP session. Each type of route is assigned its own administrative distance value.

Neighbor Relationships

Using Hello messages, EIGRP sessions establish and maintain neighbor relationships with neighboring routers. This is a quality of a link-state routing protocol. EIGRP uses the Hello protocol just like OSPF does, as discussed in Chapter 5, to establish and maintain the peering relationships with directly connected routers. The Hello packets sent between EIGRP neighboring routers determine the state of the connection between them. Once the neighbor relationship is established using the Hello protocol, the routers then exchange route information.

Each EIGRP session running on a router establishes a neighbor table in which each router stores information on all the routers known to be directly connected neighbors. The neighboring routers' IP address, hold time interval, smooth round-trip timer (SRTT), and queue information are all kept in the table, which is used to help determine when there are topology changes that need to be propagated to the neighboring routers.

The only time EIGRP advertises its entire routing table is when two neighbors initiate communication. When this happens, both neighbors advertise their entire routing tables to one another. After each has learned its neighbor's directly connected or known routes, only changes to the routing table are propagated.

When Hello messages are sent out each of the routers' interfaces, replies to the Hello packets are sent with the neighboring router's topology table (which is not the routing table) and include each route's metric information with the exception of any routes that were already advertised by the router receiving the reply. As soon as the reply is received, the receiving router sends out what is called an ACK (acknowledgement) packet to acknowledge receipt, and the routing table is updated if any new information is received from the neighboring router. Once the topology table has been updated, the originating router will then advertise its entire table to any new neighbors that come online. Then when the originating router receives information from its neighbors, the route calculation process begins. Let's now take a look at how EIGRP uses metrics to calculate the best routes through the network.

Route Calculation

EIGRP uses multicasts instead of broadcasts. Therefore, only identified stations are affected by routing updates or queries. Where IGRP updates use a 24-bit format, EIGRP uses a 32-bit format for granularity. Only changes in the network topology are advertised instead of the entire topology table.

EIGRP is called an advanced distance-vector protocol although it contains properties of both distance-vector and link-state routing protocols when calculating routes. DUAL is much faster and calculates new routes only when updates or Hello messages cause a change in the routing table. And then recalculation occurs only when the changes directly affect the routes contained in the routing table.

This last statement may be confusing. If a change occurs to a network that is directly connected to a router, all of the relevant information is used to calculate a new metric and route entry for it. If a link between two EIGRP peers becomes congested, both routers would have to calculate a new route metric, then advertise the change to any other directly connected routers.

Now that we understand the difference between a route update and a route calculation, we can summarize the steps that a router takes to calculate, learn, and propagate route update information.

Redundant Link Calculation

The topology database stores all known routes to a destination and the metrics used to calculate the least-cost path. Once the best routes have been calculated, they are moved to the routing table. The topology table can store up to six routes to a destination network, meaning that EIGRP can calculate the best path for up to six redundant paths. Using the known metrics to the destination, the router must make a decision as to which path to make its primary path and which path to use as a standby or secondary path to a destination network. Once the decision is made, the primary route will be added to the routing table as the *active route*, or successor, and the standby will be listed as a *passive route*, or the *feasible successor*, to the destination.

The path-cost calculation decisions are made from information contained in the routing table using the bandwidth and delay from both the local and adjacent routers. Using this information, a composite metric is calculated. The local router adds its cost to the cost advertised by the adjacent router. The total cost is the metric. Figure 6.1 shows how cost is used to select the best route (successor) and the backup route (feasible successor).

FIGURE 6.1   The best-route selection process

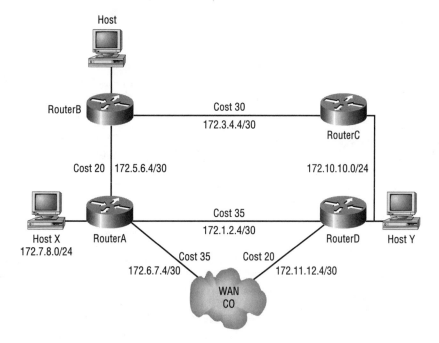

Using RouterA as a starting point, we see that there are three different routes to Host Y. Each link has been assigned a cost. Numbers in bold represent *advertised distances,* and numbers in italics represent *feasible distances*. Advertised distances are costs that routers advertise to neighbors.

In this example, RouterD and the WAN all have advertised costs that they send to RouterA. In turn, RouterA has a feasible distance for every router to which it is connected. The feasible distance is the cost assigned to the link that connects adjacent routers.

The feasible and advertised costs are added together to provide a total cost to reach a specific network. Let's calculate the lowest cost for Host X to get to Host Y. We will use the path from Host X to RouterA to RouterB to Router C and finally to Host Y for our first path calculation. To calculate the total cost, we add 20 (RouterA to RouterB) to 30 (RouterB to RouterC), for a final value of 50. For the feasible successor calculation, RouterA tells RouterB the cost of 35, which is the advertised cost. B then adds its cost to get to RouterA. This becomes 35 + 20, for a total path cost of 55.

The next path calculated is from Host X to RouterA to RouterD to Host Y. In this case, there is no advertised cost, so the final value consists of only the feasible cost of 35. The final path is calculated in the same manner to give us the result of 55.

Since the lowest cost was 35, the route to 172.10.10.0/24 learned via RouterD will be chosen as the successor or primary route. The other two routes remain in the topology table as feasible successors and are used if the successor to Host Y fails.

Information given in Table 6.4 closely represents what is contained in an actual topology table, though not exactly. The Status field shows whether a new route is being calculated or if a primary route has been selected. In our example, the route is in passive state because it has already selected the primary route.

TABLE 6.3 Topology Table Information

Status	Route—Adjacent Router's Address (Metrics)	Number of Successors	Feasible Distance
P	172.10.10.0/24 via 172.1.2.6 (3611648/3609600) via 172.5.6.6 (4121600/3609600) via 172.6.7.6 (5031234/3609600)	1 (Router C)	3611648

The route with the best metric contains the lowest metric value and is chosen as the primary route. If there is more than one route to a destination, the route with the second-lowest metric will be chosen as the feasible successor, as long as the advertised distance of the potential feasible successor is not greater than the distance of the successor. Primary routes are moved to the routing table after selection. More than one route can be made a primary route in order to load balance. This will be discussed in the "Load Balancing" section later in this chapter.

EIGRP uses the same metrics as IGRP. Those metrics are:

- Bandwidth
- Delay
- Reliability
- Load

 Just as with IGRP, there is no specific calculation for the maximum transmission unit (MTU) as a metric. The MTU, however, is used as a tiebreaker for equal metric paths.

Bandwidth and delay are the two metrics used by default. The other metrics can be configured manually. When you configure reliability, load and MTU can cause the topology table to be calculated more often.

Updates and Changes

EIGRP also has link-state properties. One of these properties is that it propagates only changes in the routing table instead of sending an entire new routing table to its neighbors. EIGRP relies on IP to deliver updates to its neighbors, as shown in a breakdown of an EIGRP packet in Figure 6.2. When changes occur in the network, a regular distance-vector protocol will send the entire routing table to neighbors. By avoiding sending the entire routing table, less bandwidth is consumed. Neighboring routers don't have to re-initialize the entire routing table; all the routers need to do is insert the new route changes. This is one of the big advantages that EIGRP has over IGRP.

FIGURE 6.2 An IP frame showing the protocol type to be EIGRP

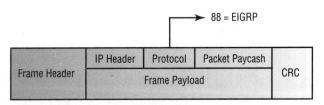

Updates can follow two paths. If a route update contains a better metric or a new route, the routers simply exchange the information. If the update contains information that a network is unavailable or that the metric is worse than before, an alternate path must be found. When a new path must be found, the router first searches the topology database for feasible successors. If no feasible successors are found, a multicast request is sent to all adjacent routers. Each router will then respond to the query. Depending on how the router answers, different paths will be taken. After the intermediate steps are taken, two final actions can occur:

1. If route information is eventually found, the route is added to the routing table, and an update is sent.

2. If the responses from the adjacent routers do not contain any route information, the route is removed from the topology and routing tables.

After the routing table has been updated, the new information is sent to all adjacent routers via a multicast.

EIGRP Metrics

EIGRP utilizes several databases or tables of information to calculate routes. These databases are as follows:

- The route database (routing table) where the best routes are stored

- The topology database (topology table) where all route information resides

- A neighbor table that is used to house information concerning other EIGRP neighbors

Each of these databases exists separately for each routed protocol configured for EIGRP. The following characteristics identify each session of EIGRP:

- The IP session is called IP-EIGRP.

- The IPX session is called IPX-EIGRP.

- The AppleTalk session is called AT-EIGRP.

Therefore, it is possible for EIGRP to have nine active databases when all three protocols are configured on the router.

As stated above, the metrics used by EIGRP are the same as those used by IGRP. As with IGRP, metrics decide how routes are selected. The higher the metric associated with a route, the less desirable the route is. The overall metric assigned to a route is created by the Bellman-Ford algorithm, using the following equation:

metric = [K1 × Bw + (K2 × Bw) / (256 − Load) + K3 × Delay] × [K5 / (Rel + K4)]

- By default: K1 = 1, K2 = 0, K3 = 1, K4 = 0, K5 = 0.

- Delay is the sum of all the delays of the links along the paths.

- Delay = [Delay in 10s of microseconds] × 256.

- BW is the lowest bandwidth of the links along the paths.

- BW = [10000000 / (bandwidth in Kbps)] × 256.

- By default, metric = bandwidth + delay.

Just as with IGRP, you can set the metrics manually from within the Configuration mode. We'll provide the details on how to change metrics after we discuss how EIGRP is configured.

Configuring EIGRP

Although EIGRP can be configured for IP, IPX, and AppleTalk, as a Cisco Certified Network Professional, you should focus on the configuration of IP. An autonomous system must be defined for each EIGRP session on a router. To start an EIGRP session on a router, use the `router eigrp` command followed by the autonomous system number of your network. You must then enter the network numbers connected to the router using the `network` command followed by the network number. The network mask is optional for network statements entered on the Cisco IOS 12.0 or later.

Let's look at an example of enabling EIGRP on a router connected to two networks with the network numbers 10.0.0.0 and 172.16.0.0:

```
Router#conf t
Enter configuration commands, one per line. End with CNTL/Z.
Router#router eigrp 20
Router(config-router)#network 172.16.0.0
```

```
Router(config-router)#network 10.0.0.0
Router(config-router)#^Z
Router#
```

Unfortunately, EIGRP assumes that all serial connections use T1 speeds. In order to identify slower links, such as a 128K link, you must identify it manually. Bandwidth is one of the two default metrics used to calculate a route's metric. If the bandwidth is slower or faster than T1 speeds, use the `bandwidth` command followed by the bandwidth in kilobits in Interface Configuration mode. The possible values are between 1 and 10,000,000.

If you need to stop routing updates from being sent on an interface, such as a BRI interface, you can flag the interface as a passive interface. To do this from an EIGRP session, use the `passive-interface interface-type interface-number` command. The `interface-type` portion defines the type of interface, and the `interface-number` portion defines the number of the interface.

EIGRP Tuning

The metrics used with EIGRP are tuned in the same manner as the metrics for IGRP. Metrics are tuned to change the manner in which routes are calculated. The same command as for IGRP is also used:

```
metric weights tos K1 K2 K3 K4 K5
```

Each constant is used to assign a weight to a specific variable. This means that when the metric is calculated, the algorithm will assign a greater importance to the specified metric. By assigning a weight, you are able to specify what is most important. If bandwidth is of greatest concern to a network administrator, a greater weight should be assigned to *K1*. If delay is unacceptable, the *K2* constant should be assigned a greater weight. The *tos* variable is the type of service. Refer back to Table 6.2 for the relationship between the constant and the metric it affects. Also, remember that EIGRP uses bandwidth and delay by default only when calculating routes.

Other tuning is possible. All routing protocols have an administrative distance associated with the protocol type. If multiple protocols are running on one router, the administrative distance value helps the router decide which path is best. The protocol with the lower administrative distance will be chosen. EIGRP has a default administrative distance of 90 for internal routes and 170 for external routes. Use the following command to make changes:

```
distance 1-255
```

Valid values for the administrative distance range from 1 to 255. Again, the lower the value, the better. If an administrative distance of 255 is chosen, routes will be considered unreachable and will be ignored.

When redistributing static routes or other protocol types within EIGRP, metrics may be set for these routes as well by using the `default-metric` command:

`default-metric bandwidth delay reliability load mtu`

Bandwidth and *delay* have a range of values from 0 to 4,294,967,295 (in Kbps) and 0 to 4,294,967,295 (in 10-microsecond units), respectively. *Reliability* ranges from 0 to 255, with 255 being the most reliable. *Load* ranges from 0 to 255; however, a value of 255 means that the link is completely loaded. Finally, the value of *MTU* has the same range as the bandwidth variable: 0 to 4,294,967,295.

Most of this information should be a review, since it's basically the same information associated with IGRP.

Load Balancing

One of EIGRP's major enhancements is its ability to select more than one primary route or successor. We have discussed how route costs are calculated and shown that up to six routes for every destination can be stored in the topology database. EIGRP capitalizes on this information.

By using multiple LAN or WAN connections from one router to another, multiple routes can exist to the next-hop address. When the links are symmetric (meaning they have the same circuit type and the same bandwidth capacity), the same local cost is assigned to each link.

Since both links have the same feasible distance, the metrics for destinations accessible via the links will be equal. As EIGRP chooses the successor for a route, it looks for the route with the lowest cost. When it sees multiple routes with the same metric, it selects them all as successors. EIGRP will then share traffic loads across each of the multiple links. This is called *load balancing*.

Let's look at an example of a topology table with multiple routes:

```
IP-EIGRP topology entry for 172.10.10.0/24
  State is Passive, Query origin flag is 1, 1
↳Successor(s),
     FD is 283648
  Routing Descriptor Blocks:
  172.16.1.6 (Serial1), from 172.16.1.6, Send flag is 0x0
     Composite metric is (283648/281600), Route is
↳Internal
     Vector metric:
        Minimum bandwidth is 1544 Kbit
        Total delay is 1080 microseconds
        Reliability is 255/255
        Load is 1/255
        Minimum MTU is 1500
        Hop count is 1
  172.16.1.10 (Serial2), from 172.16.1.10, Send flag is 0x0
     Composite metric is (283648/281600), Route is Internal
     Vector metric:
        Minimum bandwidth is 1544 Kbit
        Total delay is 1080 microseconds
        Reliability is 255/255
        Load is 1/255
        Minimum MTU is 1500
        Hop count is 1
  172.16.1.14 (Serial3),from 172.16.1.14, Send flag is 0x0
     Composite metric is (283648/281600), Route is Internal
     Vector metric:
        Minimum bandwidth is 1544 Kbit
        Total delay is 1080 microseconds
        Reliability is 255/255
        Load is 1/255
        Minimum MTU is 1500
        Hop count is 1
```

In this output, the feasible distance is the same for all three links. This means that traffic will be load balanced (shared) across all three links equally.

There will also be situations where there are multiple links to a given destination, but the links have different next-hops. The metric for these links will not likely be the same. Even though each link may have a different cost assigned to it, EIGRP does allow for unequal-cost load balancing.

This is achieved by using the `variance` command—the same command used in IGRP for unequal-cost load balancing:

```
variance multiplier
```

The `variance` command uses a multiplier, which can be a value from 1 to 128. The default setting for the multiplier is 1. This command must be used inside the EIGRP protocol configuration.

Route Redistribution

When a router has more than one routed protocol configured, each EIGRP session is defined by the autonomous system number used when enabling EIGRP. With all of the different protocols and sessions running on a router, it becomes important that the information learned by each session can be shared with the other protocols and sessions. *Route redistribution* is the feature that allows for the exchange of route information among multiple protocols and multiple sessions.

The router where multiple protocols or sessions meet is called the *Autonomous System Boundary Router (ASBR)*. When routes from one protocol or session are injected or redistributed into another protocol or session, the routes are tagged as external routes. Let's look at a simple example of a routing table that has external routes:

```
Router#show ip route eigrp
   172.16.0.0/16 is variably subnetted, 301 subnets, 10 masks
D EX    172.16.27.230/32
   [170/24827392] via 172.16.131.82, 11:39:32, ATM6/0/0.3114
D EX    172.16.237.16/29
   [170/40542208] via 172.16.131.82, 11:41:32, ATM6/0/0.3114
   [170/40542208] via 172.16.131.74, 11:41:32, ATM6/0/0.3113
D EX    172.16.237.24/29
```

```
              [170/40542208] via 172.16.131.82, 11:40:32, ATM6/0/0.3114
              [170/40542208] via 172.16.131.74, 11:41:32, ATM6/0/0.3113
D EX     172.16.52.192/26
              [170/2202112] via 172.16.131.82,  11:41:27, ATM6/0/0.3114
D EX     172.16.41.216/29
              [170/46232832] via 172.16.131.82, 11:41:28, ATM6/0/0.3114
D EX     172.16.38.200/30
              [170/2176512] via 172.16.131.82,  11:41:27, ATM6/0/0.3114
D EX     172.16.237.0/29
              [170/40542208] via 172.16.131.82, 11:41:32, ATM6/0/0.3114
              [170/40542208] via 172.16.131.74, 11:41:32, ATM6/0/0.3113
D        172.16.236.0/24
         [90/311808] via 172.16.131.82, 11:41:32, ATM6/0/0.3114
         [90/311808] via 172.16.131.74, 11:41:32, ATM6/0/0.3113
D        172.16.235.0/24
         [90/311808] via 172.16.131.82, 11:41:32, ATM6/0/0.3114
```

There are internal routes and external routes in this routing table. The external routes are flagged with EX, while the internal routes have no flag. The D stands for an EIGRP learned route.

While redistribution allows multiple protocols to share routing information, it can cause routing loops, slow convergence, and inconsistent route information. This is caused by the different algorithms and methods used by each protocol. It is not a good practice to redistribute bi-directionally. For example, if you have both EIGRP 10 using IP-EIGRP and EIGRP 20 using AT-EIGRP routing sessions, then bi-directional redistribution would occur if you entered redistribution commands under each protocol session. Here is an example:

```
Router#conf t
Enter configuration commands, one per line. End with CNTL/Z.
Router(config)#router eigrp 10
Router(config-router)#redistribute eigrp 20
Router(config-router)#router eigrp 20
Router(config-router)#redistribute eigrp 10
Router(config-router)#^Z
Router#
```

If a route from RIP, IGRP, or OSPF is injected into EIGRP, the route loses its identity, and its metrics are converted from the original format to EIGRP's format. This can cause confusion within the router.

You can reset EIGRP metrics to help alleviate certain problems by using the `default-metric` command, as follows:

`default-metric` *bandwidth delay reliability load MTU*

This command takes the metrics for the protocol being injected into EIGRP and converts them directly to values that EIGRP can use. The *bandwidth* is the capacity of the link. The *delay* is the time in microseconds, and *reliability* and *load* are values from 1 to 255. The *MTU* is the maximum transmission unit size in bytes.

Finally, you can change the distance values that are assigned to EIGRP (90 internal and 170 external). The distance value tells the router which protocol to believe. The lower the distance value, the more believable the protocol. The distance values for EIGRP are changed with the following command from within the EIGRP session:

`distance eigrp` *internal-distance external-distance*

Internal-distance and *external-distance* have a range of values from 1 to 255.

Remember that a value of 255 tells the router to ignore the route. So unless you want the routes from the protocol to be ignored, never use the value 255.

Troubleshooting EIGRP

There are several commands that can be used on a router to aid in troubleshooting EIGRP. Table 6.5 contains all of the commands that are used in conjunction with verifying EIGRP operation and offers a brief description of what each command does.

TABLE 6.4 EIGRP Troubleshooting Commands

Command	Description/Function
show ip route eigrp	Shows EIGRP entries in the routing table.
show ip eigrp neighbors	Shows all EIGRP neighbors.
show ip eigrp topology	Shows entries in the EIGRP topology table.
show ip eigrp traffic	Shows the packet count for EIGRP packets sent and received.
show ip protocols	Shows information about the active protocol sessions.
show ip eigrp events	Shows a log of EIGRP events. These are routes being added or removed from the routing table.

When troubleshooting an EIGRP problem, it is always a good idea to get a picture of the network. The most relevant picture is provided by the show ip eigrp neighbors command. This command shows all adjacent routers that share route information within a given autonomous system. If neighbors are missing, check the configuration and link status on both routers to verify that the protocol has been configured correctly.

If all neighbors are present, verify the routes learned. By executing the show ip route eigrp command, you gain a quick picture of the routes in the routing table. If the route does not appear in the routing table, verify the source of the route. If the source is functioning properly, check the topology table.

The topology table is displayed by using the show ip eigrp topology command. If the route is in the topology table, it is safe to assume that there is a problem between the topology database and the routing table. There must be a reason why the topology database is not injecting the route into the routing table.

Other commands such as `show ip eigrp traffic` can be used to see if updates are being sent. If the counters for EIGRP input and output packets don't increase, no EIGRP information is being sent between peers.

The `show ip eigrp events` command is an undocumented command. This command displays a log of every EIGRP event—when routes are injected and removed from the routing table, and when EIGRP adjacencies reset or fail. This information can be used to see if there are routing instabilities in the network.

All of these commands are intended to be used at the discretion of the system administrator when troubleshooting a problem in the network. The information provided by these commands can be used for many more issues than have been discussed in this section.

Summary

This chapter has been fairly extensive. Just to refresh your memory, we discussed the differences between and limitations of distance-vector and link-state routing protocols. Link-state routing protocols or a hybrid of link-state routing and distance-vector protocols provide for greater scalability and stability.

EIGRP, which was the main focus of the chapter, is a hybrid of link-state routing and distance-vector protocols. It provides greater stability than IGRP, which was also discussed, and allows for equal-cost load balancing, controlled routing updates, and formal neighbor adjacencies.

We also looked at how to configure, tune, and troubleshoot EIGRP, how to load balance, and how to redistribute routes using EIGRP.

So far in this book we have covered OSPF, a touch of RIP, IGRP, and EIGRP. So what's left? The Border Gateway Protocol and its components. This protocol is so complex that it will be covered in not one, not two, but the next three chapters.

Key Terms

Before taking the exam, make sure you're familiar with the following terms:

active route

Autonomous System Boundary Router (ASBR)

Enhanced IGRP (EIGRP)

feasible successor

gateway of last resort

Interior Gateway Routing Protocol (IGRP)

load balancing

passive route

route redistribution

Commands Used in This Chapter

Command	Description
distance	When multiple protocols are running, this command allows a distance value from 1 to 255 to decide which path is the best. The lowest value wins.
passive-interface interface-type interface-number	Identifies interfaces that do not participate in EIGRP updates.
router eigrp	Starts EIGRP processes on a router.
show ip route eigrp	Shows all EIGRP neighbors.
show ip eigrp neighbors	Shows directly connected EIGRP-enabled routers.
show ip eigrp topology	Shows entries in the EIGRP topology table.
show ip eigrp traffic	Shows the packet count for EIGRP packets sent and received.
show ip protocols	Shows information about the active protocol sessions.
show ip eigrp events	Shows a log of EIGRP events. These are routes being added to or removed from the routing table.
variance	Assigns a weight to each feasible successor.

Written Lab

1. What three routed protocols are supported by EIGRP?

2. When is redistribution required for EIGRP?

3. What command would be used to enable EIGRP with an ASN of 300?

4. What command will tell EIGRP that it is connected to network 172.10.0.0?

5. What type of EIGRP interface will listen to routing updates but not propagate them?

6. What command allows you to make an interface passive?

7. Which command is used to ensure proper metric conversion when redistributing routes from different protocols?

8. Which two commands show all known EIGRP routes?

9. Which command can be used to see all the router's known EIGRP neighbors?

10. Which command can be used for troubleshooting EIGRP events?

Hands-on Lab

Using the graphic shown below, we will walk through configuring all three routers for EIGRP and then view the configuration.

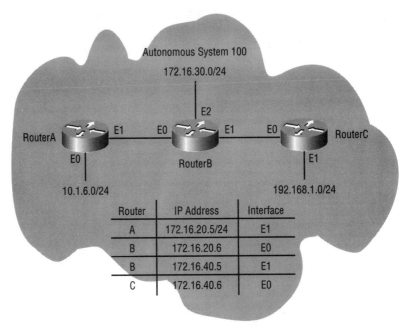

Router	IP Address	Interface
A	172.16.20.5/24	E1
B	172.16.20.6	E0
B	172.16.40.5	E1
C	172.16.40.6	E0

1. Implement EIGRP on RouterA, as shown here:

```
RouterA#conf t
Enter configuration commands, one per line.  End with CNTL/Z.
RouterA(config)#router eigrp 100
RouterA(config-router)#network 10.0.0.0
RouterA(config-router)#network 172.16.0.0
RouterA(config-router)#^Z
RouterA#
```

2. Implement EIGRP on RouterB, as shown here:

```
RouterB#conf t
Enter configuration commands, one per line.  End with CNTL/Z.
```

```
RouterB(config)#router eigrp 100
RouterB(config-router)#network 172.16.0.0
RouterB(config-router)#exit
RouterB#
```

3. Implement EIGRP on RouterC, as shown here:

```
RouterC#conf t
Enter configuration commands, one per line.  End with CNTL/Z.
RouterC(config)#router eigrp 100
RouterC(config-router)#network 172.16.0.0
RouterC(config-router)#network 192.168.1.0
RouterC(config-router)#^Z
RouterC#
```

4. Display the topology table for RouterB, as shown here:

```
RouterB#show ip eigrp topology
Codes: P - Passive, A - Active, U - Update, Q - Query,
       R - Reply, r - Reply status

P 172.0.0.0/8, 1 successors, FD is 307200
        via 172.16.20.5 (307200/281600), Ethernet0/0
P 192.168.1.0/24, 1 successors, FD is 307200
        via 172.16.40.6 (307200/281600), Ethernet0/1
P 172.16.40.4/30, 1 successors, FD is 281600
        via Connected, Ethernet0/1
P 172.16.20.4/30, 1 successors, FD is 281600
        via Connected, Ethernet0/0
RouterB#
```

Review Questions

1. When does EIGRP recalculate its topology table?

   A. On a synchronized schedule

   B. When an administrator uses the redirect command

   C. Automatically every 120 seconds

   D. Only when there is a change in the network topology

2. The neighbor table uses which of the following timers? (Choose all that apply.)

   A. SRTT

   B. RTO

   C. Hold timer

   D. FwdDelay timer

   E. MaxAge timer

3. When there are no feasible successors and only one link to a destination network, even if the link cost is set to 100,000, the link will always be in which of the following modes?

   A. On

   B. Standby

   C. Active

   D. Sending

4. Which of the following are not routed protocols supported by EIGRP?

   A. TCP

   B. IP

   C. IPX

   D. AppleTalk

5. What are benefits of using a link-state routing protocol? (Choose all that apply.)

   A. It uses the Hello protocol to establish adjacencies.

   B. It uses several components to calculate the metric of a route.

   C. Updates are sent only when changes occur in the network.

   D. It is a better protocol than distance-vector is.

6. Which route type must be redistributed by a routing protocol if other routers are to learn about it?

   A. RIP

   B. Default routes

   C. Connected routes

   D. Static routes

7. Why are passive interfaces used on interfaces where the router participates in EIGRP Global mode processes?

   A. To stop unwanted route information from entering the specified interface

   B. To allow route information to be filtered by an access list

   C. To allow routes to be sent out the specified interface, but deny route information to enter the interface

   D. To allow routes to enter the interface, but deny any route information to exit the specified interface

8. How is a feasible successor chosen when the successor fails (assuming that a redundant route exists)? (Choose all that apply.)

   A. The route with the next-lowest metric is chosen.

   B. If a router doesn't have a feasible successor, queries are multicast to neighboring routers in search of a feasible successor.

   C. The route is removed from the routing table.

   D. The route is flagged as an active state.

9. Which command should be used to ensure proper metric conversion when redistributing routes from different protocols?

   A. `distance distance-value`

   B. `default-metric`

   C. `distribute-list`

   D. `default-information`

10. How is EIGRP implemented on a router?

    A. `ip router eigrp autonomous-system-number`

    B. `router ip eigrp autonomous-system-number`

    C. `router eigrp process-id`

    D. `router eigrp autonomous-system-number`

11. Which of the following are not features of EIGRP? (Choose all that apply.)

    A. Incremental updates

    B. Only one route per destination

    C. Support for IP, IPX, and AT

    D. Hybrid distance-vector and link-state routing protocol

    E. Not a scalable protocol

    F. Hello protocol used to establish adjacencies

12. Which of the following problems may occur if route redistribution occurs?

    A. Non-optimal route choices

    B. Slow convergence

    C. Routing loops

    D. All of the above

13. When using the show ip route command, which of the following codes indicate an EIGRP learned route?

A. D

B. R

C. S

D. I

14. When using EIGRP, the process number indicates which of the following?

A. Link-state value

B. Autonomous system number

C. Path cost

D. Number of ACKs

15. Which of the following commands can be used to learn the number of EIGRP packets sent and received?

A. `show ip eigrp mail`

B. `show ip eigrp sent`

C. `show ip eigrp traffic`

D. `show ip eigrp data`

E. `show ip eigrp counters`

16. Which of the following is not a route type recognized by IGRP?

A. Network

B. Interior

C. System

D. Exterior

17. Which of the following are used by IGRP to calculate the best path to a destination network? (Choose all that apply.)

A. Bandwidth

B. Load

C. Delay

D. Reliability

18. By default, what is the maximum number of feasible links that IGRP may use to load balance over unequal-cost links?

A. Two

B. Four

C. Six

D. Eight

19. What is the maximum number of feasible successors that EIGRP can place in its routing table?

A. Two

B. Four

C. Six

D. Eight

20. Which of the following algorithms is used by EIGRP to determine the best path?

A. Open Shortest Path First

B. DUAL

C. Distance-vector

D. Link-state routing

E. Advanced Distance Vector

Answers to Written Lab

1. The three EIGRP routed protocols supported by EIGRP are IP, IPX, and AppleTalk.

2. Redistribution is required when more than one EIGRP session is running and they are identified with different ASNs. Redistribution shares topology information between EIGRP sessions.

3. `router eigrp 300`

4. `network 172.10.0.0`

5. Passive interface

6. `passive-interface` *interface-type interface-number*

7. `default-metric`

8. `show ip route eigrp and show ip route`

9. `show ip eigrp neighbors`

10. `show ip eigrp events`

Answers to Review Questions

1. D.   One of the great benefits of EIGRP is that it advertises only changes, and only when there is a change in the network topology does it recalculate routes. Hello packets continue to be sent in order to verify that all the attached links are still connected and did not go down.

2. A, B, C.   The neighbor table uses the smooth round-trip timer (SRTT), the retransmission timer (RTO), and the hold timer to track its neighboring routers. The FwdDelay and MaxAge timers are both used by the Spanning Tree Protocol to keep Layer 2 switches from creating data loops.

3. C.   The link will always be in Active mode regardless of the link cost because there is no other feasible successor. If the link goes down, there is no other redundant link to use.

4. A.   This is a trick question. IP is a routed protocol but TCP is not. Both IPX and AppleTalk are examples of routed protocols.

5. A, C.   Link-state routing protocols use the Hello protocol and update neighbors of changes without sending the entire routing or topology table.

6. D.   Static routes must always be redistributed by a routing protocol and always have the smallest administrative distance.

7. D.   Passive interfaces are used for such interfaces as BRI, where you do not want to have routing updates sent out the interface. If routing updates were sent out of a BRI interface, the interface would never disconnect. You can also configure the routing traffic to be uninteresting traffic to perform a similar function.

8. A, B.   The feasible successor, which would be the path with the next-lowest metric, would be chosen. Or, if the router has not learned of any secondary routes, the router will query its neighbors to see if they know of any routes.

9. B. Use the `default-metric` command to ensure proper metric conversion when redistributing routes from different protocols.

10. D. The command `router eigrp` followed by the ASN is used to implement EIGRP. You must then identify the attached networks using the network command.

11. B, E. Answer B is not a feature because redundant paths are supported, and answer E is not a feature because EIGRP is the most scalable routing protocol.

12. D. All of these problems may occur when using route redistribution.

13. A. EIGRP uses D, RIP uses R, S identifies a static route, and I indicates IGRP.

14. B. The EIGRP process number is always the number assigned to an autonomous system. Multiple processes can run simultaneously on a router.

15. C. The `show ip eigrp traffic` command shows the sent and received packets. The other commands are not real commands that can be used on a router.

16. A. The network route is not recognized by IGRP. An interior route is a network directly connected to a router interface. A system route is a route advertised by other IGRP neighbors within the same AS. An exterior route is learned using IGRP from a different ASN.

17. A, B, C, D. All of these are used by IGRP by the distance-vector algorithm to determine the best path to a destination network. By default however, only bandwidth and delay are used.

18. B. IGRP can use up to four feasible successors to load balance. The default is four, and the maximum is six.

19. C.   There may be more routes in the topology table, but the maximum number of feasible successors listed in the routing table is six.

20. B.   The Diffusing Update Algorithm (DUAL) is used to calculate routes in EIGRP.

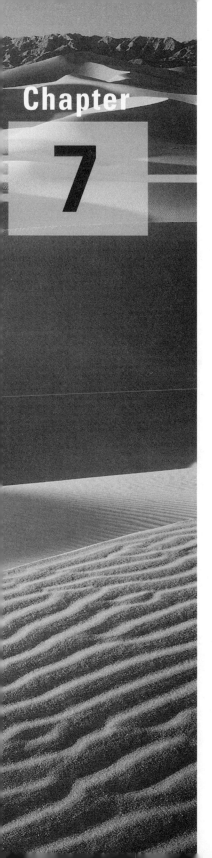

Chapter

7

BGP's Basic Components

THE CCNP ROUTING EXAM TOPICS COVERED IN THIS CHAPTER ARE AS FOLLOWS:

✓ Describe how to connect to another autonomous system using an alternative to BGP, static routes

✓ Describe BGP operations and features

✓ Describe and configure external and internal BGP

✓ Compare distance-vector and link-state protocol operation

✓ Explain how BGP peering functions

his chapter covers BGP, which stands for Border Gateway Protocol. BGP will be discussed in great detail, not only in this chapter but in the two following this one as well. Here we'll focus on BGP terminology and its basics components. Chapter 8, "Configuring Basic BGP," will focus on how BGP works and configuring BGP. Chapter 9, "Monitoring, Troubleshooting, and Scaling BGP," will focus on the more advanced uses of BGP, including scaling, policy implementation, and optimization techniques.

For some time now, Cisco has required an understanding of BGP as a requirement for obtaining your CCIE. But in order to fulfill the CCNP requirements, you needed only a basic overview and never had to deal with BGP configurations or advanced configurations. There is no way that we can project to you the actual complexities of configuring BGP for an ISP needing 20 or more paths going through ISPs. This is not an uncommon scenario, and we will prepare you to configure and support BGP in a real Internet environment.

BGP is one of the most complex routing protocols I have ever seen. It is used to connect multiple autonomous systems, which we'll discuss in detail. In this chapter, we'll focus on the following:

- Autonomous systems, including stud autonomous systems and transit autonomous systems

- BGP peers

- Internal BGP

- External BGP

- Routing protocols

- When to use and when not to use BGP

- Ingress filtering

- BGP update messages

BGP has been used for quite some time on routers connecting to the Internet. The Internet can be really thought of as the backbone of thousands of small and large companies. This book focuses on the latest version of BGP: BGP version 4(BGPv4). BGPv4 is an *exterior routing protocol*. Interior routing protocols such as RIP, IGRP, and OSPF run inside a company's network. BGP is the glue that connects the different networks to the Internet. BGP also helps in finding and distributing route information.

Are you ready for all of this? Let's get started and see what an autonomous system is.

Autonomous Systems

You can imagine the Internet as a Lego castle. In order to build a Lego™ castle, you need many pieces. The same goes for the Internet. The Internet is built with many autonomous systems, which we will think of as Lego pieces. These pieces are then assembled to form a much larger piece. Autonomous systems (AS) are the basic building blocks of network-to-network routing. An autonomous system can be the entire corporate network comprised of multiple locations connecting to the network.

An AS uses BGP to advertise routes in its network that need to be visible outside of the network; it also uses BGP to learn about the reachability and routes by listening to advertisement announcements from other autonomous systems. Each AS can have a specific policy regarding the routes it wishes to advertise externally. These policies can be different for every point in which the AS attaches to the outside world.

The Internet consists of a number of commercial networks that connect to each other via tier-one providers, such as Sprint, Qwest, WorldCom/MCI, UUNet, and many others. Each enterprise network or ISP must be identified by an autonomous system number (ASN). This number allows a hierarchy to be maintained when sharing route information.

RFC 1930 defines an autonomous system as a set of routers under one or more administrations that presents a common routing policy to the internet (lowercase i). By definition, an internet is a set of interconnected networks that cooperate with each other, advertise policies, and contain a specified level of independence. There are many organizations, such as the government, state departments, and financial institutions, with networks large enough to need BGP and to split into multiple autonomous systems.

Inside autonomous networks, interior routing protocols called interior gateway protocols (IGP) are used to discover the connectivity among a set of IP subnets. IGPs are well-known protocols such as the Routing Information Protocol (RIP), Interior Gateway Routing Protocol (IGRP), Open Shortest Path First (OSPF), and Enhanced Interior Gateway Routing Protocol (EIGRP). In Figure 7.1, we see an example of two corporate networks being connected by BGP.

FIGURE 7.1 Two corporate networks being connected by BGP

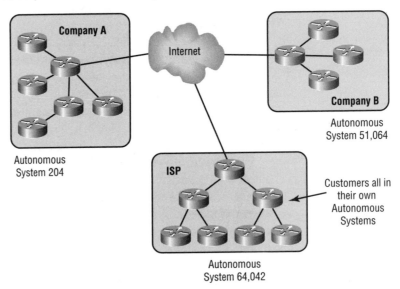

Variations of BGP terms will be used in the next two chapters. These terms are internal BGP (iBGP) and external BGP (eBGP), also known as an interdomain routing protocol. These are the same BGP protocol, but iBGP runs inside an AS while eBGP runs outside an AS and connects one AS to another AS.

So what type of routing protocol is used to find the paths and connect these autonomous systems? An Exterior Gateway Protocol (EGP). That is exactly what BGP is, an External Gateway Protocol used to connect and find routes to and from autonomous systems.

BGP is defined in many Requests For Comments (RFCs), which include 1771-1774, 1863, 1965-1966, 1997-1998, 2042, 2283, 2385, and 2439. BGPv4, the latest version, and autonomous systems are defined in RFC 1771.

Now we have to remember another routing protocol that learns the networks and can keep loops from forming in the network. In this book, there are three mapping protocol types to remember that help to determine paths and eliminate data loops:

Internal routing protocols   These are protocols like OSPF, IGRP, EIGRP, and RIP, which operate at Layer 3 of the OSI Reference Model. They are used to learn the network topology on the internal network and IP subnets to create routes that guarantee that there are no data loops in the Layer 3 network.

External routing protocols   These protocols are used to learn the network topology of multiple autonomous systems or networks and connect them with loop-free paths.

Spanning Tree Protocol   This protocol is used at Layer 2 inside a segment of an AS. It ensures that the internal network topology is learned at Layer 2 and verifies that there is a path through the network without data loops.

BGP uses reliable session management, using TCP port 179 for triggered UPDATE and KEEPALIVE messages to its neighbors to propagate and update the BGP routing table. Triggered updates are updates that are sent for a certain reason and not on a schedule.

A router can be a member of only one autonomous system and must appear to other autonomous systems to have one routing plan. All the destinations must be reachable through that plan.

There are 65,535 available autonomous system numbers that can be assigned, from 1 to 65,535. Autonomous system numbers (ASN) are 16-bit integers. Of those 65,535 ASNs, the numbers 64,512 to 65,535 are reserved for private use. This obviously means that there must be some authority available to assign these numbers to those who need them, right? Yes, there is.

RFC 1930 provides guidelines for assigning BGP autonomous system numbers. When you request a BGP ASN, you will be required to provide the following information:

- All administrative contacts in the company.

- The Internet address of your routers.

- A preferred autonomous system name.

- A hardware profile of your routing hardware and the software being used. In the case of Cisco, this would be the model and IOS version.

- Expected deployment schedule when you will begin using two or more upstream providers.

- All networks in your organization connected by the routers.

The Internet Assigned Numbers Authority (IANA) is the organization that assigns BGP autonomous system numbers. The IANA allows the American Registry for Internet Numbers (ARIN) to assign autonomous system numbers for North America, South America, the Caribbean, and Africa. Reseaux IP Eurpeennes-Network Information Center (RIPE-NIC) assigns the AS numbers for Europe, and the Asia Pacific-NIC (AP-NIC) assigns the numbers for Asia.

Stub AS

A *stub AS* is a single-homed network with only one entry and exit point, as shown in Figure 7.2. In this type of network, the stub network does not need to learn Internet routes. The reason? The local service provider or Internet Service Provider is the next hop, and all the traffic is sent to one exit interface to the provider. The provider then can have the responsibility for advertising its customers' static routes. This type of situation works well if there are relatively few static routes to manually configure and advertise. If there are many routes, then taking the time to manually configure these static routes can become burdensome.

FIGURE 7.2 A stub AS

In this situation, where there are many routes through the network, you have some choices. You can maintain static routes, use an IGP to determine the network topology and choose the most efficient paths between the AS and the service provider, use eBGP between the customer and the local service provider, or use any combination of these, as shown in Figure 7.3.

FIGURE 7.3 A stub AS to an ISP

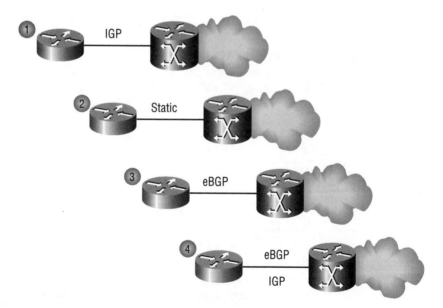

Obtaining an AS number for a stub network may be somewhat difficult when using an ISP. The ISP considers your AS an extension of their AS, and it must abide by the ISP's AS policies. What we have seen in most cases is that the ISP assigns the customer a number out of the private pool discussed earlier. The private pool of numbers runs from 64,512 to 65,535.

Transit AS

A transit AS is an AS through which data from one AS must travel to get to another AS. A non-transit AS is an AS that does not pass data through to another AS. A non-transit AS can be used to pass data from two service providers but never between them, as shown in Figure 7.4.

FIGURE 7.4   A non-transit AS connected to three ISPs

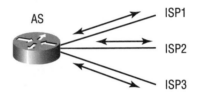

An enterprise network can have a transit AS if the network uses multiple ASes. In this situation, we would look at this as a backbone of backbones in the enterprise network. A good example of a transit AS is a local service provider. Local service providers carry traffic for many other ASes as this is the local service provider's primary business.

Now let's take a more in-depth look at eBGP and iBGP.

BGP Peers

In BGP, the word *peer* is somewhat confusing because it has two meanings. It can be used at both the protocol level and the policy level. The first usage is simple: Two BGP routers that have a BGP session running between them over a TCP connection are called *peers* or *neighbors*.

The second usage occurs at the BGP policy level and refers to a relationship within an entire AS. Peering is used to pair two ASes of the same status or an AS at one level with an AS at a higher level. If two ASes decide that they are peers, then they assume that they are equal in relationship. Usually an administrator has decided that it is beneficial for his customers to reach one another. These peers advertise their customers' routes to one another. This does not mean that they exchange their full Internet routing tables.

Let's take a more in-depth look at iBGP and eBGP.

iBGP

The *internal Border Gateway Protocol (iBGP)* is used by routers that all belong to the same autonomous system. These routers may use loopback interfaces to provide greater reachability in the AS. This is possible because an IGP can provide multiple routes to any given destination address if the network has redundant or multiple links to each router. If one interface on a router goes down, the TCP connection to the loopback address can be maintained by using redundant interfaces.

Before any BGP route information can be exchanged between two routers, a TCP connection has to be established. And another routing protocol other than BGP can be used to establish the TCP connection. The TCP connection is made by a three-way handshake using a SYN, ACK, SYN sequence. Once a TCP connection has been established, route information can be exchanged.

Routing information from one peer is not advertised from one iBGP to another iBGP peer. This prevents inconsistent route information and routing loops in the network. To share route information among all iBGP routers, you must establish a logical mesh, as shown in Figure 7.5. Routing information is then exchanged only between routers who are members of this mesh. RouterB can learn BGP networks only from RouterA. When RouterC sends its BGP information, only its own information is sent. Routing information learned from RouterA is not included.

FIGURE 7.5 iBGP information exchange

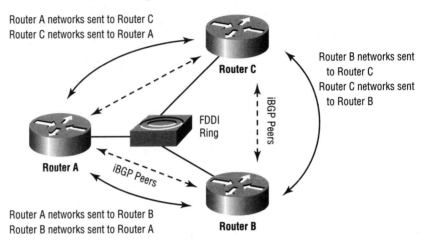

Router A networks sent to Router C
Router C networks sent to Router A

Router B networks sent
to Router C
Router C networks sent
to Router B

FDDI
Ring

iBGP Peers

Router A networks sent to Router B
Router B networks sent to Router A

Configuring BGP will be covered in Chapter 8.

eBGP

The *external Border Gateway Protocol (eBGP)* is used to exchange route information between different autonomous systems. When only one link connects two autonomous systems, the IP addresses of the connected interfaces are used to establish a BGP session between the two.

You can use any other IP address on the interfaces, but the address must be reachable without using an IGP. You can use a static route or a few other commands, which will be discussed in the Chapter 9. If multiple links are used to connect to the other autonomous systems, then using a loopback addresses is your best option.

Outside of each AS, eBGP is used to inject routes owned by one AS through the enterprise network and into another AS. Two prerequisites need to be met for internal routes to be propagated via BGP:

- In order for a router to advertise routes to BGP, the route must exist in an IGP's routing table on the router.

- The BGP must be able to learn the route.

The router can place routes in its routing table by using an IGP to learn the network topology. It uses its own table and calculates its own routes. A default (static) route can be configured, or a directly connected network can advertise the route. BGP has a synchronization option that requires the BGP's learned routes and the IGP's learned routes to synchronize before BGP will advertise the IGP's learned network topologies.

BGP can also learn routes through the network from other BGP advertisements, network statements, and redistribution of an IGP into a BGP. Since redistribution can cause routing loops and route flapping, this method is not recommended except in a lab scenario.

Routing Protocols

In a stub network, which we discussed earlier, there is only one way in or out of the AS or network—there is no need to use another protocol to find routes in the network. A static address mapping can be used for any unknown routes. This means that if the router has determined that the destination in a packet is not on the local network, it merely forwards the packet to the static default mapping.

As networks grow, however, and there begin to be many routes throughout the network, a static route becomes too difficult to maintain. This occurs when the network has expanded to the extent at which a routing protocol will scale well and is the point at which you want to discontinue using static routes.

The increased network growth imposes a greater number of topology changes in the network environment. The number of hops between end systems, the number of routes in the routing table, the various ways a route has to be learned, and route convergence are all seriously affected by network growth.

To maintain a stable routing environment, it's absolutely crucial to use a scalable protocol. When the results of network growth manifest themselves, whether your network's routers will be able to meet those challenges is up to the routing protocol the routers are using. For instance, if you use a protocol that's limited by the number of hops it can traverse, how many routes it can store in its table, or even the inability to communicate with other protocols, you have a protocol that will likely hinder the growth of your network.

BGP keeps its acquired routing table information separate from the IGP's routing tables. BGP literally steals information the IGPs have learned of their local network environments and stored on their routing tables. BGP handles the translation of information from one routing protocol to another routing protocol when multiple routing protocols are used in an AS.

Cisco supports two different types of algorithms for IGPs to find and calculate paths through the network. These two types are distance-vector and link-state routing protocols. In the next two sections, we'll take a look at these in greater detail.

Distance-Vector Protocols

BGP is considered an advanced distance-vector protocol. Distance-vector protocols such as RIP were designed when network topologies were small. Distance-vector refers to a routing protocol that uses hop counts or vectors to determine the distance from one device in the network to another. Each device that a packet must encompass to get to another destination is considered a hop. For example, if you have to go through two routers to get to a destination node, then there are three devices including the destination node, making it three hops away from your local workstation or two hops from your local router.

In small networks (less than 100 routers) where the environment contains less than 15 hops (the count-to-infinity restriction) between any destination, the network topology is much more forgiving of routing updates and calculations, and distance-vector protocols perform pretty well. Scaling a distance-vector protocol to a larger network creates higher convergence times, high router overhead CPU utilization, and increased bandwidth utilization, all of which become factors that hinder scalability.

Other drawbacks to distance-vector protocols include no support for Variable Length Subnet Masks (VLSM) or for Classless Interdomain Routing (CIDR) and that they don't take into account the speed of each link. For example, if the network topology contains two ways to a destination, one contains an ISDN link (128K) and the other is a Frame Relay link (768K) circuit. The Frame Relay link contains an extra hop. What this means is that a distance-vector protocol would choose the slow boat, which is the ISDN link, because it calculates only the hops to a destination and doesn't care that there is a faster way to the destination. Your 12MB ZIP file will now take an additional hour to get to its destination.

RIPv2 provides support for VLSM and CIDR. RIPv1 does not.

A network's convergence time is determined by the ability of RIP to propagate changes within the network topology. Distance-vector protocols don't use formal neighbor relationships between routers. A router using distance-vector algorithms becomes aware of a topology change in two ways and ages out entries in its routing information base (RIB):

- When a router fails to receive a routing update from a directly connected router

- When a router receives an update from a neighbor notifying it of a topology change somewhere in the network

Each routing protocol sends out routing updates at default intervals or at a manually configured time interval. This means that when a topology change occurs, using the defaults, it could take 90 seconds or longer before a neighboring router realizes that there has been a link-state change and switches to an alternate path. Ninety seconds can be an eternity to the network, causing application timeouts and other problems for network users. When the router does finally update its RIB with the change, it recalculates its route table. Then instead of just advertising the change, it advertises its entire table to all its neighboring routers.

Imagine having 50 routers advertising their entire routing tables and the impact that this can have on the bandwidth in your network. It compounds one problem with another. Not only do you lose a link that provides bandwidth, but the more problems you have the worse it gets because a greater percentage of bandwidth is needed for routing updates.

When the size of the routing table increases, so does the router's CPU utilization. The reason is that it takes a lot more processing power to calculate the routing table changes, converge using the new information, and advertise its new table. This utilization can also be compounded by more routes populating a routing table. The table becomes increasingly complex in order to determine the best path and next hop for a given destination.

Link-State Routing Protocols

One of the best features of a link-state routing protocol is its ability to count to infinity. This means that there is no hop count limit. A link-state routing protocol works on the theory that routers send out a link state, which carries information about each interface and the nodes attached.

A link-state-type of routing protocol—as well as the Spanning Tree Protocol—uses an algorithm called "graph theory" or the shortest path algorithm, which was developed by Edgar Dijkstra. This theory is used to construct a loop-free subset of the network topology using bits of information contained in each link-state message to create a directed graph where each link is represented by vertices and weighted edges, as shown in Figure 7.6. Each link represents a cost.

The weighted edges usually have more hops in the link than the straight-through points, so these are assigned higher values. When the paths are calculated, each link in the path has a given value, and the total of the values to a given point or destination is the total weighted value of the path. The lowest total weighted value represents the most efficient path from one point to another point.

FIGURE 7.6 An example of a directed graph

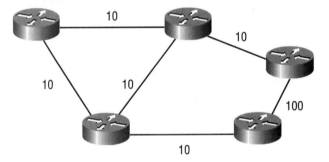

The graph takes into account that each link's bandwidth has better convergence times, supports VLSM, and supports CIDR. Link-state routing protocols also differ from distance-vector protocols because of their procedure for route calculation and advertisement. This procedure enables link-state routing protocols to scale well with the growth of a network.

Link-state routing protocols also maintain a formal neighbor relationship with directly connected routers, which allows for faster route convergence.

Link-state routers establish a peering by exchanging Hello packets (also known as link-state messages) during a session, which cements the neighbor relationship between two directly connected routers. This relationship expedites network convergence because neighbors are immediately notified of topology changes.

Hello packets are sent at short intervals, typically every 10 seconds, and if an interface fails to receive Hello packets from a neighbor within a predetermined hold time, the neighbor is considered down, and the router will then flood the update out all physical interfaces. This occurs before the new route table is calculated, so it saves time. Neighbors receive the update, copy it, flood it out their interfaces, and then calculate the new routing table—this procedure is followed until the topology change has been propagated throughout the network.

Unlike distance-vector protocols, which send the entire routing table, link-state routing protocols advertise only updates or changes, making the messages much smaller, which saves both bandwidth and CPU utilization. Plus, if there are no network changes, updates are sent out only at specified, or default, intervals, which differ among specific routing protocols and can range from as short as 30 minutes to as long as two hours. EIGRP, which is a link-state routing protocol, sends updates only when there is a topology change to a directly connected neighboring router. These updates are called *triggered updates*.

IGPs can be used with BGP; however, there are certain instances where BGP should be used and certain instances where it should not be used. In the following sections, we will outline these instances.

When to Use and When Not to Use BGP

Static or default routes, which were discussed earlier, may be used in situations where the complexity of BGP is not required. First let's take a look at when you should use BGP. The following scenarios are examples of when BGP should be used:

- When you need to send traffic through one AS to get to another AS

- When the flow of data traffic out of your network must be manipulated

- When you are connecting two or more ISPs, network access points (NAPs), and exchange points

- When you are using multi-homing in an enterprise network that connects to more than one ISP

One of the main reasons not to use BGP is if your router can't support the huge routing tables needed to support BGP. Remember that there are about 7,000 AS numbers in use today, and the router learning those huge tables requires a lot of RAM and processing power.

In a lab scenario, using two Cisco 2500 series routers works fine since the tables it has to learn are small. But once the table acquires over 70,000 routes and gets above 35MB, the router begins to develop serious processing problems. This increases the latency dramatically to the point where the throughput through the router is…well…you might as well disconnect the cable to the router and use *sneakernet* (placing the data on a disk and walking it to its destination) because the data will get to its destination faster.

There are some other reasons not to use BGP, including:

- When there is a single connection to the Internet. Use a default route instead. You'll just be wasting bandwidth, memory, and processing power.

- When your network does not have the bandwidth to support the amount of data needed to be passed, including BGP's huge routing tables.

Ingress Filtering

*I*ngress filtering allows you to decide the routes that you will advertise to other BGP neighbors or peers. When using BGP in your AS, you have the ability to announce the routes in your AS that you want to be seen by the Internet. To safeguard this process, many ISPs have policies in place to accept the announcements of routes that belong to your AS.

RFC 2267 outlines how ISPs should filter ingress routes and traffic.

There are some ISPs, however, that do not use any of the outlined techniques from RFC 2267 and that do not filter your announcements. In fact, some actually announce to the rest of the Internet all the routes that exist in your network. Ingress traffic filtering is a condition in which an ISP accepts only packets with a source address in an administrative range that belongs to one of the ISP's customers. If all the ISPs on the Internet filtered using ingress filtering based on source addresses, the Internet as a whole would gain considerable immunity to malicious hackers' denial-of-service attacks.

The reason is that hackers would not be able to insert a randomly generated or invalid source address in the packets used to attack other networks. Hackers use these addresses to prevent the attacked network from learning the true source. Ingress source filtering would block these packets before they could enter the network.

BGP Update Messages

The biggest difference between an IGP and a BGP is the amount of additional information passed between protocol-running devices because of the amount of routing information that must be passed. IGPs sometimes use a prefix, metric, tagging, or a shortest path algorithm such as that found in the Open Shortest Path First (OSPF) protocol. The updates used by an IGP can be small compared to the routing updates for BGP, which have the potential of carrying many path attributes.

RIP is a simple IGP that carries only a few attributes, such as metric information and the next hop. OSPF is a much more complex routing protocol that has path attributes such as intra-area, inter-area, and external status. BGP has the ability to attach many attributes to a given route. The minimum set of path attributes that can be included in an update message is the source of the update, called the ORIGIN attribute, and the hop information, called the AS_PATH attribute.

When two routers running BGP begin a communication process to exchange dynamic routing information, they use a TCP port at Layer 4 of the OSI Reference Model. Specifically, TCP port 179 is used. The two routers are called *endpoints*, *BGP peers*, or *BGP neighbors*, and their communications, which are reliable connection-oriented connections, are referred to as *sessions*. When a router advertises its prefixes or routes, this router is known as a *BGP speaker*. The routes that it advertises are considered valid by the other endpoints until a specific message is sent that the route is no longer valid or that the TCP session is lost.

BGP uses TCP so that it does not have to provide a component that controls the orderly delivery of messages, recognizes when data packets have been lost, detects duplicates, and controls buffering for both ends of the reliable session. Before a session between two or more BGP routers has been initiated, the endpoints are considered to be in the *Idle state*.

As soon as one endpoint tries to open a TCP session, the endpoint is considered to be in the *Connection state*. If there is a problem in establishing a connection between two endpoints, the router trying to initiate the session will transition to the *Active state*, where it will periodically try to establish a TCP session.

When the TCP connection has been established, the endpoints can be assured that as long as the session is active, there is a reliable connection-oriented path between the endpoints. Messages between the endpoints can be sent reliably. This connection allows BGP messages to be very simple and include only the information necessary with little overhead.

BGP must rely on the connection-oriented TCP session to provide the Connection state as BGP cannot use a keepalive signal but sends a message with a KEEPALIVE type in a common header to allow routers to verify sessions are active. Standard *keepalives* are signals sent from one router to another on a circuit not using a TCP session. Routers use these signals on circuits to verify that there are no failures on the circuit or that the circuit has not terminated.

Once the TCP connection has been established, BGP sends messages back and forth in a specific format. The first message is an identification message from the endpoints. As soon as this message is sent, the router transitions to the *OpenSent state*. When the router receives a reply to the identification message, it transitions to the *OpenConfirm state*. If a connection is received and accepted by the endpoints, the Connection state becomes the *Established state*. From then on, when a message is sent to the endpoint routers, the routers can respond to the sent message, update their routing table with new information in the message, or have no reaction to the sent message whatsoever.

Using the identification message information, the endpoints can accept or refuse a connection from their BGP neighbor.

Endpoints typically stay in the Established state until there is a loss of the session or an error. If this occurs, then the connection returns to the Idle state and all the information that the BGP endpoints have learned from their neighboring endpoint will be purged from the BGP routing table.

BPG Common Header

A common header precedes all BGP messages. This header, shown in Figure 7.7, contains the following fields:

- Marker

- Length

- Type

We will discuss those fields in the following sections.

FIGURE 7.7 The BGP common header

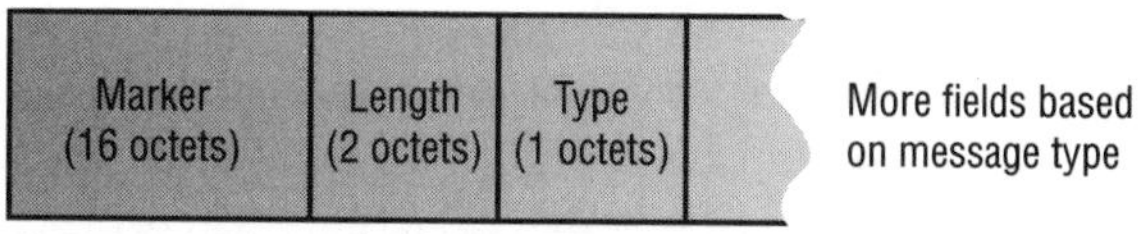

More fields based on message type

Marker (16 octets) Length (2 octets) Type (1 octets)

Marker

The Marker field is a field up to two bytes long. It is used for security and synchronization. The value of this field depends on the type of message being sent.

Length

The Length field indicates the size of the entire BGP message including the header.

Type

The Type field indicates the type of message being sent. There are four possible values, as shown in Table 7.1.

TABLE 7.1 Values for the Type Field

Type Value	Message Type
1	OPEN message
2	UPDATE message
3	NOTIFICATION message
4	KEEPALIVE message

Let's look at the different message types.

OPEN Message

This is the first message sent after a TCP session has been established between one or more peers. This message is used to identify the AS that the router is a member of, to agree on protocol parameters, and to determine the protocol timers the session will use. Figure 7.8 shows the additional fields included in the BGP header for an OPEN message.

FIGURE 7.8 The additional fields added to the BGP common header for an OPEN message type

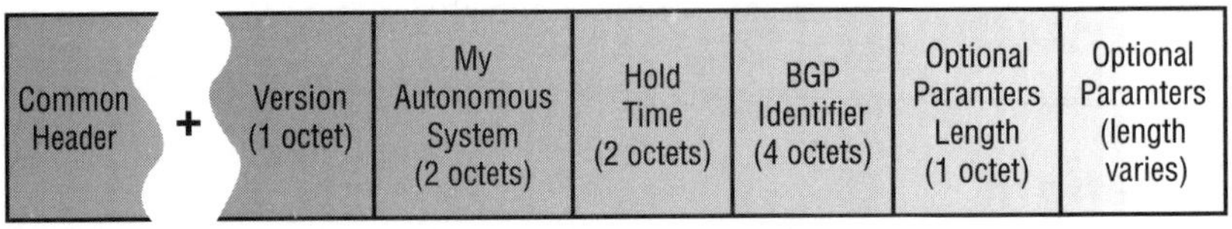

Let's take a look at each of the additional field types added to the OPEN message type.

Version

The Version field indicates the BGP version being used by the router sending the OPEN message. This field allows the BGP speakers to informally negotiate the highest common version numbers that each supports. If a BGP version speaker receives a packet indicating a version number of 4, and the BGP speaker receiving the packet is running a lower version of BGP, then it will send an error message stating that it does not understand 4 and will terminate the TCP session. The BGPv4 speaker must then reopen the TCP session using the parameters used in the lower version of BGP.

My Autonomous System

This field indicates the autonomous system number (ASN) membership of the BGP router sending this OPEN message. Every AS must be identified by its own unique ASN, which we discussed earlier in the chapter.

Hold Time

This field indicates the amount of time that the sender of the OPEN message wants to use for its hold-down timer. This hold time indicates the maximum amount of time that each endpoint will wait for another to send a message before considering the connection terminated. This means that if an UPDATE or a KEEPALIVE message is not sent in the indicated amount of time, the session is considered closed. A value of zero indicates that the sender does not want to exchange KEEPALIVE messages. This mode is not recommended since one side will not know if the other has lost communication.

The hold time value is the minimum value set locally on the router or the advertised hold time value. If the hold time value is not zero, then the hold time must be at least three seconds. A neighboring endpoint can reject an OPEN message if the hold time value is unacceptable.

BGP Identifier

This field contains a value that identifies the BGP speaker. This is a random value chosen by the BGP router when sending an OPEN message. The value must be unique to all the other BGP speakers communicating with one another. Although the number can be random, BGP speakers will typically use the logical IP address assigned to the interface. This number is then used for every BGP session.

Optional Parameters Length

This field is used to indicate the length of the Optional Parameters field in the OPEN message. If there are no optional parameters in the field, then this length is set to zero.

Optional Parameters

This field contains any optional parameters inserted into the OPEN message. Each optional parameter includes a one-octet parameter type, a one-octet parameter length, and a variable-length parameter value.

UPDATE Message

This type of message is the actual topology information sent between two BGP speakers. An UPDATE messages can contain a new route, routes to be withdrawn, or both. However, only one new route can be advertised by an UPDATE message.

The UPDATE message adds additional fields to the BGP common header, as shown in Figure 7.9.

FIGURE 7.9 The additional fields added to the BGP common header when using the UPDATE message type

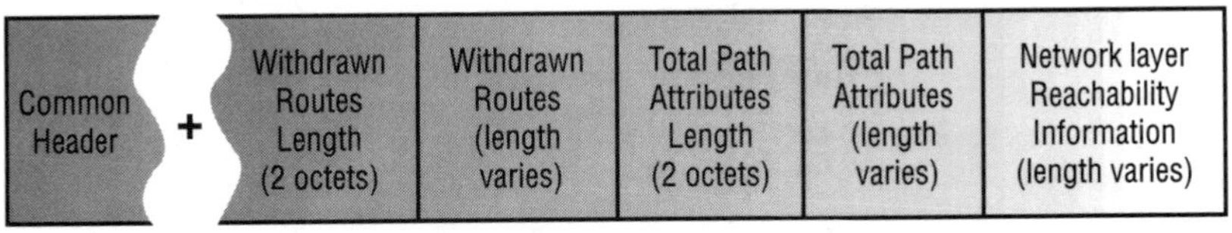

Let's look at the additional fields added to the BGP common header when the UPDATE message type is used.

Withdrawn Routes Length

This field is used to indicate the length of the Withdrawn Routes field and specifies this information in the number of octets. The BGP specification itself officially calls this field the Unfeasible Routes Length field.

Withdrawn Routes

The Withdrawn Routes field can contain a list of IP prefixes for which the BGP speaker sending the UPDATE message wants to notify its BGP peer that a route path either no longer exists or cannot be accessed due to the addition of a policy. We'll discuss this topic in more detail in Chapter 9. Each IP prefix being withdrawn adds two fields to the Withdrawn Routes field. An IP Prefix Length, which is one octet, identifies the length of the second field, called the IP Prefix field. This field is of variable length and identifies the IP prefix for the route that needs to be withdrawn. If the prefix does not equal at least eight bits, then the rest of the field is padded with additional bits to make each integer a multiple of eight bits.

Total Path Attributes Length

This field is used to indicate how large the Total Path Attributes field is.

Total Path Attributes

There are many path attributes that can be placed in the Total Path Attributes field. Each attribute has a type code and several bits that describe each attribute's usage. These attributes are associated with prefixes found in the Network Layer Reachability Information (NLRI) field. Each bit indicates a different attribute type. Table 7.2 describes the attribute types (A 0 bit equals OFF and a 1 bit equals ON).

TABLE 7.2 Attribute Types

Bit	Attribute Type
1	ON=optional.
	OFF=well-known.
2	ON=transitive.
	OFF=non-transitive.
3	ON=partial optional attribute; must be passed on.
	OFF=well-known non-transitive; does not need to be passed on.
4	ON=extended length bit; the total length of the attribute is more than one octet. (By setting the extended length bit, attributes can be longer than 255 bytes.)
	OFF=the length of the attribute is one octet.

By turning on the first bit, this flag indicates that all well-known attributes must be passed along to downstream peers after the peers receive and process the message. BGP does not require every implementation to support every option. The second bit specifies how implementations handle options they do not recognize. If the second bit, which is known as the *transitive flag*, is on, then if the option is recognized it will pass the information downstream to its BGP neighbors. If the bit is turned off, then the option is ignored and not passed downstream to other neighbors.

All well-known attributes are considered transitive.

Some attributes appear only in iBGP or in eBGP. For this book, we consider that iBGP and eBGP are the same protocol but with differences in the peering points and the types of attributes of each. Remember where each is used. In iBGP, each peer communicates between speakers in the same AS, and in eBGP, peers communicate between speakers in different ASes.

Path attributes can be considered as the metrics used by BGP routers that are passed in UPDATE messages to other BGP peers. These messages can contain notifications of local routes, foreign routes, or route topology changes. An attribute can be placed in one of four categories, as listed below:

- Well-known mandatory
- Well-known discretionary
- Optional transitive
- Optional non-transitive

Let's take a look at the characteristics of each attribute in the next sections and the attributes that can be associated with each type.

WELL-KNOWN MANDATORY

A well-known mandatory attribute is used by a totally compliant BGP implementation to propagate all the network's BGP neighbors. Well-known mandatory attributes must appear in all BGP update messages. This means that a well-known mandatory attribute must appear in an advertised route and must be supported by all implementations of BGP. These attributes are as follows:

Autonomous System Path   The *AS_PATH* (Type Code 2) is a well-known mandatory attribute. The AS_PATH attribute is composed of a variable-length series of AS path segments. Each AS path segment contains a path type, a length, and a value. The path segment type is a one-octet-long field with the values shown in Table 7.3.

The AS_PATH's fields above are modified only by eBGP speakers that advertise the route outside the local AS. These eBGP speakers prepend their own AS numbers to the end of the path vector in each of the fields. When a BGP speaker originates a route, it should include its own ASN in UPDATE messages sent to other ASes. The field is empty for an AS_PATH attribute advertised to iBGP speakers belonging to its own ASN. This allows iBGP to avoid data loops by implementing a rule that specifies that each iBGP router must ignore any route learned from an iBGP peer.

The AS_PATH attribute makes BGP a *path-vector protocol*. BGP messages carry the sequence of AS numbers indicating the complete path a message has traversed.

Next-hop   The *NEXT_HOP* (Type Code 3) attribute is a well-known mandatory attribute that indicates the IP address of the next-hop destination router. The next hop for all destinations is listed in the NLRI field of the UPDATE message. The BGP speaker should never advertise the address of a peer as the NEXT_HOP of a route the current speaker is originating to that peer. Likewise, the speaker should not install a route that has itself as the next hop unless the NEXT_HOP_SELF configuration option is used.

An iBGP speaker can advertise any internal BGP router as the next hop as long as the IP address of the iBGP border router is on the same subnet as the local and remote BGP speakers. This means that one router can handle all the announcements on the same subnet.

A BGP speaker can also advertise any external border router as the next hop if the IP address of the proposed next-hop router is learned from one of the advertising router's peers, and if the connected interface for the router is on the same subnet as both the local and remote BGP speakers.

Origin   The *ORIGIN* (Type Code 1) attribute is a well-known mandatory attribute used to tell the receiving BGP router the BGP type of the original source of the NLRI information. The ORIGIN type can be one of the type codes shown in Table 7.4.

You can override the second option if an eBGP_MULTIHOP configuration is used. The eBGP_MULTIHOP configuration, which we will discuss in Chapter 8, can be used when configuring the next hop if two eBGP speakers need to peer across multiple subnets and the physical connectivity between two eBGP speakers runs over more than one load-shared link. Do not use this feature if both iBGP speakers are in the same AS. Another reason to use the eBGP_MULTIHOP configuration is if you are using a single point-to-multipoint, non-broadcast multi-access (NBMA) medium, such as Frame Relay.

TABLE 7.3   Path Segment Values

Bit Value	Path Segment Type
0	Non-defined
1	AS_SET (an unordered list of ASes that the UPDATE message has traversed)
2	AS_SEQUENCE (an ordered list of ASes that the UPDATE message has traversed)
3	AS_CONFED_SET (an unordered list of ASes in the local confederation that the UPDATE message has traversed)
4	AS_CONFED_SEQUENCE (an ordered list of ASes that the UPDATE message has traversed in the local confederation)

TABLE 7.4 ORIGIN Type Codes

Code Value	Type
0	IGP (the originating AS, which has learned about this NLRI from its own IGP)
1	EGP (the AS sending the NLRI, which was first learned from an eBGP speaker)
2	INCOMPLETE (the NLRI obtained this route statically, such as from a configured static route) This code may also be used when any redistributed route from an IGP to BGP has an incomplete flag.

WELL-KNOWN DISCRETIONARY

A well-known discretionary attribute might be included in a route description but does not have to be included. These attributes are as follows:

Local Preference The *LOCAL_PREF* (Type Code 5) attribute is a well-known discretionary attribute that can contain only a single AS and can be used only with iBGP.

Atomic Aggregate The *ATOMIC_AGGREGATE* (Type Code 6) attribute is a well-known, discretionary attribute that is used to inform BGP speakers of policy routing decisions that have been made when there is more than one route, also known as *overlapping routes*. This attribute is basically used to indicate that a prefix is or is not to be used. Therefore, the ATOMIC_AGGREGATE has a path length of 0.

OPTIONAL TRANSITIVE

An optional transitive attribute may not be recognized by some implementations of BGP and is not expected to be. These attributes are used in many private BGP-enabled networks. If an implementation of BGP does not recognize the optional transitive attribute of a message, it will mark the message as a partial message but still propagate the message to its neighbors. The optional transitive attributes are as follows:

Aggregator The *AGGREGATOR* (Type Code 7) attribute is an optional transitive attribute of six octets in length: two octets identifying the ASN and four octets identifying the IP address. This attribute can be attached to a message that is performing aggregation to identify the AS and the router that performed the aggregation.

Communities   The *COMMUNITIES* (Type Code 8) attribute is an optional transitive attribute that allows a given route to belong to one or more *communities*. Communities are routes that share some common property. This attribute was included in BGP to simplify the configuration of complex BGP routing policies. For example, an academic network that handles both academic and commercial traffic under an acceptable-use policy might set a community attribute on the university updates; this community attribute value would indicate that the route meets the acceptable-use policy. More than one community can be associated with a route.

Community attributes are optional, transitive, and variable in length. Current communities are 32-bits long, structured as two 16-bit fields. By convention, the first 16 bits are either zero, denoting a "well-known" community known to the Internet, or the AS number that "owns" the community value. The second 16 bits are meaningful either as defined by the owning AS or, in the case of well-known communities, by the IETF.

OPTIONAL NON-TRANSITIVE

An optional non-transitive attribute may not be recognized by some implementations. These attributes are used in many private BGP-enabled networks. Even if the implementation of BGP does recognize the optional non-transitive attribute of the message, it is not passed on.

If the network sees the message as an optional non-transitive attribute, say good-bye to the message. The message is deleted and not sent to other networks. The following are the optional non-transitive attributes:

MED   The MULTI_EXIT_DISCRIMINATOR (Type Code 4) attribute is an optional non-transitive attribute that is used by BGP as an extensive route-selection component. This component starts to work before the general route-selection process begins, using a BGP attribute called multi-exit discriminator (MED), which was originally called the Inter-AS metric or the BGP metric. While the previous metrics inform the local AS routers which path to select when leaving the AS, MEDs inform the neighboring AS which link to use to receive traffic.

MED routes are used when two autonomous systems are connected by multiple links or multiple routers. MED values are not propagated to other autonomous systems and are considered only as part of the BGP route-selection process. The general route-installation process never sees these routes.

Originator ID and Cluster List   Both the ORIGINATOR_ID (Type Code 9) and CLUSTER_LIST (Type Code 10) optional non-transitive attributes are used to support the route-reflector feature used to scale iBGP meshes. These attributes are detailed in BGPv2 and are not covered in this book. The ORIGINATOR_ID is four octets long, and a CLUSTER_LIST attribute can vary in length in multiples of four octets.

The ORIGINATOR_ID attribute is used to identify the router that originated a particular route into an iBGP mesh. This way, if an iBGP router learns of a route again, it will know the source of the original routing information and not re-advertise this information to those peers that have already been sent the routing information.

The CLUSTER_LIST attribute is used to detect updates that are looping inside the cluster. This way, if a route has already been advertised to a cluster, the advertisement message will be rejected.

Route reflectors and iBGP meshes will be covered in detail in Chapter 9.

Multiprotocol Reachable NLRI   The *MP_REACH_NLRI* (Type Code 14) attribute is used in the Multiprotocol Extensions for BGP. This attribute identifies a newly reachable route in a particular address family other than global IP version 4. This attribute is not covered in this book.

Multiprotocol Unreachable NLRI   The *MP_UNREACH_NLRI* (Type Code 15) attribute is carried in a BGP UPDATE message for which the ORIGIN and AS_PATH attributes pertain to the native IPv4 BGP communications that carry the message. The Type Code of 15 identifies a route that has been withdrawn. This attribute is not covered in this book.

Type Code 11 (Destination Preference) is defined by MCI. Type Code 12 (Advertiser) and Type Code 13 (RCID_PATH) are both defined by Baynet. Type Code 255 is reserved for development. These type codes will not be covered in this book.

Network Layer Reachability Information

The *Network Layer Reachability Information (NLRI)* lists the prefixes that must be updated. One thing to understand is that all the prefixes listed in this field must match all the attributes listed in the Path Attributes field.

This means that more than one route can be withdrawn in the same UPDATE message, but if you want to add a route, you must do so in another UPDATE message. As opposed to the length of the overall Withdrawn Routes field, prefix lengths apply to specific routes. A length of zero here implies the default route.

Each prefix in the NLRI field contains a one-octet prefix length and a variable-length prefix, which does not necessarily contain an IP address.

NOTIFICATION Message

If an error occurs during a BGP session, a BGP NOTIFICATION message is generated. As soon as the BGP speaker sends the NOTIFICATION message, it immediately terminates its BGP connection. The administrator can use this message to help troubleshoot why the connection was terminated.

There are two types of error codes in NOTIFICATION message fields to watch for. These are the Error Code and Error Subcode, which are shown in Figure 7.10.

FIGURE 7.10 The NOTIFICATION message fields added to the BGP common header

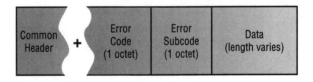

Table 7.5 lists the Error Code field's error codes.

TABLE 7.5   Error Codes

Code Number	Type
1	Indicates an error in the common header or a general message error
2	Indicates an OPEN message error
3	Indicates an UPDATE message error
4	Indicates a Hold Time Expired error
5	Indicates an illegal event for the current state
6	Used when no other error codes apply

Table 7.6 lists the Error Subcode field's error codes for general message errors.

TABLE 7.6   Error Subcodes for General Message Errors

Code Number	Type
1	Connection not synchronized or marker field incorrect
2	Bad message length
3	Bad message type

Table 7.7 lists the Error Subcode field's error codes for OPEN message errors.

TABLE 7.7 Error Subcodes for OPEN Message Errors

Code Number	Type
1	Unsupported version number
2	Bad peer AS information passed
3	Bad BGP Identifier field
4	Unsupported optional parameter
5	Authentication failure
6	Unexcepted Hold Time value

Table 7.8 lists the Error Subcode field's error codes for UPDATE message errors.

TABLE 7.8 Error Subcodes for UPDATE Message Errors

Code Number	Type
1	Error parsing the Path Attributes field
2	Unrecognized well-known path attribute
3	Missing required well-known attribute
4	Attribute flag field not understood
5	Attribute length mismatch or not understood
6	An invalid ORIGIN attribute

TABLE 7.8 Error Subcodes for UPDATE Message Errors *(continued)*

Code Number	Type
7	AS routing loop or looping prefix error
8	Invalid NEXT_HOP prefix
9	Optional attribute error
10	Invalid network field when processing a prefix update
11	Error encountered processing the AS_PATH attribute

KEEPALIVE Message

BGP neighbors use a KEEPALIVE message to confirm that the connection between the neighbors is still active. A BGP speaker sends a KEEPALIVE to each peer, usually at an interval of one-third of the agreed hold time, which is no more than once per second. If an UPDATE message is not sent during the established hold time, a KEEPALIVE message is sent in its place. A KEEPALIVE message consists only of a 19-byte header and can be turned off by setting the hold time to zero.

Summary

This chapter focused on BGP terminology and the basics components of BGP. Let's quickly review what this chapter covered:

- Autonomous systems, which are used to identify routers operating in a common network.

- Transit autonomous systems, which are between two autonomous systems.

- BGP peers, which are two routers running BGP and connecting through a TCP session to exchange messages. BGP peering is a reference to a specific relationship at the policy level, which will be covered in more detail in Chapter 8.

- The differences between Internal BGP and External BGP.

- The differences between distance-vector protocols and link-state routing protocols. Link-state routing protocols (or a hybrid of link-state routing and distance-vector) provide for greater scalability and stability.

- When to use BGP and when not to use BGP.

- Ingress filtering, which filters BGP messages and announcements based on the source address and an administrative range.

- BGP message types identified in the BGP common header, which are the OPEN, UPDATE, NOTIFICATION, and KEEPALIVE message types.

- BGP path attributes associated with the UPDATE message type.

BGP should be used only when a network meets a few specific criteria, as outlined in this chapter. In Chapter 8, we'll look at how BGP works, how the BGP metrics are used, how to change the metrics, as well as how to configure BGP.

Key Terms

Before taking the exam, make sure you're familiar with the following terms:

Active state

AGGREGATOR

ATOMIC_AGGREGATE

autonomous system

AS_PATH

COMMUNITIES

Connection state

Established state

exterior routing protocol

external Border Gateway Protocol (eBGP)

ingress filtering

Idle state

internal Border Gateway Protocol (iBGP)

keepalive

LOCAL_PREF

MP_REACH_NLRI

MP_UNREACH_NLRI

Network Layer Reachability Information (NLRI)

NEXT_HOP

OpenConfirm state

OpenSent state

ORIGIN

path-vector protocol

sneakernet

stub AS

Written Lab

1. What BGP autonomous system numbers are reserved for private use?

2. What authority allows the distribution of BGP autonomous system numbers?

3. BGP uses what TCP port number to establish a session between peers?

4. What type of attribute is required to be in every BGP UPDATE message?

5. How many entry and exit points can be found in a stub network?

6. Which type of BGP is used inside of an autonomous system?

7. What is the total range of assignable autonomous system numbers?

8. Which type of BGP is used between autonomous systems?

9. An autonomous system in the center of two other autonomous systems is referred to as what?

10. What RFC defines BGP autonomous systems?

Review Questions

1. What are the benefits of using a link-state routing protocol? (Choose all that apply.)

   A. It uses the Hello packet to establish adjacencies.

   B. It uses several components to calculate the metric of a route.

   C. Updates are sent only when changes occur in the network.

   D. It is a better protocol than distance-vector is.

2. BGP is used to advertise which of the following?

   A. Network hosts

   B. Network paths

   C. Network switches

   D. Network servers

3. Which of the following RFCs explains autonomous systems as a set of routers under one or more administrations that present a common routing policy to the Internet?

   A. RFC 1930

   B. RFC 2047

   C. RFC 2047

   D. RFC 31

4. Which of the following is not an IGP?

   A. RIPv2

   B. IGRP

   C. IPv4

   D. OSPF

5. Which of the following BGP types runs outside of an AS?

   A. oBGP

   B. iBGP

   C. eBGP

   D. xBGP

6. Interior routing protocols operate at what layer of the OSI Reference Model?

   A. Shared layer

   B. Network layer

   C. Data Link layer

   D. Physical layer

   E. Routing layer

7. When an AS must traverse another AS to get to its destination, the traversed AS is called which of the following?

   A. Complete AS

   B. Forwarding AS

   C. Transit AS

   D. Transistor AS

8. BGP uses which of the following TCP ports to open a session with another BGP peer?

   A. Port 20

   B. Port 21

   C. Port 80

   D. Port 179

9. Which of the following message types must be sent by a BGP peer during the configured hold time to keep a session from terminating? (Choose the two best answers.)

   A. Non-terminate message

   B. KEEPALIVE message

   C. UPDATE message

   D. TIMER message

10. Which of the following authorities is responsible for assigning ASNs?

   A. ANSI

   B. Internet Police

   C. IEEE

   D. IANA

11. An autonomous system number is comprised of how many bits?

   A. 8

   B. 16

   C. 32

   D. 64

12. How many entry and exit points can be found in a stub network?

   A. Five

   B. Four

   C. Two

   D. One

13. When a BGP peer tries to open a session with another endpoint, the peer is in which of the following states?

    A. Active state

    B. Connection state

    C. Open state

    D. Established state

14. Withdrawn routes are advertised in which of the following message types?

    A. OPEN

    B. UPDATE

    C. NOTIFICATION

    D. KEEPALIVE

15. Which of the following attributes must be included in a BGP UPDATE message?

    A. Well-known mandatory

    B. Well-known discretionary

    C. Optional transitive

    D. Optional non-transitive

    E. All of the above

16. Which of the following is not a well-known mandatory attribute?

    A. AS_PATH

    B. COMMUNITIES

    C. ORIGIN

    D. NEXT_HOP

17. Which of the following attributes is considered to be BGP's extensive route-selection component?

   A. ORIGINATOR_ID

   B. MULTI_EXIT_DISCRIMINATOR

   C. CLUSTER_LIST

   D. AS_PATH

18. The Network Layer Reachability Information (NLRI) field is used to identify prefixes associated with which of the following fields found in an UPDATE message?

   A. CLUSTER_LIST

   B. MED

   C. Total Path Attributes

   D. ORIGINATOR_ID

19. Which of the following fields is not found in a BGP common header?

   A. Marker

   B. Length

   C. Version

   D. Type

20. Which of the following is not a BGP message type?

   A. OPEN

   B. UPDATE

   C. NOTIFICATION

   D. KEEPALIVE

   E. WAIT

   F. All of the above.

Answers to Written Lab

1. 64,512 through 65,535

2. The Internet Assigned Numbers Authority (IANA)

3. Port 179

4. Well-known mandatory

5. One

6. iBGP (Internal BGP)

7. 1 through 65,535

8. eBGP (External BGP)

9. Transit AS

10. RFC 1930

Answers to Review Questions

1. **A, C.** Link-state routing protocols use the Hello protocol to establish adjacencies, and they send updates only when there is a change in the network topology.

2. **B.** BGP is a complex external routing protocol used to advertise and distribute available networks and paths to those networks.

3. **A.** RFC 1930 is the RFC that defines an AS.

4. **C.** An IGP is an interior routing protocol that is used to determine the network topology inside of an AS. RIP, OSPF, and IGRP are all interior routing protocols. IPv4 is a Layer 3 routed protocol, not a routing protocol.

5. **C.** Exterior BGP (eBGP) runs outside of an AS to distribute routing information and AS policies. Interior BGP (iBGP) runs inside the AS and uses its own route map separate from that used by the IGPs.

6. **B.** Interior routing protocols operate at Layer 3 of the OSI Reference Model, which is called the Network layer.

7. **C.** A transit AS is an AS through which data from one AS must travel to get to another AS.

8. **D.** Port 179 is used by BGP to establish a session with another BGP peer. Ports 20 and 21 are used by FTP, and port 23 is used by Telnet.

9. **B, C.** Either a KEEPALIVE message type or an UPDATE message must be sent in order to keep a session open during the configured hold time. The Hold Time option can be set to zero in order to disable it. If it is not disabled, then it can be set to no less than three seconds.

10. D. The Internet Assigned Numbers Authority (IANA) is responsible for delegating autonomous system numbers. Other organizations may assign numbers, but only if they are authorized by the IANA.

11. B. An autonomous systems number is 16 bits long and can range from 1 through 65,535.

12. D. In a stub network, there is one entry and exit point. In this type of network, it is recommended that you not use BGP but use a static route instead.

13. B. This peer is in the Connection state until a message is sent to identify each peer. When the connection is established, it transitions to the Open state. Once the other peer accepts the connection, the peer transitions to Established state. If the connection is lost, possibly due to a version mismatch, the peer goes to the Active state and actively tries to reestablish the connection using the proper version properties.

14. B. An UPDATE message is used to advertise topology updates and changes, including added or withdrawn routes.

15. A. A well-known mandatory attribute is known to all versions of BGP and must be included in an UPDATE message.

16. B. The COMMUNITIES attribute is an optional transitive attribute, which means that it is not required but, if included, can traverse more than one AS.

17. B. MULTI_EXIT_DISCRIMINATOR (MED) is considered to be BGP's extensive route-selection component. The ORIGINATOR_ID attribute identifies a router that first advertised a route. The CLUSTER_LIST attribute is used to detect updates that can cause data loops. The AS_PATH attribute makes BGP a path-vector protocol by logging all the autonomous systems a message has traveled through.

18. C. The NLRI field shows route prefixes with attributes identified in the Total Path Attributes field. The other answers listed are all attributes found in the Total Path Attributes field.

19. C. The Version field is not found in a BGP common header. If the common header specifies this to be a BGP OPEN message, then the Version field will be found in the message but not in the BGP common header.

20. E. There is no WAIT message type. The OPEN message type is used to establish a connection between BGP peers. The NOTIFICATION message type is used to advertise errors. The UPDATE message type is used to advertise topology updates and changes, and the KEEP-ALIVE message type is sent to keep a session active when no UPDATE messages are exchanged during the established hold time.

Configuring Basic BGP

THE CCNP ROUTING EXAM TOPICS COVERED IN THIS CHAPTER ARE AS FOLLOWS:

- ✓ Configure a basic BGP environment
- ✓ Identify how to disable BGP synchronization with an IGP
- ✓ Explain how to configure attributes
- ✓ Use show commands to verify a BGP configuration
- ✓ Identify commands used to troubleshoot BGP

In Chapter 7, "BGP's Basic Components," we talked about BGP and what it was used for, and we maintained a focus on the path attributes that are used in BGP. In this chapter, we will step into the basic configuration of BGP. I say *basic* because Chapter 9, "BGP Scalability and Advanced Features," will focus on more advanced configurations, scaling, and other important properties of BGP.

The process of configuring BGP routing is much more complex than setting up any of Cisco's supported interior routing protocols. Using BGP, we must configure both interior and exterior protocols. Obviously, this will involve additional configuration steps to establish a routing process and indicate which networks can be advertised to other networks.

Minimal Configuration

Before the configuration process for BGP can begin, we need to determine some basic information. Table 8.1 contains important BGP router checklist information. You can refer to this information whenever you need to configure BGP.

TABLE 8.1   BGP Router Checklist Information

Item	Meaning
Identifier	BGP needs a router ID. This can be the address of the loopback interface or the IP address of a directly connected interface. This ID is usually the IP address of the loopback interface, making the interface easy to identify.
BGP process number	Our assigned autonomous system number (ASN) or a private ASN.
Neighbors	We will assign those in our own AS, but the service provider should provide you the addresses and ASNs under the provider's control.
NLRI (Network Layer Reachability Information) to advertise	These are our assigned ASNs that need to be advertised over the Internet.
Filters/policy mechanisms	Our internal routing policy.
Peers	With BGP, you also need to specify the peers. Peers are not automatically discovered. This is a matter of intentional protocol design, not a limitation. Peers are other routers running BGP.

Once you have collected this information, you are ready to begin the BGP configuration process. Since BGP is very complex, it is best to learn it by starting with a very basic configuration. Our example does not have real-world applicability, but by doing it this way, we will see how to work with the basic functions of BGP.

Let's look at Figure 8.1, which shows a very simple configuration of BGP. If you can get this configuration to work, you should be able to understand how to create more complex configurations of BGP. The 69.78.0.0 network is real. I added routers to simulate the 172.16.0.0 and 130.77.0.0 networks.

FIGURE 8.1 A practice BGP topology

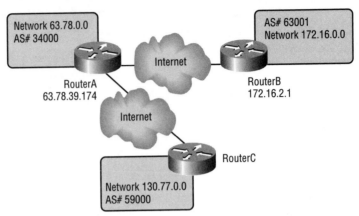

Starting the BGP process is similar to configuring an internal routing protocol. BGP is initiated on the router by using the following command and syntax:

`router bgp autonomous-system`

Let's take a look at an example of initiating BGP on RouterA based on Figure 8.1:

```
RouterA>enable
RouterB#config t
Enter configuration commands, one per line. End with CNTL/Z.

RouterA(config)#router ?
```

bgp	Border Gateway Protocol (BGP)
egp	Exterior Gateway Protocol (EGP)
eigrp	Enhanced Interior Gateway Routing Protocol (EIGRP)
igrp	Interior Gateway Routing Protocol (IGRP)
isis	ISO IS-IS
iso-igrp	IGRP for OSI networks
mobile	Mobile routes
odr	On Demand stub Routes
ospf	Open Shortest Path First (OSPF)
rip	Routing Information Protocol (RIP)

```
static              Static routes
traffic-engineering Traffic engineered routes

RouterA(config)#router bgp ?
 <1-65535>  Autonomous system number
RouterA(config)#router bgp 34000
RouterA(config-router)#
```

So far, we have configured the router with the autonomous system number (ASN) to which it belongs. Next, we must add network statements to identify the networks that the router must propagate information to in order for another AS to learn about ours. We are using network statements to avoid redistribution from an IGP into BGP, which is not recommended. The network statement establishes those address ranges to be advertised, such as those learned by the IGPs running in the network. It will not actually advertise anything until peering is established or the route to be advertised is reachable by the advertising router, meaning that a route makes its way into the routing table.

When taking the exam, you may need to know what a peer group is. A *peer group* is a way of defining a template containing parameters that more than one peer will use. This becomes useful when many different neighbors use identical outbound routing policies, which will be discussed in Chapter 9. The parameters set by a peer group affect only the outbound parameters, and the inbound parameters can be configured differently. This can simplify the configuration, as updates need to occur only once. BGP peer configurations will not be discussed in this course.

The next step is to identify peers. In BGP, as opposed to IGPs, with the exception of certain OSPF configurations, you must explicitly specify the IP addresses of the routers with which you want to exchange information. Internal peers will have the same ASN used in the source router's router bgp command. External peers are those with a different AS from the AS defined on the source router. Let's look at the command and the syntaxes:

neighbor *address* remote-as *autonomous-system-number*

The *address* is the IP address of the neighboring (peer) router. It can be the loopback address or the directly connected IP address. The *autonomous-system-number* is the peer's ASN. An iBGP peer will have the same ASN as the source router. An eBGP peer will have a different ASN than the source router.

Now let's look at an example based on Figure 8.1. We'll add RouterB, which is at 172.16.2.1, and identify the network in which to advertise to our neighbor:

```
RouterB (config-router)#neighbor 172.16.2.1
    remote-as 63001
```

The loopback IP address can be used for both iBGP and eBGP peers. Additional commands must be used when creating a peering session with a loopback interface. For iBGP sessions, the only additional command is the update-source command. The available syntaxes are as follows:

```
neighbor [address | peer-group-name] update-source
interface-type interface-number
```

The IP address of the loopback should be used for the peer address. Since the loopback interface is being used as the source of the BGP session, the interface-type should be entered as the loopback. The interface-number is the number of the loopback interface that is being used for BGP peering. This is configured on the router using the loopback address.

The following command adds networks and creates a route in the BGP table if the route is present in the IP table:

```
network network-number
```

Let's look at an example adding our own network 63.78.0.0:

```
RouterA(config-router)#network 63.78.0.0 ?
  backdoor    Specify a BGP backdoor route
  mask        Network mask
  route-map   Route-map to modify the attributes
  weight      Set BGP weight for network
  <cr>

RouterA(config-router)#network 63.78.0.0 mask
↳255.255.255.0 ?
  backdoor    Specify a BGP backdoor route
  route-map   Route-map to modify the attributes
  weight      Set BGP weight for network
  <cr>

RouterA(config-router)#network 63.78.0.0 mask 255.255.0.0
RouterA(config-router)#
```

Again, *network-number* represents the network that is to be advertised using the BGP process. The IP network specified in the BGP network statement does not have to be directly connected to the router. Network statements within the BGP protocol session allow BGP to advertise routes learned by an IGP that are contained in the route table. The network mask is applied because BGPv4 can support subnetting and supernetting. When a logical BGP mesh is in place, each IGP session should have network statements configured for only those routes learned from the IGP. Network statements should not be duplicated among internal BGP routers.

 BGP configuration can be very complicated. Several different options may be configured to optimize BGP routing. When only one link is used to peer with another AS or ISP, the configuration can be straightforward. As more links are used, or multiple ISPs or autonomous systems are connected to a router, the configuration becomes increasingly complex.

Verifying BGP Configurations

After BGP is configured, several commands will allow us to verify the BGP configuration and troubleshoot the operation of BGP. We can also use these commands to monitor the BGP process and its operations.

Table 8.2 summarizes all of the commands that can be used to verify BGP.

TABLE 8.2   BGP Monitoring Command Summary

Command	Description
show ip bgp	Shows all BGP configuration information for the selected interface.
show ip bgp neighbors	Shows all configured BGP neighbors. It provides detailed statistics and information about each neighbor.
show ip bgp community	Displays routes belonging to the specified community.

TABLE 8.2 BGP Monitoring Command Summary *(continued)*

Command	Description
show ip bgp cidr-only	Displays classless routes.
show ip bgp filter-list	Displays AS path lists.
show ip bgp paths	Displays all path information for the local router.
show ip bgp peer-group	Provides information on the members of the specified peer group.
show ip bgp summary	Shows the status of all BGP connections.

The detailed use of some of these commands will be explained in the section "Troubleshooting BGP."

In earlier versions of the Cisco IOS, in particular versions 11.1 and 11.3, some of the show commands listed above can cause the router to reload. Cisco became aware of the problem and has resolved it in later versions.

Cisco has a configurable proprietary attribute that allows us to use weights as a metric in deciding the best route. Let's take a look at this attribute in the next section. We'll also see how to configure the MED attribute discussed in Chapter 7.

Configuring BGP Route-Selection Attributes

BGP uses several metrics as criteria when selecting the best possible route to a destination. Each metric can be configured manually. Other criteria that influence BGP route selection may also be configured.

To quickly understand how BGP selects a route, review Figure 8.2. This figure summarizes the steps that the BGP process takes to choose the best route. Ten different criteria are used in path selection, several of which are configurable.

FIGURE 8.2 BGP path-selection diagram

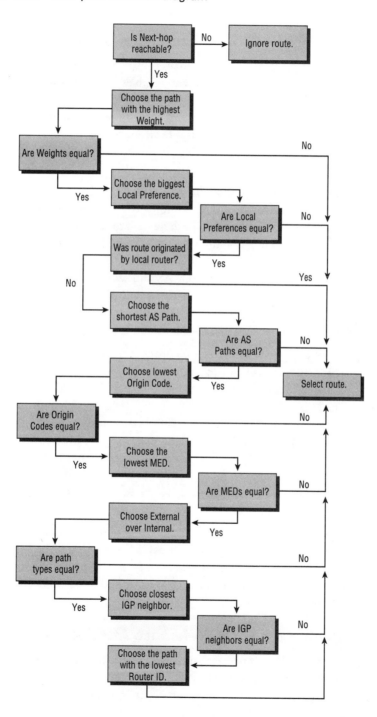

Now let's discuss some of these criteria separately. We will also learn how to configure them.

Configuring the Atomic Aggregate Attribute

When using classless interdomain routing (CIDR), you can create aggregate routes to minimize the size of routing tables. You can configure aggregate routes in BGP by redistributing an aggregate route into BGP. The Atomic Aggregate attribute can be configured using the `aggregate-address` command. This command allows you to configure an aggregate or summary entry in the BGP table. The command has several syntaxes. Let's look at the command and the possible syntaxes:

`aggregate-address ip-address mask [summary-only] [as-set]`

The *ip-address* and *mask* indicate the aggregate address to be created. By default, BGP advertises both aggregate routes and more specific routes. By using the `summary-only` syntax, the BGP router will advertise only the aggregate route. If you use the `as-set` syntax, the BGP router will advertise the route as coming from your AS and will set the Atomic Aggregate attribute to show that information regarding the route may be missing.

Configuring the Weight Attribute

The Weight attribute is a Cisco proprietary attribute used for path selection. This attribute, which is also considered a metric, allows a system administrator to manually assign a value to all paths learned from other BGP peers. The larger the weight value, the more desirable the path.

This metric is particularly helpful when a router is connected to multiple autonomous systems. The weight assigned stays local to the router on which it is configured. When paths are learned from multiple sources, the Weight metric can be used to force BGP to select a specified interface over the others.

This metric is configured using the following command from within the BGP routing session:

`neighbor [ip-address | peer-group-name] weight weight`

The *ip-address* is the IP address of the neighbor. The *peer-group-name* may be used when assigning weight to all routes learned via the BGP peer group. The *weight* value has a range from 0 to 65,535. The default value is 32,768.

Configuring the Local Preference Attribute

The Local Preference attribute is used to assign metric values that are used among IBGP peers. We learned that the Weight metric remains local to a router. The Local Preference attribute is useful when multiple iBGP peers have their own eBGP peers.

When a path is learned via two different border routers, both paths are advertised to other iBGP peers. Either path is valid and can be used. However, if one path is to be used only as a backup route, you can set local preference values on both routers.

The Local Preference attribute is configured by using the following command:

```
bgp default local-preference value
```

The command must be issued within the BGP session Configuration mode. The configured values for the Local Preference range from 0 to 4,294,967,295. Higher values are preferred over lower values.

Configuring in an NBMA Network

When you have a non-broadcast multi-access (NBMA) network in which the router you are configuring needs to advertise itself as the next hop to a destination, use the `next-hop-self` syntax for the `neighbor` command. This allows the normal BGP process to override what it's learned and forces updates to advertise this router as the next hop, even if there is another way to the destination. The command is as follows:

```
neighbor ip address | peer-group-name next-hop-self
```

Configuring MED

While the previous metrics inform local AS routers which path to select when leaving the AS, Multi-Exit Discriminators (MEDs) inform the neighboring AS which link to use to receive traffic.

MEDs are used when two autonomous systems are connected via multiple links or multiple routers. MED values are not propagated to other autonomous systems.

Configuring MEDs is more complicated than configuring Weight or Local Preference values. Because of the complexity of the configuration, more CPU resources are needed. MEDs are set using route maps. Route maps are a form of access list. Here is an example of a BGP configuration using MEDs:

```
Router1#conf t
Enter configuration commands, one per line. End with CNTL/Z.
Router1(config)#router bgp 63001
Router1(config-router)#neighbor 172.16.2.1 route-map
⮡ANEXAMPLE out
Router1(config-router)#exit
```

```
Router1(config)#route-map ANEXAMPLE permit 10
Router1(config-rou)#match ip address 1
Router1(config-rou)#set metric 25
Router1(config-rou)#exit
Router1(config)#route-map ANEXAMPLE permit 20
Router1(config-rou)#exit
Router1(config)#access-list 1 permit 172.16.0.0
↳0.0.255.255
Router1(config)#^Z
Router1#
```

```
router bgp 63001
 network 172.16.0.0
 neighbor 172.16.1.1 remote-as 59000
 neighbor 172.16.2.1 route-map ANEXAMPLE out
!
ip classless
access-list 1 permit 172.16.0.0 0.0.255.255
route-map ANEXAMPLE permit 10
 match ip address 1
 set metric 25
!
route-map ANEXAMPLE permit 20
 !
```

This configuration sets a MED of 25 for all networks belonging to 172.16.0.0. ASN 59000 will use this value. Lower MED values are preferred. The second `permit` statement of the `route-map ANEXAMPLE` permits all other networks to be advertised but does not assign a MED value. We'll discuss route maps in more detail in Chapter 9.

Clearing BGP Routes

The BGP configurations can easily be removed from the router using the `clear ip bgp` command. Let's look at the command and the available syntaxes that are used in Privileged EXEC mode, and then we'll explain each syntax:

```
clear ip bgp *|address [soft[in|out]
```

Using the * means that you wish to clear the entire BGP routing table. You can use the soft syntax so that the router advertises all its routing updates again and the configuration is not cleared. Using the address syntax instead of the asterisk, only the network address identified is removed from the BGP table. The in and out syntaxes are used with the soft syntax to identify that the triggered updates are to occur either on triggered inbound updates or outbound updates.

Disabling BGP Synchronization

If all of the routers in your AS are running BGP, then there is no need to have synchronization turned on between BGP and your IGPs that are running. When BGP Synchronization is turned on, the router will wait to learn about internal routes from an IGP instead of advertising routes learned by BGP. With BGP Synchronization turned off, you can carry fewer IGP learned routes in the topology table and BGP can converge much more quickly. To turn off BGP Synchronization, use the following command in BGP Configuration mode:

```
Router1(config-router)# no synchronization
```

Troubleshooting BGP

The most important part of troubleshooting is verifying the status of the peering router. When you issue the show ip bgp neighbors command, the basic troubleshooting information is displayed on the screen. Let's first take a look at the command syntaxes and then view a problem configuration where the BGP peers have not synchronized.

```
2514#show ip bgp ?
  A.B.C.D          IP prefix <network>/<length>, e.g.,
                   35.0.0.0/8
  A.B.C.D          Network in the BGP routing table to
                   ⮡display
  cidr-only        Display only routes with non-natural
                   ⮡netmasks
  community        Display routes matching the communities
  community-list   Display routes matching the community-
                   ⮡list
  dampened-paths   Display paths suppressed due to
                   ⮡dampening
```

filter-list	Display routes conforming to the ↳filter-list
flap-statistics	Display flap statistics of routes
inconsistent-as	Display only routes with inconsistent ↳origin ASes
neighbors	Detailed information on TCP and BGP ↳neighbor connections
paths	Path information
peer-group	Display information on peer-groups
regexp	Display routes matching the AS path ↳regular expression
summary	Summary of BGP neighbor status
<cr>	

Notice in the output below that no connections are established, as indicated by the bottom line. This means that the peer has not synchronized. If the number of connections established keeps incrementing, there could be a problem with the link between the two neighbors. This output is from IOS version 12.0(5):

```
2514#show ip bgp neighbors
BGP neighbor is 172.16.2.1, remote AS 63001, external link
 Index 1, Offset 0, Mask 0x2
  BGP version 4, remote router ID 0.0.0.0
  BGP state = Idle, table version = 0
  Last read 00:00:07, hold time is 180, keepalive interval
  ↳is 60 seconds
  Minimum time between advertisement runs is 30 seconds
  Received 0 messages, 0 notifications, 0 in queue
  Sent 0 messages, 0 notifications, 0 in queue
  Prefix advertised 0, suppressed 0, withdrawn 0
  Connections established 0; dropped 0
  Last reset never
  0 accepted prefixes consume 0 bytes
  0 history paths consume 0 bytes
  External BGP neighbor not directly connected.
  No active TCP connection
2514#
```

Now let's look at the same router with the connection established:

2514#**show ip bgp neighbors**

BGP neighbor is 172.16.2.1, remote AS 63001, external
↳link

  Index 1, Offset 0, Mask 0x2

    BGP version 4, remote router ID 172.16.2.1

    BGP state = Idle, table version = 0

    Last read 00:00:07, hold time is 180, keepalive interval
↳is 60 seconds

    Minimum time between advertisement runs is 30 seconds

    Received 4582 messages, 0 notifications, 0 in queue

    Sent 3552 messages, 0 notifications, 0 in queue

    Prefix advertised 0, suppressed 0, withdrawn 0

    Connections established 1; dropped 0

    Last reset never

    0 accepted prefixes consume 0 bytes

    0 history paths consume 0 bytes

    External BGP neighbor not directly connected.

    2514#

On an older IOS, the output will look similar to this output from version 11.1:

Router#**show ip bgp neighbors**

 BGP neighbor is 172.16.2.1, remote AS 63001, external link

  Index 1, Offset 0, Mask 0x2

    BGP version 4, remote router ID 172.16.2.1

    BGP state = Established, table version = 508, up for
↳3d20h

    Last read 00:00:45, hold time is 180, keepalive interval
↳is 60 seconds

    Minimum time between advertisement runs is 30 seconds

    Received 5579 messages, 0 notifications, 0 in queue

    Sent 5703 messages, 0 notifications, 0 in queue

    Inbound path policy configured

    Outbound path policy configured

    Incoming update AS path filter list is 10

    Outgoing update AS path filter list is 1

```
   Connections established 1; dropped 0
   Last reset never
   No. of prefix received 10
Connection state is ESTAB, I/O status: 1, unread input
↳bytes: 0
Local host: 172.16.65.1, Local port: 179
Foreign host: 172.16.65.10, Foreign port: 29768

Enqueued packets for retransmit: 0, input: 0  mis-ordered:
↳0 (0 bytes)

Event Timers (current time is 0x14322791):
Timer          Starts     Wakeups          Next
Retrans          5677          1           0x0
TimeWait            0          0           0x0
AckHold          5578       4246           0x0
SendWnd             0          0           0x0
KeepAlive           0          0           0x0
GiveUp              0          0           0x0
PmtuAger            0          0           0x0
DeadWait            0          0           0x0

iss: 1337567913  snduna: 1337679159  sndnxt: 1337679159
↳sndwnd:   15066
irs: 4270375806  rcvnxt: 4270482004  rcvwnd:       15548
↳delrcvwnd:     836

SRTT: 309 ms, RTTO: 708 ms, RTV: 45 ms, KRTT: 0 ms
minRTT: 4 ms, maxRTT: 453 ms, ACK hold: 300 ms
Flags: passive open, nagle, gen tcbs

Datagrams (max data segment is 1460 bytes):
Rcvd: 11252 (out of order: 0), with data: 5579, total data
↳bytes: 106216
Sent: 9996 (retransmit: 1), with data: 5675, total data
↳bytes: 111245
Router#
```

A great deal of information is provided by the `show ip bgp neighbor` command. When a peering relationship has trouble getting established, use this command to see if the TCP connection has failed. This will give you a starting point for troubleshooting.

When the problem seems to be route information-oriented, you can use the following command:

`show ip bgp regexp` *regular-expression*

Use this command to see which routes are being learned from the neighboring AS. If the neighboring AS is not receiving given routes from your AS, you can use the following command to see what you are advertising to the AS:

`show ip bgp neighbor` *address* `advertised-routes`

A quick `summary` command can be used to verify connectivity via BGP:

`show ip bgp summary`

These are just a few of the commands that you can use when troubleshooting BGP. Many other commands and procedures can be used to accomplish this task, but they are beyond the scope of this book.

Using Debug with BGP

The `debug ip bgp` command can be used to display events as they occur. The only drawback to this command is that not only does the BGP process being used to advertise ASNs across the Internet use considerable processing power, but the `debug` command is assigned a high priority on the router and can kill your processing power. To stop all debugging on a router, use the `undebug all` command or the `no debug all` command. Let's look at a short summary of the `debug` commands in Table 8.3.

TABLE 8.3 The Debug Commands Related to BGP

Command	Description
debug ip bgp dampening	Displays BGP dampening events as they occur.
debug ip bgp events	Displays all BGP events as they occur.
debug ip bgp keepalives	Displays all events related to BGP keepalive packets.
debug ip bgp updates	Displays information on all BGP update packets.

Summary

In Chapter 7 we looked at how BGP is used, when to use BGP, when not to use BGP, and the type of protocol BGP is, and we focused on the attributes sent in BGP update messages. In this chapter, we looked at how to enable BGP, identify the network number the router belongs to so it can be advertised to its neighbors, identify the BGP neighbors, and assign the Weight attribute.

In addition, we covered how to configure several other attributes, such as the Next-hop, MED, Atomic Aggregate, and Local Preference attributes. Then we covered the show commands that can be used to verify the configuration and troubleshoot problems that might arise in the configuration of BGP.

As you may have noticed while looking at some of the output that appeared throughout the chapter, BGP has many command syntaxes that make configuring BGP very complex—much more complex than we will cover in the following Hands-on Lab section below. In Chapter 9, we will cover many more aspects of BGP, including the addition of filters and policies, route flapping, and using BGP in large-scale networks.

Key Terms

Before taking the exam, make sure you are familiar with the following term:

peer group

Commands Used in This Chapter

aggregate-address	Allows you to configure aggregate routes in BGP and CIDR addressing.
bgp default local-preference	Allows you to assign a Local Preference attribute value in the range of 0 to 4,294,967,295. Higher values are preferred over lower values.
clear ip bgp	Allows you to clear all or an identified set of routes from the BGP table.

`debug ip bgp dampening`	Displays BGP dampening events as they occur.
`debug ip bgp events`	Displays all BGP events as they occur.
`debug ip bgp keepalives`	Displays all events related to BGP keepalive packets.
`debug ip bgp updates`	Displays information on all BGP update packets.
`neighbors`	This command has many syntaxes that allow you to identify the internal and external neighbors and assign different metrics to each.
`network`	Identifies the networks and masks associated with the local router.
`no synchronization`	Allows you to turn off synchronization between the IGPs and BGP for faster convergence.
`router bgp`	Begins the BGP process and identifies the local ASN.
`show ip bgp community`	Used to display routes belonging to the specified community.
`show ip bgp cidr-only`	Displays classless routes.
`show ip bgp filter-list`	Displays AS path lists.
`show ip bgp paths`	Displays all path information for the local router.
`show ip bgp peer-group`	Provides information on the members of the specified peer group.
`Show ip bgp summary`	Shows the status of all BGP connections.

Written Lab

1. What command in BGP Configuration mode allows you to identify a BGP peer with the IP address 172.16.1.1 in the 55009 AS?

2. What command would you use to clear the entire BGP routing table on a router?

3. What command allows you to display all of the BGP events as they occur?

4. What command would you use to identify a CIDR aggregate address?

5. What command displays all the BGP path information learned by the router?

6. What command shows all the BGP peers?

7. If your AS resides in the network 63.78.0.0 and you use a 24-bit subnet mask, how do you identify this in the BGP configuration?

8. What command allows you to view all events related to BGP updates?

9. What command can be used to view routes belonging to a specific community?

10. What command can be used to view the status of all connections?

Hands-on Lab

In this lab, we will demonstrate a very simple configuration of BGP over three routers in two autonomous systems using information found in the graphic below:

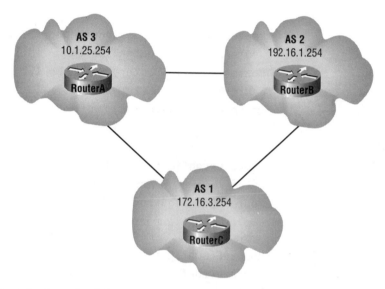

Let's look at the following objectives:

- On each router, enable BGP with its autonomous system number.
- Identify the network each resides in.
- Identify both of each router's neighbors and the AS they reside in.
- Assign the Weight attribute to each neighbor, giving any router in AS 2 a Weight of 10 and the rest a Weight of 1.

Let's now look at an example of the configuration of all three routers, which are identified by the hostname on each router.

```
RouterA#conf terminal
Enter configuration commands, one per line. End with CNTL/Z.
RouterA(config)#router bgp 3
RouterA(config-router)#network 10.0.0.0 mask 255.255.255.0
RouterA(config-router)#neighbor 192.16.1.254 remote-as 2
RouterA(config-router)#neighbor 172.16.3.254 remote-as 1
RouterA(config-router)#neighbor 192.16.1.254 weight 10
```

```
RouterA(config-router)#neighbor 172.16.3.254 weight 1

RouterB#config terminal
Enter configuration commands, one per line. End with CNTL/Z.
RouterB(config)#router bgp 2
RouterB(config-router)#network 192.16.1.0 mask
↳255.255.255.0
RouterB(config-router)#neighbor 172.16.3.254 remote-as 1
RouterB(config-router)#neighbor 10.1.25.254 remote-as 3
RouterB(config-router)#neighbor 172.16.3.254 weight 1
RouterB(config-router)#neighbor 10.1.25.254 weight 1
RouterB(config-router)#


RouterC#config terminal
Enter configuration commands, one per line. End with CNTL/Z.
RouterC(config)#router bgp 1
RouterC(config-router)#network 172.16.0.0 mask
↳255.255.255.0
RouterC(config-router)#neighbor 10.1.25.254 remote-as 3
RouterC(config-router)#neighbor 192.16.1.254 remote-as 2
RouterC(config-router)#neighbor 192.16.1.254 weight 10
RouterC(config-router)#neighbor 10.1.25.254 weight 1
```

Review Questions

1. Which of the following are needed when configuring BGP?

    A. Router ID

    B. BGP process number

    C. External neighbors

    D. Internal peers

    E. All of the above

2. Which command shows the BGP routes?

    A. `show ip bgp routes`

    B. `show ip bgp all`

    C. `show ip route bgp`

    D. `show ip bgp paths`

3. Which of the following is an example of properly enabling BGP on a router and identifying an internal network?

    A. `router ip bgp 10`
        `network 10.1.1.1 100`

    B. `router bgp 10`
        `network 10.1.1.1 remote-as 10`

    C. `router bgp 100`
        `neighbor 10.1.1.1 remote-as 100`

    D. `router bgp 100`
        `neighbor 10.1.1.1 remote-as 200`

4. Which of the following is an example of how to configure BGP with an external BGP neighbor?

A. `router ip bgp 10`
   `network 10.1.1.1 100`

B. `router bgp 10`
   `network 10.1.1.1 remote-as 10`

C. `router bgp 100`
   `neighbor 10.1.1.1 remote-as 100`

D. `router bgp 100`
   `neighbor 10.1.1.1 remote-as 200`

5. Which of the following are valid BGP `show` commands?

A. `show ip bgp`

B. `show ip bgp paths`

C. `show ip bgp summary`

D. `show bgp all`

E. `show bgp ip debug`

6. In the command `neighbor 172.16.2.2 remote-as 500`, what is the function of the `remote-as` syntax?

A. The syntax identifies the AS of the remote router that the local router will initiate a session with.

B. It identifies the local remote ASN.

C. It tells the local router to find the remote autonomous system.

D. It allows BGP to bypass the TCP connection process because you have identified the ASN.

7. Which of the following commands creates a route in the BGP table and identifies the networks that are part of the internal AS?

A. `aggregate-paths`

B. `show ip bgp`

C. `neighbors summary-only`

D. `network`

8. Which of the following identifies the function of the `clear ip bgp *` command?

    A. It clears an identified entry in the BGP routing.

    B. It clears all entries in the BGP table.

    C. It clears all entries in the IGP's topology table.

    D. It resets IP sessions.

9. Which of the following BGP attributes informs neighboring AS routers as to which link to use to receive traffic?

    A. Atomic Aggregate

    B. Next-hop

    C. MED

    D. Weight

10. In the following list of attributes, which of the following is a Cisco proprietary attribute?

    A. Weight attribute

    B. Next-hop attribute

    C. MED attribute

    D. Atomic Aggregate attribute

11. Which of the following commands displays the status of all BGP connections?

    A. `show ip bgp`

    B. `show ip bgp status`

    C. `show ip bgp all`

    D. `show ip bgp summary`

12. Using the `clear ip bgp` command, which syntax is used to identify that the command is to affect inbound or outbound triggered updates?

    A. inbound

    B. soft

    C. triggered

    D. outbound

13. When using `debug` commands with BGP, which of the following displays all the BGP events as they occur?

    A. debug ip bgp dampening

    B. debug ip bgp summary

    C. debug ip bgp events

    D. debug ip bgp all

14. The Weight attribute can be set to a value in which of the following ranges?

    A. 1 through 65,535

    B. 1 through 32,768

    C. 1 through 512

    D. 0 through 65,535

15. Using the BGP `aggregate-address` command, which of the following syntaxes can be used to advertise routes as coming from your AS?

    A. as-local

    B. as-set

    C. as-summary

    D. as-well-known

16. Which of the following commands would be used to troubleshoot a problem with an external AS not receiving updates from your AS? (Choose all that apply.)

    A. `show ip bgp events`

    B. `show ip bgp neighbors`

    C. `show ip bgp all`

    D. `show ip bgp`

17. To disable synchronization when all of the routers in an AS are running BGP, which of the commands would be used?

    A. `disable synchronization`

    B. `no ip bgp synchronization`

    C. `synchronization disable`

    D. `no synchronization`

18. Which of the following attributes can be used to help identify the correct networks for CIDR implementations?

    A. Atomic Aggregate

    B. Next-hop

    C. MED

    D. Weight

    E. Local Preference

19. When using the `neighbor` command with the `weight` syntax, in which range of values can the `weight` syntax be set?

    A. No limit

    B. 1 to 255

    C. 0 to 65,535

    D. 1 to 1000

20. Which of the following commands will begin a BGP process on a router and place you in BGP Configuration mode?

A. router enable bgp

B. router ip bgp 45323

C. router bgp 32455

D. router enable bgp 34657

Answers to Written Lab

1. neighbor 172.16.1.1, remote-as 55009

2. clear ip bgp *

3. debug ip bgp events

4. aggregate-address ip-address mask [summary-only] [as-set]

5. show ip bgp paths

6. show ip bgp neighbors

7. (config-router)#network 63.78.0.0 mask 255.255.255.0

8. debug ip bgp updates

9. show ip bgp community

10. show ip bgp summary

Answers to Review Questions

1. E. The Router ID, BGP process number, external neighbors, and internal peers are all needed to configure BGP.

2. A. The `show ip bgp routes` command is used to view all the learned BGP routes.

3. D. The only valid command statements shown above for configuring BGP are `router bgp 100` and `neighbor 10.1.1.1 remote-as 200`.

4. D. The only commands that are shown above that are valid to enable BGP and identify an external BGP neighbor are `router bgp 100` and `neighbor 10.1.1.1 remote-as 200`.

5. A, B, C. The valid BGP `show` commands listed above are `show ip bgp`, `show ip bgp paths`, and `show ip bgp summary`. The `show ip bgp` command displays the BGP routing table. The `show ip bgp paths` command displays all the router's known BGP paths. The `show ip bgp summary` command tells you the status on every BGP connection. The other two commands are not valid.

6. A. The `remote-as` syntax identifies the peer router that the local router will enable a session with. The IP address identifies the interface attached to the peer router. If the ASN is the same number as the internal ASN, it identifies an internal AS; if it is different, it identifies an external AS.

7. D. The `network` command creates a route in the BGP table if the route is present in the IP table.

8. B. The `clear ip bgp *` command is used to clear all the entries in the BGP table.

9. C. The MED attribute is used to inform other external AS routers as to which route to use in order to receive traffic.

10. A. The Weight attribute is a Cisco proprietary BGP attribute used as a metric to find the best routes through the networks.

11. B. The show ip bgp status command displays the status of all BGP connections. The show ip bgp summary command displays the BGP configuration. The other two commands are not valid.

12. B. Using the soft syntax followed by the in and out syntaxes, you can identify whether the clear ip bgp command is to affect inbound or outbound triggered updates.

13. C. The debug ip bgp events command is used to display all BGP events as they occur. The only other valid command listed is debug ip bgp dampening.

14. D. The Weight attribute can be set between 0 and 65,535 using the neighbors command. The default value is 32,768.

15. B. If you use the as-set syntax, the BGP router will advertise the route as coming from your AS. This syntax will also set the Atomic Aggregate attribute to show that information regarding the route may be missing.

16. B, D. The show ip bgp neighbors and the show ip bgp commands are both troubleshooting commands that would be used to solve this problem. The show ip bgp neighbors command displays all the advertised routes, and the show ip bgp command looks at all the connections.

17. D. The no synchronization command disables synchronization, allowing much faster convergence.

18. A. The Atomic Aggregate attribute is used to help identify the correct networks for networks that implement CIDR.

19. C. The weight value can be set to a range from 0 to 65,535. The default value is 32,768.

20. C. The router bgp 32455 command is the only valid command listed to place the router in BGP Configuration mode, which is identified by the (config-router) prompt.

Chapter

9

BGP Scalability and Advanced Features

THE CCNP ROUTING EXAM TOPICS COVERED IN THIS CHAPTER ARE AS FOLLOWS:

- ✓ Understanding BGP management problems
- ✓ Configuring BGP route reflectors
- ✓ Configuring BGP confederations
- ✓ Configuring AS_PATH attribute filters
- ✓ Understanding BGP policies
- ✓ Understanding prefix lists and distribute lists
- ✓ Understanding BGP communities and peer groups
- ✓ Configuring prefix lists
- ✓ Configuring distribute lists
- ✓ Configuring BGP communities
- ✓ Configuring BGP peer groups
- ✓ Understanding multi-homing classifications
- ✓ Configuring default routes for more than one ISP
- ✓ Understanding and configuring route maps

Large BGP networks have several methods for managing large BGP networks, such as using filters, configuring private AS numbers (ASNs), creating peer groups, creating confederations, and using route reflectors. All of these methods are quite complex. In this chapter, we will learn more about all of these problems.

When a router reaches more than 100 BGP sessions running concurrently, most network administrators fluent in BGP recommend that you configure route reflectors. When route reflectors are used, a router needs to become a peer only with a route reflector instead of with each individual router. The route reflector's responsibility is to maintain a routing table for all internal peers connected to the reflector. The route reflector can collect the same number of routes that a router can learn from a full mesh.

You can use confederations to control the size of interior BGP meshes and allow an AS to be broken up. Several sub-AS numbers can be configured inside of a real AS. Sub-ASes must use the private reserved ASNs. All of the routers within a sub-AS must be fully meshed, and one of the routers in a sub-AS creates a peer with one of the routers from the other sub-AS. This enables the overhead on each router to be reduced and a complete BGP table to be shared to the entire AS.

Before we look at the more advanced features just described, let's first take a look at different methods of applying policies to the routes advertised by BGP, such as using distribute lists, route maps, and prefix lists.

Filters

When configuring BGP, the AS path length is considered in selecting a route. With the use of route maps, the AS path may be lengthened by adding false AS numbers. This is called *AS path pre-pending*. It is another way to influence route selection.

In addition to manipulating route selection, BGP has features that allow network advertisements to be aggregated before they are advertised to neighboring autonomous systems. There are many reasons to influence the routes that are advertised. You will mainly want to control the route-selection process to stop unnecessary advertisements in order to eliminate router confusion and the high CPU utilization that can occur when routes flap. A *route flap* is defined as a change in the state of the route. Once a route is established and then removed from the BGP table, one flap has occurred. You can prevent routing problems by using the bgp dampening command. The bgp dampening command maintains a threshold for route flaps. This means that when the threshold is exceeded, the route is put into a hold-down. Hold-downs implement a timing mechanism, and during the hold-down time, BGP uses internal processes to monitor the route's status to see if the route comes back up. If the route stops flapping for a given period of time, the route is allowed back into the BGP table and can be advertised.

One of the most important items to define is the type of AS you are administering. When multiple autonomous systems interconnect, one or all of the ASes can become a transit AS, which we discussed in Chapter 7, "BGP's Basic Components." Depending on your network policy, this can be a good thing or a bad thing.

One of the biggest problems occurs when you connect to another ISP and the ISP uses your circuits, equipment, and bandwidth to connect to a neighboring AS instead of using their own resources. You can eliminate this situation by using AS path filters. Using regular expressions, you can compare AS path information and then either permit or deny it. Let's look at a sample configuration detailing how to implement AS filters:

```
router bgp 200
 no synchronization
 bgp dampening
 neighbor 172.16.65.10 remote-as 100
 neighbor 172.16.65.10 filter-list 10 in
```

```
neighbor 172.16.65.10 filter-list 1 out
neighbor 172.16.65.11 remote-as 300
neighbor 172.16.65.11 filter-list 11 in
neighbor 172.16.65.11 filter-list 1 out
!
!
ip as-path access-list 1 permit ^200$
ip as-path access-list 10 permit ^100$
ip as-path access-list 11 permit ^300$
!
!
```

To implement filters, use the `neighbor` command. Using the AS path syntax, you can configure filters to block routes that contain the AS path information that does not match the regular expression. The output above shows access list 1 allowing only routes that originate from AS 200 to be sent to the respective neighbors. Access lists 10 and 11 above allow only routes that do not originate within AS 100 and AS 300 to be sent.

Creating BGP Policies

We use policies with BGP to tell other BGP neighbors the paths through our own network. By not advertising certain routes through our network, we keep other networks from learning about them; it is difficult to route a packet through a network you don't know about. We can modify routes that we wish to advertise using both *prefix lists* and *distribute lists*. Distribute lists use access lists to control the routes advertised by a routing protocol. A prefix list is similar to an access list but is more flexible and less complicated to configure than an access list.

Distribute Lists

Distribute lists are standard or extended access lists applied to a router's BGP session to permit or deny advertised routes through the network. Distribute lists can be applied to filter BGP advertisements either coming in or going out of the router. Let's look at an example of an access list that allows routes from network 172.16.0.0.

```
RouterA(config)#access-list 105 permit ip 172.16.0.0
↳0.0.255.255 host 255.255.0.0
```

There is always an implicit deny all at the end of the access list that can't be seen. We're permitting only network 172.16.0.0 in this access list. However, although the access list has been created, we need to filter all of the BGP traffic coming in. Let's take a look at how to do this:

```
RouterA(config)#router bgp 31400

RouterA(config-router)#neighbor 172.16.11.254 remote-as
↳31400

RouterA(config-router)#neighbor 172.16.12.254 remote-as
↳31400

RouterA(config-router)#neighbor 172.16.11.254 distribute-
↳list 105 in
```

Prefix Lists

Prefix lists are actually new and have been added to version 12.0 and later of the Cisco IOS. You can use a prefix list as an alternative to the access lists used in many of the BGP route-filtering commands. There are many advantages to using prefix lists. Prefix lists don't tax the processor as much as access lists, which can improve the router's performance.

With a prefix list, you need to make configuration modifications to each router, but you can do this incrementally just as you can with route reflectors. This means that you can implement prefix lists on just a few routers in your network at a time instead of all at once.

The biggest advantage of prefix lists over distribute lists is that prefix lists have much greater flexibility and are considerably easier to configure. If you make a mistake with an access list, you must start over because access lists are read in the order you type them in, making them hard to modify. Prefix lists allow you to add and delete lines without starting over.

Prefix lists use the same line-by-line read rule as access lists, which says that as soon as I have a match in my list to the data I receive, I start processing. You need to also remember that, just as in access lists, the same implicit deny all still exists at the bottom of the list for the data that does not have a match in our prefix list. However, if there are no lines in our prefix list, instead of an implicit deny all, there is an implicit permit any.

The rule to remember when using prefix lists is that if a prefix is permitted, the route is advertised; if a prefix is denied, the route is not advertised.

One improvement from access lists is the use of sequence numbers for each statement in the prefix list. The statement with the smallest sequence numbers is read first. This also allows us to modify a sequence statement without starting over when there is a change in the network that must be applied to our prefix list.

Configuring Prefix Lists

We create a prefix list using the prefix-list command followed by a list name, which we will call list1. We can then optionally identify the sequence value using the seq syntax followed by the sequence number we wish to use. The sequence number can be any number. The lowest number gets read first. This means that if our first sequence number is 15 and our second is 18, then we can add 16 and 17 later if we need to modify the prefix list with a new statement.

If we now create this prefix list, our prefix list is called ip prefix-list list1 seq 15; if no sequence number is identified, the number is automatically assigned in increments of 5, meaning that the first would be 10 and then 15 and so on. We now need to permit a network using the permit syntax. If we do not have at least one permit statement, then we effectively deny all the routes. It is best to start with permit statements and then move on to selective deny statements.

If you wish to stop the incremental sequence numbers, you can use the no ip prefix-list sequence-number command. To re-enable the sequence numbering, use the ip prefix-list sequence-number command.

We now must identify the network in which we wish to permit. In this case, I would like to advertise the 172.16.0.0 network. To do this, I must also identify the 32-bit subnet mask either as the number of bits or a decimal value. So the statement would read

```
prefix-list list1 seq 15 172.16.0.0/24 permit
```

Let's now walk through the whole process step by step, looking at all the options available:

```
Cisco3640(config)#ip prefix-list ?
  WORD              Name of a prefix list
  WORD              Name of a prefix list


Cisco3640(config)#ip prefix-list list1 ?
  deny         Specify packets to reject
  description  Prefix-list specific description
  permit       Specify packets to forward
  seq          sequence number of an entry

Cisco3640(config)#ip prefix-list list1 seq ?
  <1-4294967294>  Sequence number

Cisco3640(config)#ip prefix-list list1 seq 15 ?
  deny    Specify packets to reject
  permit  Specify packets to forward

Cisco3640(config)#ip prefix-list list1 seq 15 permit ?
  A.B.C.D  IP prefix <network>/<length>, e.g., 35.0.0.0/8

Cisco3640(config)#ip prefix-list list1 seq 15 permit
↳172.16.0.0/24 ?
  ge  Minimum prefix length to be matched
  le  Maximum prefix length to be matched
  <cr>
```

The ge-value syntax is used to specify the range of the prefix length that is to be matched for prefixes that are more than the subnet mask identified in the network/len syntax. If the range runs from the /len value to 32, then only the ge syntax needs to be specified. The le-value syntax is used to specify the range of the prefix length to be matched, for prefixes that are of higher value specified in the specific network/len syntax. The le syntax identifies the values from the len to le-value specified, indicating a range of networks. Both ge and le are optional syntaxes and are used only when you need to specify a range of the prefix that is more specific than that identified in the network/len syntax. Just remember this rule: len < ge-value < le-value <= 32.

An exact match is assumed when neither ge nor le is specified, as shown below:

```
Cisco3640(config)#ip prefix-list list1 seq 15 permit
↳172.16.0.0/24
Cisco3640(config)#
```

The available syntaxes for the ip prefix-list command are shown below:

```
ip prefix-list list-name [seq seq-value] {deny | permit}
network/len [ge ge-value] [le le-value]
```

Now that we have created the prefix list, we need to apply it to BGP using the neighbor command. Let's look at the syntaxes and then apply the small prefix list we created above:

```
neighbor {ip-address | peer-group-name} prefix-list
prefix-listname {in | out}
```

Now let's apply the access list created above:

```
RouterA(config)#router bgp 31400
RouterA(config-router)#neighbor 172.16.11.254 remote-as
↳31400
RouterA(config-router)#neighbor 172.16.12.254 remote-as
↳31400
RouterA(config-router)#neighbor 172.16.12.254 prefix-list
↳list1 in
RouterA(config-router)#exit
```

The no `ip prefix-list` command followed by the list name is used to delete a prefix list.

Monitoring Prefix Lists

To view a prefix list, use the `show ip prefix-list` command. Let's take a look at the available syntaxes and the output:

```
RouterA#show ip prefix-list ?
  WORD     Name of a prefix list
  detail   Detail of prefix lists
  summary  Summary of prefix lists
  <cr>


RouterA#show ip prefix-list
ip prefix-list list1: 1 entries
   seq 15 permit 172.16.0.0/24
RouterA#show ip prefix-list list1
ip prefix-list list1: 1 entries
   seq 15 permit 172.16.0.0/24
RouterA#
```

You can use the `clear ip prefix-list` command to clear the hit count of the prefix list entries. You can also select the prefix list name to clear, as shown below:

```
RouterA#clear ip prefix ?
  WORD  Name of a prefix list
  <cr>


RouterA#clear ip prefix-list ?
  WORD  Name of a prefix list
  <cr>


RouterA#clear ip prefix-list list1
RouterA#
```

Route Maps

Route maps are used with BGP to control as well as modify routing table information and to define when routes are redistributed between ASes. *Route maps* can be defined as very complex access lists that allow some conditions to be applied to identified routes. If the conditions find a match, then an action you identify as the administrator using the set command takes place.

Route maps are used in communities, which we will discuss later in this chapter.

Unlike standard and extended access lists for filtering incoming and outgoing data on interfaces, the statements in route maps are sequentially numbered, allowing statements to be edited, inserted, and deleted. A collection of route-map statements using an identical route-map name is considered a single route map. One way that route maps are similar to access lists is that you must specify the source and destination address as well as the subnet mask.

To configure route maps, you begin in the Global Configuration mode. You then issue the route-map command followed by the name of the route map. You must then identify a condition you would like to set for the routing information. You have two choices: either deny or permit the routing information. You can then optionally identify a sequence number. You then press the Enter key, which will take you into a new command-line interface mode called Route Map Configuration mode, which is indicated by the Router(config-route-map)# prompt. This is a new mode that you probably have never seen on a router. Let's look at the command and the syntaxes, and then we'll demonstrate how to use this command on a router:

```
route-map map-tag [permit|deny] [sequence-number]
```

Now we will create a route map using 10 as the first sequence number (which is the default first sequence number):

```
RouterA(config)#route-map routemap1 permit 10
RouterA(config-route-map)#
```

We must now match conditions. Let's assume that previously we set an access list for the AS_PATH attribute numbered 6, permitting only the IP network 172, as shown below:

```
RouterA(config-router)# ip as-path access-list 6 permit
 172
```

We then need to add a `match` statement to allow us to use this in our route map, as shown below:

```
RouterA(config)#route-map routemap1 permit 10
RouterA(config-route-map)#match as-path 6
```

We now can use a `set` statement to add a local preference of 50 to all the matching routes:

```
RouterA(config)#route-map routemap1 permit 10
RouterA(config-route-map)#match as-path 6
RouterA(config-route-map)#set local-preference 50
```

Upon creating this list, we have effectively denied all the other routing updates including all the non-route updates. In order to keep those non-update packets going through our router, we need to create a permit route map, which we will number 25, as shown below:

```
RouterA(config)#route-map routemap1 permit 25
```

Statements in a route list are processed from the top down just like a standard or extended access list. If a match is found for a route, the set conditions are applied and the match is no longer looked for. The sequence number is used only for inserting or deleting specific route-map statements.

Just like in ACLs, there is an implicit deny any at the end of a route map. If all the statements in the route map are checked and there are no matches, then there is an automatic denial of the route. The following are the `match` and `set` commands that can be used for route maps:

```
match as-path
match community
match clns
```

```
match interface
match ip address
match ip next-hop
match ip route-source
match length
match metric
match route-type
match tag
set as-path
set clns
set automatic-tag
set community
set interface
set default interface
set ip default next-hop
set ip next-hop
set ip precedence
set level
set local-preference
set metric
set metric-type
set next-hop
set origin
set tag
set weight
```

Route Reflectors

Before you can truly understand the beauty of route reflectors, you need to understand some things about BGP split-horizon rules and the reason for a full mesh of routers. A *full mesh* means that every router has a direct connection to all the other routers in the network. This is easy to maintain in a network where there are only three routers, but what happens when you have 20 or 1000 routers? There is an easy method of calculating how many circuits or connections you will need in a full-mesh network by using the formula n(n-1)/2. This means that for 20 routers, there are 190 circuits or connections between the routers. Let's look at Figure 9.1 to see a full-mesh network.

FIGURE 9.1 A small full-mesh network

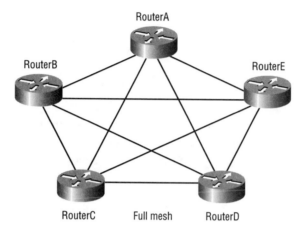

In a normal network, *split-horizon rules* mean that if we have two routers, one named RouterA and another named RouterB, when RouterA sends RouterB an update, RouterB will never send that information back to RouterA. BGP split-horizon rules mean that if an iBGP peer in AS 100 sends an update to a peer in AS 200, it will never send another router in AS 200 the same update. This is the reason for the full mesh in the internal network—so that all the routers in the network can share information they have learned with one another.

Having 190 connections or peers in a network can be a problem, however—not just the severe cost, but the overhead on the routers that are sending updates to one another. You can configure one router as a concentration router to handle all of the BGP updates. Making a router a route reflector places the main concentration of your configuration on only one router and eliminates the need for a full mesh.

The route reflector is allowed to propagate iBGP routes to other iBGP peers. Route reflectors can be very beneficial when ISPs use a considerable number of internal `neighbor` statements. The concentration router needs to be the only router configured with `neighbor` statements and becomes the concentration router for the entire network. All the other BGP routers in the AS need only peer with the concentration router; they become known as *clients*.

Route reflectors reduce the number of BGP neighbor peering relationships in an AS by maintaining a single central source for updates to their route reflector clients.

Some of the main things to remember when using route reflectors are listed below:

- Route reflectors are used when the internal `neighbor` statements become excessive.

- Route reflectors do not affect the paths that IP packets take through the network; they only identify how the routing information is distributed through the network.

- Route reflectors relieve iBGP of a full-mesh requirement.

- An IGP is still used in order to carry local routes and next-hop addresses.

- Route reflectors receive updates from their configured peers whether they are clients or non-clients.

Non-client refers to any iBGP peer that is not participating in the route reflector cluster as a client.

- Non-client updates are sent to route reflector clients in the cluster only.

- Updates from eBGP peers are sent to all clients and non-clients.

- Updates that the route reflector receives from a route reflector client are sent to all non-client peers and all route reflector clients, with the exception of the client listed in the ORIGINATOR_ID attribute field.

- You can configure multiple route reflectors for redundancy purposes.

- Other iBGP and eBGP peers can co-exist.

- Route reflectors modify the BGP split-horizon rule by allowing the router configured as the route reflector (the concentration router) to be the only router that propagates routes learned by iBGP to other iBGP peers.

The router being used as the concentration router needs to have its normal BGP configuration, neighbor statements, and routers configured as clients. On the concentration router (the route reflector), we need to identify the clients using the `neighbor <peer clients IP address> route-reflector-client` command. You need not migrate all the routers that you need to migrate to using route reflectors at once since non-route-reflector BGP routers can co-exist with route reflectors within an AS.

The concentration router needs to have a peer connection with the other BGP routers that are non-clients of route reflectors and the other route reflectors in the AS. The route-reflector clients need only have a `neighbor` statement to peer with the route reflector. Let's look at some of the terms you need to know when configuring route reflectors:

Route reflector   A router configured to be able to advertise the routes it learns from iBGP peers.

Client   A router that is not configured as a route reflector but will share information with the routers configured as route reflectors. Two route reflectors can be configured as clients.

Cluster   The combination of the routers configured as route reflectors and the clients.

Cluster ID   Used when a cluster has more than one route reflector, the cluster ID allows route reflectors to recognize updates from other route reflectors in the same cluster. A cluster that has a single route reflector is identified by the Router ID of the route reflector.

The route reflector creates the ORIGINATOR_ID BGP attribute. This attribute is used to carry the Router ID of the router that originated route information in the local AS. This allows the originator to know if it receives back any information it sent out. For more information on the ORIGINATOR_ID attribute, see Chapter 7, "BGP's Basic Components."

Configuring a Route Reflector

When you configure route reflectors, you must configure them one at a time and then configure the clients. Make sure that the routes propagate correctly. Always remember that when you are trying to control BGP routes, you are controlling all the routes in the organization. You can affect routes and information not only in your organization but in others' as well. If you have a hub and spoke network, you should first configure the hub as the route reflector and then configure the routers in the spokes as clients.

WARNING You should be especially careful that you know BGP thoroughly if your system is a transit AS. A transit AS means that another AS or organization uses your AS to connect to another AS. Transit ASes are discussed in Chapter 7.

Let's look at an example of configuring RouterA as the route reflector for the other two routers in autonomous system 100, shown in Figure 9.2.

FIGURE 9.2 A small route reflector configuration

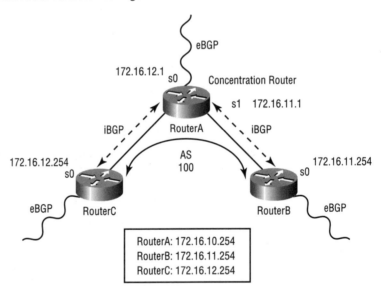

```
RouterA(config)#router bgp 100
RouterA(config-router)#neighbor 172.16.11.254 remote-as
↳100
RouterA(config-router)#neighbor 172.16.11.254 route-
↳reflector-client
RouterA(config-router)#neighbor 172.16.12.254 remote-as
↳100
RouterA(config-router)#neighbor 172.16.12.254 route-
↳reflector-client
```

If you have more than one route reflector, do not forget to peer them with one another.

Both RouterB and RouterC merely need to become peers with the concentration router and do not require `neighbor` statements identifying each other. To verify the configuration, we would use the `show ip bgp neighbor` command. Let's look at an example of the output:

```
RouterA# show ip bgp neighbor
BGP neighbor is 172.16.11.254, remote AS 100, internal
↳link
Index 1, Offset 0, Mask 0x2
Route-Reflector Client
BGP version 4, remote router ID 10.16.1.1
BGP state = Established, table version = 1, up for
↳12:10:16
Last read 00:00:06, hold time is 180,
keepalive interval is 60 seconds
Minimum time between advertisement runs is 5 seconds
Received 143 messages, 0 notifications, 0 in queue
Sent 52 messages, 0 notifications, 0 in queue
Prefix advertised 0, suppressed 0, withdrawn 0
Connections established 2; dropped 1
Last reset 12:10:16, due to User reset
53 accepted prefixes consume 32 bytes
0 history paths consume 0 bytes

--More-

BGP neighbor is 172.16.12.254, remote AS 100, internal
↳link
Index 1, Offset 0, Mask 0x2
Route-Reflector Client
BGP version 4, remote router ID 10.16.1.1
BGP state = Established, table version = 1, up for
↳12:10:16
```

```
Last read 00:00:05, hold time is 180,
keepalive interval is 60 seconds
Minimum time between advertisement runs is 5 seconds
Received 14 messages, 0 notifications, 0 in queue
Sent 12 messages, 0 notifications, 0 in queue
Prefix advertised 0, suppressed 0, withdrawn 0
Connections established 2; dropped 1
Last reset 12:10:16, due to User reset
53 accepted prefixes consume 32 bytes
0 history paths consume 0 bytes
```

Confederations

A *confederation* is another extension of using route reflectors. The difference is that instead of looking from the iBGP standpoint, BGP now looks at the entire autonomous system. Using confederations allows you to divide an AS into sub-ASes running eBGP between them. A confederation is a conglomerate of all the sub-ASes being advertised to the outside world as one giant AS. To the outside world, a confederation is invisible.

Confederations are a little more difficult to configure than route reflectors, unfortunately. The reason I say this is that when using confederations, you must perform a reconfiguration on each of the routers in the AS and also let non-optimal routes seep in to the BGP table, creating routing problems in your network. The way around learning the non-optimal routes is to reconfigure your BGP policies on each individual router participating in the confederation.

When you use confederations, you use the `router bgp` command to configure all of the sub-AS routers with their own BGP ASN. You then configure the confederation's ASN on each of the routers using the `bgp confederation identifier` command. Next, you configure each of the peer sub-ASNs using the `bgp confederation peers` command.

To get a better idea of how to configure confederations, let's examine Figure 9.3. You see that all of the routers are part of confederation AS 31,400, but it been broken down into three sub-ASes.

FIGURE 9.3 A small confederation

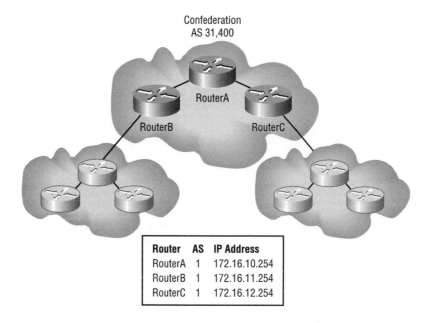

To make this easy to understand, we'll do the configuration on all three routers displayed above. First, let's take a look at the configuration of RouterA in our confederation.

```
RouterA(config)#router bgp 1
RouterA(config-router)#bgp confederation identifier 31400
RouterA(config-router)#bgp confederation peers 2 3
RouterA(config-router)#neighbor 172.16.11.254 remote-as 2
RouterA(config-router)#neighbor 172.16.12.254 remote-as 3
```

Now let's look at RouterB's configuration.

```
RouterB(config)#router bgp 2
RouterB(config-router)#bgp confederation identifier 31400
RouterB(config-router)#bgp confederation peers 1 3
RouterB(config-router)#neighbor 172.16.10.254 remote-as 1
```

Lastly, let's look at RouterC's configuration, which is very similar to that of RouterB.

```
RouterC(config)#router bgp 3
RouterC(config-router)#bgp confederation identifier 31400
RouterC(config-router)#bgp confederation peers 1 2
RouterC(config-router)#neighbor 172.16.10.254 remote-as 1
```

Peer Groups and Communities

Peer groups and communities are used to eliminate some of the overhead associated with BGP. BGP, as you can see, is a very complex protocol with many configuration options. Communities are a way of tagging routes to make sure that a consistent filtering or route-selection policy exists when using route maps.

All the BGP routers can tag routes coming into or going out of their interfaces when doing routing updates. The COMMUNITIES attribute (Type Code 8) is used to carry the communities information in the BGP update packets. BGP routers can then filter routes in incoming or outgoing updates or use preferred routes based on the COMMUNITIES attribute. By default, the communities information is stripped from any outgoing BGP update. Without any communities configured, each individual BGP neighbor would require either a statement in an access list for a distribute list or a statement in a prefix list.

Some implementations do not understand the concept of communities. When such is the case, the router will still send the information onto the next router. When the implementation does understand the concept of communities, then the router must be configured to propagate the COMMUNITIES attribute—otherwise, the communities information will be dropped.

The COMMUNITIES attribute can contain a value in the range of 0 to 4,294,967,200. Remember that a network can be a member of multiple communities and that you can use route maps to set the community attributes. The COMMUNITIES attribute can be 32 bits long, with the upper 16 bits indicating the AS number that was defined in the community. The lower 16 bits have only local significance and are the community number. Enter the value as a single decimal number in the format AS:nn, where AS is the AS number and nn is the lower 16-bit local community number. The total community value is displayed as one long decimal number by default.

There are a few well-known communities, shown here:

Internet   All routers by default belong to this community and can be used to advertise routes to all other routers.

No-export   Indicates that the route will not be passed outside the AS using eBGP.

No-advertise   Keeps the route secret from every other router.

Local-as   Used in confederations and was introduced in version 12.0 of the Cisco IOS. We do not cover this topic in this book. You can visit Cisco's Web site for more information on this community.

The community name is set in the Route Map Configuration mode after the route map is created. Let's look at the syntaxes shown below:

```
set community { community-number [additive]}|none
```

Here's an example of using the command:

```
RouterA(config-route-map)#route-map COM1 permit 10
RouterA(config-route-map)#match ip address 1
RouterA(config-route-map)#set community 1 additive
```

The `additive` syntax is used to add the router to an existing community. You must then instruct BGP to perform community propagations. To do so, you need to use the `send community` syntax with the `neighbor` command. Let's look at the `neighbor` command and the syntaxes used with it:

```
neighbor { ip-address|peer-group-name} send-community
```

This command tells BGP that the BGP COMMUNITIES attribute should be sent to a BGP neighbor. Let's look at an example of using the command:

```
RouterA(config)#router bgp 31400
Router(config-router)#network 172.16.0.0
Router(config-router)#neighbor  10.1.1.254 remote-as 500
Router(config-router)#neighbor  10.1.1.254 send-community
Router(config-router)#neighbor 10.1.1.254 route-map
↳Routemap1 out
```

Peer Groups

When you maintain a large BGP network, there tend to be many small configuration changes that need to be made to a number of BGP routers. To avoid making an individual change to each and every router, peer groups were created. This allows you to place those routers that share common policies into a group. You then make policy changes to the peer group instead of to each individual router. Policies in your peer group can be overridden, but only for incoming updates. The outgoing policies must always be identical for all of the members in your peer group. Peer group policies include outbound route maps, distribute lists, filter lists, and prefix lists.

All members of the peer group are internal members of an AS and always share the same ASN. You can assign a peer group name, but the name is local only to the router it is configured on; it is not passed to any other router.

To configure a peer group, use the `neighbor` command followed by the peer group name and then the `peer-group` syntax, as shown below:

```
neighbor peer-group-name peer-group
```

Let's look at an example of configuring a peer group using the command and assigning the peer group name of group1 to AS 31,400:

```
RouterA(config)#router bgp 31400
RouterA(config-router)#neighbor group1 peer-group
```

We now have to identify the neighboring routers in our peer group using the `neighbor` command followed by our BGP peer's IP address, the `peer-group` syntax, and the peer group's name. Let's take a look at the command and the syntaxes:

```
neighbor ip-address peer-group peer-group-name
```

Let's now use the command to add the two neighbors to RouterA that we have used in most of the demonstrations in this chapter, those being RouterB using IP address 172.16.11.254 and RouterC using IP address 172.16.12.254.

```
RouterA(config)#router bgp 31400
RouterA(config-router)#neighbor group1 peer-group
RouterA(config-router)#neighbor 172.16.11.254 peer-group
 group1
RouterA(config-router)#neighbor 172.16.12.254 peer-group
 group1
```

You can clear the BGP connection of a peer on any BGP router using the clear ip bgp peer-group *peer-group-name* command in Privilege mode.

Multi-homing

Multi-homing is the process of connecting two or more service providers to one network in an effort to provide redundancy to the outside world. Multi-homing can be used with or without BGP. If you are not using BGP, you can use default routes. Default routes must be manually configured on a router. Remember, a manually configured route is a static route. BGP finds its own routes, and the routes do not need to be manually configured. These routes are called dynamic routes when the administrator does not need to manually configure them. Static routes can be configured with BGP; regardless of whether BGP knows a better route through the network, it will use the static route. BGP does this by trusting a static route more than a route that it has learned itself.

Static routes give only the interface of the destination for the next hop. BGP learns the entire route from one point to another.

Using default static routes relieves the processor on the router from handling BGP processes that tax the processor heavily. It also frees RAM in the router for other uses.

In the example below, BGP is not configured. We use the ip route command followed by 0.0.0.0, which means any destination IP address; the second 0.0.0.0 indicates any mask the router doesn't know about from the IGP. In this case, we use OSPF as the IGP. We then use the default-information orginate always command to instruct all the other OSPF routers to learn this default route. Figure 9.4 shows our network using a single static route.

FIGURE 9.4 A single static (default) route to an ISP

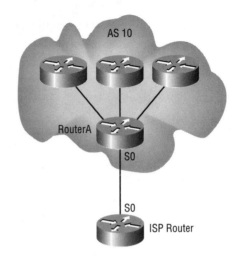

```
RouterA(config)#ip route 0.0.0.0 0.0.0.0 serial 0
RouterA(config)#router ospf 10
RouterA(config-router)#network 172.16.0.0 0.0.255.255 area 1
RouterA(config-router)#default-information ?
  originate  Distribute a default route

RouterA(config-router)#default-information originate ?
  always       Always advertise default route
  metric       OSPF default metric
  metric-type  OSPF metric type for default routes
  route-map    Route-map reference
  <cr>

RouterA(config-router)#default-information originate
↳always
RouterA(config-router)#
```

You can configure static routes for multiple ISPs as well. In Figure 9.5, we see that there are two ISP routers from two different ISPs. The primary link uses a 1.544Mbps link; the other uses a 512Kbps link as a backup. We can tell the router to use one link over another by assigning an administrative distance. In this case, we assign 200 to one link and 201 to the other in the following code. The link used will be the link with the lowest administrative distance.

FIGURE 9.5 Configuring static routes to multiple ISPs

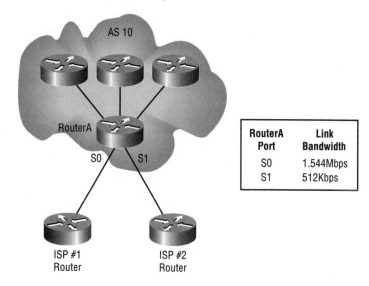

RouterA Port	Link Bandwidth
S0	1.544Mbps
S1	512Kbps

```
RouterA(config)#ip route 0.0.0.0 0.0.0.0 serial 0 ?
  <1-255>    Distance metric for this route
  A.B.C.D    Forwarding router's address
  permanent  permanent route
  tag        Set tag for this route
  <cr>

RouterA(config)#ip route 0.0.0.0 0.0.0.0 s0 200
RouterA(config)#ip route 0.0.0.0 0.0.0.0 s1 201
RouterA(config)#router ospf 10
RouterA(config-router)#network 172.16.0.0 0.0.255.255
↳area 0
RouterA(config-router)#default-information originate
↳always
```

When multi-homing two networks, three classifications are possible:

- Basic

- Medium

- Full

Basic multi-homing is the simplest and requires only that the AS attach to the ISP. The ISP will offer only default routes to the Internet. The internal AS (your AS) decides the ISP connection to use, similar to the one portrayed in Figure 9.5. This method uses the least amount of CPU time and the least amount of RAM on the router.

Medium multi-homing uses default routes and BGP. In this case, the internal AS gets more routing information and can select the best ISP to use based on that information.

Full multi-homing uses only BGP, and all the routes are learned using the AS-PATH attribute information to make routing decisions. This is the most processor-intensive type and requires a lot of RAM.

Summary

This was one of the most complex chapters that we have ever written. Not only was it the most complex, it was the longest to write and we used more equipment and cabling than we have ever used writing a chapter. If you implement BGP incorrectly, you can not only screw up advertising your own internal network, but you can also wreak havoc on other organizations' networks as well, and this includes your own ISP's network. If you do not know how to configure or maintain BGP in a network, you should not implement it.

For the exam, you need a firm understanding of route maps, prefix lists, communities, peer groups, multi-homing, static routes, access lists, distribute lists, and confederations. We covered all of these in detail in this chapter.

Key Terms

Before taking the exam, make sure you're familiar with the following terms:

AS path pre-pending

confederation

distribute list

full mesh

multi-homing

prefix list

route flap

route map

Written Lab

1. What command is used to instruct a route map what to do when it finds a match?

2. In which command mode would you use the show ip bgp neighbors command?

3. A grouping of BGP routers that share the same common policies is called what?

4. What command would you use to assign peer group group6 to a router?

5. What are the three classifications for multi-homing BGP networks?

6. What command will assign a static default route to Serial 0 on a router?

7. What command would you use if you needed to assign an administrative distance of 200 to a default route on serial 0?

8. What command would you use to clear a peer group named group3 from a router?

9. What command can be used to place a hold-down time on a link that has flapped before it is re-advertised?

10. When using the set command, what mode should the router be in?

Hands-on Lab

In this lab, we will take what we learned about configuring basic BGP and add to it. We will configure RouterA as a route reflector, and we need to configure the router's basic configuration as well. If you have forgotten how to do this, refer to the Hands-on Lab section in Chapter 8, "Configuring Basic BGP." Let's look at the graphic below to see the three routers in our network. This graphic seems somewhat complex but is very easy to configure step by step since it is only a small configuration with five routers. While there is more than one way to configure the routers in the diagram below, I will give a suggested configuration example based on the information from Chapter 8 and this one.

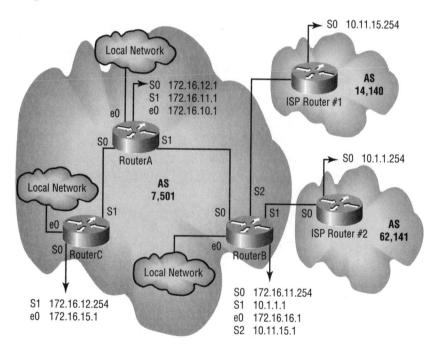

Let's look at the lab objectives in the following list:

- On each router, enable BGP with its autonomous system number (ASN).

- Identify the network each resides in.

- Identify both of the route reflector's neighboring routers and the AS they reside in.

- Assign an IGP. (We will use OSPF with the ASN of 10 and assign all the routers in the internal AS to Area 1.)

- Configure multi-homing on RouterB using the links to the two-ISP number router and configure ISP Router #1 as the primary link. Assign an administrative distance of 100 to one link to the ISP and 150 to the other.

- Configure RouterA as the route reflector, making RouterB and RouterC clients.

Let's now look at an example of the configuration of all three routers, which are identified by the hostname on each router. We'll start with RouterA:

```
RouterA(config)#router bgp 7501
RouterA(config-router)#network 172.16.0.0 mask 255.255.0
RouterA(config-router)#network 10.0.0.0 mask 255.0.0
RouterA(config-router)#neighbor 172.16.11.254 remote-as
↳7501
RouterA(config-router)#neighbor 172.16.11.254 route-
↳reflector-client
RouterA(config-router)#neighbor 172.16.12.254 remote-as
↳7501
RouterA(config-router)#neighbor 172.16.11.254 route-
↳reflector-client
RouterA(config-router)#exit
RouterA(config)#router ospf 10
RouterA(config-router)#network 172.16.0.0 0.0.255.255 area 0
RouterB(config-router)#default-information originate
↳always
RouterA(config-router)#exit
RouterA(config)#interface ethernet 0
RouterA(config-if)#ip address 172.16.10.1 255.255.255.0
RouterA(config-if)#no shut
RouterA(config-if)#interface serial 0
RouterA(config-if)#ip address 172.16.12.1 255.255.255.0
RouterA(config-if)#no shut
RouterA(config-if)#exit
```

```
RouterA(config)#interface serial 1
RouterA(config-if)#ip address 172.16.11.1 255.255.255.0
RouterA(config-if)#no shut
RouterA(config-if)#
```

Now let's look at the suggested configuration for RouterB:

```
RouterB#conf t
Enter configuration commands, one per line.  End with
↪CNTL/Z.
RouterB(config)#router bgp 7501
RouterB(config-router)#network 172.16.0.0 mask
↪255.255.255.0
RouterB(config-router)#network 10.0.0.0 mask 255.0.0
RouterB(config-router)#neighbor 172.16.12.1 remote-as 7501
RouterB(config-router)#neighbor 10.11.15.254 remote-as
↪14140
RouterB(config-router)#neighbor 10.1.1.254 remote-as 62141
RouterB(config-router)#redist static
RouterB(config-router)#exit
RouterB(config)#router ospf 10
RouterB(config-router)#network 172.16.0.0 0.0.255.255 area 0
RouterB(config-router)#default-information originate
↪always
RouterB(config)#ip route 0.0.0.0 0.0.0.0 serial 1 100
RouterB(config)#ip route 0.0.0.0 0.0.0.0 serial 2 150
RouterB(config)# interface ethernet 0
RouterB(config-if)#ip address 172.16.16.1 255.255.255.0
RouterB(config-if)#no shut
RouterB(config-if)#exit
RouterB(config)#interface serial 0
RouterB(config-if)#ip address 172.16.11.254 255.255.255.0
RouterB(config-if)#no shut
RouterB(config-if)#exit
RouterB(config)#interface serial 1
RouterB(config-if)#ip address 10.1.1.1 255.0.0
RouterB(config-if)#no shut
RouterB(config-if)#exit
```

```
RouterB(config)#interface serial 2
RouterB(config-if)#ip address 10.11.15.1 255.0.0
RouterB(config-if)#no shut
RouterB(config-if)#
```

Connecting to two or more simulated ISPs might be a problem because it requires the use of more than two serial ports on the router. I used a 3600 series. If you do not have a router available with more than two serial links, simulate only one ISP. BGP can load balance over as many as six external links to ISPs.

Here's the suggested configuration for RouterC:

```
RouterC(config)#router bgp 7501
RouterC(config-router)#network 172.16.0.0 mask
%255.255.255.0
RouterC(config-router)#neighbor 172.16.11.1 remote-as 7501
RouterC(config-router)#exit
RouterC(config)#router ospf 10
RouterC(config-router)#network 172.16.0.0 0.0.255.255 area 0
RouterC(config-router)#default-information originate
%always
RouterC(config-router)#exit
RouterC(config)#interface ethernet 0
RouterC(config-if)#ip address 172.16.15.1 255.255.255.0
RouterC(config-if)#no shut
RouterC(config-if)#exit
RouterC(config)#interface serial 1
RouterC(config-if)#ip address 172.16.12.254 255.255.255.0
RouterC(config-if)#no shut
RouterC(config-if)#exit
```

Review Questions

1. Access lists are read from top to bottom. Therefore, which of the following should be near the top?

   A. Least restrictive

   B. Most restrictive

   C. Permit or deny

   D. Deny only

2. Which of the following should be used to reduce the number of routes in a routing table?

   A. EIGRP

   B. DDR

   C. Route carving

   D. Route summarization

3. Which of the following are true of a prefix list? (Choose all that apply.)

   A. Statements can be added at any time.

   B. Statements can be assigned a sequence number.

   C. Statements use the `set` command to tell the prefix list what to do.

   D. Any statements can be deleted at any time.

4. A router acting as a route reflector should have a peer connection with which of the following routers?

   A. Other route reflectors

   B. The route reflector's clients

   C. Non-clients

   D. All of the above

5. If multiple ISPs are connected to your network, BGP can load balance over up to how many links?

    A. Eight

    B. Thirty-two

    C. Six

    D. One

6. You can define communities using which type of filters?

    A. Standard access lists

    B. Route maps

    C. Prefix lists

    D. Extended access lists

7. Which of the following can be used to avoid creating a full-mesh network? (Choose all that apply.)

    A. Confederations

    B. Route maps

    C. Prefix lists

    D. Route reflectors

8. Which of the following commands shows the configured peer BGP routers and the current connection state?

    A. show ip bgp all

    B. show cdp bgp neighbors

    C. show running-config

    D. show ip bgp neighbors

9. What router command mode is used to start BGP using the `router bgp 100` command?

    A. User mode

    B. Privilege mode

    C. Global Configuration mode

    D. Interface Configuration mode

    E. Route Map Configuration mode

10. What are two advantages of prefix lists over distribute lists?

    A. Less CPU usage

    B. Easy to configure

    C. Affect advertised routes and data coming into an interface

    D. Can be configured on individual interfaces

11. Which of the following is *not* a way of managing routes advertised by BGP routers?

    A. Using route maps

    B. Using prefix lists

    C. Using distribute lists

    D. Using path filters

    E. Using redistribution lists

12. You can lengthen the AS-PATH length by doing which of the following?

    A. Add a new value using the `ip bgp as-path value` command.

    B. Add false AS numbers

    C. Add a new value using the `set as-path extended` command.

    D. Use the `bgp dampening` command.

13. Statements in distribute lists are processed in which order? (Choose all that apply.)

    A. The order in which they were entered

    B. From the top down

    C. The order given by the sequence number

    D. All of the above

14. When configuring a prefix list, if the seq syntax is not used, in what sequence are numbers assigned and in what increment?

    A. 1 (1,2,3...)

    B. 5 (10,15,20...)

    C. 10 (10,20,30...)

    D. 25 (25,50,75...)

15. A BGP router not participating in a route reflector cluster is called which of the following?

    A. Non-cluster client

    B. Non-BGP router

    C. Non-client

    D. Non-iBGP client

16. The COMMUNITIES attribute can contain a value in what range of numbers?

    A. 1 to 1012

    B. 1 to 255

    C. 0 to 512

    D. 1 to 4,294,967,200

17. Which of the following is *not* used in confederations?

   A. iBGP

   B. eBGP

   C. Sub-ASes

   D. Sequence numbers

   E. Confederation identifier

18. Which command can be used to disable sequence numbering when creating prefix lists?

   A. `ip bgp prefix-list sequence-number disable`

   B. `no ip prefix-list sequence-number`

   C. `disable ip bgp prefix-list sequence-number`

   D. `no ip prefix-list`

19. Which of the following ranges of numbers can be assigned to a BGP distribute list?

   A. 299 to 399

   B. 1 to 200

   C. 1 to 199

   D. 1 to 2,000

20. When creating prefix lists, which of the following are optional syntaxes?

   A. `list-name`

   B. `ge`

   C. `le`

   D. `seq`

Answers to Written Lab

1. The set command

2. Privileged mode

3. Peer group

4. neighbor group6 peer-group

5. Basic, Medium, and Full

6. ip route 0.0.0.0 0.0.0.0 serial 0

7. ip route 0.0.0.0 0.0.0.0 serial 0 200

8. clear ip peer-group group3

9. bgp dampening

10. Route Map Configuration mode displayed on the router prompt as Router(config-route-map)#

Answers to Review Questions

1. A. The least restrictive statements should be placed at the top of an access list. This means that if the last statement is the implicit deny all, then the permit statements should be first unless you want to deny a subset of what was permitted. A good rule to remember is that the most specific statements should be at the top.

2. D. Route summarization reduces the number of entries found in the routing table, creating a single summarized route for all the entries in the routing table for networks residing out a single interface.

3. A, B, D. A prefix list can be reconfigured with new statements, or you can delete statements at any time as long as they are numbered with sequence numbers. The set command is used to tell the router what to do when a match is made in a route map.

4. D. A route reflector is used to manage larger networks. A route reflector should be peered with other route reflectors, its own route reflector clients, and those routers not participating in a route reflector cluster.

5. C. You can have up to six physical links to ISPs and use those links to send data traffic back and forth from your network to your ISP's network. This effectively allows you to not only have redundant links, but to use those redundant links to load balance your traffic.

6. B. The COMMUNITIES attribute can be used in route maps. The COMMUNITIES attribute identifies a common set of BGP routers participating in a community.

7. A, D. Confederations and route reflectors can both be configured to avoid creating a full-mesh network where the neighbors command is used excessively.

8. D. The show bgp neighbors command shows the configured BGP peers and the current connection status.

9. C. The router bgp command is used in the Global Configuration mode.

10. A, B. Prefix lists use considerably less CPU space and are much easier to configure than access lists. They cannot affect advertised routes coming into an interface and are configured globally on a router, not on each interface.

11. E. There is no such thing as a redistribution list using BGP. The other ways listed are all valid ways of manipulating routes advertised by BGP.

12. B. You can increase the AS-PATH length by adding false AS numbers. Although the `ip bgp as-path value` command and the `set as-path extended` command appear convincing enough, they are not real commands. The `bgp dampening` command is used by BGP to set a hold time before a route can be re-advertised after route flapping.

13. A, B. Statements are entered in a distribute list by configuring an access list. The statements are processed in the order in which they were entered and from the top down. Sequence numbers are not used in distribute lists.

14. B. Sequence numbers are assigned in increments of five when no sequence number was assigned when the prefix list statements were configured.

15. C. BGP routers not participating in a route reflector client are called non-client routers.

16. D. The COMMUNITIES attribute value can be any number between 1 and 4,294,967,200.

17. D. The sequence number is used in prefix lists. Confederations use iBGP on routers in sub-ASes and then use eBGP to connect the sub-ASes.

18. B. The `no ip prefix-list sequence-number` command is used to disable sequence numbering for prefix lists. The only other real command is the `no ip prefix-list` command, which is used to delete a prefix list.

19. C. This is sort of a trick question. The reason is that distribute lists are created using access lists. IP standard access lists are numbered 1 to 99, and extended access lists are numbered 100 to 199.

20. B, C, D. The `prefix-list` command is followed by the `list-name` syntax. The `ge`, `le`, and `seq` syntaxes are all optional and not required.

Chapter

10

Route Optimization

THE CCNP ROUTING EXAM TOPICS COVERED IN THIS CHAPTER ARE AS FOLLOWS:

✓ Show the need for route redistribution

✓ Review the metrics of commonly used routing protocols

✓ Illustrate how to redistribute routing protocols, including RIP, OSPF, IGRP, and EIGRP

✓ Learn how to verify and troubleshoot route redistribution

✓ Explore how to fine-tune route redistribution through the use of access lists and route maps

✓ Recognize the benefits of policy routing

✓ Detail how to direct traffic flows through the use of policy routing

✓ Configure route maps to control traffic flows

In this chapter, we will discuss how to take networks running different routing protocols and allow them to exchange routing information, through a process called *route redistribution*. One of the challenges of route redistribution is that many routing protocols use different metrics. To overcome this challenge, we will show you how to set default metrics for various routing protocols. After examining several redistribution examples, we will review commands for verifying and troubleshooting route redistribution.

We will discuss many advanced route-manipulation techniques, including setting metrics on a protocol-by-protocol basis and setting metrics for specific routes. We'll introduce the `distribute-list` feature as a tool for filtering the receiving or advertising of routes, and we'll show the virtual interface *Null0* to be an efficient way of discarding packets destined for specified networks. We will also detail how to redistribute static and connected routes. In addition, we'll introduce the powerful features of route maps.

Route Redistribution

We have previously discussed various routing protocols available on Cisco routers. Some of the more common routing protocols are RIP, IGRP, EIGRP, and OSPF. However, we have not considered what happens when we interconnect networks that are running differing routing protocols. To illustrate this situation, let's consider the implications of when two businesses (or divisions within the same business) merge. Let's say that Company A had a network infrastructure that used the Cisco proprietary EIGRP protocol, as shown in Figure 10.1.

FIGURE 10.1 Company A's EIGRP configuration

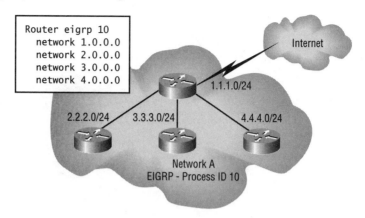

```
Router eigrp 10
  network 1.0.0.0
  network 2.0.0.0
  network 3.0.0.0
  network 4.0.0.0
```

Internet

1.1.1.0/24

2.2.2.0/24   3.3.3.0/24   4.4.4.0/24

Network A
EIGRP - Process ID 10

Company B ran RIP as its interior routing protocol, as shown in Figure 10.2, because Company B's network had mixture of routing vendors. One day, Company A and Company B merged.

FIGURE 10.2 Company B's RIP configuration

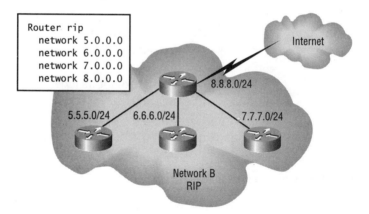

```
Router rip
  network 5.0.0.0
  network 6.0.0.0
  network 7.0.0.0
  network 8.0.0.0
```

Internet

8.8.8.0/24

5.5.5.0/24   6.6.6.0/24   7.7.7.0/24

Network B
RIP

When the backbone routers of each company were interconnected, as illustrated in Figure 10.3, the Company A routers did not automatically learn the routes from the Company B routers, nor vice versa. A common misconception is that if the router joining two networks runs both routing protocols, then route redistribution will just happen—this is not so.

FIGURE 10.3 Improper redistribution

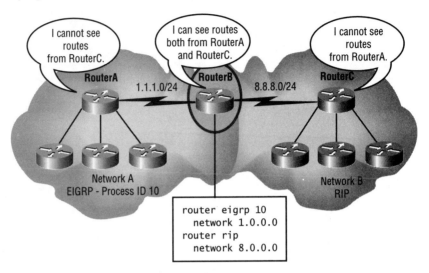

The solution to this problem of mixed routing protocols is route redistribution. The reason that route redistribution does not happen automatically between diverse routing protocols is that the protocols have different methods of representing the desirability of a route. This desirability is called a *metric*. Also, some routing protocols include subnet information (prefix information) within routing updates (e.g., classless routing protocols), and some routing protocols do not include subnet information (e.g., classful routing protocols). Therefore, to better understand how we redistribute one routing protocol into another, let's first review some characteristics of various routing protocols.

Routing Protocol Metrics

In this section, we will discuss the various routing protocols and metrics used to calculate the best path to all remote networks. It is important to remember that a router first used the administrative distance as a tool to find the best path to a remote network. For example, if you have a network route being advertised to a router with both RIP and IGRP, the IGRP route will be used and the RIP route will be ignored. If two or more routes are being advertised as available routes to the remote network, then the metric of a routing protocol is used to determine the best path. If the metrics are the same, the routing protocol will perform load balancing over the available routes. It is important that you understand the default administrative distance of each routing protocol and the metrics used so that you can effectively troubleshoot and maintain an internetwork.

IP RIP

RIP (Routing Information Protocol) uses a simple metric called the hop count. The *hop count* for a network is simply the number of routers that a packet must pass through to reach that network. The hop-count metric does not take into account such things as the speed or reliability of a link, just the number of hops. In this way, RIP is similar to the AppleTalk routing protocol of RTMP (Routing Table Maintenance Protocol). Novell's NetWare IPX RIP uses ticks to determine the best path to a remote network. Ticks are calculated as approximately $1/18$ of a second and are Novell's way of using load and delay of the line as metrics. If the IPX RIP finds multiple paths to the same location with the same tick count, then hops are used as a tiebreaker.

The other important characteristic of RIP that we are considering is that RIP is a classful routing protocol. This means that the subnet mask (prefix information) is not sent with the route updates as it is with classless routing protocols. RIP cannot effectively work with classless routing protocols like EIGRP and OSPF because of this reason. However, RIP version 2 sends prefix information with the router updates and its routes can be redistributed with OSPF and EIGRP, for example. To configure RIP version 2, you just add the command version 2 under the router rip process command, as shown below:

```
Router#config t
Router(config)#router rip
Router(config-router)#network 172.16.0.0
Router(config-router)#network 10.0.0.0
Router(config-router)#version 2
```

It is important to remember to advertise your directly attached networks as classful addresses. However, if you have a router attached to network 172.16.0.0/24 but are using subnets 172.16.30.0 and 172.16.40.0, you would advertise 172.16.0.0, and the routing process would find and advertise your subnets. However, we see many students type the network 172.16.30.0 as the network number under RIP; this command works because the router will change it to 172.16.0.0 (the classful boundary) for you. You need to remember that even though the router will fix it for you, the Cisco certification exam will not, and you will get a wrong answer. Just remember that a classful routing protocol is always configured with all subnet and host bits off.

Another thought to keep in mind regarding RIP version 1 is that it doesn't work with VLSM because subnet mask information is not sent with the route updates. Since RIP version 2 does send prefix information, you absolutely must use RIP version 2 if you are trying to perform any type of VLSM networking.

OSPF

*O*SPF *(Open Shortest Path First)* uses an algorithm to determine a composite metric. Specifically, the algorithm used is based on the Dijkstra Algorithm, named after its inventor, Edsger Dijkstra. This algorithm uses only the bandwidth of a link to determine the cost to a remote network. Remember that OSPF does not summarize by default like IGRP, EIGRP, and RIP. However, unlike RIP, OSPF is a classless routing protocol, which means that it includes subnet information (prefix information) in its routing updates. OSPF is typically the fastest converging routing protocol for IP. However, we have found that EIGRP can give it a run for the money in smaller networks in regards to convergence times.

IGRP

*I*GRP *(Internet Gateway Routing Protocol)* is a Cisco proprietary protocol and therefore cannot run on routers from other vendors. Similar to RIP, IGRP is a classful, distance-vector protocol. However, IGRP uses a much more complex metric than RIP. Specifically, the metric for IGRP is made up of the following five components:

Bandwidth   The bandwidth value is represented by the number of Kbps that a particular interface is capable of. For example, a 10Mbps Ethernet port would, by default, have a bandwidth value of 10,000 (10,000Kbps = 10Mbps). Similarly, a 56Kbps serial interface would have a bandwidth value of 56. All Cisco routers have a default bandwidth of 1.544Mbps on the router's serial interfaces. It is important to change the bandwidth of an interface if you are using a routing protocol that uses the bandwidth of a link to calculate the best path to a remote network, for example, IGRP, EIGRP, and OSPF. However, it is also important to understand that the bandwidth command has absolutely nothing to do with the speed of the link. Yes, it would be nice to type in a command on a serial interface and boost your bandwidth. Unfortunately, the only thing the bandwidth command is used for on an interface is to help routing protocols make smart decisions.

Delay   The delay value is calculated by adding up the delay (in 10-microsecond increments) along the path to the next router.

Reliability   The reliability component of the metric is determined by how many errors are occurring on the interface. The best possible reliability value is 255. So, if we had an interface that was experiencing multiple errors, and its reliability value was 128, then we would know that its reliability was approximately 50 percent.

Load   The load value, like the reliability value, has a maximum value of 255. However, in the case of load, lower values are better. If a particular serial link were being used at approximately 25 percent of capacity, its load value would be 63 (255 x .25 = 63.25). A value of 1 is the best.

MTU   MTU is the Maximum Transmit Unit size, in bytes, allowed over an interface. An Ethernet and serial interface, for example, has a default MTU size of 1500 bytes. Traffic over an interface is more efficient at larger MTU sizes (assuming the link is not experiencing multiple errors, requiring retransmission), because with a larger MTU size, a message does not have to be broken up into as many packets. Therefore, with fewer packets, there is lower overhead (header information that is contained in each packet). With lower overhead, there is a higher rate of data throughput.

An easy way to remember the metric components of IGRP is to recall the acrostic "**B**ig **D**ogs **R**eally **L**ike **M**e," where **B** is bandwidth, **D** is delay, **R** is reliability, **L** is load, and **M** is MTU size.

If you were to look at a network analyzer, you would see that IGRP sends route updates with all the metric information described above. However, by default, IGRP routing protocols use only bandwidth and delay of the line to determine the best route. MTU, reliability, and load have to be configured by the administrator. I don't recommend this unless it is a rainy Saturday and you have absolutely nothing else to do in the world and you want to amaze your friends at work on Monday morning.

EIGRP

*E*IGRP *(Enhanced IGRP)* is a Cisco proprietary protocol, like IGRP. The good news is that EIGRP uses the same metric components as IGRP (bandwidth, delay, reliability, load, and MTU size) but also uses only bandwidth and delay of the line by default as IGRP does. The news gets even better. Since EIGRP and IGRP use the same metrics, they can automatically be redistributed into each other, provided that they are using the same autonomous system number. Later we'll present an example that will clarify this automatic redistribution. Unlike IGRP, however, EIGRP is a classless routing protocol. Therefore, EIGRP is capable of sending subnet information in its routing updates.

Configuring Route Redistribution

Now that we have an understanding of the issues involved in route redistribution (metrics and classless versus classful), we will examine some basic scenarios of route redistribution. Let's first consider the situation presented at the beginning of the chapter—two companies merging and needing to redistribute RIP and EIGRP into each other.

As you already know, we have two networks that are merging together. RouterB's routing table knows the routes from both RouterA and RouterC, because it is configured to run both the RIP and EIGRP routing processes. However, RouterA and RouterC cannot see the routes from each other, as shown in Figure 10.4.

FIGURE 10.4   Improper redistribution

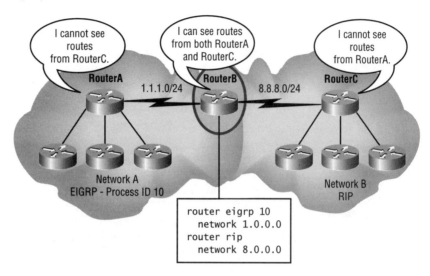

Since RouterB connects to both the EIGRP and RIP networks, RouterB is the router where we can redistribute EIGRP and RIP into each other. The syntax on router RouterB to redistribute EIGRP and RIP into one another is as follows:

`router eigrp 10`

where 10 is the AS number.

`redistribute rip`

which tells the router to take routes learned via RIP and re-advertise them via EIGRP.

`network 1.0.0.0`

where `network` is the network that is part of the EIGRP routing process.

`default-metric 56 10 255 1 1500`

where `default-metric` is the metric to be used when redistributing routes from other routing protocols, 56 is the bandwidth (56Kbps), 10 is the delay (in 10-microsecond increments), 255 is the reliability (100 percent reliable), 1 is the load (no load), and 1500 is the MTU size (1,500 bytes).

```
!
router rip
```
which enables the RIP routing process.

```
redistribute eigrp 10
```
which tells the router to take routes learned via EIGRP AS 10 and re-advertise them via RIP.

```
network 8.0.0.0
```
where `network` is the network that is part of the RIP routing process.

```
default-metric 3
```
where 3 is to be used as the default metric (hop count) when other routing protocols are injected into RIP.

At this point, both RouterA and RouterC can see each other's routes. Also note that it would have been possible to do a one-way redistribution. A one-way redistribution is where one routing protocol is redistributed into another, but not vice versa. For example, if we had omitted the RouterB configuration command `redistribute rip` under the `router eigrp 10` section of the configuration, then routes learned via RIP would not have been re-advertised by EIGRP. In some situations, it is good design practice to use one-way redistribution, to avoid routing loops. This is of particular importance when a router's *split-horizon* function (which prevents routing loops) has been disabled.

EIGRP and IGRP Route Redistribution

We mentioned earlier that EIGRP and IGRP use the same metrics and can therefore automatically redistribute their routes into each other without the need for manual redistribution, which was required in the previous example. The one caveat is that the EIGRP and IGRP AS must be the same.

For example, consider a variation on our original scenario. This time, Company B's network uses IGRP, as shown in Figure 10.5.

FIGURE 10.5 EIGRP and IGRP redistribution

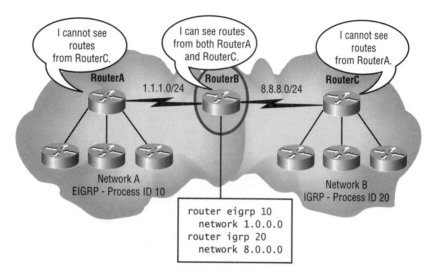

However, with the syntax shown, route redistribution still doesn't work. The reason is that Network A is using a process ID of 10 for EIGRP, and Network B is using an AS of 20 for IGRP. If we change the IGRP AS of Network B from 20 to 10, route redistribution functions correctly. The final syntax of RouterB would be as follows:

```
router eigrp 10
network 1.0.0.0
!
router igrp 10
   network 8.0.0.0
```

Notice that no `redistribute` or `default-metric` commands are necessary. Since the AS for both EIGRP and IGRP is now set to 10, redistribution occurs automatically.

Before considering more advanced concepts of route redistribution, we will examine one final scenario of route summarization. This time, we will be redistributing EIGRP and OSPF.

EIGRP and OSPF Route Redistribution

In this variation of our original example, let us say that Company B ran OSPF as its internal routing process. Figure 10.6 shows the appropriate syntax for redistributing EIGRP and OSPF into one another.

FIGURE 10.6 EIGRP and OSPF redistribution

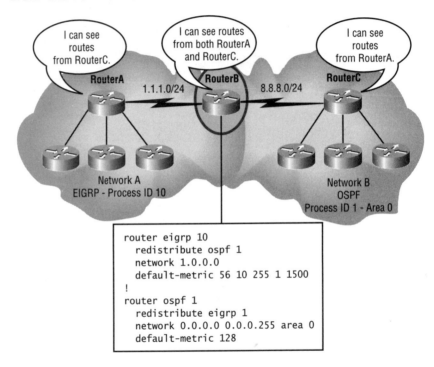

```
router eigrp 10
  redistribute ospf 1
  network 1.0.0.0
  default-metric 56 10 255 1 1500
!
router ospf 1
  redistribute eigrp 1
  network 0.0.0.0 0.0.0.255 area 0
  default-metric 128
```

Verifying and Troubleshooting Route Redistribution

You can use various commands to verify and troubleshoot route redistribution. The best commands to use on your router are `trace`, `show ip route`, and `show ip protocol`. Let's take a closer look at each of these commands:

trace   This command is useful for verifying and troubleshooting route redistribution. Using the `trace` command, you can determine over which path your traffic is flowing and decide if the optimal path is being used.

show ip route   This command displays what routes the router has learned and by which routing protocol it learned them. You can verify that all the networks are in the routing table.

show ip protocols   This command displays the IP routing protocols configured on the router and shows what each routing process is redistributing. Let's look at an example:

```
Routing Protocol is "ospf 1"
  Sending updates every 0 seconds
  Invalid after 0 seconds, hold down 0, flushed after 0
  Outgoing update filter list for all interfaces is not
⮡set
  Incoming update filter list for all interfaces is not
⮡set
  Default redistribution metric is 128
  Redistributing: ospf 1, eigrp 10
```

In addition to the above listed commands, protocol-specific **debug** commands may be useful. For example, if you are viewing RIP updates (by using the `debug ip rip` command), you may see a network advertised as unreachable. An unreachable network will not show up in the routing table. This situation can occur when you forget to set a protocol's default metric.

Advanced Redistribution

Our redistribution examples up to this point have set the default metric for a particular routing protocol. That metric is then used every time another routing protocol is redistributed into that particular routing protocol. Also, in our examples, all the routes have been redistributed; that is, we have not been filtering the content of our routing updates.

We will now examine how to control redistribution with a higher degree of granularity. For example, we may want RIP to apply one metric to OSPF and another metric to IGRP, as these products are redistributed into the RIP routing process.

Also, in some cases, we may want only a subset of routes redistributed. When, in our example, the two companies merge, perhaps we don't want the users on Network B to be able to access the services on network 2.0.0.0 in Network A, for security reasons. In other instances, we may not want to advertise or accept advertisements from all available routes, due to the sheer volume of routes. For example, if our router is connected to an Internet Service Provider and is accepting full routes from the Internet, we would have over 65,000 routing entries in our routing table. Such a large number of routing entries consumes a significant amount of RAM and processor overhead.

Protocol-Specific Metrics

Let's examine how to set up redistribution such that we set the metric for a redistributed protocol as part of the redistribute command. To illustrate, let's consider the first example given in the chapter, where Network A is running EIGRP and Network B is running RIP. Figure 10.7 shows how we could configure RouterB to accomplish route redistribution. This syntax gives us the flexibility to specify alternate metrics for EIGRP and RIP to use if other routing protocols, such as OSPF, were being redistributed into them.

FIGURE 10.7   Protocol-specific metrics

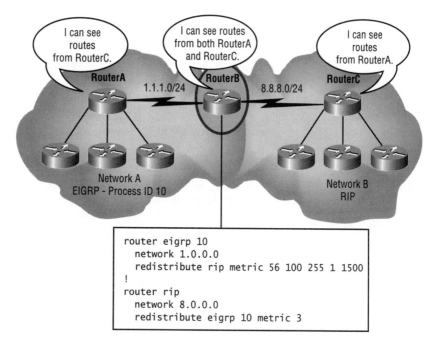

Route-Specific Metrics

To get even greater control over how metrics are assigned, we can use access lists and route maps to set metrics for specific routes. As an example, let's examine how to set a specific metric for network 5.0.0.0 as it is redistributed from RIP in Network B into EIGRP in Network A.

First, we create an access list that permits only network 5.0.0.0. Since we're not concerned with destination addresses, a standard IP access list (an access list numbered from 1 through 99) will be fine for our purposes. Following is the syntax to create an access list that permits only network 5.0.0.0:

```
access-list 1 permit 5.0.0.0
```

Next, we need to create a route map. We will examine route maps in more detail later in the chapter. However, for now we can think of a route map as an IF-THEN-ELSE statement. IF the advertised route is permitted by our access list, THEN apply a specific metric, or ELSE apply a different metric. Following is the syntax to create our route map:

- `route-map test 1`

  assigns the name `test` to our `route-map`, and designates this section as sequence number 1.

- `match ip address 1`

  checks `access-list` 1 to see if a `permit` condition is met.

- `set metric 56 100 255 100 1500`

  If the `permit` condition was met in the previous statement, then assign the given metric. Notice that we have set this metric to indicate that the link is partially loaded (load is set to 100, indicating that the link is approximately 39 percent [100/255] loaded).

- `route-map test 2`

  designates this section as sequence number 2 of the `route-map` named `test`.

- `set metric 56 100 255 1 1500`

  If the `match` condition in sequence number 1 was not met, then apply the given `metric`. Notice that this `metric` specifies an unloaded link (load is set to 1).

Finally, we need to apply the route map to the EIGRP routing process with the following syntax:

```
router eigrp 10
redistribute rip route-map test
```

Here we `redistribute` routes learned via RIP into EIGRP, with the parameters specified in the `route-map` named `test`.

Now, when network 5.0.0.0 is being redistributed into EIGRP, it will have a different metric than other networks, as shown in Figure 10.8.

FIGURE 10.8   Route-specific metrics

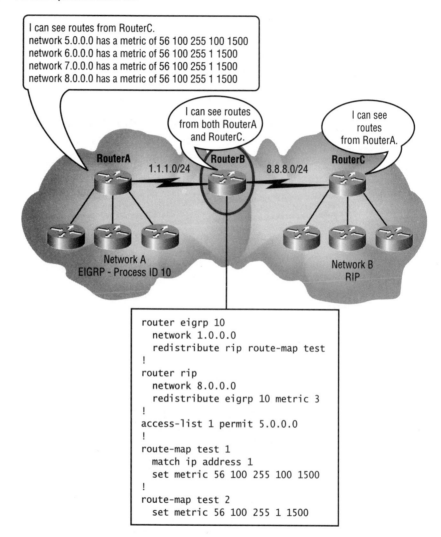

Filtering Routes

In the previous section, we explored how we could specify different metrics
for different routes. However, as we mentioned earlier, there are many
instances where we want only a subset of routes advertised or received. We

can use the `distribute-list` command to accomplish this goal. To illustrate how to use the `distribute-list` command, consider a variation of our original example. This time, Network A is running EIGRP, Network B is running RIP, and we want only the 1.0.0.0 network and the 2.0.0.0 network to be advertised to Network B.

First, we create an access list that specifies which networks we want to be learned by RouterB:

```
access-list 2 permit 1.0.0.0 0.255.255.255
access-list 2 permit 2.0.0.0 0.255.255.255
```

Next, we use the `distribute-list` command to permit only the networks specified in the access list:

```
router eigrp 10
  distribute-list 2 in
```

Notice the `in` argument in the `distribute-list` command. The `in` argument tells the EIGRP routing process to learn only routes that are permitted by the access list, as shown in Figure 10.9.

FIGURE 10.9 Distribute list

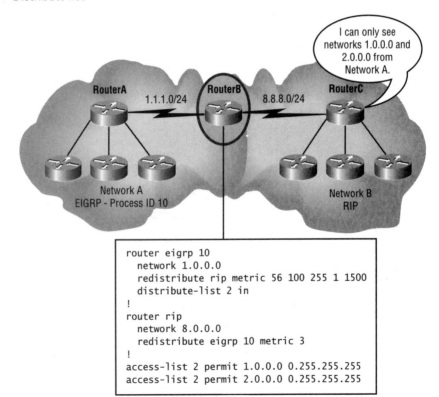

Alternatively, we could have used the out argument with the RIP routing process. The out argument tells the RIP routing process to advertise only routes that are permitted by the access list. If we had used the out argument, the syntax would be

```
router rip
  distribute-list 1 out
```

Using the Null0 Interface

Like the distribute-list feature, the Null0 interface can be used to creatively control routes. Specifically, Null0 is a logical interface, and when traffic is directed (routed) to this interface, the traffic is discarded. In some of the literature, you may see Null0 referred to as a "bit bucket" or a "black hole," because whatever goes in does not come out. Traffic can be directed into the Null0 interface using a static route. Consider the following example.

In order to conserve IP numbers, some networks use private IP addresses (e.g., 10.0.0.0/8, 172.16.0.0/12, or 192.168.0.0/16). If we were using private address space inside our network, then we would certainly not want to advertise these networks outside our network, because we might accidentally advertise these routes to someone else who was using private addressing. Therefore, we could use our distribute-list command to prevent the advertisement of private address space. Alternatively, we could create a static route that directed all traffic destined for this private address space to be discarded, as shown in Figure 10.10.

FIGURE 10.10   The bit bucket

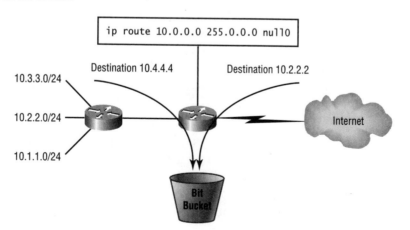

Let's examine the syntax used in Figure 10.10:

`ip route 10.0.0.0 255.0.0.0 null0`

The standard syntax of the `ip route` command is

`ip route network network_mask {`*`address`* `|` *`interface`*`}`

where *`address`* is the IP number of the next-hop address (the next router on the way to the destination network) and *`interface`* is the interface on the local router to which traffic should be forwarded.

In our example, *`interface`* is the logical interface Null0. Therefore, all traffic destined for network 10.0.0.0/8 is discarded.

Static, Connected, and Default Routes

So far in this chapter, we have examined how to take routes from one routing protocol and re-advertise them into a different routing protocol. We'll now take a look at some special redistribution cases.

If we want to redistribute static routes that we have created or routes that are part of directly connected interfaces on a router, we can use the following commands:

`redistribute static`

which redistributes routes that have been manually configured.

`redistribute connected`

which redistributes routes of networks that are connected directly to the local router. These routes may or may not be a part of a routing process.

The Null0 interface example we considered earlier would be an example of a static route, as would a default route. A default route tells a router where to send packets if the destination network is not in its routing table. For example, if a client were trying to reach an IP address on the Internet, and the local router did not have an explicit route to the destination, then the packet would be sent along the default route to either a particular router interface or to the IP address of the next-hop router. When creating a static default route, the syntax is as follows:

`ip route 0.0.0.0 0.0.0.0 {`*`address`* `|` *`interface`*`}`

where `0.0.0.0 0.0.0.0` is the network number for a default route.

Redistributing a default route can be particularly useful for systems such as older Unix hosts that run RIP. In the case of these hosts, some do not have a default gateway setting. Rather, these hosts rely on RIP advertisements to find the default gateway, as shown in Figure 10.11.

FIGURE 10.11 Redistributing static default routes

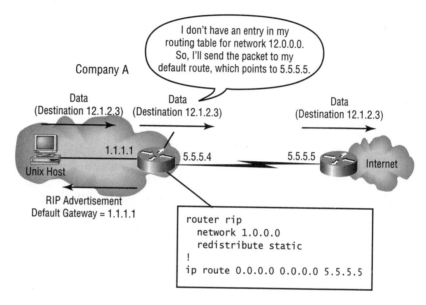

Route Maps

Earlier in the chapter, we saw how route maps can be used to fine-tune route redistribution. Other examples of policy-based routing benefits include

- Load sharing, based on the type of traffic

- Sending low-priority or non-interactive traffic (e.g., routine batch processes) over slower, low-cost links

- Traffic prioritization, based on the type of traffic

Route maps have two primary components: a match clause and a set clause. The function of the match clause is to specify the traffic that is to be policy routed. The traffic may be specified by using an access list (either standard or extended), packet length, metric value, route type, or tag value. The route map processes the match statements sequentially until a match is found. As with access lists, there is an implicit deny statement at the end of the match list.

Once the `match` clause is satisfied, the `set` clause can manipulate the routing of the traffic by setting the next-hop or default interface or IP address, setting the IP TOS (Type of Service), or setting the IP precedence of the traffic. Note that route maps are set on the source router (the first router to receive the packet), not the destination router. To better understand how policy routing works, let's consider a couple of examples.

Policy-Routing TCP Services

As shown in Figure 10.12, Company A has two connections to the Internet: one to ISP A and the other to ISP B. The connection to ISP A is much faster than the connection to ISP B. Therefore, Company A wants to send all latency-sensitive traffic over the link to ISP A and all non-interactive traffic over the link to ISP B. So, for our example, we will configure RouterA to direct SMTP (Simple Mail Transfer Protocol) traffic over the link to ISP B, and all other traffic will be sent over the link to ISP A.

FIGURE 10.12   Policy routing example 1

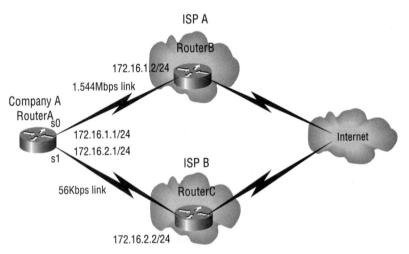

First we need to create an access list that will define the traffic we are interested in, specifically SMTP traffic:

```
access-list 101 permit tcp any any eq 25
```
where 25 is the `tcp` port number for SMTP.

Next, we need to create a route map. In this example, we will name it "routemail":

```
route-map routemail permit 10
```

where `routemail` is an arbitrary name chosen for the route map, 10 is the route map sequence number, and the sequence number is 10 by default, unless another number is specified.

We will now set the criteria for the first `match` clause:

`match ip address 101`

where 101 is the access list that the `match` clause is checking traffic against.

We will now use the `set` clause to specify the `next-hop` address of traffic satisfying the `match` clause:

`set ip next-hop 172.16.2.2`

where `172.16.2.2` is the IP address of the `next-hop` router.

Finally, we need to specify where to send traffic if the match condition is not met:

`route-map routemail permit 20`
`  set ip next-hop 172.16.1.2`

where 20 is the sequence number and `172.16.1.2` is the `next-hop` router.

RouterA will now send all SMTP traffic over the 56Kbps link to RouterC and all other traffic over the 1.544Mbps link to RouterB, as shown in Figure 10.13.

FIGURE 10.13   Policy routing configuration for example 1

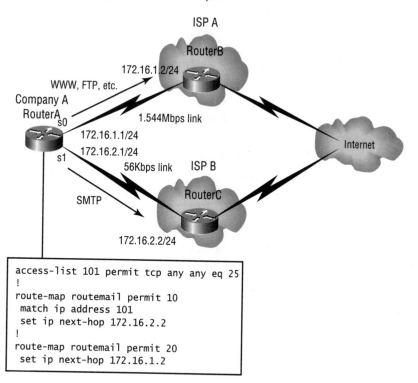

Policy Routing Subnets

As another example, consider the following scenario. Company A has the same ISP connections as in the previous example. Inside Company A, we have two VLANs, the Engineering VLAN (172.16.3.0/24) and the Accounting VLAN (172.16.4.0/24), as illustrated in Figure 10.14. Our goal is to direct traffic from the Engineering VLAN (172.16.3.0/24) out the 1.544Mbps link (interface s0) and to direct traffic from the Accounting VLAN (172.16.4.0/24) out the 56Kbps link (interface s1).

FIGURE 10.14 Policy routing example 2

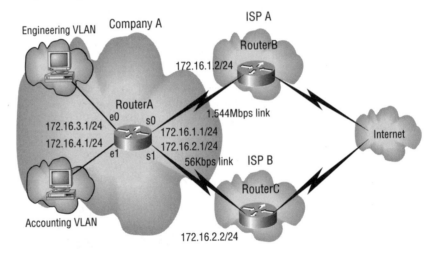

First, we need to create our access lists, specifying the conditions we're looking for, that is, whether a packet was sourced from the Engineering or Accounting VLAN:

```
access-list 1 permit 172.16.3.0 0.0.0.255
access-list 2 permit 172.16.4.0 0.0.0.255
```

Next, we need to create our route map and specify the match and set parameters. In this example, we will use the name "routevlan":

```
route-map routevlan permit 10
  match ip address 1
  set interface serial0
!
```

```
route-map routevlan permit 20
  match ip address 2
  set interface serial1
```

The Accounting users will now have their Internet traffic directed to ISP B, while the Engineering users will have their Internet traffic directed to ISP A, as shown in Figure 10.15.

FIGURE 10.15 Policy routing configuration for example 2

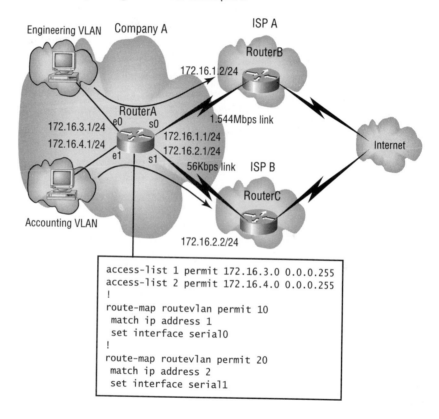

```
access-list 1 permit 172.16.3.0 0.0.0.255
access-list 2 permit 172.16.4.0 0.0.0.255
!
route-map routevlan permit 10
 match ip address 1
 set interface serial0
!
route-map routevlan permit 20
 match ip address 2
 set interface serial1
```

Summary

In this chapter, we discussed how to take networks running different routing protocols and allow them to exchange routing information, through a process called route redistribution. One of the challenges of route redistribution is that many routing protocols use different metrics. To overcome this challenge, we set default metrics for various routing protocols. After examining several redistribution examples, we reviewed commands for verifying and troubleshooting route redistribution.

We explored various advanced route-manipulation techniques including setting metrics on a protocol-by-protocol basis and setting metrics for specific routes. We introduced the `distribute-list` feature as a tool for filtering the receiving or advertising of routes, and we showed the virtual interface Null0 to be an efficient way of discarding packets destined for specified networks. We also detailed how to redistribute static and connected routes.

Finally, we introduced the powerful features of route maps. We used the route map components, `match` and `set` clauses, in examples where we routed traffic based on the source network and Layer 4 information (TCP port numbers).

Key Terms

Before taking the exam, make sure you are familiar with the following terms:

hop count

metric

Null0

route redistribution

Written Lab

Write the configuration for the RouterA, such that HTTP traffic is directed to RouterC, and all other traffic is directed to RouterB, as shown in the following graphic:

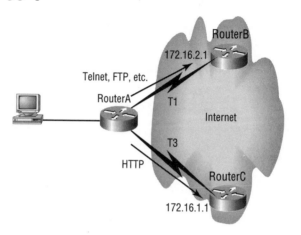

Solution

The first step is to create an access list that specifies the traffic we are interested in, which in this case is HTTP traffic. By default, HTTP uses TCP port 80. Therefore, our access list would be

```
access-list 101 permit tcp any any eq 80
```

Next, we need to create a route map. In this exercise, we will name it "routeweb":

```
route-map routeweb permit 10
```

We'll now set the criteria for the first match clause:

```
match ip address 101
```

Next, we will use the set clause to specify the next-hop address of traffic satisfying the match clause:

```
set ip next-hop 172.16.1.1
```

Finally, we need to specify where to send traffic if the `match` condition is not met:

```
route-map routeweb permit 20
  set ip next-hop 172.16.2.1
```

RouterA will now send all HTTP traffic over the T3 link to RouterC and all other traffic over the T1 link to RouterB.

Hands-on Lab

Add a `distribute-list` command to RouterA, such that RouterB can see network 1.1.1.0/24 in its routing table, but not network 2.2.2.0/24, as shown in the following graphic:

Solution

RouterA and RouterB should have their s0 interfaces interconnected with a serial crossover cable. We will arbitrarily designate RouterB as the DCE side and RouterA as the DTE side.

First, we create an access list on RouterA that specifies which networks we want to be advertised:

```
access-list 1 permit 1.0.0.0 0.255.255.255
```

Next, we use the `distribute-list` command to permit only the network specified in the access list:

```
router rip
  distribute-list 1 out
```

Following are possible configurations for RouterA and RouterB:

RouterA

```
!
version 11.2
!
hostname RouterA
!
interface Loopback0
 ip address 1.1.1.1 255.255.255.0
!
interface Loopback1
 ip address 2.2.2.2 255.255.255.0
!
interface Serial0
 ip address 3.3.3.1 255.255.255.0
!
router rip
 distribute-list 1 out
 network 1.0.0.0
 network 2.0.0.0
 network 3.0.0.0
!
access-list 1 permit 1.0.0.0 0.255.255.255
!
no ip classless
!
line con 0
line aux 0
line vtp 0 4
 login
!
end
```

RouterB

```
!
version 11.2
!
hostname RouterB
!
interface Serial0
 ip address 3.3.3.1 255.255.255.0
 clockrate 56000
!
router rip
 network 3.0.0.0
!
no ip classless
!
line con 0
line aux 0
line vtp 0 4
 login
!
end
```

Issuing the show ip route command on RouterB reveals that RouterB has entries for networks 1.1.1.0 and 3.3.3.0 but not for network 2.2.2.0.

Review Questions

1. Which of the following is the metric used by RIP?

   A. Ticks

   B. Bandwidth

   C. Delay

   D. Hop count

2. Which of the following is the network address and subnet mask of the default route?

   A. 127.0.0.1 255.255.255.255

   B. 0.0.0.0 0.0.0.0

   C. 255.255.255.255 0.0.0.0

   D. 255.255.255.255 255.255.255.255

3. What are the two clauses used by route maps?

   A. metric

   B. match

   C. access

   D. set

4. Which of the following are Cisco proprietary protocols? (Choose all that apply.)

   A. RIP

   B. IGRP

   C. OSPF

   D. EIGRP

5. Which of the following are metric components of IGRP? (Choose all that apply.)

   A. Delay

   B. Hops

   C. Bandwidth

   D. Ticks

6. What number would we assign to the load component of an EIGRP metric to indicate that a link was approximately 10 percent loaded?

   A. 10

   B. 1

   C. 2.5

   D. 25

7. What is the default MTU size metric component for an Ethernet interface?

   A. 1500 bytes

   B. 1518 bytes

   C. 64 bytes

   D. 4000 bytes

8. What is the most desirable value for the reliability metric component?

   A. 255

   B. 0

   C. 1

   D. 100

9. Which of the following protocols share similar metrics?

   A. RIP and OSPF

   B. IGRP and EIGRP

   C. BGP and RTMP

   D. NLSP and RIP

10. What command, under the `router eigrp 10` command, would you enter to set the default metric for EIGRP to use, regardless of which protocol was being distributed into the EIGRP process?

   A. `redistribute eigrp metric 56 10 255 1 1500`

   B. `default-metric 56 10 255 1 1500`

   C. `metric 10`

   D. `default metric 10`

11. Given the access list access-list 1 permit 10.0.0.0 0.255.255.255, what command would allow only network 10.0.0.0/8 to be added to a router's routing table?

   A. `access-list 1 in`

   B. `distribute-list 1 out`

   C. `distribute-list 1 in`

   D. `distribute 1 out`

12. What happens to packets that are forwarded to the Null0 interface?

   A. The packets are sent to the gateway of last resort.

   B. The packets are policy-routed.

   C. The packets are marked as discard eligible.

   D. The packets are discarded.

13. Which of the following commands will display the default redistribution metric for a protocol?

    A. show ip route

    B. trace

    C. show ip protocols

    D. debug ip route

14. Which of the following commands will redistribute manually configured routes into a specified routing process?

    A. redistribute connected

    B. redistribute static

    C. redistribute default

    D. redistribute local

15. If a local interface is not part of a routing process, what command may be used to inject its route into a routing process?

    A. redistribute connected

    B. redistribute static

    C. redistribute default

    D. redistribute local

16. Which of the following are possible applications of route maps? (Choose all that apply.)

    A. Load sharing

    B. Directing different traffic types over different links

    C. Route redistribution

    D. Traffic prioritization

17. Given the command `route-map routemail permit` 20, what does 20 represent?

A. The sequence number of the route map

B. The access list number being used

C. The TCP port number being routed

D. The percent of bandwidth to be allocated

18. In order for IGRP and EIGRP to automatically redistribute routes into each other, what must be true?

A. They must be advertising subnets of the same major network.

B. They must have the same process ID (the same Autonomous System).

C. They must be in different areas.

D. They must both be in totally stubby areas.

19. What command could you use to view RIP updates as they occur?

A. `show ip protocols`

B. `show ip route`

C. `show ip rip`

D. `debug ip rip`

20. What does the command `distribute-list 2 out` do?

A. It prevents or permits the routes specified in access-list 2 from being added to the local routing table.

B. It prevents or permits the routes specified in access-list 2 from being advertised.

C. It redirects the routes specified in access-list 2 to the Null0 interface.

D. It redistributes routes specified in access-list 2 to all routing protocols.

Answers to Review Questions

1. D.   RIP considers only the number of routers (hops) to be traversed en route to a destination network.

2. B.   Cisco uses 0.0.0.0 0.0.0.0 to indicate a default route in a static routing statement.

3. B and D.   Route maps have two primary components, a `match` clause and a `set` clause. The function of the `match` clause is to specify the traffic that is to be policy routed. The purpose of the `set` clause is to manipulate the routing of traffic by adjusting such parameters as next-hop address.

4. B and D.   IGRP and EIGRP are similar in that they use the same metric components, and they are both Cisco proprietary.

5. A and C.   The metric components of IGRP are bandwidth, delay, reliability, load, and MTU size.

6. D.   The values for load range from 1 through 255, where 1 is unloaded and 255 is completely loaded. A 10 percent load may be calculated by multiplying 255 by .1, which equals 25.5. Since we need to specify load in terms of an integer, we choose 25.

7. A.   Even though the maximum MTU size for Ethernet is 1518 bytes, the default MTU value used in the metric calculation for an Ethernet interface is 1500 bytes.

8. A.   Reliability values range from 1 through 255, where 1 is completely unreliable and 255 is completely reliable.

9. B.   Both IGRP and EIGRP use bandwidth, delay, reliability, load, and MTU size as their metric components.

10. B.   The command `default-metric 56 10 255 1 1500` can be used to specify the metric to be used for any route being redistributed into EIGRP. This may not be optimal if you want to specify different metrics for different protocols.

11. C. The `in` parameter on a `distribute-list` command specifies routes to be added to a router's routing table. The `out` parameter specifies routes to be advertised from a router.

12. D. The Null0 interface is a virtual interface, which is sometimes referred to as a bit bucket. Packets sent to the Null0 interface are discarded. Since a static route requires less processing than an access list, a route to Null0 is sometimes preferable to an access list denying a particular host or network.

13. C. The `show ip protocols` command will display such information as redistribution parameters.

14. B. The `redistribute static` command redistributes routes that have been manually configured.

15. A. The `redistribute connected` command redistributes routes of networks that are connected directly to the local router. These routes may or may not be a part of a routing process.

16. A, B, C, and D. Route maps, which use a combination of `match` and `set` clauses, can be used for all of the listed applications.

17. A. The 20 is the sequence number of the route map. The sequence numbers of the route map determine in what order the `match` and `set` clauses will be evaluated.

18. B. If IGRP and EIGRP processes are both running on the same router, and they both have the same process ID, then their routes will automatically be redistributed into each other.

19. D. The `debug ip rip` command can be used to view the contents of RIP updates as they occur.

20. B. The `out` parameter of the `distribute-list` command deals with advertising routes, while the `in` parameter deals with adding routes to the local routing table.

Appendix A

Practice Exam

1. How is a BGP session established between two routers?

   A. Telnet

   B. TCP (SYN, ACK, SYN)

   C. UDP (SYN, ACK, SYN)

   D. IPX SAP

2. Which of the following is true concerning a stub area?

   A. It does not receive summary Link State Advertisements.

   B. It does not receive Type 5 LSAs.

   C. It is configured with the IOS command area `stub area-id`.

   D. Only the ABR needs to be configured as stubby.

3. Which two of the following would you use to avoid creating a full-mesh BGP network?

   A. Confederations

   B. Route maps

   C. Prefix lists

   D. Route reflectors

4. Which of the following are used by EIGRP to send queries to other EIGRP neighbors?

   A. Broadcasts

   B. Multicasts

   C. ACKs

   D. Unicasts

5. Which of the following is the IOS command to clear all dynamic IP routes from a router's routing table?

A. `clear ip route *`

B. `clear ip route 0.0.0.0`

C. `clear ip route all`

D. `clear ip route 127.0.0.1`

6. When should BGP be used? (Choose all that apply.)

A. When multi-homing

B. When connecting multiple ISPs

C. When connecting routers within the same AS

D. When configuring backup links

7. What route/subnet mask combination indicates a default route?

A. 127.0.0.1 255.255.255.255

B. 255.255.255.255 255.255.255.255

C. 0.0.0.0 255.255.255.255

D. 0.0.0.0 0.0.0.0

8. Which Cisco layer is responsible for breaking up collision domains?

A. Core

B. Backbone

C. Distribution

D. Access

9. What does the IOS command `show ip ospf virtual-links` do?

    A. It shows the router link states.

    B. It shows the network link states.

    C. It shows the status of a router's virtual links.

    D. It shows the virtual memory that a router is using to maintain its link state database.

10. What does the command `redistribute static` do?

    A. It makes dynamically learned routes permanent.

    B. It takes manually configured routes and redistributes them into a specified routing protocol.

    C. It takes routes from directly connected interfaces and redistributes them into a specified routing protocol.

    D. It causes the same metric to be used for a routing protocol, regardless of which routing protocol it is being redistributed into.

11. Which syntax used with the `clear ip bgp` command is used to identify that the command is to affect inbound or outbound triggered updates?

    A. open in

    B. soft

    C. triggered inbound

    D. triggered outbound

12. What is the default administrative distance of EIGRP?

    A. 0

    B. 1

    C. 90

    D. 100

    E. 110

13. If an external AS is not receiving updates from your AS, which of the following show commands can be used to troubleshoot this? (Choose all that apply.)

A. show ip bgp events

B. show ip bgp neighbor

C. show ip bgp all

D. show ip bgp

14. If you wanted to summarize networks 172.16.100.0/24 and 172.16.106.0/24, which network and mask would you use?

A. 172.16.0.0/24

B. 172.16.100.0/20

C. 172.16.106.0/20

D. 172.16.96.0/20

15. Which of the following statements are true? (Choose all that apply.)

A. Every OSPF network must have an Area 0.

B. A router with one or more interfaces in Area 0 is said to be a backbone router.

C. If an IGRP routing process connects to a multi-area OSPF network, the router through which it enters the OSPF network is called an ABR.

D. An ASBR separates two or more OSPF areas.

16. If you wanted to reduce bandwidth usage, which Cisco IOS features could you use? (Choose all that apply.)

A. Access lists

B. Snapshot routing

C. Compression of WANs

D. TTL

E. DDR

F. Incremental updates

17. Which IOS command will display redistribution parameters?

   A. `show ip protocols`

   B. `debug ip protocols`

   C. `debug ip redistribution`

   D. `show ip redistribution`

18. If you wanted to manually summarize an EIGRP, which of the following commands must you use under the EIGRP configuration?

   A. `no summary`

   B. `no auto-summary`

   C. `no summary stub`

   D. `no route-summary`

19. Which is true regarding routing protocols?

   A. Classless routing protocols send periodic subnet mask information.

   B. Classless routing protocols send incremental subnet mask information.

   C. Classless routing protocols send prefix mask information.

   D. All devices on a network running classless routing protocols must use the same mask.

20. Which of the following commands is used to specify the NBMA network type?

   A. `ip ospf nmba network`

   B. `ip ospf network`

   C. `ip ospf nmba-network`

   D. `ip ospf network-nmba`

21. The following output is an example of using which command?

```
BGP neighbor is 172.16.11.254, remote AS 100, internal
↳link
Index 1, Offset 0, Mask 0x2
Route-Reflector Client
BGP version 4, remote router ID 10.16.1.1
BGP state = Established, table version = 1, up for
↳12:10:16
Last read 00:00:06, hold time is 180,
keepalive interval is 60 seconds
Minimum time between advertisement runs is 5 seconds
Received 143 messages, 0 notifications, 0 in queue
Sent 52 messages, 0 notifications, 0 in queue
Prefix advertised , suppressed 0, withdrawn 0
Connections established 2; dropped 1
Last reset 12:10:16, due to User reset
53 accepted prefixes consume 32 bytes
0 history paths consume 0 bytes
```

A. show ip bgp all

B. show cdp bgp neighbors

C. show running-config

D. show ip bgp neighbors

22. When an AS must traverse another AS to get to its destination, the traversed AS is called which of the following?

A. Transfer AS

B. Forwarding AS

C. Transit AS

D. Transmitting AS

23. How many steps (neighbor states) are involved in establishing an OSPF adjacency?

A. Five

B. Six

C. Seven

D. Four

24. Which of the following is true regarding route summarization?

A. It's used primarily with discontiguous networks.

B. It's used primarily with contiguous networks.

C. Do not use with VLSM.

D. It's used with non-hierarchical addressing.

25. The OSPF _____ state is simply the state of receiving Hello packets on the interface.

A. Down

B. Up

C. Init

D. Active

26. What happens to traffic that is sent to the Null0 interface?

A. It is set to a full CIR.

B. It is discarded.

C. It is sent to the default interface.

D. It is multiplexed with other traffic leaving the router on interface Null0.

27. Which of the following are true regarding IP unnumbered? (Choose all that apply.)

    A. It does not work over HDLC networks.

    B. It is not compatible with SNMP.

    C. It does not work over X.25 networks.

    D. You cannot ping an unnumbered interface.

28. Which of the following is true regarding routing protocols?

    A. Classful routing protocols send periodic subnet mask information.

    B. Classful routing protocols send incremental subnet mask information.

    C. Classful routing protocols send prefix mask information.

    D. All devices on a network running classful routing protocols must use the same mask.

29. In the IOS command used to create an OSPF virtual link, `area area-id virtual-link router-id`, what is the `area-id`?

    A. The transit area's ID

    B. The IP address of the highest loopback interface configured on the router

    C. The ID of the area that is not physically adjacent to the backbone area

    D. The highest IP address configured on the router

30. If you wanted to see the configured peer BGP routers and the current connection state, which Cisco IOS command would you use?

    A. `show ip bgp all`

    B. `show cdp bgp neighbors`

    C. `show running-config`

    D. `show ip bgp neighbors`

31. If you wanted to provide stability and availability, which Cisco IOS features could you use? (Choose all that apply.)

   A. Reachability

   B. Convergence

   C. Alternative path routing

   D. Snapshot routing

   E. Tunneling

   F. Dial backup

   G. Load balancing

32. Which of the following is a disadvantage to segmenting a network with bridges?

   A. Bridges do not segment the network.

   B. Bridges only create internetworks.

   C. Bridges forward all broadcasts.

   D. Bridges only filter frames.

33. Which of the following indicates EIGRP process numbers?

   A. Link-state value

   B. Autonomous system number

   C. Path cost

   D. Number of ACKs

34. What is the default administrative distance of static routes?

   A. 0

   B. 1

   C. 90

   D. 100

   E. 110

35. The IOS commands `router bgp 100` and `neighbor 10.1.1.1 remote-as 200` provide what function?

    A. They configure BGP with an internal iBGP neighbor.

    B. They configure BGP with an external iBGP neighbor.

    C. They configure BGP with an internal BGP neighbor.

    D. They configure BGP with an external BGP neighbor.

36. Which of the following are problems that may occur if route redistribution occurs across multiple EIGRP processes? (Choose all that apply.)

    A. Non-optimal route choices

    B. Slow convergence

    C. Routing loops

    D. Broadcast storms

37. If you want to allow routes to enter a route interface, but deny any route information from exiting the specified interface, which IOS command must you use?

    A. `no routing`

    B. `access filters`

    C. `access lists`

    D. `passive interface`

38. In the IOS command `match ip address 1`, what does the 1 indicate?

    A. Sequence number

    B. Access list number

    C. Process ID

    D. Apply to incoming traffic

39. If you have a subnet mask of 255.255.255.224, what is the CIDR?

  A. /17

  B. /23

  C. /24

  D. /27

40. Which of the following are timers used by the EIGRP neighbor table? (Choose all that apply.)

  A. SRTT

  B. RTO

  C. Hold timer

  D. Time To Live timer

  E. Stop timer

41. If you wanted to connect to your company network and load balance with connections to four different ISPs, which routing protocol must you use?

  A. RIP

  B. OSPF

  C. BGP

  D. EIGRP

42. What is port 179 used for in a BGP session?

  A. Route updates

  B. To set up FTP between BGP peers

  C. To close a session with another BGP peer

  D. To open a session with another BGP peer

43. Which of the following commands can be used on a router when routes continuously flap to make sure that a link is up before it is advertised?

A. `ip bgp as-path`

B. `ip bgp hold time`

C. `set as-path extended`

D. `bgp dampening`

44. Which of the following is a Cisco proprietary BGP attribute?

A. Atomic Aggregate

B. Next-hop

C. MED

D. Weight

45. What is the default administrative distance of OSPF?

A. 0

B. 1

C. 90

D. 100

E. 110

46. If OSPF Hello packets are not received from the neighbor, what state will the neighbor interface be in?

A. Down

B. Up

C. Init

D. Active

47. The BGP hold timer is established in which of the following BGP message types?

A. OPEN

B. UPDATE

C. NOTIFICATION

D. KEEPALIVE

48. Which is a solution for a large internetwork that has thousands of route entries in the routing tables?

A. Route summarization

B. Incremental updates

C. IP filtering

D. VLANs

49. What is the router configuration IOS command to configure a router as totally stubby?

A. `area area-id stub`

B. `area area-id totally-stubby`

C. `area area-id stub no-summary`

D. `area area-id nssa`

50. To verify BGP on your Cisco router, which of the following commands should you use?

A. `show ip bgp`

B. `show ip bgp paths`

C. `show ip bgp summary`

D. `show bgp all`

E. `show bgp ip debug`

Answers to Practice Exam

1. B. Using TCP port 179, a BGP session is established.

2. B. A stub area does not receive AS External Link Advertisements (Type 5 LSAs).

3. A, D. Confederations and route reflectors can both be configured to avoid creating a full-mesh network where the `neighbors` command is used excessively.

4. B. EIGRP relies on multicasts to send queries and updates to other EIGRP peers.

5. A. The IOS command `clear ip route *` will clear dynamically established routes from a router's routing table. When troubleshooting routing problems, this command can be useful in clearing route tables immediately, instead of waiting for convergence processes to complete. The other options are invalid syntax.

6. A, B. BGP should be used when multi-homing is used or when you are connecting more than one ISP to your network.

7. D. Cisco uses 0.0.0.0 0.0.0.0 to represent a default route.

8. D. The Access layer is responsible for breaking up collision domains.

9. C. To show the status of a router's virtual links (links that span a transit area in order to reach the backbone area), you can use the IOS command `show ip ospf virtual-links`.

10. B. The `redistribute static` command takes routes that have been manually configured (static routes) and redistributes them into a specified dynamic routing protocol.

11. B. Using the `soft` syntax followed by the `in` and `out` syntaxes, you can identify whether the `clear ip bgp` command is to affect inbound or outbound triggered updates.

12. C. EIGRP routes have a default administrative distance of 90.

13. B, D. The `show ip bgp neighbor` command displays all the advertised routes, and the `show ip bgp` command looks at all the connections.

14. D. If you write out the networks 172.16.100.0/24 and 172.16.106.0/24 in binary and see how many leading bits that they have in common, you will find that the first 20 bits are the same for both networks. If you then convert these 20 bits back into decimal, you will have the address of the summarized route.

15. A and B. In an OSPF network, there must always be a backbone area, which is numbered as Area 0. If a router has any of its interfaces connected to Area 0, that router is said to be a backbone router.

16. A, B, C, E, F. Access lists, snapshot routing, compression techniques, Dial-on-Demand Routing (DDR), and incremental updates all can help reduce bandwidth usage.

17. A. The `show ip protocols` command will display such information as redistribution parameters.

18. B. The command `no auto-summary` is a router-configuration command that disables the automatic summarization of routes.

19. C. Classless routing protocols send prefix routing information with each update.

20. B. The other options are invalid syntax.

21. D. The `show bgp neighbors` command shows the configured BGP peers and the current connection status as shown above.

22. C. A transit AS is an AS through which data from one AS must travel to get to another AS.

23. B. The answer here can be tricky. There are six initialization steps, but not all of them are always seen. Many times the Loading phase is not necessary between the Exchange state and the Full state.

24. B. Route summarization is most effective when used with contiguous address space, because contiguous address space tends to have the most higher-order bits in common.

25. C. The init state is simply the state of receiving Hello packets on the interface; no adjacencies or other information have been exchanged at this point.

26. B. Traffic sent to the virtual interface Null0 is discarded.

27. C, D. IP unnumbered is not supported on X.25 or SMDS networks. Since the serial interface has no IP number, you will not be able to ping the interface to see if it is up. However, you can determine the interface status with SNMP. Also, IP security options are not supported on an IP unnumbered interface.

28. D. Classful routing protocols send no subnet mask information with the routing updates, so all devices on the network must use the same subnet mask.

29. A. The `area-id` parameter in the `area area-id virtual-link router-id` command refers to the ID of the transit area. The transit area connects the backbone area to the area requiring the virtual link.

30. D. The `show bgp neighbors` command shows the configured BGP peers and the current connection status.

31. C, D, E, F. Alternate path routing, which provides redundancy and load balancing, along with snapshot routing, tunneling, and dial backup all provide stability and availability in an internetwork.

32. C. Both switches and bridges break up collision domains but are one large broadcast domain by default. All broadcasts are forwarded to all network segments with a bridge or switch.

33. B. The EIGRP process number is always the number assigned to an autonomous system.

34. B. Static routes have a default administrative distance of 1.

35. D. The commands `router bgp 100` and `neighbor 10.1.1.1 remote-as` 200 configure BGP with an external BGP neighbor.

36. A, B, C. Slow convergence, non-optimal routes, and routing loops are all problems that can occur by using route redistribution.

37. D. Passive interfaces are used for such interfaces as BRI where you do not want to have routing updates sent out the interface. If routing updates were sent out of a BRI interface, then the interface would never disconnect.

38. B. The 1 refers to the access list against which the match command is testing traffic.

39. D. If you write out 255.255.255.224 in binary, you will find that the first 27 bits are ones, and the remaining five bits are zeros. Therefore, we say that it is a /27.

40. A, B, C. The smooth round-trip timer (SRTT), the retransmission timer (RTO), and the hold timer are all used by the neighbor table to track its neighboring routers. The Time To Live and Stop timers are not used by the EIGRP neighbor table.

41. C. Border Gateway Protocol can load balance connections with as many as six different ISPs.

42. D. Port 179 is used by BGP to establish a session with another BGP peer. Ports 20 and 21 are used by FTP, and port 23 is used by Telnet.

43. D. The `bgp dampening` command is used by BGP to set a hold time before a route can be re-advertised after route flapping.

44. D. The Weight attribute is a Cisco proprietary attribute used as a metric only in Cisco implementations of BGPv4.

45. E. OSPF has an administrative distance of 110.

46. A. This status could result from an interface being down, but the specific OSPF definition is the lack of Hello packets received from the neighbor.

47. A. The OPEN message type is used to establish a connection between BGP peers and to negotiate the hold time. The UPDATE message type is used to advertise topology updates and changes. The NOTIFICATION message type is used to advertise errors. The KEEP-ALIVE message type is sent to keep a session active when no UPDATE messages are exchanged during the established hold time.

48. A. Route summarization is used to send fewer route entries in an update. This can reduce the routing table entries.

49. C. The `area area-id stub no-summary` IOS router configuration command is used to configure a router as totally stubby for the specified area. Remember that by becoming totally stubby, a router stops receiving summary Link State Advertisements.

50. A, B, C. The valid BGP `show` commands listed above are `show ip bgp`, `show ip bgp paths`, and `show ip bgp summary`. The `show ip bgp` command displays the BGP routing table. The `show ip bgp paths` command displays all the router's known BGP paths. The `show ip bgp summary` command tells you the status on every BGP connection. The other two commands are not valid.

Appendix B

Commands in This Study Guide

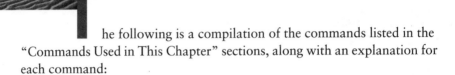

The following is a compilation of the commands listed in the "Commands Used in This Chapter" sections, along with an explanation for each command:

Command	Description	Chapter
aggregate-address	Allows you to configure aggregate routes in BGP and CIDR addressing.	8
bgp default local-preference	Allows you to assign a Local Preference attribute value in the range of 0 to 4,294,967,295. Higher values are preferred over lower values.	8
clear ip bgp	Allows you to clear all or an identified set of routes from the BGP table.	8
debug ip bgp dampening	Displays BGP dampening events as they occur.	8
debug ip bgp events	Displays all BGP events as they occur.	8
debug ip bgp keepalives	Displays all events related to BGP keepalive packets.	8

Command	Description	Chapter
`debug ip bgp updates`	Displays information on all BGP update packets.	8
`distance`	When multiple protocols are running, this command allows a distance value from 1 to 255 to decide which path is the best. The lowest value wins.	6
`ip unnumbered`	Allows serial interfaces to borrow an IP number from another router interface (which may or may not be specified), so that it can joint two contiguous address spaces.	3
`neighbors`	This command has many syntaxes that allow you to identify the internal and external neighbors and assign different metrics to each.	8
`network`	Identifies the networks and masks associated with the local router.	8
`no auto-summary`	Used to disable the automatic route summarization performed by various classless routing protocols, such as RIPv2 and EIGRP.	3
`no synchronization`	Allows you to turn off synchronization between the IGPs and BGP for faster convergence.	8
`passive-interface` *`interface-type`* *`interface-number`*	Identifies interfaces that do not participate in EIGRP updates.	6

Command	Description	Chapter
`router bgp`	Begins the BGP process and identifies the local ASN.	8
`router eigrp`	Starts EIGRP processes on a router.	6
`show ip bgp cidr-only`	Displays classless routes.	8
`show ip bgp community`	Used to display routes belonging to the specified community.	8
`show ip bgp filter-list`	Displays AS path lists.	8
`show ip bgp paths`	Displays all path information for the local router.	8
`show ip bgp peer-group`	Provides information on the members of the specified peer group.	8
`show ip bgp summary`	Shows the status of all BGP connections.	8
`show ip eigrp events`	Shows a log of EIGRP events. These are routes being added to or removed from the routing table.	6
`show ip eigrp neighbors`	Shows directly connected EIGRP-enabled routers.	6
`show ip eigrp topology`	Shows entries in the EIGRP topology table.	6
`show ip eigrp traffic`	Shows the packet count for EIGRP packets sent and received.	6
`show ip protocols`	Shows information about the active protocol sessions.	6

Command	Description	Chapter
show ip route eigrp	Shows all EIGRP neighbors.	6
variance	Assigns a weight to each feasible successor.	6

Appendix C

Route Summarization

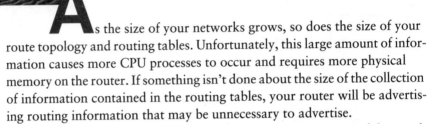

As the size of your networks grows, so does the size of your route topology and routing tables. Unfortunately, this large amount of information causes more CPU processes to occur and requires more physical memory on the router. If something isn't done about the size of the collection of information contained in the routing tables, your router will be advertising routing information that may be unnecessary to advertise.

Summarization provides an excellent way to reduce the size of the topology and routing tables and significantly reduce the load on the router. Summarization provides a way to aggregate routing information, summarize the known routes, and reduce the lines in the IGP tables. If summarization doesn't occur, every route—including those the router doesn't need to know about—will be learned by the router and stored in the tables. This appendix covers route summarization related to Open Shortest Path First (OSPF), Enhanced Interior Gateway Routing Protocol (EIGRP), and Border Gateway Protocol (BGP).

Route Summarization for OSPF

By implementing route summarization for OSPF, you help to eliminate the number of Link State Advertisements that are sent when there is a change in the topology of the network. When route summarization is applied to OSPF, and when there are frequent changes in the router's topology, you can eliminate the advertising of those changes, particularly in the backbone (Area 0).

Three individual route types can be found with OSPF and its various configured areas. The route types are as follows:

Intra-area routes (Type O)   Routes that are explicit network or subnet routes. These must be carried inside a configured area, and all area member routers must know about them.

Intra-area routes (Type IA)   Routes that exist in the internal autonomous system but not in the router's configured area.

External routes (Types E1 and E2)   Routes that exchange routing information between autonomous systems.

Configured areas help divide shared routing information. Area Border Routers (ABR) advertise IA routers from one area to another area.

Route Summarization for EIGRP

EIGRP does not build the same hierarchy tables that OSPF does but is capable of reducing the learned routes. By default, EIGRP automatically summarizes its routes when Variable-Length Subnet Masking (VLSM) is not used. This means that if your addressing scheme uses an 8-, 16-, or 24-bit mask with a class A, B, or C network, EIGRP will handle route summarization just fine. If you do use VLSM, then you need to disable the default summarization by using the `no auto summary` command in the Router Configuration mode. Then you can manually configure a summarized route using the `ip summary eigrp` command on each interface. The command and syntaxes are as follows:

```
ip summary-address eigrp <AS number> <network> <mask>
```

Let's look at an example of the command where the IP address of 172.16.5.254 is connected to another a router that is connected to two other routers with a network range of 172.16.16.0 to 172.16.24.0. If we write out the network numbers in bits, we see that the first 20 bits are identical in each network address. These first 20 bits are referred to as a *CIDR Block*. This block allows the network to be advertised as a single route to the outside world. Instead of keeping a giant routing table of all the networks individually, the tables have only one entry for all the networks contained in the

CIDR Block. This does mean that all those network numbers must be well planned, and they must reside only out Serial 0 on RouterA in Figure C.1.

FIGURE C.1 Summarizing Routes EIGRP

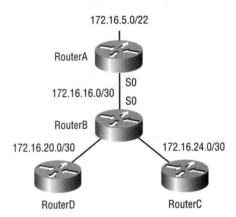

Let's take a look at an example of using the ip summary-address eigrp command:

```
Cisco3640(config)#interface serial 0
Cisco3640(config-if)#ip address 172.16.16.254
↳255.255.255.0
Cisco3640(config-if)#ip summary-address eigrp 10
↳172.16.0.0 255.255.240.0
Cisco3640(config-if)#bandwidth 64
Cisco3640(config-if)#no shut
```

Route Summarization for BGP

We employ route summarization with BGP to limit the number of routes in the routing table by using the aggregate-address command in the BGP router configuration mode. This command creates an atomic aggregate, or summarized, entry in the BGP table. The syntax summary-only tells BGP to advertise only the summary and not the specific routes to each destination. You can use the as-set syntax to include a list of all of the AS numbers that the more specific routes have passed through. The command and the syntaxes are as follows:

```
aggregate-address ip-address mask [summary-only]
[as-set]
```

Let's take a look at a sample configuration using this command:

```
RouterA(config)#router bgp 65000
RouterA(config-router)#network 172.16.0.0 mask 255.255.0.0
RouterA(config-router)#neighbor 10.1.1.2 remote-as 64500
RouterA(config-router)#neighbor 172.16.1.50 remote-as
 ⮡65000
RouterA(config-router)#network 172.16.10.0 mask
 ⮡255.255.255.0
RouterA(config-router)#network 172.16.1.0 mask
 ⮡255.255.255.0
RouterA(config-router)#no synchronization
RouterA(config-router)#neighbor 172.16.1.50 next-hop-self
RouterA(config-router)#aggregate-address 172.16.0.0
 ⮡255.255.0.0 summary-only
```

Advertising Networks into BGP

Redistribution of routing information occurs in a number of ways. The primary way is the network command, which was discussed in Chapters 8, "Configuring Basic BGP" and 9, "BGP Scalability and Advanced Features." The network command allows BGP to advertise a network that is already in the IP table. When using the network command, you must identify all the networks in the AS that you want to advertise.

You can also use the ip route command to create a static route. The static route is then redistributed into BGP. Redistribution occurs when a router uses different protocols to advertise routing information received between the protocols. BGP considers a static route to be a protocol. Static route information is advertised to BGP.

The third way to create a static route is to redistribute dynamically learned routes (routes learned through an IGP) into BGP. In Chapter 8 we learned the commands to enable this; however, Cisco does not recommend this approach because of convergence issues and the possibility of introducing routing loops into the network. Convergence is the time it takes for the network to recover from a change in the network's topology.

Glossary

A&B bit signaling Used in T1 transmission facilities and sometimes called "24th channel signaling." Each of the 24 T1 subchannels in this procedure uses one bit of every sixth frame to send supervisory signaling information.

AAA Authentication, authorization, and accounting: A Cisco description of the processes that are required to provide a remote access security solution. Each is implemented separately, but each can rely on the others for functionality.

AAL ATM Adaptation Layer: A service-dependent sublayer of the Data Link layer, which accepts data from other applications and brings it to the ATM layer in 48-byte ATM payload segments. CS and SAR are the two sublayers that form AALs. Currently, the four types of AAL recommended by the ITU-T are AAL1, AAL2, AAL3/4, and AAL5. AALs are differentiated by the source-destination timing they use, whether they are CBR or VBR, and whether they are used for connection-oriented or connectionless mode data transmission. *See also: AAL1, AAL2, AAL3/4, AAL5, ATM,* and *ATM layer.*

AAL1 ATM Adaptation Layer 1: One of four AALs recommended by the ITU-T, it is used for connection-oriented, time-sensitive services that need constant bit rates, such as isochronous traffic and uncompressed video. *See also: AAL.*

AAL2 ATM Adaptation Layer 2: One of four AALs recommended by the ITU-T, it is used for connection-oriented services that support a variable bit rate, such as voice traffic. *See also: AAL.*

AAL3/4 ATM Adaptation Layer 3/4: One of four AALs (a product of two initially distinct layers) recommended by the ITU-T, supporting both connectionless and connection-oriented links. Its primary use is in sending SMDS packets over ATM networks. *See also: AAL.*

AAL5 ATM Adaptation Layer 5: One of four AALs recommended by the ITU-T, it is used to support connection-oriented VBR services primarily to transfer classical IP over ATM and LANE traffic. This least complex of the AAL recommendations uses SEAL, offering lower bandwidth costs and simpler processing requirements but also providing reduced bandwidth and error-recovery capacities. *See also: AAL.*

AARP AppleTalk Address Resolution Protocol: The protocol in an Apple-Talk stack that maps data-link addresses to network addresses.

AARP probe packets Packets sent by the AARP to determine whether a given node ID is being used by another node in a nonextended AppleTalk network. If the node ID is not in use, the sending node appropriates that node's ID. If the node ID is in use, the sending node will select a different ID and then send out more AARP probe packets. *See also: AARP.*

ABM Asynchronous Balanced Mode: When two stations can initiate a transmission, ABM is an HDLC (or one of its derived protocols) communication technology that supports peer-oriented, point-to-point communications between both stations.

ABR area border router: An OSPF router that is located on the border of one or more OSPF areas. ABRs are used to connect OSPF areas to the OSPF backbone area.

access control Used by Cisco routers to control packets as they pass through a router. Access lists are created and then applied to router interfaces to accomplish this.

Access layer One of the layers in Cisco's three-layer hierarchical model. The Access layer provides users with access to the internetwork.

access link Is a link used with switches and is only part of one Virtual LAN (VLAN). Trunk links carry information from multiple VLANs.

access list A set of test conditions kept by routers that determines "interesting traffic" to and from the router for various services on the network.

access method The manner in which network devices approach gaining access to the network itself.

access rate Defines the bandwidth rate of the circuit. For example, the access rate of a T1 circuit is 1.544Mbps. In Frame Relay and other technologies, there may be a fractional T1 connection—256Kbps, for example—however, the access rate and clock rate is still 1.544Mbps.

access server Also known as a "network access server," it is a communications process connecting asynchronous devices to a LAN or WAN through network and terminal emulation software, providing synchronous or asynchronous routing of supported protocols.

acknowledgment   Verification sent from one network device to another signifying that an event has occurred. May be abbreviated as ACK or Ack. *Contrast with: NAK.*

accounting   One of the three components in AAA. Accounting provides auditing and logging functionalities to the security model.

ACR   allowed cell rate: A designation defined by the ATM Forum for managing ATM traffic. Dynamically controlled using congestion control measures, the ACR varies between the minimum cell rate (MCR) and the peak cell rate (PCR). *See also: MCR and PCR.*

active monitor   The mechanism used to manage a Token Ring. The network node with the highest MAC address on the ring becomes the active monitor and is responsible for management tasks such as preventing loops and ensuring that tokens are not lost.

address learning   Used with transparent bridges to learn the hardware addresses of all devices on an internetwork. The switch then filters the network with the known hardware (MAC) addresses.

address mapping   By translating network addresses from one format to another, this methodology permits different protocols to operate interchangeably.

address mask   A bit combination descriptor identifying which portion of an address refers to the network or subnet and which part refers to the host. Sometimes simply called the mask. *See also: subnet mask.*

address resolution   The process used for resolving differences between computer addressing schemes. Address resolution typically defines a method for tracing Network layer (Layer 3) addresses to Data Link layer (Layer 2) addresses. *See also: address mapping.*

adjacency   The relationship made between defined neighboring routers and end nodes, using a common media segment, to exchange routing information.

administrative distance   A number between 0 and 225 that expresses the value of trustworthiness of a routing information source. The lower the number, the higher the integrity rating.

administrative weight   A value designated by a network administrator to rate the preference given to a network link. It is one of four link metrics exchanged by PTSPs to test ATM network resource availability.

ADSU   ATM Data Service Unit: The terminal adapter used to connect to an ATM network through an HSSI-compatible mechanism. *See also: DSU.*

advertising   The process whereby routing or service updates are transmitted at given intervals, allowing other routers on the network to maintain a record of viable routes.

AEP   AppleTalk Echo Protocol: A test for connectivity between two AppleTalk nodes where one node sends a packet to another and receives an echo, or copy, in response.

AFI   Authority and Format Identifier: The part of an NSAP ATM address that delineates the type and format of the IDI section of an ATM address.

AFP   AppleTalk Filing Protocol: A Presentation layer protocol, supporting AppleShare and Mac OS File Sharing, that permits users to share files and applications on a server.

AIP   ATM Interface Processor: Supporting AAL3/4 and AAL5, this interface for Cisco 7000 series routers minimizes performance bottlenecks at the UNI. *See also: AAL3/4 and AAL5.*

algorithm   A set of rules or processes used to solve a problem. In networking, algorithms are typically used for finding the best route for traffic from a source to its destination.

alignment error   An error occurring in Ethernet networks in which a received frame has extra bits; that is, a number not divisible by eight. Alignment errors are generally the result of frame damage caused by collisions.

all-routes explorer packet   An explorer packet that can move across an entire SRB network, tracing all possible paths to a given destination. Also known as an all-rings explorer packet. *See also: explorer packet, local explorer packet,* and *spanning explorer packet.*

AM   Amplitude Modulation: A modulation method that represents information by varying the amplitude of the carrier signal. *See also: modulation.*

AMI   Alternate Mark Inversion: A line-code type on T1 and E1 circuits that shows zeros as "01" during each bit cell, and ones as "11" or "00," alternately, during each bit cell. The sending device must maintain ones density in AMI but not independently of the data stream. Also known as binary-coded, alternate mark inversion. *Contrast with: B8ZS. See also: ones density.*

amplitude   An analog or digital waveform's highest value.

analog   Analog signaling is a technique to carry voice and data over copper and wireless media. When analog signals are transmitted over wires or through the air, the transmission conveys information through a variation of some type of signal amplitude, frequency, and phase.

analog connection   Provides signaling via an infinitely variable waveform. This differs from a digital connection, in which a definite waveform is used to define values. Traditional phone service is an analog connection.

analog transmission   Signal messaging whereby information is represented by various combinations of signal amplitude, frequency, and phase.

ANSI   American National Standards Institute: The organization of corporate, government, and other volunteer members that coordinates standards-related activities, approves U.S. national standards, and develops U.S. positions in international standards organizations. ANSI assists in the creation of international and U.S. standards in disciplines such as communications, networking, and a variety of technical fields. It publishes over 13,000 standards for engineered products and technologies ranging from screw threads to networking protocols. ANSI is a member of the IEC and ISO.

anycast   An ATM address that can be shared by more than one end system, allowing requests to be routed to a node that provides a particular service.

AppleTalk   Currently in two versions, the group of communication protocols designed by Apple Computer for use in Macintosh environments. The earlier Phase 1 protocols support one physical network with only one network number that resides in one zone. The later Phase 2 protocols support more than one logical network on a single physical network, allowing networks to exist in more than one zone. *See also: zone.*

Application layer   Layer 7 of the OSI Reference Model, supplying services to application procedures (such as electronic mail or file transfer) that are outside the OSI model. This layer chooses and determines the availability of communicating partners along with the resources necessary to make the connection, coordinates partnering applications, and forms a consensus on procedures for controlling data integrity and error recovery.

ARA   AppleTalk Remote Access: A protocol for Macintosh users establishing their access to resources and data from a remote AppleTalk location.

area   A logical, rather than physical, set of segments (based on either CLNS, DECnet, or OSPF) along with their attached devices. Areas are commonly connected to others using routers to create a single autonomous system. *See also: autonomous system.*

ARM   Asynchronous Response Mode: An HDLC communication mode using one primary station and at least one additional station, in which transmission can be initiated from either the primary or one of the secondary units.

ARP   Address Resolution Protocol: Defined in RFC 826, the protocol that traces IP addresses to MAC addresses. *See also: RARP.*

ASBR   Autonomous System Boundary Router: An area border router placed between an OSPF autonomous system and a non-OSPF network that operates both OSPF and an additional routing protocol, such as RIP. ASBRs must be located in a non-stub OSPF area. *See also: ABR, non-stub area,* and *OSPF.*

ASCII   American Standard Code for Information Interchange: An 8-bit code for representing characters, consisting of seven data bits plus one parity bit.

ASICs   Application-Specific Integrated Circuits: Used in Layer 2 switches to make filtering decisions. The ASIC looks in the filter table of MAC addresses and determines which port the destination hardware address of a received hardware address is destined for. The frame will be allowed to traverse only that one segment. If the hardware address is unknown, the frame is forwarded out all ports.

ASN.1 Abstract Syntax Notation One: An OSI language used to describe types of data that is independent of computer structures and depicting methods. Described by ISO International Standard 8824.

ASP AppleTalk Session Protocol: A protocol employing ATP to establish, maintain, and tear down sessions, as well as sequence requests. *See also: ATP.*

AST Automatic Spanning Tree: A function that supplies one path for spanning explorer frames traveling from one node in the network to another, supporting the automatic resolution of spanning trees in SRB networks. AST is based on the IEEE 802.1 standard. *See also: IEEE 802.1 and SRB.*

asynchronous connection Defines the start and stop of each octet. As a result, each byte in asynchronous connections requires two bytes of overhead. Synchronous connections use a synchronous clock to mark the start and stop of each character.

asynchronous dial-up Asynchronous dial-up is interchangeable with analog dial-up. Both terms refer to traditional modem-based connections.

asynchronous transmission Digital signals sent without precise timing, usually with different frequencies and phase relationships. Asynchronous transmissions generally enclose individual characters in control bits (called start and stop bits) that show the beginning and end of each character. *Contrast with: isochronous transmission and synchronous transmission.*

ATCP AppleTalk Control Program: The protocol for establishing and configuring AppleTalk over PPP, defined in RFC 1378. *See also: PPP.*

ATDM Asynchronous Time-Division Multiplexing: A technique for sending information, it differs from normal TDM in that the time slots are assigned when necessary rather than preassigned to certain transmitters. *Contrast with: FDM, statistical multiplexing, and TDM.*

ATG Address Translation Gateway: The mechanism within Cisco DECnet routing software that enables routers to route multiple, independent DECnet networks and to establish a user-designated address translation for chosen nodes between networks.

ATM   Asynchronous Transfer Mode: The international standard, identified by fixed-length 53-byte cells, for transmitting cells in multiple service systems, such as voice, video, or data. Transit delays are reduced because the fixed-length cells permit processing to occur in the hardware. ATM is designed to maximize the benefits of high-speed transmission media, such as SONET, E3, and T3.

ATM ARP server   A device that supplies logical subnets running classical IP over ATM with address-resolution services.

ATM endpoint   The initiating or terminating connection in an ATM network. ATM endpoints include servers, workstations, ATM-to-LAN switches, and ATM routers.

ATM Forum   The international organization founded jointly by Northern Telecom, Sprint, Cisco Systems, and NET/ADAPTIVE in 1991 to develop and promote standards-based implementation agreements for ATM technology. The ATM Forum broadens official standards developed by ANSI and ITU-T and creates implementation agreements before official standards are published.

ATM layer   A sublayer of the Data Link layer in an ATM network that is service-independent. To create standard 53-byte ATM cells, the ATM layer receives 48-byte segments from the AAL and attaches a 5-byte header to each. These cells are then sent to the Physical layer for transmission across the physical medium. *See also: AAL.*

ATMM   ATM Management: A procedure that runs on ATM switches, managing rate enforcement and VCI translation. *See also: ATM.*

ATM user-user connection   A connection made by the ATM layer to supply communication between at least two ATM service users, such as ATMM processes. These communications can be uni- or bidirectional, using one or two VCCs, respectively. *See also: ATM layer and ATMM.*

ATP   AppleTalk Transaction Protocol: A Transport-level protocol that enables reliable transactions between two sockets, where one requests the other to perform a given task and to report the results. ATP fastens the request and response together, assuring a loss-free exchange of request-response pairs.

attenuation In communication, weakening or loss of signal energy, typically caused by distance.

AURP AppleTalk Update-based Routing Protocol: A technique for encapsulating AppleTalk traffic in the header of a foreign protocol that allows the connection of at least two noncontiguous AppleTalk internetworks through a foreign network (such as TCP/IP) to create an AppleTalk WAN. The connection made is called an AURP tunnel. By exchanging routing information between exterior routers, the AURP maintains routing tables for the complete AppleTalk WAN. *See also: AURP tunnel.*

AURP tunnel A connection made in an AURP WAN that acts as a single, virtual link between AppleTalk internetworks separated physically by a foreign network such as a TCP/IP network. *See also: AURP.*

authentication The first component in the AAA model. Users are typically authenticated via a username and password, which are used to uniquely identify them.

authority zone A portion of the domain-name tree associated with DNS for which one name server is the authority. *See also: DNS.*

authorization The act of permitting access to a resource based on authentication information in the AAA model.

auto duplex A setting on Layer 1 and 2 devices that sets the duplex of a switch or hub port automatically.

automatic call reconnect A function that enables automatic call rerouting away from a failed trunk line.

autonomous confederation A collection of self-governed systems that depend more on their own network accessibility and routing information than on information received from other systems or groups.

autonomous switching The ability of Cisco routers to process packets more quickly by using the ciscoBus to switch packets independently of the system processor.

autonomous system (AS) A group of networks under mutual administration that share the same routing methodology. Autonomous systems are subdivided by areas and must be assigned an individual 16-bit number by the IANA. *See also: area.*

autoreconfiguration   A procedure executed by nodes within the failure domain of a Token Ring, wherein nodes automatically perform diagnostics, trying to reconfigure the network around failed areas.

Auto-RP   An IOS feature that allows multicast-enabled routers to detect RP and forward the summary information to other routers and hosts.

auxiliary port   The console port on the back of Cisco routers that allows you to dial the router and make console configuration settings.

AVVID   Architecture for Voice, Video and Integrated Data: This is a Cisco marketing term to group their convergence efforts. Convergence is the integration of historically distinct services into a single service.

B8ZS   Binary 8-Zero Substitution: A line-code type, interpreted at the remote end of the connection, that uses a special code substitution whenever eight consecutive zeros are transmitted over the link on T1 and E1 circuits. This technique assures ones density independent of the data stream. Also known as bipolar 8-zero substitution. *Contrast with: AMI. See also: ones density.*

backbone   The basic portion of the network that provides the primary path for traffic sent to and initiated from other networks.

back end   A node or software program supplying services to a front end. *See also: server.*

backup designated router (BDR)   Used in OSPF routing to make sure area information is still advertised if the designated router goes down.

bandwidth   The gap between the highest and lowest frequencies employed by network signals. More commonly, it refers to the rated throughput capacity of a network protocol or medium.

BoD   Bandwidth on Demand: This function allows an additional B channel to be used to increase the amount of bandwidth available for a particular connection.

baseband   A feature of a network technology that uses only one carrier frequency. For example, Ethernet. Also named "narrowband." *Compare with: broadband.*

Basic Management Setup Used with Cisco routers when in setup mode. Provides only enough management and configuration to get the router working so someone can telnet into the router and configure it.

baud Synonymous with bits per second (bps), if each signal element represents one bit. It is a unit of signaling speed equivalent to the number of separate signal elements transmitted per second.

B channel Bearer channel: A full-duplex, 64Kbps channel in ISDN that transmits user data. *Compare with: D channel, E channel, and H channel.*

beacon An FDDI device or Token Ring frame that points to a serious problem with the ring, such as a broken cable. The beacon frame carries the address of the station thought to be down. *See also: failure domain.*

bearer service Used by service providers to provide DS0 service to ISDN customers. A DS0 is one 64K channel. An ISDN bearer service provides either two DS0s, called two bearer channels, for a Basic Rate Interface (BRI), or 24 DS0s, called a Primary Rate Interface (PRI).

BECN Backward Explicit Congestion Notification: BECN is the bit set by a Frame Relay network in frames moving away from frames headed into a congested path. A DTE that receives frames with the BECN may ask higher-level protocols to take necessary flow control measures. *Compare with: FECN.*

BGP4 BGP Version 4: Version 4 of the interdomain routing protocol most commonly used on the Internet. BGP4 supports CIDR and uses route-counting mechanisms to decrease the size of routing tables. *See also: CIDR.*

bidirectional shared tree A method of shared tree multicast forwarding. This method allows group members to receive data from the source or the RP, whichever is closer. *See also: RP (rendezvous point).*

binary A two-character numbering method that uses ones and zeros. The binary numbering system underlies all digital representation of information.

BIP Bit Interleaved Parity: A method used in ATM to monitor errors on a link, sending a check bit or word in the link overhead for the previous block or frame. This allows bit errors in transmissions to be found and delivered as maintenance information.

BISDN   Broadband ISDN: ITU-T standards created to manage high-bandwidth technologies such as video. BISDN presently employs ATM technology along SONET-based transmission circuits, supplying data rates between 155Mbps and 622Mbps and beyond. *See also: BRI, ISDN, and PRI.*

bit-oriented protocol   Regardless of frame content, the class of Data Link layer communication protocols that transmits frames. Bit-oriented protocols, as compared with byte-oriented, supply more efficient and trustworthy full-duplex operation. *Compare with: byte-oriented protocol.*

Boot ROM   Used in routers to put the router into bootstrap mode. Bootstrap mode then boots the device with an operating system. The ROM can also hold a small Cisco IOS.

border gateway   A router that facilitates communication with routers in different autonomous systems.

border router   Typically defined within Open Shortest Path First (OSPF) as a router that connected an area to the backbone area. However, a border router can be a router that connects a company to the Internet as well. *See also: OSPF.*

BPDU   Bridge Protocol Data Unit: A Spanning Tree Protocol initializing packet that is sent at definable intervals for the purpose of exchanging information among bridges in networks.

BRI   Basic Rate Interface: The ISDN interface that facilitates circuit-switched communication between video, data, and voice; it is made up of two B channels (64Kbps each) and one D channel (16Kbps). *Compare with: PRI. See also: BISDN.*

bridge   A device for connecting two segments of a network and transmitting packets between them. Both segments must use identical protocols to communicate. Bridges function at the Data Link layer, Layer 2 of the OSI Reference Model. The purpose of a bridge is to filter, send, or flood any incoming frame, based on the MAC address of that particular frame.

bridge ID   Used to find and elect the root bridge in a Layer 2 switched internetwork. The bridge ID is a combination of the bridge priority and base MAC address.

bridging   A Layer 2 process to block or forward frames based on MAC layer addresses. Bridges are lower speed, lower port density switches.

broadband   A transmission methodology for multiplexing several independent signals onto one cable. In telecommunications, broadband is classified as any channel with bandwidth greater than 4kHz (typical voice grade). In LAN terminology, it is classified as a coaxial cable on which analog signaling is employed. Also known as "wideband." *Contrast with: baseband.*

broadcast   A data frame or packet that is transmitted to every node on the local network segment (as defined by the broadcast domain). Broadcasts are known by their broadcast address, which is a destination network and host address with all the bits turned on. Also called "local broadcast." *Compare with: directed broadcast.*

broadcast domain   A group of devices receiving broadcast frames initiating from any device within the group. Because they do not forward broadcast frames, broadcast domains are generally surrounded by routers.

broadcast storm   An undesired event on the network caused by the simultaneous transmission of any number of broadcasts across the network segment. Such an occurrence can overwhelm network bandwidth, resulting in time-outs.

brute force attack   A brute force attack bombards the resource with attempted connections until successful. In the most common brute force attack, different passwords are repeatedly tried until a match is found that is then used to compromise the network.

buffer   A storage area dedicated to handling data while in transit. Buffers are used to receive/store sporadic deliveries of data bursts, usually received from faster devices, compensating for the variations in processing speed. Incoming information is stored until everything is received prior to sending data on. Also known as an "information buffer."

bursting   Some technologies, including ATM and Frame Relay, are considered burstable. This means that user data can exceed the bandwidth normally reserved for the connection; however, this cannot exceed the port speed. An example of this would be a 128Kbps Frame Relay CIR on a T1—depending on the vendor, it may be possible to send more than 128Kbps for a short time.

bus topology   A linear LAN architecture in which transmissions from various stations on the network are reproduced over the length of the medium and are accepted by all other stations. *Compare with: ring* and *star.*

bus   Any physical path, typically wires or copper, through which a digital signal can be used to send data from one part of a computer to another.

BUS   broadcast and unknown servers: In LAN emulation, the hardware or software responsible for resolving all broadcasts and packets with unknown (unregistered) addresses into the point-to-point virtual circuits required by ATM. *See also: LANE, LEC, LECS,* and *LES.*

BX.25   AT&T's use of X.25. *See also: X.25.*

bypass mode   An FDDI and Token Ring network operation that deletes an interface.

bypass relay   A device that enables a particular interface in the Token Ring to be closed down and effectively taken off the ring.

byte   Eight bits of binary.

byte-oriented protocol   Any type of data-link communication protocol that, in order to mark the boundaries of frames, uses a specific character from the user character set. These protocols have generally been superseded by bit-oriented protocols. *Compare with: bit-oriented protocol.*

cable modem   A cable modem is not actually an analog device, like an asynchronous modem, but rather a customer access device for linking to a broadband cable network. These devices are typically bridges that have a COAX connection to link to the cable network and a 10BaseT Ethernet connection to link to the user's PC.

cable range   In an extended AppleTalk network, the range of numbers allotted for use by existing nodes on the network. The value of the cable range can be anywhere from a single to a sequence of several touching network numbers. Node addresses are determined by their cable range value.

CAC   Connection Admission Control: The sequence of actions executed by every ATM switch while connection setup is performed in order to determine if a request for connection is violating the guarantees of QoS for established connections. Also, CAC is used to route a connection request through an ATM network.

call admission control   A device for managing traffic in ATM networks, determining the possibility of a path containing adequate bandwidth for a requested VCC.

call priority   In circuit-switched systems, the defining priority given to each originating port; it specifies in which order calls will be reconnected. Additionally, call priority identifies which calls are allowed during a bandwidth reservation.

call set-up time   The length of time necessary to effect a switched call between DTE devices.

candidate packets   Packets identified by the MLS-SE as having the potential for establishing a flow cache. This determination is made based on the destination MAC (DMAC) address. The DMAC address must be a MAC address associated with a known MLS-RP. *See also: MLS-SE, MLS-SE, and MLS-RP.*

CBR   Constant Bit Rate: An ATM Forum QoS class created for use in ATM networks. CBR is used for connections that rely on precision clocking to guarantee trustworthy delivery. *Compare with: ABR and VBR.*

CD   Carrier Detect: A signal indicating that an interface is active or that a connection generated by a modem has been established.

CDP   Cisco Discovery Protocol: Cisco's proprietary protocol that is used to tell a neighboring Cisco device about the type of hardware, software version, and active interfaces that the Cisco device is using. It uses a SNAP frame between devices and is not routable.

CDVT   Cell Delay Variation Tolerance: A QoS parameter for traffic management in ATM networks specified when a connection is established. The allowable fluctuation levels for data samples taken by the PCR in CBR transmissions are determined by the CDVT. *See also: CBR and PCR.*

cell   In ATM networking, the basic unit of data for switching and multiplexing. Cells have a defined length of 53 bytes, including a 5-byte header that identifies the cell's data stream and 48 bytes of payload. *See also: cell relay.*

cell payload scrambling The method by which an ATM switch maintains framing on some medium-speed edge and trunk interfaces (T3 or E3 circuits). Cell payload scrambling rearranges the data portion of a cell to maintain the line synchronization with certain common bit patterns.

cell relay A technology that uses small packets of fixed size, known as cells. Their fixed length enables cells to be processed and switched in hardware at high speeds, making this technology the foundation for ATM and other high-speed network protocols. *See also: cell.*

Centrex A local exchange carrier service, providing local switching that resembles that of an on-site PBX. Centrex has no on-site switching capability. Therefore, all customer connections return to the CO. *See also: CO.*

CER Cell Error Ratio: In ATM the ratio of the number of transmitted cells having errors to the total number of cells sent in a transmission within a certain span of time.

CGMP Cisco Group Management Protocol: A proprietary protocol developed by Cisco. The router uses CGMP to send multicast membership commands to Catalyst switches.

Challenge Used to provide authentication in Challenge Handshake Authentication Protocol (CHAP) as part of the handshake process. This numerically unique query is sent to authenticate the user without sending the password unencrypted across the wire. *See also: CHAP.*

channelized E1 Operating at 2.048Mpbs, an access link that is sectioned into 29 B channels and one D channel, supporting DDR, Frame Relay, and X.25. *Compare with: channelized T1.*

channelized T1 Operating at 1.544Mbps, an access link that is sectioned into 23 B channels and one D channel of 64Kbps each, where individual channels or groups of channels connect to various destinations, supporting DDR, Frame Relay, and X.25. *Compare with: channelized E1.*

CHAP Challenge Handshake Authentication Protocol: Supported on lines using PPP encapsulation, it is a security feature that identifies the remote end, helping keep out unauthorized users. After CHAP is performed, the router or access server determines whether a given user is permitted access. It is a newer, more secure protocol than PAP. *Compare with: PAP.*

character mode connections   Character mode connections are typically terminated at the access server and include Telnet and console connections.

checksum   A test for ensuring the integrity of sent data. It is a number calculated from a series of values taken through a sequence of mathematical functions, typically placed at the end of the data from which it is calculated, and then recalculated at the receiving end for verification. *Compare with: CRC.*

choke packet   When congestion exists, it is a packet sent to inform a transmitter that it should decrease its sending rate.

CIDR   Classless Interdomain Routing: A method supported by classless routing protocols, such as OSPF and BGP4, based on the concept of ignoring the IP class of address, permitting route aggregation and VLSM that enable routers to combine routes in order to minimize the routing information that needs to be conveyed by the primary routers. It allows a group of IP networks to appear to other networks as a unified, larger entity. In CIDR, IP addresses and their subnet masks are written as four dotted octets, followed by a forward slash and the numbering of masking bits (a form of subnet notation shorthand). *See also: BGP4.*

CIP   Channel Interface Processor: A channel attachment interface for use in Cisco 7000 series routers that connects a host mainframe to a control unit. This device eliminates the need for an FBP to attach channels.

CIR   Committed Information Rate: Averaged over a minimum span of time and measured in bps, a Frame Relay network's agreed-upon minimum rate of transferring information.

circuit switching   Used with dial-up networks such as PPP and ISDN. Passes data, but needs to set up the connection first—just like making a phone call.

Cisco FRAD   Cisco Frame-Relay Access Device: A Cisco product that supports Cisco IPS Frame Relay SNA services, connecting SDLC devices to Frame Relay without requiring an existing LAN. May be upgraded to a fully functioning multiprotocol router. Can activate conversion from SDLC to Ethernet and Token Ring, but does not support attached LANs. *See also: FRAD.*

CiscoFusion   Cisco's name for the internetworking architecture under which its Cisco IOS operates. It is designed to "fuse" together the capabilities of its disparate collection of acquired routers and switches.

Cisco IOS software   Cisco Internet Operating System software. The kernel of the Cisco line of routers and switches that supplies shared functionality, scalability, and security for all products under its CiscoFusion architecture. *See also: CiscoFusion.*

CiscoView   GUI-based management software for Cisco networking devices, enabling dynamic status, statistics, and comprehensive configuration information. Displays a physical view of the Cisco device chassis and provides device-monitoring functions and fundamental troubleshooting capabilities. May be integrated with a number of SNMP-based network management platforms.

Class A network   Part of the Internet Protocol hierarchical addressing scheme. Class A networks have only 8 bits for defining networks and 24 bits for defining hosts on each network.

Class B network   Part of the Internet Protocol hierarchical addressing scheme. Class B networks have 16 bits for defining networks and 16 bits for defining hosts on each network.

Class C network   Part of the Internet Protocol hierarchical addressing scheme. Class C networks have 24 bits for defining networks and only 8 bits for defining hosts on each network.

classical IP over ATM   Defined in RFC 1577, the specification for running IP over ATM that maximizes ATM features. Also known as "CIA."

classless routing   Routing that sends subnet mask information in the routing updates. Classless routing allows Variable-Length Subnet Mask (VLSM) and supernetting. Routing protocols that support classless routing are RIP version 2, EIGRP, and OSPF.

CLI   Command Line Interface: Allows you to configure Cisco routers and switches with maximum flexibility.

clocking   Used in synchronous connections to provide a marker for the start and end of data bytes. This is similar to the beat of a drum with a speaker talking only when the drum is silent.

CLP   Cell Loss Priority: The area in the ATM cell header that determines the likelihood of a cell being dropped during network congestion. Cells with CLP = 0 are considered insured traffic and are not apt to be dropped. Cells with CLP = 1 are considered best-effort traffic that may be dropped during congested episodes, delivering more resources to handle insured traffic.

CLR   Cell Loss Ratio: The ratio of discarded cells to successfully delivered cells in ATM. CLR can be designated a QoS parameter when establishing a connection.

CO   Central Office: The local telephone company office where all loops in a certain area connect and where circuit switching of subscriber lines occurs.

collapsed backbone   A nondistributed backbone where all network segments are connected to each other through an internetworking device. A collapsed backbone can be a virtual network segment at work in a device such as a router, hub, or switch.

collapsed core   A collapsed core is defined as one switch performing both Core and Distribution layer functions. Typically found in a small network, the functions of the Core and Distribution layers are still distinct.

collision   The effect of two nodes sending transmissions simultaneously in Ethernet. When they meet on the physical media, the frames from each node collide and are damaged. *See also: collision domain.*

collision domain   The network area in Ethernet over which frames that have collided will spread. Collisions are propagated by hubs and repeaters, but not by LAN switches, routers, or bridges. *See also: collision.*

composite metric   Used with routing protocols, such as IGRP and EIGRP, that use more than one metric to find the best path to a remote network. IGRP and EIGRP both use bandwidth and delay of the line by default. However, maximum transmission unit (MTU), load, and reliability of a link can be used as well.

compression   A technique to send more data across a link than would be normally permitted by representing repetitious strings of data with a single marker.

configuration register   A 16-bit configurable value stored in hardware or software that determines how Cisco routers function during initialization. In hardware, the bit position is set using a jumper. In software, it is set by specifying specific bit patterns used to set startup options, configured using a hexadecimal value with configuration commands.

congestion   Traffic that exceeds the network's ability to handle it.

congestion avoidance   To minimize delays, the method an ATM network uses to control traffic entering the system. Lower-priority traffic is discarded at the edge of the network when indicators signal it cannot be delivered, thus using resources efficiently.

congestion collapse   The situation that results from the retransmission of packets in ATM networks where little or no traffic successfully arrives at destination points. It usually happens in networks made of switches with ineffective or inadequate buffering capabilities combined with poor packet discard or ABR congestion feedback mechanisms.

connection ID   Identifications given to each Telnet session into a router. The show sessions command will give you the connections a local router will have to a remote router. The show users command will show the connection IDs of users telnetted into your local router.

connectionless   Data transfer that occurs without the creating of a virtual circuit. No overhead, best-effort delivery, not reliable. *Contrast with: connection-oriented. See also: virtual circuit.*

connection-oriented   Data transfer method that sets up a virtual circuit before any data is transferred. Uses acknowledgments and flow control for reliable data transfer. *Contrast with: connectionless. See also: virtual circuit.*

console port   Typically an RJ-45 port on a Cisco router and switch that allows command line interface capability.

contention media   Media access method that is a baseband media; that is, first come, first served. Ethernet is an example of a contention media access.

control direct VCC   One of three control connections defined by Phase I LAN Emulation; a bidirectional virtual control connection (VCC) established in ATM by an LEC to an LES. *See also: control distribute VCC.*

control distribute VCC   One of three control connections defined by Phase 1 LAN Emulation; a unidirectional virtual control connection (VCC) set up in ATM from an LES to an LEC. Usually, the VCC is a point-to-multipoint connection. *See also: control direct VCC.*

convergence   The process required for all routers in an internetwork to update their routing tables and create a consistent view of the network, using the best possible paths. No user data is passed during a convergence time.

core block   If you have two or more switch blocks, the Cisco rule of thumb states that you need a core block. No routing is performed at the core, only transferring of data. It is a pass-through for the switch block, the server block, and the Internet. The core is responsible for transferring data to and from the switch blocks as quickly as possible. You can build a fast core with a frame, packet, or cell (ATM) network technology.

Core layer   Top layer in the Cisco three-layer hierarchical model, which helps you design, build, and maintain Cisco hierarchical networks. The Core layer passes packets quickly to Distribution layer devices only. No packet filtering should take place at this layer.

cost   An arbitrary value, based on hop count, bandwidth, or other calculation, that is typically assigned by a network administrator and used by the routing protocol to compare different routes through an internetwork. Routing protocols use cost values to select the best path to a certain destination: The lowest cost identifies the best path. Also known as "path cost." *See also: routing metric.*

count to infinity   A problem occurring in routing algorithms that are slow to converge where routers keep increasing the hop count to particular networks. To avoid this problem, various solutions have been implemented into each of the different routing protocols. Some of those solutions include defining a maximum hop count (defining infinity), route poisoning, poison reverse, and split horizon.

CPCS Common Part Convergence Sublayer: One of two AAL sublayers that are service-dependent, it is further segmented into the CS and SAR sublayers. The CPCS prepares data for transmission across the ATM network; it creates the 48-byte payload cells that are sent to the ATM layer. *See also: AAL* and *ATM layer*.

CPE Customer Premises Equipment: Items such as telephones, modems, and terminals installed at customer locations and connected to the telephone company network.

crankback In ATM, a correction technique used when a node somewhere on a chosen path cannot accept a connection setup request, blocking the request. The path is rolled back to an intermediate node, which then uses GCAC to attempt to find an alternate path to the final destination.

CRC Cyclic Redundancy Check: A methodology that detects errors, whereby the frame recipient makes a calculation by dividing frame contents with a prime binary divisor and compares the remainder to a value stored in the frame by the sending node. *Contrast with: checksum*.

CSMA/CD Carrier Sense Multiple Access Collision Detect: A technology defined by the Ethernet IEEE 802.3 committee. Each device senses the cable for a digital signal before transmitting. Also, CSMA/CD allows all devices on the network to share the same cable, but one at a time. If two devices transmit at the same time, a frame collision will occur and a jamming pattern will be sent; the devices will stop transmitting, wait a predetermined amount of time, and then try to transmit again.

CST Common Spanning Tree: The IEEE uses what is called Common Spanning Tree (CST), which is defined with IEEE 802.1q. The IEEE 802.1q defines one spanning tree instance for all VLANs.

CSU Channel Service Unit: A digital mechanism that connects end-user equipment to the local digital telephone loop. Frequently referred to along with the Data Service Unit as CSU/DSU. *See also: DSU*.

CTD Cell Transfer Delay: For a given connection in ATM, the time period between a cell exit event at the source user-network interface (UNI) and the corresponding cell entry event at the destination. The CTD between these points is the sum of the total inter-ATM transmission delay and the total ATM processing delay.

custom queuing   Used by Cisco router IOS to provide a queuing method to slower serial links. Custom queuing allows an administrator to configure the type of traffic that will have priority over the link.

cut-through frame switching   A frame-switching technique that flows data through a switch so that the leading edge exits the switch at the output port before the packet finishes entering the input port. Frames will be read, processed, and forwarded by devices that use cut-through switching as soon as the destination address of the frame is confirmed and the outgoing port is identified.

data compression   *See: compression.*

data direct VCC   A bidirectional point-to-point virtual control connection (VCC) set up between two LECs in ATM and one of three data connections defined by Phase 1 LAN Emulation. Because data direct VCCs do not guarantee QoS, they are generally reserved for UBR and ABR connections. *Compare with: control distribute VCC and control direct VCC.*

data encapsulation   The process in which the information in a protocol is wrapped, or contained, in the data section of another protocol. In the OSI Reference Model, each layer encapsulates the layer immediately above it as the data flows down the protocol stack.

data frame   Protocol Data Unit encapsulation at the Data Link layer of the OSI Reference Model. Encapsulates packets from the Network layer and prepares the data for transmission on a network medium.

datagram   A logical collection of information transmitted as a Network layer unit over a medium without a previously established virtual circuit. IP datagrams have become the primary information unit of the Internet. At various layers of the OSI Reference Model, the terms *cell, frame, message, packet,* and *segment* also define these logical information groupings.

data link control layer   Layer 2 of the SNA architectural model, it is responsible for the transmission of data over a given physical link and compares somewhat to the Data Link layer of the OSI model.

Data Link layer   Layer 2 of the OSI reference model, it ensures the trustworthy transmission of data across a physical link and is primarily concerned with physical addressing, line discipline, network topology, error notification, ordered delivery of frames, and flow control. The IEEE has further segmented this layer into the MAC sublayer and the LLC sublayer. Also known as the Link layer. Can be compared somewhat to the data link control layer of the SNA model. *See also: Application layer, LLC, MAC, Network layer, Physical layer, Presentation layer, Session layer,* and *Transport layer.*

DCC   Data Country Code: Developed by the ATM Forum, one of two ATM address formats designed for use by private networks. *Compare with: ICD.*

DCE   data communications equipment (as defined by the EIA) or data circuit-terminating equipment (as defined by the ITU-T): The mechanisms and links of a communications network that make up the network portion of the user-to-network interface, such as modems. The DCE supplies the physical connection to the network, forwards traffic, and provides a clocking signal to synchronize data transmission between DTE and DCE devices. *Compare with: DTE.*

D channel   1) Data channel: A full-duplex, 16Kbps (BRI) or 64Kbps (PRI) ISDN channel. *Compare with: B channel, E channel,* and *H channel.* 2) In SNA, anything that provides a connection between the processor and main storage with any peripherals.

DDP   Datagram Delivery Protocol: Used in the AppleTalk suite of protocols as a connectionless protocol that is responsible for sending datagrams through an internetwork.

DDR   dial-on-demand routing: A technique that allows a router to automatically initiate and end a circuit-switched session per the requirements of the sending station. By mimicking keepalives, the router fools the end station into treating the session as active. DDR permits routing over ISDN or telephone lines via a modem or external ISDN terminal adapter.

DE   Discard Eligibility: Used in Frame Relay networks to tell a switch that a frame can be discarded if the switch is too busy. The DE is a field in the frame that is turned on by transmitting routers if the Committed Information Rate (CIR) is oversubscribed or set to 0.

DE bit   The DE bit marks a frame as discard eligible on a Frame Relay network. If a serial link is congested and the Frame Relay network has passed the Committed Information Rate (CIR), then the DE bit will always be on.

default route   The static routing table entry used to direct frames whose next hop is not spelled out in the dynamic routing table.

delay   The time elapsed between a sender's initiation of a transaction and the first response they receive. Also, the time needed to move a packet from its source to its destination over a path. *See also: latency.*

demarc   The demarcation point between the customer premises equipment (CPE) and the telco's carrier equipment.

demodulation   A series of steps that return a modulated signal to its original form. When receiving, a modem demodulates an analog signal to its original digital form (and, conversely, modulates the digital data it sends into an analog signal). *See also: modulation.*

demultiplexing   The process of converting a single multiplex signal, comprising more than one input stream, back into separate output streams. *See also: multiplexing.*

denial-of-service attack   A denial-of-service attack, or DoS, blocks access to a network resource by saturating the device with attacking data. Typically, this is targeted against the link (particularly lower bandwidth links) or the server. DDoS attacks, or distributed denial-of-service attacks, make use of multiple originating attacking resources to saturate a more capable resource.

designated bridge   In the process of forwarding a frame from a segment to the route bridge, the bridge with the lowest path cost.

designated port   Used with the Spanning Tree Protocol (STP) to designate forwarding ports. If there are multiple links to the same network, STP will shut a port down to stop network loops.

designated router   An OSPF router that creates LSAs for a multi-access network and is required to perform other special tasks in OSPF operations. Multi-access OSPF networks that maintain a minimum of two attached routers identify one router that is chosen by the OSPF Hello protocol, which makes possible a decrease in the number of adjacencies necessary on a multi-access network. This in turn reduces the quantity of routing protocol traffic and the physical size of the database.

destination address   The address for the network devices that will receive a packet.

dial backup   Dial backup connections are typically used to provide redundancy to Frame Relay connections. The backup link is activated over an analog modem.

digital   A digital waveform is one where distinct ones and zeros provide the data representation. *See also: analog.*

directed broadcast   A data frame or packet that is transmitted to a specific group of nodes on a remote network segment. Directed broadcasts are known by their broadcast address, which is a destination subnet address with all the bits turned on.

discovery mode   Also known as dynamic configuration, this technique is used by an AppleTalk interface to gain information from a working node about an attached network. The information is subsequently used by the interface for self-configuration.

distance-vector protocol   Type of routing protocol that sends complete routing table on periodic intervals to neighbor routers.

distance-vector routing algorithm   In order to find the shortest path, this group of routing algorithms repeats on the number of hops in a given route, requiring each router to send its complete routing table with each update, but only to its neighbors. Routing algorithms of this type tend to generate loops, but they are fundamentally simpler than their link-state counterparts. *See also: link-state routing algorithm and SPF.*

Distribution layer   Middle layer of the Cisco three-layer hierarchical model, which helps you design, install, and maintain Cisco hierarchical networks. The Distribution layer is the point where Access layer devices connect. Routing is performed at this layer.

distribution lists Access lists used to filter incoming and outgoing route table entries on a router.

DLCI Data-Link Connection Identifier: Used to identify virtual circuits in a Frame Relay network.

DNS Domain Name System: Used to resolve host names to IP addresses.

DSAP Destination Service Access Point: The service access point of a network node, specified in the destination field of a packet. *See also: SSAP and SAP.*

DSL Digital Subscriber Line: DSL technologies are used to provide broadband services over a single copper pair, typically to residential customers. Most vendors are providing DSL services at up to 6Mbps downstream, but the technology can support 52Mbps service.

DSR Data Set Ready: When a DCE is powered up and ready to run, this EIA/TIA-232 interface circuit is also engaged.

DSU Data Service Unit: This device is used to adapt the physical interface on a data terminal equipment (DTE) mechanism to a transmission facility such as T1 or E1 and is also responsible for signal timing. It is commonly grouped with the Channel Service Unit and referred to as the CSU/DSU. *See also: CSU.*

DTE data terminal equipment: Any device located at the user end of a user-network interface serving as a destination, a source, or both. DTE includes devices such as multiplexers, protocol translators, and computers. The connection to a data network is made through data communications equipment (DCE) such as a modem, using the clocking signals generated by that device. *See also: DCE.*

DTR data terminal ready: An activated EIA/TIA-232 circuit communicating to the DCE the state of preparedness of the DTE to transmit or receive data.

DUAL Diffusing Update Algorithm: Used in Enhanced IGRP, this convergence algorithm provides loop-free operation throughout an entire route's computation. DUAL grants routers involved in a topology revision the ability to synchronize simultaneously, while routers unaffected by this change are not involved. *See also: Enhanced IGRP.*

DVMRP Distance Vector Multicast Routing Protocol: Based primarily on the Routing Information Protocol (RIP), this Internet gateway protocol implements a common, condensed-mode IP multicast scheme, using IGMP to transfer routing datagrams between its neighbors. *See also: IGMP.*

DXI Data Exchange Interface: Described in RFC 1482, DXI defines the effectiveness of a network device such as a router, bridge, or hub to act as an FEP to an ATM network by using a special DSU that accomplishes packet encapsulation.

dynamic entries Used in Layer 2 and 3 devices to create a table of either hardware addresses or logical addresses dynamically.

dynamic routing Also known as adaptive routing, this technique automatically adapts to traffic or physical network revisions.

dynamic VLAN An administrator will create an entry in a special server with the hardware addresses of all devices on the internetwork. The server will then assign dynamically used VLANs.

E1 Generally used in Europe, a wide-area digital transmission scheme carrying data at 2.048Mbps. E1 transmission lines are available for lease from common carriers for private use.

E.164 1) Evolved from standard telephone numbering system, the standard recommended by ITU-T for international telecommunication numbering, particularly in ISDN, SMDS, and BISDN. 2) Label of field in an ATM address containing numbers in E.164 format.

E channel Echo channel: A 64Kbps ISDN control channel used for circuit switching. Specific description of this channel can be found in the 1984 ITU-T ISDN specification, but was dropped from the 1988 version. *See also: B channel, D channel,* and *H channel.*

edge device A device that enables packets to be forwarded between legacy interfaces (such as Ethernet and Token Ring) and ATM interfaces based on information in the Data Link and Network layers. An edge device does not take part in the running of any Network layer routing protocol; it merely uses the route description protocol in order to get the forwarding information required.

EEPROM Electronically Erasable Programmable Read-Only Memory: Programmed after their manufacture, these nonvolatile memory chips can be erased if necessary using electric power and reprogrammed. *See also: EPRO and PROM.*

EFCI Explicit Forward Congestion Indication: A congestion feedback mode permitted by ABR service in an ATM network. The EFCI may be set by any network element that is in a state of immediate or certain congestion. The destination end system is able to carry out a protocol that adjusts and lowers the cell rate of the connection based on the value of the EFCI. *See also: ABR.*

80/20 rule The 80/20 rule means that 80 percent of the users' traffic should remain on the local network segment and only 20 percent or less should cross the routers or bridges to the other network segments

EIGRP *See: Enhanced IGRP.*

EIP Ethernet Interface Processor: A Cisco 7000 series router interface processor card, supplying 10Mbps AUI ports to support Ethernet Version 1 and Ethernet Version 2 or IEEE 802.3 interfaces with a high-speed data path to other interface processors.

ELAN Emulated LAN: An ATM network configured using a client/server model in order to emulate either an Ethernet or Token Ring LAN. Multiple ELANs can exist at the same time on a single ATM network and are made up of a LAN Emulation Client (LEC), a LAN Emulation Server (LES), a Broadcast and Unknown Server (BUS), and a LAN Emulation Configuration Server (LECS). ELANs are defined by the LANE specification. *See also: LANE, LEC, LECS, and LES.*

ELAP EtherTalk Link Access Protocol: In an EtherTalk network, the link-access protocol constructed above the standard Ethernet Data Link layer.

enable packets Packets that complete the flow cache. Once the MLS-SE determines that the packet meets enable criteria, such as source MAC (SMAC) address and destination IP, the flow cache is established and subsequent packets are Layer 3 switched. *See also: MLS-SE and MLS-RP.*

encapsulation The technique used by layered protocols in which a layer adds header information to the protocol data unit (PDU) from the layer above. As an example, in Internet terminology, a packet would contain a header from the Physical layer, followed by a header from the Network layer (IP), followed by a header from the Transport layer (TCP), followed by the application protocol data.

encryption   The conversion of information into a scrambled form that effectively disguises it to prevent unauthorized access. Every encryption scheme uses some well-defined algorithm, which is reversed at the receiving end by an opposite algorithm in a process known as decryption.

end-to-end VLANs   VLANs that span the switch-fabric from end to end; all switches in end-to-end VLANs understand about all configured VLANs. End-to-end VLANs are configured to allow membership based on function, project, department, and so on.

Enhanced IGRP   Enhanced Interior Gateway Routing Protocol: An advanced routing protocol created by Cisco, combining the advantages of link-state and distance-vector protocols. Enhanced IGRP has superior convergence attributes, including high operating efficiency. *See also: IGP, OSPF,* and *RIP.*

enterprise network   A privately owned and operated network that joins most major locations in a large company or organization.

enterprise services   Defined as services provided to all users on the internetwork. Layer 3 switches or routers are required in this scenario because the services must be close to the core and would probably be based in their own subnet. Examples of these services include Internet access, e-mail, and possibly videoconferencing. If the servers that host these enterprise services were placed close to the backbone, all users would have the same distance to them, but this also means that all users' data would have to cross the backbone to get to these services.

EPROM   Erasable Programmable Read-Only Memory: Programmed after their manufacture, these nonvolatile memory chips can be erased if necessary using high-power light and reprogrammed. *See also: EEPROM* and *PROM.*

error correction   Error correction uses a checksum to detect bit errors in the data stream.

ESF   Extended Superframe: Made up of 24 frames with 192 bits each, with the 193rd bit providing other functions including timing. This is an enhanced version of SF. *See also: SF.*

Ethernet   A baseband LAN specification created by the Xerox Corporation and then improved through joint efforts of Xerox, Digital Equipment Corporation, and Intel. Ethernet is similar to the IEEE 802.3 series standard and, using CSMA/CD, operates over various types of cables at 10Mbps. Also called DIX (Digital/Intel/Xerox) Ethernet. *See also: 10BaseT, FastEthernet, and IEEE.*

EtherTalk   A data-link product from Apple Computer that permits Apple-Talk networks to be connected by Ethernet.

excess rate   In ATM networking, traffic exceeding a connection's insured rate. The excess rate is the maximum rate less the insured rate. Depending on the availability of network resources, excess traffic can be discarded during congestion episodes. *Compare with: maximum rate.*

expansion   The procedure of directing compressed data through an algorithm, restoring information to its original size.

expedited delivery   An option that can be specified by one protocol layer, communicating either with other layers or with the identical protocol layer in a different network device, requiring that identified data be processed faster.

explorer packet   An SNA packet transmitted by a source Token Ring device to find the path through a source-route-bridged network.

extended IP access list   IP access list that filters the network by logical address, protocol field in the Network layer header, and even the port field in the Transport layer header.

extended IPX access list   IPX access list that filters the network by logical IPX address, protocol field in the Network layer header, or even socket number in the Transport layer header.

Extended Setup   Used in setup mode to configure the router with more detail than Basic Setup mode. Allows multiple-protocol support and interface configuration.

external route processor   A router that is external to the switch. An external Layer-3 routing device can be used to provide routing between VLANs.

exterior routing protocol   Routing protocol that connects and advertises autonomous systems.

failure domain   The region in which a failure has occurred in a Token Ring. When a station gains information that a serious problem, such as a cable break, has occurred with the network, it sends a beacon frame that includes the station reporting the failure, its NAUN, and everything between. This defines the failure domain. Beaconing then initiates the procedure known as autoreconfiguration. *See also: autoreconfiguration* and *beacon.*

fallback   In ATM networks, this mechanism is used for scouting a path if it isn't possible to locate one using customary methods. The device relaxes requirements for certain characteristics, such as delay, in an attempt to find a path that meets a certain set of the most important requirements.

Fast EtherChannel   Fast EtherChannel uses load distribution to share the links called a bundle, which is a group of links managed by the Fast Ether-Channel process. Should one link in the bundle fail, the Ethernet Bundle Controller (EBC) informs the Enhanced Address Recognition Logic (EARL) ASIC of the failure, and the EARL in turn ages out all addresses learned on that link. The EBC and the EARL use hardware to recalculate the source and destination address pair on a different link.

Fast Ethernet   Any Ethernet specification with a speed of 100Mbps. Fast Ethernet is 10 times faster than 10BaseT, while retaining qualities like MAC mechanisms, MTU, and frame format. These similarities make it possible for existing 10BaseT applications and management tools to be used on Fast Ethernet networks. Fast Ethernet is based on an extension of IEEE 802.3 specification (IEEE 802.3u). *Compare with: Ethernet. See also: 100BaseT, 100BaseTX,* and *IEEE.*

fast switching   A Cisco feature that uses a route cache to speed packet switching through a router. *Contrast with: process switching.*

FDM   Frequency-Division Multiplexing: A technique that permits information from several channels to be assigned bandwidth on one wire based on frequency. *See also: TDM, ATDM,* and *statistical multiplexing.*

FDDI   Fiber Distributed Data Interface: A LAN standard, defined by ANSI X3T9.5 that can run at speeds up to 200Mbps and uses token-passing media access on fiber-optic cable. For redundancy, FDDI can use a dual-ring architecture.

feasible successor   A route that is kept in a topology table and will be placed in the routing table if the current successor goes down.

FECN   Forward Explicit Congestion Notification: A bit set by a Frame Relay network that informs the DTE receptor that congestion was encountered along the path from source to destination. A device receiving frames with the FECN bit set can ask higher-priority protocols to take flow-control action as needed. *See also: BECN.*

FEIP   Fast Ethernet Interface Processor: An interface processor employed on Cisco 7000 series routers, supporting up to two 100Mbps 100BaseT ports.

firewall   A barrier purposefully erected between any connected public networks and a private network, made up of a router or access server or several routers or access servers, that uses access lists and other methods to ensure the security of the private network.

Flash   Electronically Erasable Programmable Read-Only Memory (EEPROM). Used to hold the Cisco IOS in a router by default.

flash memory   Developed by Intel and licensed to other semiconductor manufacturers, it is nonvolatile storage that can be erased electronically and reprogrammed, physically located on an EEPROM chip. Flash memory permits software images to be stored, booted, and rewritten as needed. Cisco routers and switches use flash memory to hold the IOS by default. *See also: EPROM and EEPROM.*

flat network   Network that is one large collision domain and one large broadcast domain.

flooding   When traffic is received on an interface, it is then transmitted to every interface connected to that device with the exception of the interface from which the traffic originated. This technique can be used for traffic transfer by bridges and switches throughout the network.

flow   A shortcut or MLS cache entry that is defined by the packet properties. Packets with identical properties belong to the same flow. *See also: MLS.*

flow control   A methodology used to ensure that receiving units are not overwhelmed with data from sending devices. Pacing, as it is called in IBM networks, means that when buffers at a receiving unit are full, a message is transmitted to the sending unit to temporarily halt transmissions until all the data in the receiving buffer has been processed and the buffer is again ready for action.

FRAD   Frame Relay Access Device: Any device affording a connection between a LAN and a Frame Relay WAN. *See also: Cisco FRAD and FRAS.*

fragment   Any portion of a larger packet that has been intentionally segmented into smaller pieces. A packet fragment does not necessarily indicate an error and can be intentional. *See also: fragmentation.*

fragmentation   The process of intentionally segmenting a packet into smaller pieces when sending data over an intermediate network medium that cannot support the larger packet size.

FragmentFree   LAN switch type that reads into the data section of a frame to make sure fragmentation did not occur. Sometimes called modified cut-through.

frame   A logical unit of information sent by the Data Link layer over a transmission medium. The term often refers to the header and trailer, employed for synchronization and error control, that surround the data contained in the unit.

Frame Relay   A more efficient replacement of the X.25 protocol (an unrelated packet relay technology that guarantees data delivery). Frame Relay is an industry-standard, shared-access, best-effort, switched Data Link layer encapsulation that services multiple virtual circuits and protocols between connected mechanisms.

Frame Relay bridging   Defined in RFC 1490, this bridging method uses the identical spanning-tree algorithm as other bridging operations but permits packets to be encapsulated for transmission across a Frame Relay network.

Frame Relay switching When a router at a service provider provides packet switching for Frame Relay packets.

frame tagging VLANs can span multiple connected switches, which Cisco calls a switch-fabric. Switches within this switch-fabric must keep track of frames as they are received on the switch ports, and they must keep track of the VLAN they belong to as the frames traverse this switch-fabric. Frame tagging performs this function. Switches can then direct frames to the appropriate port.

framing Encapsulation at the Data Link layer of the OSI model. It is called framing because the packet is encapsulated with both a header and a trailer.

FRAS Frame Relay Access Support: A feature of Cisco IOS software that enables SDLC, Ethernet, Token Ring, and Frame Relay-attached IBM devices to be linked with other IBM mechanisms on a Frame Relay network. *See also: FRAD.*

frequency The number of cycles of an alternating current signal per time unit, measured in Hertz (cycles per second).

FSIP Fast Serial Interface Processor: The Cisco 7000 routers' default serial interface processor, it provides four or eight high-speed serial ports.

FTP File Transfer Protocol: The TCP/IP protocol used for transmitting files between network nodes, it supports a broad range of file types and is defined in RFC 959. *See also: TFTP.*

full duplex The capacity to transmit information between a sending station and a receiving unit at the same time. *See also: half duplex.*

full mesh A type of network topology where every node has either a physical or a virtual circuit linking it to every other network node. A full mesh supplies a great deal of redundancy but is typically reserved for network backbones because of its expense. *See also: partial mesh.*

gateway of last resort Term used when the default route is set.

Gigabit EtherChannel *See: Fast EtherChannel.*

Gigabit Ethernet   1000Mbps version of the IEEE 802.3. Fast Ethernet offers a speed increase of 10 times that of the 10BaseT Ethernet specification while preserving qualities such as frame format, MAC, mechanisms, and MTU.

GNS   Get Nearest Server: On an IPX network, a request packet sent by a customer for determining the location of the nearest active server of a given type. An IPX network client launches a GNS request to get either a direct answer from a connected server or a response from a router disclosing the location of the service on the internetwork to the GNS. GNS is part of IPX and SAP. *See also: IPX and SAP.*

grafting   A process that activates an interface that has been deactivated by the pruning process. It is initiated by an IGMP membership report sent to the router.

GRE   Generic Routing Encapsulation: A tunneling protocol created by Cisco with the capacity for encapsulating a wide variety of protocol packet types inside IP tunnels, thereby generating a virtual point-to-point connection to Cisco routers across an IP network at remote points. IP tunneling using GRE permits network expansion across a single-protocol backbone environment by linking multiprotocol subnetworks in a single-protocol backbone environment.

Group of Four   Used by Cisco Local Management Interface on Frame Relay networks to manage the permanent virtual circuits (PVCs). *See also: PVC.*

guard band   The unused frequency area found between two communications channels, furnishing the space necessary to avoid interference between the two.

half duplex   The capacity to transfer data in only one direction at a time between a sending unit and receiving unit. *See also: full duplex.*

handshake   Any series of transmissions exchanged between two or more devices on a network to ensure synchronized operations.

H channel   High-speed channel: A full-duplex, ISDN primary rate channel operating at a speed of 384Kbps. *See also: B channel, D channel, and E channel.*

HDLC   High-Level Data Link Control: Using frame characters, including checksums, HDLC designates a method for data encapsulation on synchronous serial links and is the default encapsulation for Cisco routers. HDLC is a bit-oriented synchronous Data Link layer protocol created by ISO and derived from SDLC. However, most HDLC vendor implementations (including Cisco's) are proprietary. *See also: SDLC.*

helper address   The unicast address specified, which instructs the Cisco router to change the client's local broadcast request for a service into a directed unicast to the server.

hierarchical addressing   Any addressing plan employing a logical chain of commands to determine location. IP addresses are made up of a hierarchy of network numbers, subnet numbers, and host numbers to direct packets to the appropriate destination.

hierarchical network   A multi-segment network configuration providing only one path through intermediate segments between source segments and destination segments.

hierarchy   *See: hierarchical network.*

HIP   HSSI Interface Processor: An interface processor used on Cisco 7000 series routers, providing one HSSI port that supports connections to ATM, SMDS, Frame Relay, or private lines at speeds up to T3 or E3.

hold-down   The state a route is placed in so that routers can neither advertise the route nor accept advertisements about it for a defined time period. Hold-down is used to surface bad information about a route from all routers in the network. A route is generally placed in hold-down when one of its links fails.

hop   The movement of a packet between any two network nodes. *See also: hop count.*

hop count   A routing metric that calculates the distance between a source and a destination. RIP employs hop count as its sole metric. *See also: hop* and *RIP.*

host address   Logical address configured by an administrator or server on a device. Logically identifies this device on an internetwork.

HSCI   High-Speed Communication Interface: Developed by Cisco, a single-port interface that provides full-duplex synchronous serial communications capability at speeds up to 52Mbps.

HSRP   Hot Standby Router Protocol: A protocol that provides high network availability and provides nearly instantaneous hardware fail-over without administrator intervention. It generates a Hot Standby router group, including a lead router that lends its services to any packet being transferred to the Hot Standby address. If the lead router fails, it will be replaced by any of the other routers—the standby routers—that monitor it.

HSSI   High-Speed Serial Interface: A network standard physical connector for high-speed serial linking over a WAN at speeds of up to 52Mbps.

hubs   Physical layer devices that are really just multiple port repeaters. When an electronic digital signal is received on a port, the signal is reamplified or regenerated and forwarded out all segments except the segment from which the signal was received.

ICD   International Code Designator: Adapted from the subnetwork model of addressing, this assigns the mapping of Network layer addresses to ATM addresses. HSSI is one of two ATM formats for addressing created by the ATM Forum to be utilized with private networks. *See also: DCC.*

ICMP   Internet Control Message Protocol: Documented in RFC 792, it is a Network layer Internet protocol for the purpose of reporting errors and providing information pertinent to IP packet procedures.

IEEE   Institute of Electrical and Electronics Engineers: A professional organization that, among other activities, defines standards in a number of fields within computing and electronics, including networking and communications. IEEE standards are the predominant LAN standards used today throughout the industry. Many protocols are commonly known by the reference number of the corresponding IEEE standard.

IEEE 802.1   The IEEE committee specification that defines the bridging group. The specification for STP (Spanning Tree Protocol) is IEEE 802.1d. The STP uses SPA (spanning-tree algorithm) to find and prevent network loops in bridged networks. The specification for VLAN trunking is IEEE 802.1q.

IEEE 802.3   The IEEE committee specification that defines the Ethernet group, specifically the original 10Mbps standard. Ethernet is a LAN protocol that specifies Physical layer and MAC sublayer media access. IEEE 802.3 uses CSMA/CD to provide access for many devices on the same network. Fast Ethernet is defined as 802.3u, and Gigabit Ethernet is defined as 802.3q. *See also: CSMA/CD.*

IEEE 802.5   IEEE committee that defines Token Ring media access.

IGMP Internet Group Management Protocol: Employed by IP hosts, the protocol that reports their multicast group memberships to an adjacent multicast router. The first version, IGMPv1, allows hosts to subscribe to or join specified multicast groups. Enhancements were made to IGMPv2 to facilitate a host-initiated leave process.

IGMP Join process The process by which hosts may join a multicast session outside of the Membership Query interval.

IGMP Leave process IGMPv1 does not have a formal leave process; a period of three query intervals must pass with no host confirmation before the interface is deactivated. IGMPv2 does allow the host to initiate the leave process immediately.

IGMP Query process The router uses IGMP to query hosts for Membership Reports, thus managing multicast on its interfaces.

IGP Interior Gateway Protocol: Any protocol used by the Internet to exchange routing data within an independent system. Examples include RIP, IGRP, and OSPF.

ILMI Integrated (or Interim) Local Management Interface. A specification created by the ATM Forum, designated for the incorporation of network-management capability into the ATM UNI. Integrated Local Management Interface cells provide for automatic configuration between ATM systems. In LAN emulation, ILMI can provide sufficient information for the ATM end station to find an LECS. In addition, ILMI provides the ATM NSAP (Network Service Access Point) prefix information to the end station.

in-band management In-band management is the management of a network device "through" the network. Examples include using Simple Network Management Protocol (SNMP) or Telnet directly via the local LAN. *Compare with: out-of-band management.*

in-band signaling Configuration of a router from within the network. Examples are Telnet, Simple Network Management Protocol (SNMP), or a Network Management Station (NMS).

insured burst In an ATM network, it is the largest, temporarily permitted data burst exceeding the insured rate on a PVC and not tagged by the traffic policing function for being dropped if network congestion occurs. This insured burst is designated in bytes or cells.

inter-area routing   Routing between two or more logical areas. *Contrast with: intra-area routing. See also: area.*

interface processor   Any of several processor modules used with Cisco 7000 series routers. *See also: AIP, CIP, EIP, FEIP, HIP, MIP,* and *TRIP.*

Interior Gateway Routing Protocol (IGRP)   Cisco proprietary distance-vector protocol.

internal route processors   Route Switch Modules (RSM) and Route Switch Feature Cards (RSFC) are called internal route processors because the processing of Layer 3 packets is internal to a switch.

Internet   The global "network of networks," whose popularity has exploded in the last few years. Originally a tool for collaborative academic research, it has become a medium for exchanging and distributing information of all kinds. The Internet's need to link disparate computer platforms and technologies has led to the development of uniform protocols and standards that have also found widespread use within corporate LANs. *See also: TCP/IP* and *MBONE.*

internet   Before the rise in the use of the Internet, this lowercase form was shorthand for "internetwork" in the generic sense. Now rarely used. *See also: internetwork.*

Internet Protocol   Any protocol belonging to the TCP/IP protocol stack. *See also: TCP/IP.*

internetwork   Any group of private networks interconnected by routers and other mechanisms, typically operating as a single entity.

internetworking   Broadly, anything associated with the general task of linking networks to each other. The term encompasses technologies, procedures, and products. When you connect networks to a router, you are creating an internetwork.

inter-VLAN routing   Cisco has created the proprietary protocol Inter-Switch Link (ISL) to allow routing between VLANs with only one Ethernet interface. To run ISL, you need to have two VLAN-capable Fast Ethernet or Gigabit Ethernet devices like a Cisco 5000 switch and a 7000 series router.

intra-area routing   Routing that occurs within a logical area. *Contrast with: inter-area routing.*

intruder detection   Intruder detection systems operate by monitoring the data flow for characteristics consistent with security threats. In this manner, an intruder can be monitored or blocked from access. One trigger for an intruder detection system is multiple ping packets from a single resource in a brief period of time.

Inverse ARP   Inverse Address Resolution Protocol: A technique by which dynamic mappings are constructed in a network, allowing a device such as a router to locate the logical network address and associate it with a permanent virtual circuit (PVC). Commonly used in Frame Relay to determine the far-end node's TCP/IP address by sending the Inverse ARP request to the local DLCI.

IP   Internet Protocol: Defined in RFC 791, it is a Network layer protocol that is part of the TCP/IP stack and allows connectionless service. IP furnishes an array of features for addressing, type-of-service specification, fragmentation and reassembly, and security.

IP address   Often called an Internet address, this is an address uniquely identifying any device (host) on the Internet (or any TCP/IP network). Each address consists of four octets (32 bits), represented as decimal numbers separated by periods (a format known as "dotted-decimal"). Every address is made up of a network number, an optional subnetwork number, and a host number. The network and subnetwork numbers together are used for routing, while the host number addresses an individual host within the network or subnetwork. The network and subnetwork information is extracted from the IP address using the subnet mask. There are five classes of IP addresses (A–E), which allocate different numbers of bits to the network, subnetwork, and host portions of the address. *See also: CIDR, IP,* and *subnet mask.*

IPCP   IP Control Program: The protocol used to establish and configure IP over PPP. *See also: IP* and *PPP.*

IP multicast   A technique for routing that enables IP traffic to be reproduced from one source to several endpoints or from multiple sources to many destinations. Instead of transmitting only one packet to each individual point of destination, one packet is sent to a multicast group specified by only one IP endpoint address for the group.

IP unnumbered   Cisco proprietary protocol that allows two point-to-point links to communicate without an IP address.

IPX   Internetwork Packet Exchange: Network layer protocol (Layer 3) used in Novell NetWare networks for transferring information from servers to workstations. Similar to IP and XNS.

IPXCP   IPX Control Program: The protocol used to establish and configure IPX over PPP. *See also: IPX and PPP.*

IPX spoofing   Provides IPX RIP/SAP traffic without requiring a connection to the opposing network. This allows a per-minute tariffed link, such as ISDN or analog phone, to support IPX without requiring the link to remain active.

IPXWAN   Protocol used for new WAN links to provide and negotiate line options on the link using IPX. After the link is up and the options have been agreed upon by the two end-to-end links, normal IPX transmission begins.

IRDP   ICMP Router Discovery Protocol: Allows hosts to use the Internet Control Message Protocol (ICMP) to find a new path when the primary router becomes unavailable. IRDP is an extension to the ICMP protocol and not a dynamic routing protocol. This ICMP extension allows routers to advertise default routes to end stations.

ISDN   Integrated Services Digital Network: Offered as a service by telephone companies, a communication protocol that allows telephone networks to carry data, voice, and other digital traffic. *See also: BISDN, BRI, and PRI.*

ISL routing   Inter-Switch Link routing is a Cisco proprietary method of frame tagging in a switched internetwork. Frame tagging is a way to identify the VLAN membership of a frame as it traverses a switched internetwork.

isochronous transmission   Asynchronous data transfer over a synchronous data link, requiring a constant bit rate for reliable transport. *Compare with: asynchronous transmission and synchronous transmission.*

ITU-T   International Telecommunication Union Telecommunication Standardization Sector: This is a group of engineers that develops worldwide standards for telecommunications technologies.

keepalive   Used to tell directly connected neighbors that a router is still up and functioning.

LAN   local area network: Broadly, any network linking two or more computers and related devices within a limited geographical area (up to a few kilometers). LANs are typically high-speed, low-error networks within a company. Cabling and signaling at the Physical and Data Link layers of the OSI are dictated by LAN standards. Ethernet, FDDI, and Token Ring are among the most popular LAN technologies. *Compare with: MAN.*

LANE   LAN emulation: The technology that allows an ATM network to operate as a LAN backbone. To do so, the ATM network is required to provide multicast and broadcast support, address mapping (MAC-to-ATM), SVC management, in addition to an operable packet format. Additionally, LANE defines Ethernet and Token Ring ELANs. *See also: ELAN.*

LAN switch   A high-speed, multiple-interface transparent bridging mechanism, transmitting packets between segments of data links, usually referred to specifically as an Ethernet switch. LAN switches transfer traffic based on MAC addresses. Multilayer switches are a type of high-speed, special-purpose, hardware-based router. *See also: multilayer switch* and *store-and-forward packet switching.*

LAPB   Link Accessed Procedure, Balanced: A bit-oriented Data Link layer protocol that is part of the X.25 stack and has its origin in SDLC. *See also: SDLC and X.25.*

LAPD   Link Access Procedure on the D channel: The ISDN Data Link layer protocol used specifically for the D channel and defined by ITU-T Recommendations Q.920 and Q.921. LAPD evolved from LAPB and is created to comply with the signaling requirements of ISDN basic access.

latency   Broadly, the time it takes a data packet to get from one location to another. In specific networking contexts, it can mean either 1) the time elapsed (delay) between the execution of a request for access to a network by a device and the time the mechanism actually is permitted transmission, or 2) the time elapsed between when a mechanism receives a frame and the time that frame is forwarded out of the destination port.

Layer 2 switching   Layer 2 switching is hardware based, which means it uses the MAC address from the hosts' NIC cards to filter the network. Switches use Application-Specific Integrated Circuits (ASICs) to build and maintain filter tables. It is okay to think of a Layer 2 switch as a multiport bridge.

Layer 3 switch   *See: multilayer switch.*

layered architecture   Industry standard way of creating applications to work on a network. Layered architecture allows the application developer to make changes in only one layer instead of the whole program.

LCP   Link Control Protocol: The protocol designed to establish, configure, and test data link connections for use by PPP. *See also: PPP.*

leaky bucket   An analogy for the basic cell rate algorithm (GCRA) used in ATM networks for checking the conformance of cell flows from a user or network. The bucket's "hole" is understood to be the prolonged rate at which cells can be accommodated, and the "depth" is the tolerance for cell bursts over a certain time period.

learning bridge   A bridge that transparently builds a dynamic database of MAC addresses and the interfaces associated with each address. Transparent bridges help to reduce traffic congestion on the network.

LE ARP   LAN Emulation Address Resolution Protocol: The protocol providing the ATM address that corresponds to a MAC address.

leased lines   Permanent connections between two points leased from the telephone companies.

LEC   LAN Emulation Client: Software providing the emulation of the Data Link layer interface that allows the operation and communication of all higher-level protocols and applications to continue. The LEC client runs in all ATM devices, which include hosts, servers, bridges, and routers. The LEC is responsible for address resolution, data transfer, address caching, interfacing to the emulated LAN, and driver support for higher-level services. *See also: ELAN and LES.*

LECS LAN Emulation Configuration Server: An important part of emulated LAN services, providing the configuration data that is furnished upon request from the LES. These services include address registration for Integrated Local Management Interface (ILMI) support, configuration support for the LES addresses and their corresponding emulated LAN identifiers, and an interface to the emulated LAN. *See also: LES and ELAN.*

LES LAN Emulation Server: The central LANE component that provides the initial configuration data for each connecting LEC. The LES typically is located on either an ATM-integrated router or a switch. Responsibilities of the LES include configuration and support for the LEC, address registration for the LEC, database storage and response concerning ATM addresses, and interfacing to the emulated LAN. *See also: ELAN, LEC, and LECS.*

link compression *See: compression.*

link-state router Type of routing protocol run on a router that sends partial route updates incrementally.

link-state routing algorithm A routing algorithm that allows each router to broadcast or multicast information regarding the cost of reaching all its neighbors to every node in the internetwork. Link-state algorithms provide a consistent view of the network and are therefore not vulnerable to routing loops. However, this is achieved at the cost of somewhat greater difficulty in computation and more widespread traffic (compared with distance-vector routing algorithms). *See also: distance-vector routing algorithm.*

LLAP LocalTalk Link Access Protocol: In a LocalTalk environment, the Data Link–level protocol that manages node-to-node delivery of data. This protocol provides node addressing and management of bus access, and it also controls data sending and receiving to assure packet length and integrity.

LLC Logical Link Control: Defined by the IEEE, the higher of two Data Link layer sublayers. LLC is responsible for error detection (but not correction), flow control, framing, and software-sublayer addressing. The predominant LLC protocol, IEEE 802.2, defines both connectionless and connection-oriented operations. *See also: Data Link layer and MAC.*

LMI An enhancement to the original Frame Relay specification. Among the features it provides are a keepalive mechanism, a multicast mechanism, global addressing, and a status mechanism.

LNNI   LAN Emulation Network-to-Network Interface: In the Phase 2 LANE specification, an interface that supports communication between the server components within one ELAN.

load balancing   The sharing of paths to a remote network.

local explorer packet   In a Token Ring SRB network, a packet generated by an end system to find a host linked to the local ring. If no local host can be found, the end system will produce one of two solutions: a spanning explorer packet or an all-routes explorer packet.

local loop   Connection from a demarcation point to the closest switching office.

local services   Users trying to get to network services that are located on the same subnet or network are defined as local services. Users do not cross Layer 3 devices, and the network services are in the same broadcast domain as the users. This type of traffic never crosses the backbone.

LocalTalk   Utilizing CSMA/CD, in addition to supporting data transmission at speeds of 230.4Kbps, LocalTalk is Apple Computer's proprietary baseband protocol, operating at the Data Link and Physical layers of the OSI Reference Model.

local VLANs   Local VLANs are configured by geographic location; these locations can be a building or just a closet in a building, depending on switch size. Geographically configured VLANs are designed around the fact that the business or corporation is using centralized resources, like a server farm.

loop avoidance   If multiple connections between switches are created for redundancy, network loops can occur. STP is used to stop network loops and allow redundancy.

LSA   link-state advertisement: Contained inside of link-state packets (LSPs), these advertisements are usually multicast packets, containing information about neighbors and path costs, that are employed by link-state protocols. Receiving routers use LSAs to maintain their link-state databases and, ultimately, routing tables.

LSA acknowledgement   A Link State Advertisement acknowledgement is sent from a router back to an originating router to acknowledge receipt of an LSA from an OSPF router.

LSA flooding   OSPF floods the network with Link State Advertisements if a change in the network occurs, permitting rapid convergence.

LUNI   LAN Emulation User-to-Network Interface: Defining the interface between the LAN Emulation Client (LEC) and the LAN Emulation Server (LES), LUNI is the ATM Forum's standard for LAN Emulation on ATM networks. *See also: LES* and *LECS.*

LZW algorithm   A data-compression process named for its inventors, Lempel, Ziv, and Welch. The algorithm works by finding longer and longer strings of data to compress with shorter representations.

MAC   Media Access Control: The lower sublayer in the Data Link layer, it is responsible for hardware addressing, media access, and error detection of frames. *See also: Data Link layer* and *LLC.*

MAC address   A Data Link layer hardware address that every port or device needs in order to connect to a LAN segment. These addresses are used by various devices in the network for accurate location of logical addresses. MAC addresses are defined by the IEEE standard and their length is six characters, typically using the burned-in address (BIA) of the local LAN interface. Variously called "hardware address," "physical address," "burned-in address," or "MAC layer address."

MacIP   In AppleTalk, the Network layer protocol encapsulating IP packets in Datagram Delivery Protocol (DDP) packets. MacIP also supplies substitute ARP services.

MAN   metropolitan area network: Any network that encompasses a metropolitan area; that is, an area typically larger than a LAN but smaller than a WAN. *See also: LAN.*

Manchester encoding   A method for digital coding in which a mid-bit–time transition is employed for clocking, and a 1 (one) is denoted by a high voltage level during the first half of the bit time. This scheme is used by Ethernet and IEEE 802.3.

maximum burst   Specified in bytes or cells, the largest burst of information exceeding the insured rate that will be permitted on an ATM permanent virtual connection for a short time and will not be dropped even if it goes over the specified maximum rate. *Compare with: insured burst. See also: maximum rate.*

maximum rate   The maximum permitted data throughput on a particular virtual circuit, equal to the total of insured and uninsured traffic from the traffic source. Should traffic congestion occur, uninsured information may be deleted from the path. Measured in bits or cells per second, the maximum rate represents the highest throughput of data the virtual circuit is ever able to deliver and cannot exceed the media rate. *Compare with: excess rate. See also: maximum burst.*

MBS   Maximum Burst Size: In an ATM signaling message, this metric, coded as a number of cells, is used to convey the burst tolerance.

MBONE   multicast backbone: The multicast backbone of the Internet, it is a virtual multicast network made up of multicast LANs, including point-to-point tunnels interconnecting them.

MCDV   Maximum Cell Delay Variation: The maximum two-point CDV objective across a link or node for the identified service category in an ATM network. The MCDV is one of four link metrics that are exchanged using PTSPs to verify the available resources of an ATM network. Only one MCDV value is assigned to each traffic class.

MCLR   Maximum Cell Loss Ratio: The maximum ratio of cells in an ATM network that fail to transit a link or node compared with the total number of cells that arrive at the link or node. MCDV is one of four link metrics that are exchanged using PTSPs to verify the available resources of an ATM network. The MCLR applies to cells in VBR and CBR traffic classes whose CLP bit is set to zero. *See also: CBR, CLP, and VBR.*

MCR   Minimum Cell Rate: A parameter determined by the ATM Forum for traffic management of the ATM networks. MCR is specifically defined for ABR transmissions and specifies the minimum value for the allowed cell rate (ACR). *See also: ACR and PCR.*

MCTD Maximum Cell Transfer Delay: In an ATM network, the total of the maximum cell delay variation and the fixed delay across the link or node. MCTD is one of four link metrics that are exchanged using PNNI topology state packets to verify the available resources of an ATM network. There is one MCTD value assigned to each traffic class. *See also: MCDV.*

metric *See: routing metric.*

MIB Management Information Base: Used with SNMP management software to gather information from remote devices. The management station can poll the remote device for information, or the MIB running on the remote station can be programmed to send information on a regular basis.

microsegmentation: Term used to describe LAN segmentation using Layer 2 switching.

MIP Multichannel Interface Processor: The resident interface processor on Cisco 7000 series routers, providing up to two channelized T1 or E1 connections by serial cables connected to a CSU. The two controllers are capable of providing 24 T1 or 30 E1 channel groups, with each group being introduced to the system as a serial interface that can be configured individually.

mips millions of instructions per second: A measure of processor speed.

MLP Multilink PPP: A technique used to split, recombine, and sequence datagrams across numerous logical data links.

MLS Multi-Layer Switching: Switching normally takes place at Layer 2. When Layer 3 information is allowed to be cached, Layer 2 devices have the capability of rewriting and forwarding frames based on the Layer 3 information.

MLSP Multilayer Switching Protocol: A protocol that runs on the router and allows it to communicate to the MLS-SE regarding topology or security changes.

MLS-RP Multilayer Switching Route Processor: An MLS-capable router or an RSM (Route Switch Module) installed in the switch. *See also: RSM* and *MLS.*

MLS-SE Multilayer Switching Switching Engine: An MLS-capable switch (a 5000 with an NFFC or a 6000 with an MSFC and PFC). *See also: MLS, NFFC, MSFC* and *PFC.*

MMP Multichassis Multilink PPP: A protocol that supplies MLP support across multiple routers and access servers. MMP enables several routers and access servers to work as a single, large dial-up pool with one network address and ISDN access number. MMP successfully supports packet fragmenting and reassembly when the user connection is split between two physical access devices.

modem modulator-demodulator: A device that converts digital signals to analog and vice versa so that digital information can be transmitted over analog communication facilities, such as voice-grade telephone lines. This is achieved by converting digital signals at the source to analog for transmission and reconverting the analog signals back into digital form at the destination. *See also: modulation* and *demodulation.*

modemcap database Stores modem initialization strings on the router for use in auto-detection and configuration.

modem eliminator A mechanism that makes possible a connection between two DTE devices without modems by simulating the commands and physical signaling required.

modulation The process of modifying some characteristic of an electrical signal, such as amplitude (AM) or frequency (FM), in order to represent digital or analog information. *See also: AM.*

MOSPF Multicast OSPF: An extension of the OSPF unicast protocol that enables IP multicast routing within the domain. *See also: OSPF.*

MP bonding MultiPoint bonding: A process of linking two or more physical connections into a single logical channel. This may use two or more analog lines and two or more modems, for example.

MPOA Multiprotocol over ATM: An effort by the ATM Forum to standardize how existing and future Network layer protocols such as IP, Ipv6, AppleTalk, and IPX run over an ATM network with directly attached hosts, routers, and multilayer LAN switches.

MSFC Multilayer Switch Feature Card: A route processor (parallel to an RSM, or Route Switch Module) that is installed as a daughter card on Cisco Catalyst 6000 series switches. *See also: RSM.*

mtrace (multicast traceroute)   Used to establish the SPT for a specified multicast group.

MTU   maximum transmission unit: The largest packet size, measured in bytes, that an interface can handle.

multicast   Broadly, any communication between a single sender and multiple receivers. Unlike broadcast messages, which are sent to all addresses on a network, multicast messages are sent to a defined subset of the network addresses; this subset has a group multicast address, which is specified in the packet's destination address field. *See also: broadcast* and *directed broadcast.*

multicast address   A single address that points to more than one device on the network by specifying a special non-existent MAC address specified in that particular multicast protocol. Identical to group address. *See also: multicast.*

multicast group   A group set up to receive messages from a source. These groups can be established based on Frame Relay or IP in the TCP/IP protocol suite, as well as other networks.

multicast send VCC   A two-directional point-to-point virtual control connection (VCC) arranged by an LEC to a BUS, it is one of the three types of informational links specified by phase 1 LANE. *See also: control distribute VCC* and *control direct VCC.*

multilayer switch   A highly specialized, high-speed, hardware-based type of LAN router, the device filters and forwards packets based on their Layer 2 MAC addresses and Layer 3 network addresses. It's possible that even Layer 4 can be read. Sometimes called a Layer 3 switch. *See also: LAN switch.*

multilayer switching   Multilayer switching combines Layer 2, 3, and 4 switching technology and provides very high-speed scalability with low latency. This is provided by huge filter tables based on the criteria designed by the network administrator.

multiplexing   The process of converting several logical signals into a single physical signal for transmission across one physical channel. *Contrast with: demultiplexing.*

NAK negative acknowledgment: A response sent from a receiver, telling the sender that the information was not received or contained errors. *Compare with: acknowledgment.*

NAT Network Address Translation: An algorithm instrumental in minimizing the requirement for globally unique IP addresses, permitting an organization whose addresses are not all globally unique to connect to the Internet, regardless, by translating those addresses into globally routable address space.

NBP Name Binding Protocol: In AppleTalk, the Transport-level protocol that interprets a socket client's name, entered as a character string, into the corresponding DDP address. NBP gives AppleTalk protocols the capacity to discern user-defined zones and names of mechanisms by showing and keeping translation tables that map names to their corresponding socket addresses.

NCP Network Control Protocol: A protocol at the Logical Link Control sublayer of the Data Link layer used in the PPP stack. It is used to allow multiple Network layer protocols to run over a nonproprietary HDLC serial encapsulation.

neighboring routers Two routers in OSPF that have interfaces to a common network. On networks with multi-access, these neighboring routers are dynamically discovered using the Hello protocol of OSPF.

NetBEUI NetBIOS Extended User Interface: An improved version of the NetBIOS protocol used in a number of network operating systems including LAN Manager, Windows NT, LAN Server, and Windows for Workgroups, implementing the OSI LLC2 protocol. NetBEUI formalizes the transport frame not standardized in NetBIOS and adds more functions. *See also: OSI.*

NetBIOS Network Basic Input/Output System: The API employed by applications residing on an IBM LAN to ask for services, such as session termination or information transfer, from lower-level network processes.

NetView A mainframe network product from IBM, used for monitoring SNA (Systems Network Architecture) networks. It runs as a VTAM (Virtual Telecommunications Access Method) application.

NetWare   A widely used NOS created by Novell, providing a number of distributed network services and remote file access.

network address   Used with the logical network addresses to identify the network segment in an internetwork. Logical addresses are hierarchical in nature and have at least two parts: network and host. An example of a hierarchical address is 172.16.10.5, where 172.16 is the network and 10.5 is the host address.

Network layer   In the OSI reference model, it is Layer 3—the layer in which routing is implemented, enabling connections and path selection between two end systems. *See also: Application layer, Data Link layer, Physical layer, Presentation layer, Session layer,* and *Transport layer.*

NFFC   NetFlow Feature Card: A module installed on Cisco Catalyst 5000 series switches. It is capable of examining each frame's IP header as well as the Ethernet header. This in turn allows the NFFC to create flows.

NFS   Network File System: One of the protocols in Sun Microsystems' widely used file system protocol suite, allowing remote file access across a network. The name is loosely used to refer to the entire Sun protocol suite, which also includes RPC, XDR (External Data Representation), and other protocols.

NHRP   Next Hop Resolution Protocol: In a nonbroadcast multi-access (NBMA) network, the protocol employed by routers in order to dynamically locate MAC addresses of various hosts and routers. It enables systems to communicate directly without requiring an intermediate hop, thus facilitating increased performance in ATM, Frame Relay, X.25, and SMDS systems.

NHS   Next Hop Server: Defined by the NHRP protocol, this server maintains the next-hop resolution cache tables, listing IP-to-ATM address maps of related nodes and nodes that can be reached through routers served by the NHS.

NIC   network interface card: An electronic circuit board placed in a computer. The NIC provides network communication to a LAN.

NLSP   NetWare Link Services Protocol: Novell's link-state routing protocol, based on the IS-IS model.

NMP   Network Management Processor: A Catalyst 5000 switch processor module used to control and monitor the switch.

node address   Used to identify a specific device in an internetwork. Can be a hardware address, which is burned into the network interface card, or a logical network address, which an administrator or server assigns to the node.

Non-Broadcast Multi-Access (NBMA)   A type of network that does not, by default, allow LAN broadcasts to be transmitted on the network. An example of an NBMA is Frame Relay.

nondesignated port   The Spanning Tree Protocol tells a port on a Layer 2 switch to stop transmitting and creating a network loop. Only designated ports can send frames.

non-stub area   In OSPF, a resource-consuming area carrying a default route, intra-area routes, inter-area routes, static routes, and external routes. Non-stub areas are the only areas that can have virtual links configured across them and exclusively contain an anonymous system boundary router (ASBR). *Compare with: stub area. See also: ASBR and OSPF.*

NRZ   Nonreturn to Zero: One of several encoding schemes for transmitting digital data. NRZ signals sustain constant levels of voltage with no signal shifting (no return to zero-voltage level) during a bit interval. If there is a series of bits with the same value (1 or 0), there will be no state change. The signal is not self-clocking. *See also: NRZI.*

NRZI   Nonreturn to Zero Inverted: One of several encoding schemes for transmitting digital data. A transition in voltage level (either from high to low or vice versa) at the beginning of a bit interval is interpreted as a value of 1; the absence of a transition is interpreted as a 0. Thus, the voltage assigned to each value is continually inverted. NRZI signals are not self-clocking. *See also: NRZ.*

NT1   network termination 1: An ISDN designation to devices that understand ISDN standards.

NT2   network termination 2: An ISDN designation to devices that do not understand ISDN standards. To use a NT2, you must use a terminal adapter (TA).

NVRAM Non-Volatile RAM: Random-access memory that keeps its contents intact while power is turned off.

OC Optical Carrier: A series of physical protocols, designated as OC-1, OC-2, OC-3, and so on, for SONET optical signal transmissions. OC signal levels place STS frames on a multimode fiber-optic line at various speeds, of which 51.84Mbps is the lowest (OC-1). Each subsequent protocol runs at a speed divisible by 51.84. *See also: SONET.*

octet Base-8 numbering system used to identify a section of a dotted decimal IP address. Also referred to as a byte.

100BaseT Based on the IEEE 802.3u standard, 100BaseT is the Fast Ethernet specification of 100Mbps baseband that uses UTP wiring. 100BaseT sends link pulses (containing more information than those used in 10BaseT) over the network when no traffic is present. *See also: 10BaseT, FastEthernet,* and *IEEE 802.3.*

100BaseTX Based on the IEEE 802.3u standard, 100BaseTX is the 100Mbps baseband FastEthernet specification that uses two pairs of UTP or STP wiring. The first pair of wires receives data; the second pair sends data. To ensure correct signal timing, a 100BaseTX segment cannot be longer than 100 meters.

ones density Also known as pulse density, this is a method of signal clocking. The CSU/DSU retrieves the clocking information from data that passes through it. For this scheme to work, the data needs to be encoded to contain at least one binary 1 for each eight bits transmitted. *See also: CSU* and *DSU.*

one-time challenge tokens Used to provide a single-use password. This prevents replay attacks and snooping; however, it also requires the user to have a device that provides the token. This physical component of the security model works to prevent hackers from guessing or obtaining the user's password.

OSI Open Systems Interconnection: International standardization program designed by ISO and ITU-T for the development of data networking standards that make multivendor equipment interoperability a reality.

OSI reference model   Open Systems Interconnection reference model: A conceptual model defined by the International Organization for Standardization (ISO), describing how any combination of devices can be connected for the purpose of communication. The OSI model divides the task into seven functional layers, forming a hierarchy with the applications at the top and the physical medium at the bottom, and it defines the functions each layer must provide. *See also: Application layer, Data Link layer, Network layer, Physical layer, Presentation layer, Session layer,* and *Transport layer.*

OSPF   Open Shortest Path First: A link-state, hierarchical IGP routing algorithm derived from an earlier version of the IS-IS protocol, whose features include multipath routing, load balancing, and least-cost routing. OSPF is the suggested successor to RIP in the Internet environment. *See also: Enhanced IGRP, IGP,* and *IP.*

OSPF areas   Small areas within an autonomous system that share routing information.

OUI   Organizationally Unique Identifier: Assigned by the IEEE to an organization that makes network interface cards. The organization then puts this OUI on each and every card they manufacture. The OUI is 3 bytes (24 bits) long. The manufacturer then adds a 3-byte identifier to uniquely identify the host on an internetwork. The total length of the address is 48 bits (6 bytes) and is called a hardware address or MAC address.

out-of-band management   Management "outside" of the network's physical channels. For example, using a console connection not directly interfaced through the local LAN or WAN or a dial-in modem. *Compare to: in-band management.*

out-of-band signaling   Within a network, any transmission that uses physical channels or frequencies separate from those ordinarily used for data transfer. For example, the initial configuration of a Cisco Catalyst switch requires an out-of-band connection via a console port.

packet   In data communications, the basic logical unit of information transferred. A packet consists of a certain number of data bytes, wrapped or encapsulated in headers and/or trailers that contain information about where the packet came from, where it's going, and so on. The various protocols involved in sending a transmission add their own layers of header information, which the corresponding protocols in receiving devices then interpret.

packet mode connections   Packet mode connections are typically passed through the router or remote access device. This includes Point-to-Point Protocol (PPP) sessions.

packet switch   A physical device that makes it possible for a communication channel to share several connections, its functions include finding the most efficient transmission path for packets.

packet switching   A networking technology based on the transmission of data in packets. Dividing a continuous stream of data into small units—packets—enables data from multiple devices on a network to share the same communication channel simultaneously but also requires the use of precise routing information.

PAD   Packet assembler and disassembler: Used to buffer incoming data that is coming in faster than the receiving device can handle it. Typically, only used in X.25 networks.

PAP   Password Authentication Protocol: In Point-to-Point Protocol (PPP) networks, a method of validating connection requests. The requesting (remote) device must send an authentication request, containing a password and ID, to the local router when attempting to connect. Unlike the more secure CHAP (Challenge Handshake Authentication Protocol), PAP sends the password unencrypted and does not attempt to verify whether the user is authorized to access the requested resource; it merely identifies the remote end. *See also: CHAP.*

parity checking   A method of error-checking in data transmissions. An extra bit (the parity bit) is added to each character or data word so that the sum of the bits will be either an odd number (in odd parity) or an even number (even parity).

partial mesh   A type of network topology in which some network nodes form a full mesh (where every node has either a physical or a virtual circuit linking it to every other network node), but others are attached to only one or two nodes in the network. A typical use of partial-mesh topology is in peripheral networks linked to a fully meshed backbone. *See also: full mesh.*

PAT   Port Address Translation: This process allows a single IP address to represent multiple resources by altering the source TCP or UDP port number.

payload compression   Reduces the number of bytes required to accurately represent the original data stream. Header compression is also possible. *See also: compression.*

PCR   Peak Cell Rate: As defined by the ATM Forum, the parameter specifying, in cells per second, the maximum rate at which a source may transmit.

PDN   Public Data Network: Generally for a fee, a PDN offers the public access to computer communication network operated by private concerns or government agencies. Small organizations can take advantage of PDNs, aiding them creating WANs without investing in long-distance equipment and circuitry.

PDU   Protocol Data Unit: The name of the processes at each layer of the OSI model. PDUs at the Transport layer are called segments; PDUs at the Network layer are called packets or datagrams; and PDUs at the Data Link layer are called frames. The Physical layer uses bits.

PFC   Policy Feature Card: The PFC can be paralleled with the NFFC used in Catalyst 5000 switches. It is a device that is capable of examining IP and Ethernet headers in order to establish flow caches.

PGP   Pretty Good Privacy: A popular public-key/private-key encryption application offering protected transfer of files and messages.

Physical layer   The lowest layer—Layer 1—in the OSI reference model, it is responsible for converting data packets from the Data Link layer (Layer 2) into electrical signals. Physical layer protocols and standards define, for example, the type of cable and connectors to be used, including their pin assignments and the encoding scheme for signaling 0 and 1 values. *See also: Application layer, Data Link layer, Network layer, Presentation layer, Session layer,* and *Transport layer.*

PIM   Protocol Independent Multicast: A multicast protocol that handles the IGMP requests as well as requests for multicast data forwarding.

PIM DM   Protocol Independent Multicast dense mode: PIM DM utilizes the unicast route table and relies on the source root distribution architecture for multicast data forwarding.

PIM SM Protocol Independent Multicast sparse mode: PIM SM utilizes the unicast route table and relies on the shared root distribution architecture for multicast data forwarding.

PIM sparse-dense mode An interface configuration that allows the interface to choose the method of PIM operation.

ping packet Internet groper: A Unix-based Internet diagnostic tool, consisting of a message sent to test the accessibility of a particular device on the IP network. The acronym (from which the "full name" was formed) reflects the underlying metaphor of submarine sonar. Just as the sonar operator sends out a signal and waits to hear it echo ("ping") back from a submerged object, the network user can ping another node on the network and wait to see if it responds.

pinhole congestion Two links to the same remote network with equal hops but with different bandwidths. Distance vector will try to load balance and waste bandwidth.

pleisochronous Nearly synchronous, except that clocking comes from an outside source instead of being embedded within the signal as in synchronous transmissions.

PLP Packet Level Protocol: Occasionally called X.25 Level 3 or X.25 Protocol, a Network layer protocol that is part of the X.25 stack.

PNNI Private Network-Network Interface: An ATM Forum specification for offering topology data used for the calculation of paths through the network, among switches and groups of switches. It is based on well-known link-state routing procedures and allows for automatic configuration in networks whose addressing scheme is determined by the topology.

point-to-multipoint connection In ATM, a communication path going only one way, connecting a single system at the starting point, called the "root node," to systems at multiple points of destination, called "leaves." *See also: point-to-point connection.*

point-to-point connection In ATM, a channel of communication that can be directed either one way or two ways between two ATM end systems. *See also: point-to-multipoint connection.*

poison reverse updates   These update messages are transmitted by a router back to the originator (thus ignoring the split-horizon rule) after route poisoning has occurred. Typically used with DV routing protocols in order to overcome large routing loops and offer explicit information when a subnet or network is not accessible (instead of merely suggesting that the network is unreachable by not including it in updates). *See also: route poisoning.*

polling   The procedure of orderly inquiry, used by a primary network mechanism, to determine if secondary devices have data to transmit. A message is sent to each secondary, granting the secondary the right to transmit.

POP   1) Point Of Presence: The physical location where an interexchange carrier has placed equipment to interconnect with a local exchange carrier. 2) Post Office Protocol (currently at version 3): A protocol used by client e-mail applications for recovery of mail from a mail server.

port density   Port density reflects the capacity of the remote access device regarding the termination of interfaces. For example, the port density of an access server that serves four T1 circuits is 96 analog lines (non ISDN PRI).

port security   Used with Layer 2 switches to provide some security. Not typically used in production because it is difficult to manage. Allows only certain frames to traverse administrator-assigned segments.

POTS   Plain Old Telephone Service: This refers to the traditional analog phone service that is found in most installations.

PPP   Point-to-Point Protocol: The protocol most commonly used for dial-up Internet access, superseding the earlier SLIP. Its features include address notification, authentication via CHAP or PAP, support for multiple protocols, and link monitoring. PPP has two layers: the Link Control Protocol (LCP) establishes, configures, and tests a link; and then any of various Network Control Programs (NCPs) transport traffic for a specific protocol suite, such as IPX. *See also: CHAP, PAP,* and *SLIP.*

PPP callback   The point-to-point protocol supports callback to a predetermined number to augment security.

Predictor   A compression technique supported by Cisco. *See also: compression.*

prefix routing   A routing protocol that sends subnet mask information along with route updates. Used in classless routing.

Presentation layer   Layer 6 of the OSI reference model, it defines how data is formatted, presented, encoded, and converted for use by software at the application layer. *See also: Application layer, Data Link layer, Network layer, Physical layer, Session layer,* and *Transport layer.*

PRI   Primary Rate Interface: A type of ISDN connection between a PBX and a long-distance carrier, which is made up of a single 64Kbps D channel in addition to 23 (T1) or 30 (E1) B channels. *See also: ISDN.*

priority queuing   A routing function in which frames temporarily placed in an interface output queue are assigned priorities based on traits such as packet size or type of interface.

process switching   As a packet arrives on a router to be forwarded, it's copied to the router's process buffer, and the router performs a lookup on the Layer 3 address. Using the route table, an exit interface is associated with the destination address. The processor forwards the packet with the added new information to the exit interface, while the router initializes the fast-switching cache. Subsequent packets bound for the same destination address follow the same path as the first packet.

PROM   programmable read-only memory: ROM that is programmable only once, using special equipment. *Compare with: EPROM.*

propagation delay   The time it takes data to traverse a network from its source to its destination.

protocol   In networking, the specification of a set of rules for a particular type of communication. The term is also used to refer to the software that implements a protocol.

protocol stack   A collection of related protocols.

Proxy ARP   Proxy Address Resolution Protocol: Used to allow redundancy in case of a failure with the configured default gateway on a host. Proxy ARP is a variation of the ARP protocol in which an intermediate device, such as a router, sends an ARP response on behalf of an end node to the requesting host.

pruning   The act of trimming down the Shortest Path Tree. This deactivates interfaces that do not have group participants.

PSE   Packet Switch Exchange: The X.25 term for a switch.

PSN   packet-switched network: Any network that uses packet-switching technology. Also known as packet-switched data network (PSDN). *See also: packet switching.*

PSTN   Public Switched Telephone Network: Colloquially referred to as "plain old telephone service" (POTS). A term that describes the assortment of telephone networks and services available globally.

PVC   permanent virtual circuit: In a Frame-Relay network, a logical connection, defined in software, that is maintained permanently. *Compare with: SVC. See also: virtual circuit.*

PVP   permanent virtual path: A virtual path made up of PVCs. *See also: PVC.*

PVP tunneling   permanent virtual path tunneling: A technique that links two private ATM networks across a public network using a virtual path; wherein the public network transparently trunks the complete collection of virtual channels in the virtual path between the two private networks.

PVST   Per-VLAN Spanning Tree: A Cisco proprietary implementation of STP. PVST uses ISL and runs a separate instance of STP for each and every VLAN.

PVST+   Per-VLAN Spanning Tree+: Allows CST information to be passed into PVST.

QoS   Quality of Service: A set of metrics used to measure the quality of transmission and service availability of any given transmission system.

queue   Broadly, any list of elements arranged in an orderly fashion and ready for processing, such as a line of people waiting to enter a movie theater. In routing, it refers to a backlog of information packets waiting in line to be transmitted over a router interface.

queuing   A quality of service process that allows packets to be forwarded from the router based on administratively defined parameters. This may be used for time-sensitive protocols, such as SNA.

R reference point   Used with ISDN networks to identify the connection between an NT1 and an S/T device. The S/T device converts the four-wire network to the two-wire ISDN standard network.

RADIUS   Remote Access Dial-in User Service: A protocol that is used to communicate between the remote access device and an authentication server. Sometimes an authentication server running RADIUS will be called a RADIUS server.

RAM   random access memory: Used by all computers to store information. Cisco routers use RAM to store packet buffers and routing tables, along with the hardware addresses cache.

RARP   Reverse Address Resolution Protocol: The protocol within the TCP/IP stack that maps MAC addresses to IP addresses. *See also: ARP.*

rate queue   A value, assigned to one or more virtual circuits, that specifies the speed at which an individual virtual circuit will transmit data to the remote end. Every rate queue identifies a segment of the total bandwidth available on an ATM link. The sum of all rate queues should not exceed the total available bandwidth.

RCP   Remote Copy Protocol: A protocol for copying files to or from a file system that resides on a remote server on a network, using TCP to guarantee reliable data delivery.

redistribution   Command used in Cisco routers to inject the paths found from one type of routing protocol into another type of routing protocol. For example, networks found by RIP can be inserted into an IGRP network.

redundancy   In internetworking, the duplication of connections, devices, or services that can be used as a backup in the event that the primary connections, devices, or services fail.

reference point   Used to define an area in an ISDN network. Providers used these reference points to find problems in the ISDN network.

relay system   Another term for a router.

reliability   The measure of the quality of a connection. It is one of the metrics that can be used to make routing decisions.

reload   An event or command that causes Cisco routers to reboot.

remote access   A generic term that defines connectivity to distant resources using one of many technologies, as appropriate.

remote services   Network services close to users but not on the same network or subnet as the users. The users would have to cross a Layer 3 device to communicate with the network services, but they might not have to cross the backbone.

reverse Telnet   Maps a Telnet port to a physical port on the router or access device. This allows the administrator to connect to a modem or other device attached to the port.

RFC   Request for Comments: RFCs are used to present and define standards in the networking industry.

RIF   Routing Information Field: In source-route bridging, a header field that defines the path direction of the frame or token. If the Route Information Indicator (RII) bit is not set, the RIF is read from source to destination (left to right). If the RII bit is set, the RIF is read from the destination back to the source, so the RIF is read right to left. It is defined as part of the Token Ring frame header for source-routed frames, which contains path information.

ring   Two or more stations connected in a logical circular topology. In this topology, which is the basis for Token Ring, FDDI, and CDDI, information is transferred from station to station in sequence.

ring topology   A network logical topology comprising a series of repeaters that form one closed loop by connecting unidirectional transmission links. Individual stations on the network are connected to the network at a repeater. Physically, ring topologies are generally organized in a closed-loop star. *Compare with: bus topology* and *star topology.*

RIP   Routing Information Protocol: The most commonly used interior gateway protocol in the Internet. RIP employs hop count as a routing metric. *See also: Enhanced IGRP, IGP, OSPF,* and *hop count.*

RIP version 2   Newer, updated version of Routing Information Protocol (RIP). Allows VLSM. *See also: VLSM.*

RJ connector registered jack connector: Is used with twisted-pair wiring to connect the copper wire to network interface cards, switches, and hubs.

robbed bit signaling Used in Primary Rate Interface clocking mechanisms.

ROM read-only memory: Chip used in computers to help boot the device. Cisco routers use a ROM chip to load the bootstrap, which runs a power-on self test, and then find and load the IOS in flash memory by default.

root bridge Used with the Spanning Tree Protocol to stop network loops from occurring. The root bridge is elected by having the lowest bridge ID. The bridge ID is determined by the priority (32,768 by default on all bridges and switches) and the main hardware address of the device. The root bridge determines which of the neighboring Layer 2 devices' interfaces become the designated and nondesignated ports.

routed protocol Routed protocols (such as IP and IPX) are used to transmit user data through an internetwork. By contrast, routing protocols (such as RIP, IGRP, and OSPF) are used to update routing tables between routers.

route redistribution Translation of routing information from one type of routing protocol to another. *See also: redistribution.*

route poisoning Used by various DV routing protocols in order to overcome large routing loops and offer explicit information about when a subnet or network is not accessible (instead of merely suggesting that the network is unreachable by not including it in updates). Typically, this is accomplished by setting the hop count to one more than maximum. *See also: poison reverse updates.*

route summarization In various routing protocols, such as OSPF, EIGRP, and IS-IS, the consolidation of publicized subnetwork addresses so that a single summary route is advertised to other areas by an area border router.

router A Network layer mechanism, either software or hardware, using one or more metrics to decide on the best path to use for transmission of network traffic. Sending packets between networks by routers is based on the information provided on Network layers. Historically, this device has sometimes been called a gateway.

router on a stick   A term that identifies a single router interface connected to a single Distribution-layer switch port. The router is an external router that provides trunking protocol capabilities for routing between multiple VLANs. *See also: RSM, MSFC.*

routing   The process of forwarding logically addressed packets from their local subnetwork toward their ultimate destination. In large networks, the numerous intermediary destinations a packet might travel before reaching its destination can make routing very complex.

routing by rumor   Term used by a distance-vector protocol to explain how neighbor routers learn about remote networks.

routing domain   Any collection of end systems and intermediate systems that operate under an identical set of administrative rules. Every routing domain contains one or several areas, all individually given a certain area address.

routing metric   Any value that is used by routing algorithms to determine whether one route is superior to another. Metrics include such information as bandwidth, delay, hop count, path cost, load, MTU, reliability, and communication cost. Only the best possible routes are stored in the routing table, while all other information may be stored in link-state or topological databases. *See also: cost.*

routing protocol   Any protocol that defines algorithms to be used for updating routing tables between routers. Examples include IGRP, RIP, and OSPF.

routing table   A table kept in a router or other internetworking mechanism that maintains a record of only the best possible routes to certain network destinations and the metrics associated with those routes.

RP   1) rendezvous point: A router that acts as the multicast source in a multicast network. Primarily in a shared tree distribution. 2) Route Processor: Also known as a supervisory processor, a module on Cisco 7000 series routers that holds the CPU, system software, and most of the memory components used in the router.

RSFC Route Switch Feature Card: Used to provide routing between VLANs. The RSFC is a daughter card for the Supervisor engine II G and Supervisor III G cards. The RSFC is a fully functioning router running the Cisco IOS.

RSM Route Switch Module: A route processor that is inserted into the chassis of a Cisco Catalyst 5000 series switch. The RSM is configured exactly like an external router.

RSP Route/Switch Processor: A processor module combining the functions of RP and SP used in Cisco 7500 series routers. *See also: RP and SP.*

RTS Request To Send: An EIA/TIA-232 control signal requesting permission to transmit data on a communication line.

S reference point ISDN reference point that works with a T reference point to convert a four-wire ISDN network to the two-wire ISDN network needed to communicate with the ISDN switches at the network provider.

sampling rate The rate at which samples of a specific waveform amplitude are collected within a specified period of time.

SAP 1) Service Access Point: A field specified by IEEE 802.2 that is part of an address specification. 2) Service Advertising Protocol: The Novell Net-Ware protocol that supplies a way to inform network clients of resources and services availability on network, using routers and servers. *See also: IPX.*

SCR Sustainable Cell Rate: An ATM Forum parameter used for traffic management, it is the long-term average cell rate for VBR connections that can be transmitted.

scripts A script predefines commands that should be issued in sequence, typically to complete a connection or accomplish a repetitive task.

SDLC Synchronous Data Link Control: A protocol used in SNA Data Link layer communications. SDLC is a bit-oriented, full-duplex serial protocol that is the basis for several similar protocols, including HDLC and LAPB. *See also: HDLC and LAPB.*

security policy   Document that defines the business requirements and processes that are to be used to protect corporate data. A security policy might be as generic as "no file transfers allowed" to very specific, such as "FTP puts allowed only to server X."

security server   A centralized device that authenticates access requests, typically via a protocol such as TACACS+ or RADIUS. *See also: TACACS+, RADIUS.*

seed router   In an AppleTalk network, the router that is equipped with the network number or cable range in its port descriptor. The seed router specifies the network number or cable range for other routers in that network section and answers to configuration requests from nonseed routers on its connected AppleTalk network, permitting those routers to affirm or modify their configurations accordingly. Every AppleTalk network needs at least one seed router physically connected to each network segment.

server   Hardware and software that provide network services to clients.

Session layer   Layer 5 of the OSI reference model, responsible for creating, managing, and terminating sessions between applications and overseeing data exchange between Presentation layer entities. *See also: Application layer, Data Link layer, Network layer, Physical layer, Presentation layer,* and *Transport layer.*

set-based   Set-based routers and switches use the `set` command to configure devices. Cisco is moving away from set-based commands and is using the Command-Line Interface (CLI) on all new devices.

setup mode   Mode that a router will enter if no configuration is found in nonvolatile RAM when the router boots. Allows the administrator to configure a router step-by-step. Not as robust or flexible as the Command-Line Interface.

SF   super frame: A super frame (also called a D4 frame) consists of 12 frames with 192 bits each, and the 193rd bit providing other functions including error checking. SF is frequently used on T1 circuits. A newer version of the technology is Extended Super Frame (ESF), which uses 24 frames. *See also: ESF.*

shared trees   A method of multicast data forwarding. Shared trees use an architecture in which multiple sources share a common rendezvous point.

signaling packet   An informational packet created by an ATM-connected mechanism that wants to establish a connection with another such mechanism. The packet contains the QoS parameters needed for connection and the ATM NSAP address of the endpoint. The endpoint responds with a message of acceptance if it is able to support the desired QoS, and the connection is established. *See also: QoS.*

silicon switching   A type of high-speed switching used in Cisco 7000 series routers, based on the use of a separate processor (the Silicon Switch Processor, or SSP). *See also: SSE.*

simplex   The mode at which data or a digital signal is transmitted. Simplex is a way of transmitting in only one direction. Half duplex transmits in two directions but only one direction at a time. Full duplex transmits in both directions simultaneously.

sliding window   The method of flow control used by TCP, as well as several Data Link layer protocols. This method places a buffer between the receiving application and the network data flow. The "window" available for accepting data is the size of the buffer minus the amount of data already there. This window increases in size as the application reads data from it and decreases as new data is sent. The receiver sends the transmitter announcements of the current window size, and it may stop accepting data until the window increases above a certain threshold.

SLIP   Serial Line Internet Protocol: An industry standard serial encapsulation for point-to-point connections that supports only a single routed protocol, TCP/IP. SLIP is the predecessor to PPP. *See also: PPP.*

SMDS   Switched Multimegabit Data Service: A packet-switched, datagram-based WAN networking technology offered by telephone companies that provides high speed.

SMTP   Simple Mail Transfer Protocol: A protocol used on the Internet to provide electronic mail services.

SNA   System Network Architecture: A complex, feature-rich, network architecture similar to the OSI reference model but with several variations; created by IBM in the 1970s and essentially composed of seven layers.

SNAP   Subnetwork Access Protocol: SNAP is a frame used in Ethernet, Token Ring, and FDDI LANs. Data transfer, connection management, and QoS selection are three primary functions executed by the SNAP frame.

snapshot routing   Snapshot routing takes a point-in-time capture of a dynamic routing table and maintains it even when the remote connection goes down. This allows the use of a dynamic routing protocol without requiring the link to remain active, which might incur per-minute usage charges.

socket   1) A software structure that operates within a network device as a destination point for communications. 2) In AppleTalk networks, an entity at a specific location within a node; AppleTalk sockets are conceptually similar to TCP/IP ports.

SOHO   small office, home office: A contemporary term for remote users.

SONET   Synchronous Optical Network: The ANSI standard for synchronous transmission on fiber-optic media, developed at Bell Labs. It specifies a base signal rate of 51.84Mbps and a set of multiples of that rate, known as Optical Carrier levels, up to 2.5Gbps.

source trees   A method of multicast data forwarding. Source trees use the architecture of the source of the multicast traffic as the root of the tree.

SP   Switch Processor: Also known as a ciscoBus controller, it is a Cisco 7000 series processor module acting as governing agent for all CxBus activities.

span   A full-duplex digital transmission line connecting two facilities.

SPAN   Switched Port Analyzer: A feature of the Catalyst 5000 switch, offering freedom to manipulate within a switched Ethernet environment by extending the monitoring ability of the existing network analyzers into the environment. At one switched segment, the SPAN mirrors traffic onto a predetermined SPAN port, while a network analyzer connected to the SPAN port is able to monitor traffic from any other Catalyst switched port.

spanning explorer packet Sometimes called limited-route or single-route explorer packet, it pursues a statically configured spanning tree when searching for paths in a source-route bridging network. *See also: all-routes explorer packet, explorer packet,* and *local explorer packet.*

spanning tree A subset of a network topology, within which no loops exist. When bridges are interconnected into a loop, the bridge, or switch, cannot identify a frame that has been forwarded previously, so there is no mechanism for removing a frame as it passes the interface numerous times. Without a method of removing these frames, the bridges continuously forward them—consuming bandwidth and adding overhead to the network. Spanning trees prune the network to provide only one path for any packet. *See also: Spanning Tree Protocol* and *spanning tree algorithm.*

spanning-tree algorithm (STA) An algorithm that creates a spanning tree using the Spanning Tree Protocol (STP). *See also: spanning tree* and *Spanning Tree Protocol.*

Spanning Tree Protocol (STP) The bridge protocol (IEEE 802.1d) that enables a learning bridge to dynamically avoid loops in the network topology by creating a spanning tree using the spanning-tree algorithm. Spanning-tree frames called bridge protocol data units (BPDUs) are sent and received by all switches in the network at regular intervals. The switches participating in the spanning tree don't forward the frames; instead, they're processed to determine the spanning-tree topology itself. Cisco Catalyst series switches use STP 802.1d to perform this function. *See also: BPDU, learning bridge, MAC address, spanning tree,* and *spanning-tree algorithm.*

SPF Shortest Path First algorithm: A routing algorithm used to decide on the shortest-path spanning tree. Sometimes called Dijkstra's algorithm and frequently used in link-state routing algorithms. *See also: link-state routing algorithm.*

SPID Service Profile Identifier: A number assigned by service providers or local telephone companies and assigned by administrators to a BRI port. SPIDs are used to determine subscription services of a device connected via ISDN. ISDN devices use SPID when accessing the telephone company switch that initializes the link to a service provider.

split horizon   Useful for preventing routing loops, a type of distance-vector routing rule where information about routes is prevented from leaving the router interface through which that information was received.

spoofing   1) In dial-on-demand routing (DDR), where a circuit-switched link is taken down to save toll charges when there is no traffic to be sent, spoofing is a scheme used by routers that causes a host to treat an interface as if it were functioning and supporting a session. The router pretends to send "spoof" replies to keepalive messages from the host in an effort to convince the host that the session is up and running. *See also: DDR.* 2) The illegal act of sending a packet labeled with a false address, in order to deceive network security mechanisms such as filters and access lists.

spooler   A management application that processes requests submitted to it for execution in a sequential fashion from a queue. A good example is a print spooler.

SPX   Sequenced Packet Exchange: A Novell NetWare transport protocol that augments the datagram service provided by Network layer (Layer 3) protocols, it was derived from the Switch-to-Switch Protocol of the XNS protocol suite.

SQE   Signal Quality Error: In an Ethernet network, a message sent from a transceiver to an attached machine that the collision-detection circuitry is working.

SRB   Source-Route Bridging: Created by IBM, the bridging method used in Token-Ring networks. The source determines the entire route to a destination before sending the data and includes that information in route information fields (RIF) within each packet. *Contrast with: transparent bridging.*

SRT   source-route transparent bridging: A bridging scheme developed by IBM, merging source-route and transparent bridging. SRT takes advantage of both technologies in one device, fulfilling the needs of all end nodes. Translation between bridging protocols is not necessary. *Compare with: SR/TLB.*

SR/TLB   source-route translational bridging: A bridging method that allows source-route stations to communicate with transparent bridge stations aided by an intermediate bridge that translates between the two bridge protocols. Used for bridging between Token Ring and Ethernet. *Compare with: SRT.*

SSAP   Source Service Access Point: The SAP of the network node identified in the Source field of the packet. *See also: DSAP and SAP.*

SSE   Silicon Switching Engine: The software component of Cisco's silicon switching technology, hard-coded into the Silicon Switch Processor (SSP). Silicon switching is available only on the Cisco 7000 with an SSP. Silicon-switched packets are compared to the silicon-switching cache on the SSE. The SSP is a dedicated switch processor that offloads the switching process from the route processor, providing a fast-switching solution, but packets must still traverse the backplane of the router to get to the SSP and then back to the exit interface.

SS-7 signaling   Signaling System 7: The current standard for tele-communications switching control signaling. This is out-of-band signaling that establishes circuits and provides billing information.

Stac   A compression method developed by Stacker Corporation for use over serial links.

standard IP access list   IP access list that uses only the source IP addresses to filter a network.

standard IPX access list   IPX access list that uses only the source and destination IPX address to filter a network.

star topology   A LAN physical topology with endpoints on the network converging at a common central switch (known as a hub) using point-to-point links. A logical ring topology can be configured as a physical star topology using a unidirectional closed-loop star rather than point-to-point links. That is, connections within the hub are arranged in an internal ring. *See also: bus topology and ring topology.*

startup range   If an AppleTalk node does not have a number saved from the last time it was booted, then the node selects from the range of values from 65280 to 65534.

state transitions   Digital signaling scheme that reads the "state" of the digital signal in the middle of the bit cell. If it is five volts, the cell is read as a one. If the state of the digital signal is zero volts, the bit cell is read as a zero.

static route   A route whose information is purposefully entered into the routing table and takes priority over those chosen by dynamic routing protocols.

static VLANs   Static VLANs are manually configured port-by-port. This is the method typically used in production networks.

statistical multiplexing   Multiplexing in general is a technique that allows data from multiple logical channels to be sent across a single physical channel. Statistical multiplexing dynamically assigns bandwidth only to input channels that are active, optimizing available bandwidth so that more devices can be connected than with other multiplexing techniques. Also known as statistical time-division multiplexing, or stat mux.

STM-1   Synchronous Transport Module Level 1. In the European SDH standard, one of many formats identifying the frame structure for the 155.52Mbps lines that are used to carry ATM cells.

store-and-forward packet switching   A technique in which the switch first copies each packet into its buffer and performs a cyclical redundancy check (CRC). If the packet is error-free, the switch then looks up the destination address in its filter table, determines the appropriate exit port, and sends the packet.

STP   1) Shielded Twisted Pair: A two-pair wiring scheme, used in many network implementations, that has a layer of shielded insulation to reduce EMI. 2) Spanning Tree Protocol.

stub area   An OSPF area carrying a default route, intra-area routes, and inter-area routes, but no external routes. Configuration of virtual links cannot be achieved across a stub area, and stub areas are not allowed to contain an ASBR. *See also: non-stub area, ASBR,* and *OSPF.*

stub AS   An area that accepts only default routes.

stub network   A network having only one connection to a router.

STUN   Serial Tunnel: A technology used to connect an HDLC link to an SDLC link over a serial link.

subarea   A portion of an SNA network made up of a subarea node and its attached links and peripheral nodes.

subarea node   An SNA communications host or controller that handles entire network addresses.

subchannel   A frequency-based subdivision that creates a separate broad-band communications channel.

subinterface   One of many virtual interfaces available on a single physical interface.

subnet   *See: subnetwork.*

subnet address   The portion of an IP address that is specifically identified by the subnet mask as the subnetwork. *See also: IP address, subnetwork,* and *subnet mask.*

subnet mask   Also simply known as mask, a 32-bit address mask used in IP to identify the bits of an IP address that are used for the subnet address. Using a mask, the router does not need to examine all 32 bits, only those selected by the mask. *See also: address mask* and *IP address.*

subnetwork   1) Any network that is part of a larger IP network and is identified by a subnet address. A network administrator segments a network into subnetworks in order to provide a hierarchical, multilevel routing structure, and at the same time protect the subnetwork from the addressing complexity of networks that are attached. Also known as a subnet. *See also: IP address, subnet mask,* and *subnet address.* 2) In OSI networks, the term specifically refers to a collection of ESs and ISs controlled by only one administrative domain, using a solitary network connection protocol.

SVC   switched virtual circuit: A dynamically established virtual circuit, created on demand and dissolved as soon as transmission is over and the circuit is no longer needed. In ATM terminology, it is referred to as a switched virtual connection. *See also: PVC.*

switch   1) In networking, a device responsible for multiple functions such as filtering, flooding, and sending frames. It works using the destination address of individual frames. Switches operate at the Data Link layer of the OSI model. 2) Broadly, any electronic/mechanical device allowing connections to be established as needed and terminated if no longer necessary.

switch block   The switch block is a combination of Layer 3 switches and Layer 3 routers. The Layer 2 switches connect users in the wiring closet into the Access layer and provide 10 or 100Mbps dedicated connections. 1900/2820 and 2900 Catalyst switches can be used in the switch block.

switched Ethernet   Device that switches Ethernet frames between segments by filtering on hardware addresses.

switched LAN   Any LAN implemented using LAN switches. *See also: LAN switch.*

switch-fabric   The central functional block of any switch design; responsible for buffering and routing the incoming data to the appropriate output ports.

synchronous transmission   Signals transmitted digitally with precision clocking. These signals have identical frequencies and contain individual characters encapsulated in control bits (called start/stop bits) that designate the beginning and ending of each character. *See also: asynchronous transmission* and *isochronous transmission.*

T reference point   Used with an S reference point to change a 4-wire ISDN network to a 2-wire ISDN network.

T1   Digital WAN that uses 24 DS0s at 64K each to create a bandwidth of 1.536Mbps, minus clocking overhead, providing 1.544Mbps of usable bandwidth.

T3   Digital WAN that can provide bandwidth of 44.763Mbps.

TACACS+   Terminal Access Control Access Control System: An enhanced version of TACACS, this protocol is similar to RADIUS. *See also: RADIUS.*

tag switching   Based on the concept of label swapping, where packets or cells are designated to defined-length labels that control the manner in which data is to be sent, tag switching is a high-performance technology used for forwarding packets. It incorporates Data Link layer (Layer 2) switching and Network layer (Layer 3) routing and supplies scalable, high-speed switching in the network core.

tagged traffic ATM cells with their cell loss priority (CLP) bit set to 1. Also referred to as discard-eligible (DE) traffic. Tagged traffic can be eliminated in order to ensure trouble-free delivery of higher priority traffic, if the network is congested. *See also: CLP.*

TCP Transmission Control Protocol: A connection-oriented protocol that is defined at the Transport layer of the OSI reference model. Provides reliable delivery of data.

TCP header compression A compression process that compresses only the TCP header information, which is typically repetitive. This would not compress the user data. *See also: compression.*

TCP/IP Transmission Control Protocol/Internet Protocol. The suite of protocols underlying the Internet. TCP and IP are the most widely known protocols in that suite. *See also: IP* and *TCP.*

TDM time division multiplexing: A technique for assigning bandwidth on a single wire, based on preassigned time slots, to data from several channels. Bandwidth is allotted to each channel regardless of a station's ability to send data. *See also: ATDM, FDM,* and *multiplexing.*

TE terminal equipment: Any peripheral device that is ISDN-compatible and attached to a network, such as a telephone or computer. TE1s are devices that are ISDN-ready and understand ISDN signaling techniques. TE2s are devices that are not ISDN-ready and do not understand ISDN signaling techniques. A terminal adapter must be used with a TE2.

TE1 A device with a four-wire, twisted-pair digital interface is referred to as terminal equipment type 1. Most modern ISDN devices are of this type.

TE2 Devices known as terminal equipment type 2 do not understand ISDN signaling techniques, and a terminal adapter must be used to convert the signaling.

telco A common abbreviation for the telephone company.

Telnet The standard terminal emulation protocol within the TCP/IP protocol stack. Method of remote terminal connection, enabling users to log in on remote networks and use those resources as if they were locally connected. Telnet is defined in RFC 854.

10BaseT   Part of the original IEEE 802.3 standard, 10BaseT is the Ethernet specification of 10Mbps baseband that uses two pairs of twisted-pair, Category 3, 4, or 5 cabling—using one pair to send data and the other to receive. 10BaseT has a distance limit of about 100 meters per segment. *See also: Ethernet* and *IEEE 802.3.*

terminal adapter   A hardware interface between a computer without a native ISDN interface and an ISDN line. In effect, a device to connect a standard async interface to a non-native ISDN device, emulating a modem.

terminal emulation   The use of software, installed on a PC or LAN server, that allows the PC to function as if it were a "dumb" terminal directly attached to a particular type of mainframe.

TFTP   Conceptually, a stripped-down version of FTP, it's the protocol of choice if you know exactly what you want and where it's to be found. TFTP doesn't provide the abundance of functions that FTP does. In particular, it has no directory-browsing abilities; it can do nothing but send and receive files.

Thicknet   Also called 10Base5. Bus network that uses a thick cable and runs Ethernet up to 500 meters.

Thinnet   Also called 10Base2. Bus network that uses a thin coax cable and runs Ethernet media access up to 185 meters.

token   A frame containing only control information. Possessing this control information gives a network device permission to transmit data onto the network. *See also: token passing.*

token bus   LAN architecture that is the basis for the IEEE 802.4 LAN specification and employs token passing access over a bus topology. *See also: IEEE.*

token passing   A method used by network devices to access the physical medium in a systematic way based on possession of a small frame called a token. *See also: token.*

Token Ring   IBM's token-passing LAN technology. It runs at 4Mbps or 16Mbps over a ring topology. Defined formally by IEEE 802.5. *See also: ring topology* and *token passing.*

toll network   WAN network that uses the Public Switched Telephone Network (PSTN) to send packets.

trace   IP command used to trace the path a packet takes through an internetwork.

traffic shaping   Used on Frame Relay networks to provide priorities of data.

transparent bridging   The bridging scheme used in Ethernet and IEEE 802.3 networks, it passes frames along one hop at a time, using bridging information stored in tables that associate end-node MAC addresses within bridge ports. This type of bridging is considered transparent because the source node does not know it has been bridged, because the destination frames are sent directly to the end node. *Contrast with: SRB.*

Transport layer   Layer 4 of the OSI reference model, used for reliable communication between end nodes over the network. The Transport layer provides mechanisms used for establishing, maintaining, and terminating virtual circuits, transport fault detection and recovery, and controlling the flow of information. *See also: Application layer, Data Link layer, Network layer, Physical layer, Presentation layer,* and *Session layer.*

TRIP   Token Ring Interface Processor: A high-speed interface processor used on Cisco 7000 series routers. The TRIP provides two or four ports for interconnection with IEEE 802.5 and IBM media with ports set to speeds of either 4Mbps or 16Mbps set independently of each other.

trunk link   Link used between switches and from some servers to the switches. Trunk links carry information about many VLANs. Access links are used to connect host devices to a switch and carry only VLAN information that the device is a member of.

TTL   Time To Live: A field in an IP header, indicating the length of time a packet is valid.

TUD   Trunk Up-Down: A protocol used in ATM networks for the monitoring of trunks. Should a trunk miss a given number of test messages being sent by ATM switches to ensure trunk line quality, TUD declares the trunk down. When a trunk reverses direction and comes back up, TUD recognizes that the trunk is up and returns the trunk to service.

tunneling A method of avoiding protocol restrictions by wrapping packets from one protocol in another protocol's packet and transmitting this encapsulated packet over a network that supports the wrapper protocol. *See also: encapsulation.*

20/80 rule This rule means that 20 percent of what the user performs on the network is local, whereas up to 80 percent crosses the network segmentation points to get to network services.

UART The Universal Asynchronous Receiver/Transmitter: A chip that governs asynchronous communications. Its primary function is to buffer incoming data, but it also buffers outbound bits.

U reference point Reference point between a TE1 and an ISDN network. The U reference point understands ISDN signaling techniques and uses a two-wire connection.

UDP User Datagram Protocol: A connectionless Transport layer protocol in the TCP/IP protocol stack that simply allows datagrams to be exchanged without acknowledgements or delivery guarantees, requiring other protocols to handle error processing and retransmission. UDP is defined in RFC 768.

unicast Used for direct host-to-host communication. Communication is directed to only one destination and is originated only from one source.

unidirectional shared tree A method of shared tree multicast forwarding. This method allows only multicast data to be forwarded from the RP.

unnumbered frames HDLC frames used for control-management purposes, such as link startup and shutdown or mode specification.

UTP unshielded twisted-pair: Copper wiring used in small-to-large networks to connect host devices to hubs and switches. Also used to connect switch to switch or hub to hub.

VBR Variable Bit Rate: A QoS class, as defined by the ATM Forum, for use in ATM networks that is subdivided into real time (RT) class and non-real time (NRT) class. RT is employed when connections have a fixed-time relationship between samples. Conversely, NRT is employed when connections do not have a fixed-time relationship between samples, but still need an assured QoS.

VCC   Virtual Channel Connection: A logical circuit that is created by VCLs. VCCs carry data between two endpoints in an ATM network. Sometimes called a virtual circuit connection.

VIP   1) Versatile Interface Processor: An interface card for Cisco 7000 and 7500 series routers, providing multilayer switching and running the Cisco IOS software. The most recent version of VIP is VIP2. 2) Virtual IP: A function making it possible for logically separated switched IP workgroups to run Virtual Networking Services across the switch ports of a Catalyst 5000.

virtual circuit   Abbreviated VC, a logical circuit devised to assure reliable communication between two devices on a network. Defined by a virtual path connection (VPC)/virtual path identifier (VCI) pair, a virtual circuit can be permanent (PVC) or switched (SVC). Virtual circuits are used in Frame Relay and X.25. Known as virtual channel in ATM. *See also: PVC and SVC.*

virtual link   Used to attach an OSPF area to Area 0 across an area other than Area 0.

virtual ring   In an SRB network, a logical connection between physical rings, either local or remote.

VLAN   Virtual LAN: A group of devices on one or more logically segmented LANs (configured by use of management software), enabling devices to communicate as if attached to the same physical medium, when they are actually located on numerous different LAN segments. VLANs are based on logical instead of physical connections and thus are tremendously flexible.

VLSM   Variable-Length Subnet Mask: Helps optimize available address space and specify a different subnet mask for the same network number on various subnets. Also commonly referred to as "subnetting a subnet."

VPN   virtual private network: A method of encrypting point-to-point logical connections across a public network, such as the Internet. This allows secure communications across a public network.

VTP   VLAN Trunk Protocol: Used to update switches in a switch-fabric about VLANs configured on a VTP server. VTP devices can be a VTP server, client, or transparent device. Servers update clients. Transparent devices are only local devices and do not share information with VTP clients. VTPs send VLAN information down trunked links only.

VTP pruning   VLAN Trunk Protocol is used to communicate VLAN information between switches in the same VTP domain. VTP pruning stops VLAN update information from being sent down trunked links if the updates are not needed.

WAN   wide area network: A designation used to connect LANs together across a DCE (data communications equipment) network. Typically, a WAN is a leased line or dial-up connection across a PSTN network. Examples of WAN protocols include Frame Relay, PPP, ISDN, and HDLC.

weighted fair queuing   Default queuing method on serial links on all Cisco routers.

wildcard   Used with access-list, supernetting, and OSPF configurations. Wildcards are designations used to identify a range of subnets.

windowing   Flow-control method used with TCP at the Transport layer of the OSI model.

WinSock   Windows Socket Interface: A software interface that makes it possible for an assortment of applications to use and share an Internet connection. The WinSock software consists of a Dynamic Link Library (DLL) with supporting programs such as a dialer program that initiates the connection.

workgroup switching   A switching method that supplies high-speed (100Mbps) transparent bridging between Ethernet networks as well as high-speed translational bridging between Ethernet and CDDI or FDDI.

X.25   An ITU-T packet-relay standard that defines communication between DTE and DCE network devices. X.25 uses a reliable Data Link layer protocol called LAPB. X.25 also uses PLP at the Network layer. X.25 has mostly been replaced by Frame Relay.

X.25 protocol   First packet-switching network, but now mostly used in Europe. Replaced in the U.S. by Frame Relay.

XTAG   A locally significant numerical value assigned by the MLS-SE to each MLS-RP in the Layer 2 network. *See also: MLS-SE, MLS-RP.*

ZIP   Zone Information Protocol: A Session layer protocol used by Apple-Talk to map network numbers to zone names. NBP uses ZIP in the determination of networks containing nodes that belong to a zone. *See also: ZIP storm* and *zone.*

ZIP storm A broadcast storm occurring when a router running AppleTalk reproduces or transmits a route for which there is no corresponding zone name at the time of execution. The route is then forwarded by other routers downstream, thus causing a ZIP storm. *See also: broadcast storm* and *ZIP.*

zone A logical grouping of network devices in AppleTalk. *See also: ZIP.*

Index

B

C

D

F

K

L

M

N

O

S

U

GET CISCO CERTIFIED WITH THE EXPERTS!

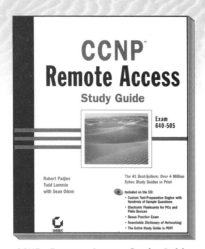

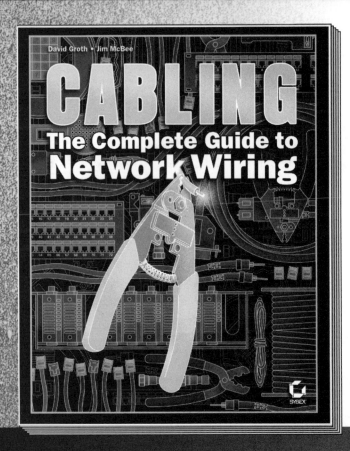

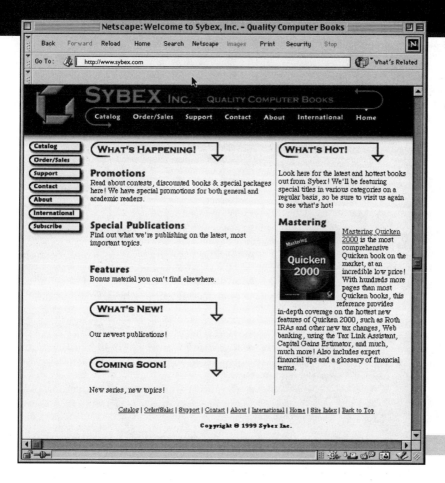